HUSSERL'S *CRISIS OF THE EUROPEAN SCIENCES AND TRANSCENDENTAL PHENOMENOLOGY*

The *Crisis of the European Sciences* is Husserl's last and most influential book, written in Nazi Germany where he was discriminated against as a Jew. It incisively identifies the urgent moral and existential crises of the age, and defends the relevance of philosophy at a time of both scientific progress and political barbarism. It is also a response to Heidegger, offering Husserl's own approach to the problems of human finitude, history and culture. The *Crisis* introduces Husserl's influential notion of the 'life-world' – the pregiven, familiar environment that includes both 'nature' and 'culture' – and offers the best introduction to his phenomenology as both method and philosophy. Dermot Moran's rich and accessible introduction to the *Crisis* explains its intellectual and political context, its philosophical motivations and the themes that characterize it. His book will be invaluable for students and scholars of Husserl's work and of phenomenology in general.

DERMOT MORAN is Professor of Philosophy at University College Dublin. He is the author of *The Philosophy of John Scottus Eriugena* (Cambridge, 1989), *Edmund Husserl: Founder of Phenomenology* (2005) and *Introduction to Phenomenology* (2000), co-author of the *Husserl Dictionary* (2011) and editor of *The Routledge Companion to Twentieth-Century Philosophy* (2008). He is founding editor of *The International Journal of Philosophical Studies*.

T0370919

CAMBRIDGE INTRODUCTIONS TO KEY
PHILOSOPHICAL TEXTS

This series offers introductory textbooks on what are considered to be the most important texts of Western philosophy. Each book guides the reader through the main themes and arguments of the work in question, while also paying attention to its historical context and its philosophical legacy. No philosophical background knowledge is assumed, and the books will be well suited to introductory university-level courses.

Titles published in the series:

HUSSERL'S *CRISIS OF THE EUROPEAN SCIENCES AND TRANSCENDENTAL PHENOMENOLOGY*

An Introduction

DERMOT MORAN

University College Dublin

CAMBRIDGE
UNIVERSITY PRESS

University Printing House, Cambridge CB2 8BS, United Kingdom

One Liberty Plaza, 20th Floor, New York, NY 10006, USA

477 Williamstown Road, Port Melbourne, VIC 3207, Australia

314-321, 3rd Floor, Plot 3, Splendor Forum, Jasola District Centre, New Delhi - 110025, India

79 Anson Road, #06-04/06, Singapore 079906

Cambridge University Press is part of the University of Cambridge.

It furthers the University's mission by disseminating knowledge in the pursuit of education, learning and research at the highest international levels of excellence.

www.cambridge.org
Information on this title: www.cambridge.org/9780521719698

© Dermot Moran 2012

First published 2012

A catalogue record for this publication is available from the British Library

Library of Congress Cataloging in Publication data
Moran, Dermot.
Husserl's Crisis of the European Sciences and Transcendental Phenomenology : an introduction / Dermot Moran.
p.   cm. – (Cambridge introductions to key philosophical texts)
Includes bibliographical references and index.
ISBN 978-0-521-89536-1 (hardback) – ISBN 978-0-521-71969-8 (paperback)
1. Husserl, Edmund, 1859–1938. Krisis der europäischen Wissenschaften und die transzendentale Phänomenologie.   2. Science–Philosophy.
3. History–Philosophy.   4. Phenomenology.   I. Title.
B3279.H93K736 2012
142′.7–dc23   2012016089

ISBN 978-0-521-89536-1 Hardback
ISBN 978-0-521-71969-8 Paperback

For Loretta, Katie, Eoin and Hannah

Contents

Acknowledgements

This book is a critical study of Edmund Husserl's last work, *Crisis of the European Sciences* (partially published in 1936 and edited posthumously in 1954), a work universally acknowledged as an enduring masterpiece. The *Crisis* is one of the more successful of Husserl's major works in terms of its philosophical range, depth and accessibility. To write it, he had to overcome not only recurrent illness and the trials of old age, but also personal discrimination and victimization at the hands of the National Socialist regime in Germany. As he himself acknowledged, the practice of philosophy is a calling, a 'vocation' (*Beruf*), and as such presents a demanding challenge to the way one lives and interprets one's life. Writing this book has made me appreciate more and more Husserl's earnest dedication to philosophy as a vocation and as a way of engaging reflectively with urgent problems concerning the future of our contemporary scientific culture and technologically shaped mode of living.

Husserl's philosophical output was vast, and much of it consists of lecture notes and private research jottings that are still being edited and published in the Husserliana series (now more than forty volumes). As a consequence, Husserl scholarship is also vast and growing strongly. Any study of Husserl's *Crisis of the European Sciences* must build on the work of previous scholars. Fortunately, Husserl has been exceptionally well served by successive generations of loyal and dedicated scholars, and by the editorial activities of the various Husserl Archives in Belgium, France, Germany and the United States, as well as by the research promulgated at the annual meetings of the Husserl Circle, founded in 1969, and in the journal *Husserl Studies*, founded in 1984. With regard to the *Crisis*, one has especially to acknowledge the original editorial work of Husserl's assistant, Eugen Fink, as well as that of Walter Biemel, the editor of Husserliana Volume vi and other Husserliana volumes.

I would like here to acknowledge gratefully the contribution of a number of Husserl scholars who in one way or another have assisted me. I am grateful to David Carr for discussions and for his lucid and fluid English translation of the main parts of the *Crisis*, which is the basis for this study. I have also benefited from consulting Gérard Granel's elegant and free-flowing French translation. I have also to acknowledge other scholars who have recently written illuminatingly on the *Crisis*, in particular two monographs – James Dodd's *Crisis and Reflection: An Essay on Edmund Husserl's Crisis of the European Sciences* (2004) and Ernst Wolfgang Orth's *Edmund Husserls Krisis der europäischen Wissenschaften und die transzendentale Phänomenologie: Vernunft und Kultur* (1999) – as well as two recent collections of essays: Jean-Claude Gens, ed., *La Krisis de Husserl: Approches contemporaines* (2008), and David Hyder and Hans-Jörg Rheinberger, eds., *Science and the Life-World: Essays on Husserl's 'Crisis of European Sciences'* (2010). Clearly, interest in Husserl's *Crisis* continues to grow, and I hope this book will continue the debate concerning the meaning of Husserl's last work.

I want to thank the Husserl Archief of the Katholieke Universiteit Leuven, Belgium, its current director, Ullrich Melle, and researchers Thomas Vongehr and Filip Mattens, for their assistance. I record my thanks here also to those with whom I have had discussions concerning the *Crisis*, especially Jocelyn Benoist, John Brough, David Carr, Steven Galt Crowell, John J. Drummond, Lester Embree, Jean-Claude Gens, George Heffernan, Elmar Holenstein, Burt Hopkins, Hanne Jacobs, Leonard Lawlor, Sebastian Luft, Jeff Malpas, Tom Nenon, Hans-Rainer Sepp, Ted Toadvine, Nicolas de Warren and Dan Zahavi. Special thanks go to Lubica Učnik and Ivan Chvatík for providing me with material on Husserl's student Jan Patočka. I would also like to thank Sara Heinämaa for inviting me to discuss the *Crisis* at a seminar at the Helsinki Collegium for Advanced Studies, Helsinki, Finland, in May 2010, and I thank the participants for their comments, especially Jussi Backman, Mirja Hartimo, Tim Miettinen, Simo Pulkkinen and Joona Taipale. I also want specially to thank Professors Cheung Chan-Fai, Kwan Tze-Wan and Lau Kwok-Ying for inviting me to participate in the Fourth International Masterclass in Phenomenology held at the Chinese University of Hong Kong in July 2010. I want in particular to thank the academic staff, especially my co-presenter, Mauro Carbone, Yu Chung-Chi and the graduate students from six Asian countries (China, Taiwan, Hong Kong, Japan, Korea and the Philippines) who actively and enthusiastically participated in this seminar, and from whom I learned a great deal.

Much of the research and writing on this book was conducted under the auspices of the Irish Research Council for Humanities and Social Sciences (IRCHSS) research project on 'The Phenomenology of Consciousness and Subjectivity (2008–2010)', of which I was principal investigator. Thanks go also to the IRCHSS postdoctoral researcher Rasmus Thybo Jensen and visiting doctoral student Ignacio de los Reyes. I also want to thank the Australian Research Council for their support for this book as part of the ARC Discovery Project, 'Judgment, Responsibility and the Life-World: The Phenomenological Critique of Formalism (2010–2013)'.

Thanks go also to my colleagues in the School of Philosophy at University College Dublin, especially Maria Baghramian, Joseph Cohen, Maeve Cooke, Tim Mooney and Jim O'Shea, for their philosophical discussions on aspects of Husserl. I would like to record my special thanks to the students who participated in my Husserl seminars in University College Dublin and Trinity College Dublin, whose ideas and questions greatly assisted me in clarifying my ideas about Husserl. Special thanks are due to visiting ERASMUS student Lukas Steinacher, who collaborated with me in the translation of Husserl's 1935 letter to Lévy-Bruhl, and UCD postgraduate David Florcyzk Jones for his assistance in the translation of Husserl's Draft Preface to Section 3 of the *Crisis*.

Thanks are also due to Cambridge University Press and especially to Hilary Gaskin for her patience and for her editorial comments on early drafts, and to the four anonymous referees and the clearance reviewer for their helpful critical comments.

Last, but not least, I would like to thank my family for their support, especially my wife, Loretta, and our three children, Katie, Eoin and Hannah, and of course, our new sheepdog, Charlie.

Abbreviations

APS	Husserl, *Analysen zur passiven Synthesis*, Hua XI (*Analyses Concerning Passive and Active Synthesis*, trans. A. J. Steinbock)
Briefwechsel	Husserl, *Briefwechsel,* ed. K. and E. Schuhmann, 10 vols.
BPP	Husserl, *Grundprobleme der Phänomenologie*, Hua XIII (*The Basic Problems of Phenomenology*, trans. I. Farin and J. G. Hart)
C	Husserl, *The Crisis of European Sciences*, trans. D. Carr.
CM	Husserl, *Cartesianische Meditationen*, Hua I (*Cartesian Meditations*, trans. D. Cairns)
Chronik	*Husserl-Chronik: Denk- und Lebensweg Edmund Husserls*, ed. K. Schuhmann
DR	Husserl, *Ding und Raum*, Hua XVI (*Thing and Space: Lectures of 1907*, trans. R. Rojcewicz)
EP I	Husserl, *Erste Philosophie (1923/1924)*. Erster Teil: *Kritische Ideengeschichte*, Hua VII
EU	Husserl, *Erfahrung und Urteil*, rev. and ed. L. Landgrebe (*Experience and Judgment*, trans. J. S. Churchill and K. Ameriks)
FTL	Husserl, *Formale und transzendentale Logik*, Hua XVII (*Formal and Transcendental Logic*, trans. D. Cairns)
GA	Heidegger, *Gesamtausgabe*
HSW	Husserl, *Shorter Works*, trans. and ed. F. Elliston and P. McCormick

Hua	Husserliana series, Edmund Husserl *Gesammelte Werke.*
Ideas I	Husserl, *Ideen zu einer reinen Phänomenologie und phänomenologischen Philosophie.* Erstes Buch: *Allgemeine Einführung in die reine Phänomenologie,* Hua III (*Ideas pertaining to a Pure Phenomenology and to a Phenomenological Philosophy, First Book,* trans. F. Kersten)
Ideas II	Husserl, *Ideen zu einer reinen Phänomenologie und phänomenologischen Philosophie.* Zweites Buch: *Phänomenologische Untersuchungen zur Konstitution,* Hua IV (*Ideas pertaining to a Pure Phenomenology and to a Phenomenological Philosophy, Second Book,* trans. R. Rojcewicz and A. Schuwer)
Ideas III	Husserl, *Ideen zu einer reinen Phänomenologie und phänomenologischen Philosophie.* Drittes Buch: *Die Phänomenologie und die Fundamente der Wissenschaften,* Hua V (*Ideas Pertaining to a Pure Phenomenology and to a Phenomenological Philosophy, Third Book,* trans. T. E. Klein and W.E. Pohl)
IP	Husserl, *Die Idee der Phänomenologie,* Hua II (*Idea of Phenomenology,* trans. L. Hardy)
K	Husserl, *Die Krisis der europäischen Wissenschaften und die transzendentale Phänomenologie,* ed. W. Biemel, Hua VI
KITP	Husserl, 'Kant and the Idea of Transcendental Philosophy', trans. T. E. Klein and W. E. Pohl; EP I, Hua VII 230–87
LU	Husserl, *Logische Untersuchungen,* Hua XVIII, XIX/1 and XIX/2 (*Logical Investigations,* trans. J. N. Findlay, ed. D. Moran, 2 vols.)
Materialen VIII	Husserl, *Späte Texte über Zeitkonstitation (1929–1934): Die C-Manuskripte,* ed. D. Lohmar, Materialen Vol. VIII
OG	Derrida, *Edmund Husserl's Origin of Geometry: An Introduction,* trans. J.P. Leavey RJr., ed. D.B. Allison.

PES	Brentano, *Psychologie vom empirischen Standpunkt* (*Psychology from an Empirical Standpoint*, trans. A.C. Rancurello, D.B. Terrell and L.L. McAlister)
Phen. Psych.	Husserl, *Phänomenologische Psychologie: Vorlesungen Sommersemester* 1925, Hua ix (*Phenomenological Psychology*, trans. J. Scanlon)
PL	Husserl, *Pariser Vorträge*, Hua i (*Paris Lectures*, trans. P. Koestenbaum)
PP	Merleau-Ponty, *Phénoménologie de la perception*, 1945 (*Phenomenology of Perception*, trans. C. Smith)
Prol.	Husserl, *Prolegomena, Logische Untersuchungen* (*Logical Investigations*, trans. J. N. Findlay)
PRS	Husserl, *Philosophie als strenge Wissenschaft*, Hua xxv ('Philosophy as Rigorous Science', trans. M. Brainard)
SZ	Heidegger, *Sein und Zeit*, 1927 (*Being and Time*, trans. J. Macquarrie and E. Robinson)
Trans. Phen.	Husserl, *Psychological and Transcendental Phenomenology and the Confrontation with Heidegger (1927–1931)*, trans. T. Palmer and R. E. Palmer

In general, citations from Husserl will give the English translation pagination (if any) followed by the Husserliana volume number and German pagination. Thus, for the *Crisis* the reference will be 'C' followed by the page number of the Carr translation (where available) followed by 'K' for Hua vi and the page number there, e.g. 'C 3; K 1'). In the case of *Ideas* i, the German pagination will be that of the first edition of 1913, printed in the margin of the Husserliana edition. For the *Logical Investigations*, the volume number of the English translation will be indicated in bold, e.g. i or ii.

Introduction

This book offers an explanatory and critical introduction to Edmund Husserl's last work, *The Crisis of European Sciences and Transcendental Phenomenology* (1936 and 1954, hereafter '*Crisis*'),[1] a disrupted, partially published and ultimately unfinished project, written when its author was in his late 70s, struggling with declining health and suffering under the adverse political conditions imposed by the German National Socialist Regime that had come to power in 1933. The *Crisis* is universally recognized as his most lucidly written, accessible and engaging published work, aimed at the general educated reader as an urgent appeal to address the impending crises – scientific, moral and existential – of the age. Husserl is writing with the authority of a life-time of practice as a phenomenologist and with a fluidity previously not often found in his tortured prose. There is the strong sense of a philosopher with a mission, a mission to defend the very relevance of philosophy itself in an era defined both by astonishing scientific and technological progress and by political barbarism. The *Crisis* is also, undoubtedly, Husserl's most influential book, continuing to this day to challenge philosophers reflecting on the meaning of the achievements of the modern sciences and their transformative impact on human culture and on the world as a whole. The *Crisis of the European Sciences* is, by any measure, a work of extraordinary

---

[1] The German edition is Edmund Husserl, *Die Krisis der europäischen Wissenschaften und die transzendentale Phänomenologie: Eine Einleitung in die phänomenologische Philosophie* (hereafter 'K'), Walter Biemel ed., Husserliana (hereafter 'Hua') VI (The Hague: Nijhoff, 1954), partially translated by David Carr as *The Crisis of European Sciences and Transcendental Phenomenology: An Introduction to Phenomenological Philosophy* (hereafter 'C') (Evanston, IL: Northwestern University Press, 1970).

range, depth and intellectual force. It reveals a thinker who, still in possession of his subject, is embarking on a powerful and sustained defence of the very phenomenology he himself had been instrumental in developing and which he was attempting to rescue from the current generation of philosophers who, he claimed, had misunderstood his efforts.

Sadly, the *Crisis* was also the last work that Husserl was able to publish in his life-time. In fact, over the course of his working life, Husserl managed to publish no more than half a dozen books, chiefly: *Logical Investigations* (1900–1),[2] *Ideas* 1 (1913),[3] *Lectures on Internal Time Consciousness* edited by Martin Heidegger (1928),[4] *Formal and Transcendental Logic* (1929)[5] and *Cartesian Meditations* (published in French in 1931).[6] The *Crisis* was Husserl's last project, and it did not appear as a book but initially in the form of two journal articles. In fact, only the first two of the projected five parts of the *Crisis* appeared in print in the newly founded *Philosophia* journal, edited by the exiled German Neo-Kantian philosopher Arthur Liebert (1878–1946)[7] and published in Belgrade in January 1937 (but

[2] See Edmund Husserl, *Logical Investigations*, 2 vols, trans. J.N. Findlay, ed., with a New Introduction by Dermot Moran and New Preface by Michael Dummett (London, New York: Routledge, 2001). Hereafter 'LU' followed by the Investigation Number, the volume number of the English translation in bold, then section and page number; followed by the Husserliana volume and page number.

[3] Edmund Husserl, *Ideen zu einer reinen Phänomenologie und phänomenologischen Philosophie. Erstes Buch: Allgemeine Einführung in die reine Phänomenologie* 1. Halbband: *Text der 1–3. Auflage*, ed. Karl Schuhmann, Hua III/1 (The Hague: Nijhoff, 1977), trans. F. Kersten as *Ideas Pertaining to a Pure Phenomenology and to a Phenomenological Philosophy, First Book* (Dordrecht: Kluwer, 1983). Hereafter '*Ideas* 1'.

[4] Edmund Husserl, *The Phenomenology of Internal Time Consciousness*, trans. J.S. Churchill ed. Martin Heidegger (London: Indiana University Press, 1964).

[5] Edmund Husserl, *Formal and Transcendental Logic*, trans. D. Cairns (The Hague: Nijhoff, 1969). Hereafter 'FTL' followed by the section number and the page number of the English translation and the Husserliana volume and page number.

[6] For the English translation, see Edmund Husserl, *Cartesian Meditations*, trans. D. Cairns (The Hague: Nijhoff, 1967). Hereafter 'CM' followed by the section number and the page number of the English translation and the Husserliana volume and page number.

[7] Arthur Liebert, a Prussian Jew, was a Neo-Kantian philosopher who became head of the Kant-Gesellschaft in 1910. He was born Arthur Levy in Berlin (he changed his name to Liebert when he converted to Christianity) and studied philosophy in Berlin. A committed humanist, he published his first book on Pico della Mirandola and completed his doctorate under Friedrich Paulsen and Alois Riehl. For many years he edited *Kant-Studien*. He lectured in Berlin from 1919 until 1933, when he was dismissed under the Nazi laws. He then went to Prague, where he founded the *Philosophia* society and organized the publication of its journal, *Philosophia*, which appeared between 1936 and 1938, aiming to be an international voice

dated 1936).[8] Husserl continued to work on further parts but fell ill in the summer of 1937 and eventually died on 27 April 1938, unable to bring his planned project to completion. An edited version, still incomplete, based on Husserl's manuscripts and containing many supplementary texts, was published in 1954, edited by Walter Biemel (b. 1918), a Romanian-German philosopher who had written his doctoral thesis with Martin Heidegger (1889–1976). Aside from his official publications, Husserl left a considerable *Nachlass* (his literary estate) consisting of extensive notes of his lecture courses, as well as more exploratory research manuscripts that continue to be edited in the Husserliana series.

The text of the *Crisis,* as we currently have it, then, is the outcome of editorial work carried out first by Husserl and his assistants Eugen Fink (1905–75) and Ludwig Landgrebe (1902–91) and then by Walter Biemel on the printed parts, together with a bundle of associated manuscripts that Husserl himself had assembled as the K-III Group of manuscripts. Given these circumstances, the *Crisis of the European Sciences* is more a collage, a patch-work of fragments, than an actual, unified book. Yet it is still a remarkable philosophical accomplishment in many respects. Husserl himself regarded the *Crisis* as containing his most important work, 'the richest results of my life's work of over forty years', as he put it in a letter to Arthur Liebert (Hua XXIX xxxiii).

The *Crisis* claims to offer an introduction to transcendental phenomenology, and, of course, Edmund Husserl is best known for founding and developing the new science of *phenomenology*, developing an insight into the *intentionality*, or directedness, of conscious

serving philosophy. In 1939 he emigrated to Birmingham, England. He returned to Berlin in 1946 as full professor and dean of the education faculty, but he died soon afterwards. He wrote several Kantian studies and three books whose titles have relevance to Husserl's theme: *Die geistige Krisis der Gegenwart* [The Present Spiritual Crisis] (Berlin 1923), *Die Krise des Idealismus* [The Crisis of Idealism] (Zurich 1936) and *Von der Pflicht der Philosophie in unserer Zeit* [On the Duty of Philosophy in Our Time] (Zurich 1938). As a Neo-Kantian, and in agreement with Husserl, he opposed irrationalism and mysticism in philosophy, on the one hand, and also naturalism, on the other, and was also worried about philosophy collapsing into a relativistic worldview.

[8] The first two parts (i.e. §§ 1–27) of the *Crisis* were published in *Philosophia* Vol. 1 (1936), 77–176. Although dated 1936, the journal was in fact held up by a printer's strike and the editor Liebert's travels, and did not actually appear until January 1937. Husserl himself received his copy on 7 January 1937.

experiences that had been proposed by his teacher Franz Brentano (1838–1917). Phenomenology, as developed by Husserl and furthered by his students (e.g. Edith Stein (1891–1942), Ludwig Landgrebe, Eugen Fink) and followers (e.g. Martin Heidegger, Maurice Merleau-Ponty (1908–61)), quickly established itself as the dominant philosophical approach on the European continent in the first half of the twentieth century. Indeed, phenomenology continues to hold its own as a movement of international significance, both within Continental philosophy and also as a specific outlook and methodological approach to human subjectivity in the cognitive and health sciences. Phenomenology may be characterized broadly as the descriptive science of consciously lived experiences and the objects of those experiences, described precisely in the manner in which they are experienced.[9]

Husserl's understanding of phenomenology evolved and changed over his life, and the *Crisis* represents the mature expression of his transcendental phenomenology. Initially, he focused on individual processes of consciousness – perception, imagination, memory, time-consciousness and so on – understood as 'lived experiences' (*Erlebnisse*), mental episodes. But gradually he came to recognize the need to address the manner in which the flowing, connected stream of conscious experiences is unified into a *life*, centred around an *ego* but interconnected with other egos in a communal life of what Husserl calls broadly 'intersubjectivity', leading, finally, to the shared experience of a world as a whole (primarily experienced as the familiar 'life-world'). This turn to the ego, especially, led Husserl's phenomenology in a transcendental direction (and Descartes (1596–1650) is, for Husserl, the father of transcendental philosophy). The *Crisis* revolutionized phenomenology with its introduction of the life-world understood as the historical world, as we shall discuss in the course of this book.

Husserl had a deep fear that his phenomenology had been misunderstood. In his draft 'Foreword to the Continuation of the *Crisis*', Husserl fears his labours in the development of phenomenology are in danger of being discarded as irrelevant and outmoded, especially with the growing interest in life-philosophy, existentialism and

---

[9] See Dermot Moran, *Introduction to Phenomenology* (London, New York: Routledge, 2000).

what Husserl broadly characterizes as 'irrationalism' in philosophy. Husserl's urgent tone reflects not just his own sense of impending mortality, his need to critically assess his own achievement, but also the need to confront the intellectual crisis shaking Europe at a time – the mid 1930s – when the Nazification process was in full swing in Germany. Husserl had a strong sense the whole scientific culture of Europe was being threatened and undermined by a descent into irrationalism. He outlines the dangers confronting European culture and the intellectual confusions lying at the very heart of the positive sciences that appear, on the surface, to be so successful. Indeed, the *Crisis* is – a decade before Heidegger's famous critique of humanist ideals in his 'Letter on "Humanism"' (1947)[10] – a profound critical interrogation and reflection on the meaning of humanity and the humanist ideals of the Enlightenment.

Husserl's aim is, therefore, extremely ambitious. He says he is seeking to understand nothing less than 'the origin of the modern spirit' (C 57; K 58), and, in particular, the nature of the particular 'bestowal of meaning' or 'sense-bestowal' (*Sinngebung*, C 58; K 58) that has brought about the intellectual edifice or construction known as modern science. In his writings on culture, Husserl explicitly employs the German term '*Geist*', which has no exact equivalent in English, but which can broadly be translated as 'culture'. Spirit signifies the collective efforts and achievements of human conscious endeavour, and can be extended to mean all conscious life, including that of animals.[11]

Husserl begins the *Crisis* by announcing a 'crisis' not just in the extraordinarily successful natural sciences, but also in the 'total meaningfulness' of cultural life (C 12; K 10). After the German defeat in 1918, an entire generation seemed to have lost its faith in Western civilization and its supposed progress. As Husserl put it, humanity

---

[10] See Martin Heidegger, 'Letter on "Humanism"', *Pathmarks*, ed. William McNeill (New York: Cambridge University Press, 1998), pp. 239–76. Heidegger's letter was originally written to the French philosopher Jean Beaufret in 1946 as a response to certain questions put to Heidegger regarding his relation to Jean-Paul Sartre's existentialism. In his letter, Heidegger believes 'humanism' is an essentially metaphysical position deriving from Roman philosophy that fails to capture what is essential to human existence: 'Humanism is opposed because it does not set the *humanitas* of the human being high enough' (p. 251).

[11] The German *Geist* can be translated as 'mind', 'spirit' or 'culture', as well as 'ghost' or 'spectre'. Husserl speaks of 'the spirit of philosophy' and 'the spiritual battles' of Western culture (*Crisis* § 3).

appeared to have lost its faith in the 'ideal of universal philosophy' (C 10; K 8). Husserl, furthermore, in Hegelian fashion but without explicit reference to Hegel (1770–1831), regards the history of modern philosophy as presenting the shape of modern humanity itself (C 16; K 14). The move towards naturalism in modern philosophy mirrors the scientific embrace of naturalism and objectivism, with a consequent loss of a way of understanding values and indeed a complete misunderstanding of the 'enigma of subjectivity'.

Husserl's extended meditation on the development and current predicament of modern science and modern philosophy includes a critical evaluation of the circumstances that give birth to the (then relatively new) science of *psychology*. As we shall discuss in Chapter 4, Husserl is concerned to show that empirical psychology is a failed science since it fundamentally misunderstands the true nature of subjectivity, due to its acceptance of the fundamental split between objectivity and subjectivity brought about by modern science and further installed into the heart of modern philosophy by Descartes and his successors. For Husserl, the crisis of psychology (with its retarded development and methodological difficulties, C 4; K 2), is emblematic of the crisis facing the cultural sciences as a whole; these sciences have a distorted conception of subjectivity which is threatening their very meaningfulness as sciences. He therefore embarks on an intensive investigation of the meaning of human cultural interpenetration with the world, the world of living experience, what he calls the 'life-world' (*Lebenswelt*), which we shall discuss in Chapter 6, as a way of re-orienting and grounding both the natural and the human sciences. The term 'life-world' – which was already in use well before Husserl – began to appear in his work from around 1917. He acknowledges the influences of the discussion of the 'pre-found' world of experience in the early positivist Richard Avenarius (1843–96),[12] and the world of naïve experience in the philosopher and physicist Ernst Mach (1838–1916). Earlier incarnations of the concept include the

---

[12] See Richard Avenarius, *Der menschliche Weltbegriff* [The Human Conception of the World] (Leipzig: O. R. Reisland, 1891; reprinted Elibron Classics, 2005). Avenarius speaks of the world as 'the pre-found' (*das Vorgefundene*). Husserl discusses Avenarius in his *The Basic Problems of Phenomenology* (hereafter 'BPP' followed by English page number and Husserliana volume and page number), trans. Ingo Farin and James G. Hart, *Husserl Collected Works* Vol. XII (Dordrecht: Springer, 2006), pp. 22–8 and 107–11.

natural, surrounding world (see, especially, *Ideas* I §§ 27–9) and the 'natural concept of the world'.[13] The life-world, as Husserl characterizes it, is the world of the pre-given, familiar, present, available, surrounding world, including both 'nature' and 'culture' (however they may be defined), that envelops us and is always there as taken for granted. The life-world also provides a set of horizons for all human activity. The life-world is, in Husserl's terms, the 'fundament' for all human meaning and purposive activity. Although he is fascinated by the idea of the evolving human historical and cultural world (which has been the object of the particular sciences for millennia), in fact, in the *Crisis*, he is not specifically interested in the life-world for its own sake (what he would regard as a 'naïve' science of the life-world), but rather in meditating on the life-world as both support and counterpoint to the world of science as a way to understanding transcendental phenomenology. Husserl wants to understand the life-world in terms of the manner in which it provides cooperating subjects with the background and horizons necessary for the whole accomplishment of the objective world.

In the *Crisis*, Husserl uses two German words more or less interchangeably for 'crisis' – '*Krise*' (e.g. C 203; K 207) and the Greek-derived term '*Krisis*' (C 3; K 1). In the opening sections (*Crisis* §§ 1–7) Husserl makes a number of bold and interrelated claims:

1. There is a crisis of foundations in exact sciences.
2. There is a crisis brought on by the positivity of the sciences.
3. There is a crisis in the human sciences, since they model themselves on the exact sciences.
4. There is an explicit crisis in psychology, the supposed science of human spirit.
5. There is a crisis in contemporary culture ('a radical life-crisis of European humanity').
6. There is a crisis in philosophy (traditionally understood as the discipline which addresses the crisis in the sciences and in life).

All these crises are interlinked and have, according to Husserl, a common solution: transcendental phenomenology, which, with its secure

---

[13] See, for instance, Husserl's discussion of the 'natural concept of the world, i.e., that concept of the world in the natural attitude', BPP, esp. 15; Hua XIII 125.

and grounded clarification of the concept of *subjectivity*, offers a way out of these crises.

The *Crisis*, then, is not only a critical study of the current state of the sciences (chiefly physics and psychology), but also Husserl's preferred way to introduce students to his mature transcendental phenomenology.[14] Husserl intended the *Crisis* to be the authoritative and final statement of his mature phenomenological method – he himself speaks of it as a kind of 'discourse on method' (C 250; K 254). For Husserl, phenomenology cannot be seen as simply one philosophy among others; rather, as he articulates in the *Crisis*, it represents the mature form of modern philosophy itself, the highest form of transcendental philosophy, the epitome of self-conscious thinking that has interrogated its own assumptions and therefore can be genuinely seen as the most radical and fundamental form of reflection. To come to terms with phenomenology is, in Husserl's opinion, to come to terms with the cultural, scientific and philosophical achievement of the West ('Europe' in his broad sense). Husserl is offering a narrative, telling a tale involving an intellectual reconstruction of some defining moments in the intellectual history of the West and seeking to introduce transcendental phenomenology as a way of making sense of this history. Indeed, in his 'Foreword to the Continuation of the *Crisis*', Husserl speaks of 'the teleological-historical way' into transcendental phenomenology (C 102; K 435). Similarly, in a late note written in the summer of 1937, he calls it his 'historical way' into transcendental phenomenology (Hua XXIX 426) and claims that it is the principal and most systematic way, as we shall explore in Chapter 5.

For Husserl, the practice of philosophy is neither a private pursuit nor a merely cultural exercise; rather, as the pursuit of truth, it is an urgent matter for humanity itself. Furthermore, philosophy mediates our humanity to ourselves. Philosophers are 'functionaries of humankind' (*Funktionäre der Menschheit*, C 17; K 15), honest bureaucrats whose function it is to steer social and cultural development on

---

[14] Husserl was particularly concerned, as we shall see, to define phenomenology as an absolutely fundamental science that deals with the entire manner in which the objective world is disclosed to and experienced by concrete living subjects. He was equally concerned, however, to distinguish phenomenology, as a science of subjectivity-correlated-with-objectivity, from all forms of empirical *psychology*, which, for him, were based on a naturalistic misconstrual of the transcendental nature of this world-constituting subjectivity and intersubjectivity (see *Crisis* § 53).

the right path. The overall crisis, for Husserl, then, is the failure of European rationality, despite the enormous advances of the sciences in the technological domination of the world and in the technical organization of society, to have supplied a cure for the social and psychic illness of the time, because of the crucial neglect of the subjective contribution to the experience of the world. Thus, in his 1935 'Vienna Lecture', he contrasts folk medicine with scientific medicine and wonders why there has been no scientific equivalent of medicine for cultural ailments. Phenomenology will provide that cultural medicine for our time.

In this study, I plan, through a guided reading of the *Crisis*, to introduce Husserl's mature transcendental phenomenology and discuss critically his main concepts and methodological moves. I shall not assume any prior familiarity with Husserl or with phenomenology. In referring to Husserl's *Crisis* I shall use the English translation by David Carr published by Northwestern University Press,[15] which is based on the Husserliana edition edited by Walter Biemel. It must be noted at the outset that Carr's version of the *Crisis* contains a significant majority – but not all – of the texts of the German Husserliana edition. Where the non-translated parts are referred to, I shall provide the relevant translations. In 1992, other important research manuscripts broadly associated with the *Crisis* – including the text of Husserl's Prague lectures of November 1935 – were published in German as Hua xxix.[16] A further large volume of writings on the 'life-world' (*Lebenswelt*) – one of the key themes of the *Crisis* – recently appeared as Hua xxxix (2008).[17] Insofar as the material published in Hua xxix and xxxix casts new light on Husserl's thinking in the *Crisis*, I shall refer to it in my commentary.

---

[15] Carr's translation is excellent but does not translate the full text of Hua vi. Certain editorial decisions have been imposed, e.g. Husserl makes great use of emphasis (in the German text represented by wider spacing of the letters, '*gesperrt*'), but Carr does not always reproduce the italics. Carr often divides long sentences into shorter ones and divides a single complex question into several shorter ones.

[16] See Edmund Husserl, *Die Krisis der europäischen Wissenschaften und die transzendentale Phänomenologie. Ergänzungsband. Texte aus dem Nachlaß 1934–1937*, ed. Reinhold N. Smid, Hua xxix (Dordrecht: Kluwer, 1992).

[17] Edmund Husserl, *Die Lebenswelt: Auslegungen der vorgegebenen Welt und ihrer Konstitution. Texte aus dem Nachlass (1916–1937)*, ed. Rochus Sowa, Hua XXXIX (Dordrecht: Springer, 2008).

Because the *Crisis* is a fragmentary and unfinished text, I shall proceed thematically. Having introduced Husserl and his philosophy, and explained the genesis of the *Crisis* project, I shall focus on the themes of the natural sciences (in the figure of Galileo Galilei (1564–1642)), the human sciences (in particular psychology and history), Husserl's discovery of the life-world and his effort to develop the most advanced form of transcendental phenomenology. Finally, I shall discuss the influence of the *Crisis* in the twentieth century and beyond. In spite of everything, the *Crisis* is a relentlessly optimistic work, a work that looks to the future, a paean in praise of the philosophical life. For these reasons, the *Crisis* has inspired philosophers as varied as Jan Patočka (1907–77), Maurice Merleau-Ponty, Alfred Schutz (1899–1959), Hans-Georg Gadamer (1900–2002), Paul Ricoeur (1913–2005), Jacques Derrida (1930–2004), Jürgen Habermas (b. 1929), and Hilary Putnam (b. 1926).

HUSSERL'S TERMINOLOGY AND METHOD

A word of warning is necessary at the outset: while the *Crisis* is undoubtedly Husserl's most accessible and readable work, it is still a difficult and challenging text. It unfolds a narrative, but it does not do so in a straightforward manner. It is not always easy to follow the flow of his argument since Husserl – ever the honest philosopher – shares his hesitations and uncertainties as he unfolds his own thoughts. In this respect, he is the paradigmatic 'self-thinker' (*Selbstdenker*), as he himself calls the philosopher.[18]

Husserl's method of exposition in the *Crisis* involves a very particular procedure of interpretation that is only occasionally explicitly addressed in the text (primarily in *Crisis* §§ 7, 9(l) and 15). Husserl is developing a narrative, a *hermeneutical recuperation of the history of modern science and philosophy*. Although he does not use the term 'hermeneutics' (the word does appear infrequently in his later writings, presumably under the influence of Dilthey and Heidegger), he does speak of 'interpretation' (*Interpretation, Deutung*) or 'exposition' (*Auslegung*, see C 11; K 9), which he characterizes as primarily

---

[18] *Selbstdenker*, literally 'self-thinker', which Carr sometimes renders as 'autonomous thinker', is one of Husserl's favourite idioms, see e.g. C 393; K 511 and C 394; K 512.

achieved through a kind of 'backwards questioning' (*Rückfragen*) or 'backward reflection' (*Rückbesinnung*) – key terms in the *Crisis*. He is trying to recover a foundational meaning that has become covered up or obscured in our present understanding. He also speaks of clarifying the original 'bestowal of meaning' (*Sinngebung*, C 58; K 58) and exposing the various 'shifts and concealments of meaning' (*Sinnverschiebungen und Verdeckungen*, C 58; K 58) that have taken place across history. But Husserl is not just looking backwards, trying to make sense of the past as it shapes the present. He is also attempting to understand how the future has been shaped and set on a particular course by the meanings instituted in the past.

At *Crisis* §9 (l), he characterizes his approach to the history of meaning as moving in a 'kind of circle' (C 58; K 59) – involving what Heidegger calls, in *Being and Time* § 2, a kind of 'relatedness backwards and forwards' (a conception often called the 'hermeneutic circle'). In the *Crisis* Husserl speaks of moving in a zig-zag manner (*im Zickzack*, C 58; K 59), but one should not assume he is borrowing from Heidegger here. In fact he is repeating a characterization of his method that is early in his *Logical Investigations* (1900–), where he first speaks of moving in a 'zig-zag' manner, *im Zickzack*, LU **I**, *Intro.* § 6, 175; Hua XIX/1 22). According to this zig-zag procedure, Husserl will begin, for instance, from the contemporary positivistic understanding of the sciences and move back to try to understand their 'origin' and their 'development of sense' (*Sinnesentwicklung*, C 58; K 59). His phenomenology always involves the uncovering of presuppositions. He assumes (in a way that recalls the later Wittgenstein (1889–1951)) that we are all caught up in the 'spell' (*Bann*, K 58) of our times and that there is a need to get out from under this bewitchment. Going backwards and forwards between current understanding and the understanding of beginnings produces an 'interplay' (*Wechselspiel*) that helps to display what is at stake in our concepts. Husserl writes: 'Relative clarification [*Klärung*] on the one hand brings some elucidation [*Erhellung*] on the other, which in turn casts light back on the former' (C 58; K 59). Reading Husserl, then, requires a hermeneutical vigilance. He is never simply narrating a historical development for its own sake, but is attempting to uncover necessary structural features that make such meaning-formation possible.

Reading the *Crisis* is difficult not just because of the narrative relating backwards and forwards, but also because Husserl employs a unique terminology. He casually introduces key technical notions (e.g. intuition, evidence, intentionality, habituality, primal institution, sedimentation, horizon and so on) and assumes his readers to be familiar with his earlier works (e.g. *Logical Investigations, Ideas* 1), to which he alludes in passing.[19] Husserl's terminology can be quite complex and confusing. He sometimes invents terms, e.g. 'sensings' (*Empfindisse*). He imports terms liberally from the philosophical tradition (essence, matter, form, transcendental, soul), including classical Greek thought (e.g. *doxa, eidos, epochē, noesis, noema, telos, theoria*), but he usually invests these terms with new meaning. He borrows from Descartes (*cogito ergo sum, cogitatio, cogitatum*), Hume (e.g. 'matters of fact'), or Kant (1724–1804) ('manifold', 'receptivity', 'synthesis', 'transcendental ego'). Similarly, he adapted terms from psychology (e.g. 'outer perception', 'inner perception', 'ideation') or other sciences (e.g. 'attitude', 'worldview'). He also gave everyday terms new technical meanings (e.g. 'adumbration', 'horizon', 'world'). He took up and adopted in a unique manner many terms that were in use in the philosophical circles of his day, e.g. 'facticity' (*Faktizität*), 'lived experience' (*Erlebnis*), 'life-world' (*Lebenswelt*), 'empathy' (*Einfühlung*) or 'intersubjectivity' (*Intersubjektivität*). But, even with all his inventions and borrowings, the outcome is uniquely Husserl's own, and his thinking is expressed in a unique and identifiable style of expression. Husserl's technical terms are linked in an interconnected web of meanings. It is often therefore impossible to explain one term without invoking another related or contrasting technical term. Fortunately, there are a number of dictionaries available to assist in clarifying his terms.[20] Throughout this work I shall explain Husserl's technical terms as they arise and situate them in the context of his overall philosophy. In this manner, I hope in the following chapters to provide an illuminating

---

[19] For instance, Husserl discusses 'manifolds' (*Mannigfaltigkeiten*, C 45–6; K 45) and refers to earlier discussions on the theory of manifolds in LU *Prol.* §§ 60, 69, 70; *Ideas* 1 § 72; and FTL § 23, p. 77; Hua XVII 67.

[20] See Dermot Moran and Joseph Cohen, *The Husserl Dictionary* (London, New York: Continuum, 2012) and Dorion Cairns, *Guide for Translating Husserl* (The Hague: Nijhoff, 1973).

explication of phenomenology and Husserl's unique contribution to this movement.

One further complicating fact that must be borne in mind is that the *Crisis* is in part the outcome of Husserl's collaboration with his brilliant young assistant Eugen Fink, who had joined him in Freiburg and who was also attending Heidegger's lectures and seminars. Husserl had a series of assistants – including Edith Stein, Martin Heidegger, Ludwig Landgrebe – on whom he relied to put his research material in order, arrange sections, give chapter headings and so on. He thought of himself more or less as a scientist working in a community of other scientists, 'co-philosophizing', as he called it. For a full decade, from 1928 until Husserl's death in 1938, Fink actively collaborated with Husserl not just in creating typescripts from Husserl's shorthand notes, but also in drafting sketches for Husserl's system and writing proposed continuations of his work with a relatively free hand.[21] Husserl publicly endorsed Fink's interpretation of his work in 1933 (in a Foreword to Fink's article in *Kant-Studien*) and seemed content to allow his assistant to act as his public advocate, although privately he disagreed with many of Fink's formulations. Indeed, there are passages in the *Crisis* (especially those praising Hegel and German Idealism) which may very well have been inspired by Fink. There is clear evidence of Fink's involvement in some of Husserl's formulations, such as his presentation of the work as a kind of self-critique of the Cartesian approach of the *Cartesian Meditations*.[22] Fink also provided all the section and subsection heading titles for the *Crisis*.[23] Fink's guiding intention at that time was to reconcile Husserl's and Heidegger's approaches, and this has the effect of making Husserl often sound more Heideggerian than his more usual formulations would lead the reader to expect. The final text of the *Crisis*, then, in part is a Fink–Husserl cooperative effort and their individual contributions may never be properly

---

[21] For a full discussion of Fink's relationship with Husserl, see Ronald Bruzina, *Edmund Husserl and Eugen Fink: Beginnings and Ends in Phenomenology 1928–1938* (Neew Haven, London: Yale Univeristy Press, 2004), and Dermot Moran, 'Fink's Speculative Phenomenology: Between Constitution and Transcendence', *Research in Phenomenology*, Vol. 37 No. 1 (2007), pp. 3–31.

[22] See Bruzina, *Edmund Husserl and Eugen Fink*, op. cit., p. 213.

[23] See Fink's letter to Stephan Strasser, 1 November 1946, in Bruzina, *Edmund Husserl and Eugen Fink*, pp. 21 and 213.

identified and disentangled. Husserl believed in 'co-philosophizing', and the *Crisis* is a product of this approach.

Even in its unfinished form, the *Crisis of European Sciences* is Husserl's attempt to provide a new and radical critique of pure reason (to rectify Kant's efforts) including a critique of the human sciences (to replace Wilhelm Dilthey's efforts to develop an account of historical life). It offers a powerful philosophical critique of the project of modernity begun by Galileo and Descartes, i.e. contemporary Western culture with its reliance on science and technological organization. The *Crisis* introduces the notion of the 'life-world' (*Lebenswelt*) and defends its primacy in a way that reads almost as a counter-proposal to the Manifesto of the Vienna Circle that promoted the adoption of a scientific worldview.[24] The *Crisis* offers a devastating critique of the problems imposed by an overly narrow promotion of the natural scientific outlook in all areas of life. It builds on Husserl's earlier critiques of naturalism and objectivism, and defends the need for a rigorous science of subjectivity (which modern scientific psychology had failed to be).

The *Crisis* is, despite everything, a resolutely optimistic work, a defence of universal critical rationalism against the irrationalism of the age. It is a critical renewal of the values of the Greek and German Enlightenments and an encomium to the enduring role of philosophy in the development of an informed, self-critical scientific culture that promotes and protects genuine human values. It vigorously defends the role of philosophy in the critique of culture; philosophers are 'functionaries' of humankind whose aim is nothing less than the creation of a 'new humanity'.

The *Crisis* offers the first published account of Husserl's mature transcendental phenomenology that paid attention to history and development of culture, offering a counter-balance to the more solipsistic reflection of the *Cartesian Meditations* (1931). The *Crisis* is

---

[24] See *Wissenschaftliche Weltauffassung: Der Wiener Kreis* (1929), trans. 'The Scientific Conception of the World: The Vienna Circle', in Sahotra Sarkar, ed., *The Emergence of Logical Empiricism: From 1900 to the Vienna Circle* (New York: Garland Publishing, 1996), pp. 321–40.

subtitled *An Introduction to Phenomenological Philosophy* but it is unique in that the main text begins not with an exposition of phenomenology, but with a discussion of modern natural science and its problems (especially *Crisis* § 9), and then moves to a discussion of the development of modern philosophy and psychology, before introducing the concept of the 'life-world', and only then arriving at the concept of transcendental phenomenology. Husserl's plan is clearly to introduce phenomenology as resolving the deep problems of the sciences (including philosophy) by offering the first truly grounded scientific account of transcendental subjectivity and of the objective world that is always and everywhere constituted in and through this subjectivity. Husserl, then, is not abandoning the *Cartesian Meditations* (published in French in 1931), but providing a new mode of access to the same domain of transcendental subjectivity.

According to Husserl in the *Crisis,* phenomenology is the final evolution of modern philosophy in its transcendental turn. It aims at a comprehensive account of what he calls the *a priori correlation* between objectivity and subjectivity.[25] As he recounts at several points in the *Crisis* (i.e. §§ 41, 46 and 48), this a priori correlation presented itself to Husserl as a new insight around 1898:

The correlation between world (the world of which we always speak) and its subjective manners of givenness never evoked philosophical wonder (that is, prior to the first breakthrough of 'transcendental phenomenology' in the *Logical Investigations*), in spite of the fact that it had made itself felt even in pre-Socratic philosophy and among the Sophists – though here only as a motive for sceptical argumentation. This correlation never aroused a philosophical interest of its own which could have made it the object of an appropriate scientific attitude. (C 165; K 168)

According to this a priori correlation, the manner in which entities in the world present themselves is always related to the subjective way of apprehending these entities. Thus, the properties of the seen object have to be understood as related to the subjective act of visual perception, and so on. As Husserl puts it in his 1917 Inaugural Address to Freiburg University: 'To every object there corresponds an ideally closed system of truths that are true of it and, on the other

---

[25] On Husserl's 'correlationism' see Quentin Meillassoux, *After Finitude* (London: Continuum, 2009).

hand, an ideal system of possible cognitive processes by virtue of which the object and the truths about it would be given to any cognitive subject.'[26]

This correlation is uncovered through a specific kind of reflection. In his *Amsterdam Lectures* given in 1928, shortly before he delivered the Paris lectures of February 1929 that formed the basis of the *Cartesian Meditations*, Husserl gives an illuminating description of how he means to proceed in phenomenological reflection:

We will refrain from any traditional prejudgments, even the most universally obvious ones of traditional logic, which already have perhaps taken from Nature unnoticed elements of meaning. We will hold ourselves resolutely to what phenomenological reflection presents to us as consciousness and object of consciousness, and purely to what comes to actual, evident self-givenness. In other words, we will interrogate exclusively the phenomenological experience, clearly and quite concretely thinking into a reflective experience of consciousness, without interest in determining concretely occurring facts. Such [phenomenological] experience does not have the individual experience [in view], but the form most immediate to all as *Self-Experience* ... I as phenomenologist thus uncover my own living (in the attitude of fantasy, directed toward concrete possibility), my concrete possible living in this or that concretely actual and concretely possible forms. One can easily see that it is there, on the basis of this immediacy of my self-experience, that all other experience of the mental (always understood as experiencing intuition) is founded, pure experience of what is strange or other (*Fremderfahrung*) as well as of the community. So it is quite natural that from the outset the method of taking pure self-experience is treated as the method appropriate to a consistently conceived phenomenological disclosure of oneself.[27]

This is a typical statement of method of the so-called 'Cartesian' way of practising phenomenology. The aim as elucidated here is to attend to

[26] See Edmund Husserl, 'Pure Phenomenology: Its Method and Field of Investigation', trans. Robert Welsh Jordan, in Husserl, *Husserl. Shorter Works* (hereafter 'HSW'), trans. and ed. Frederick Elliston and Peter McCormick (University of Notre Dame Press, 1981), pp. 10–17; reprinted in Dermot Moran and Tim Mooney, eds., *The Phenomenology Reader* (London, New York: Routledge, 2002), pp. 124–33, esp. p. 125.

[27] See Edmund Husserl, *Psychological and Transcendental Phenomenology and the Confrontation with Heidegger (1927–31): The Encyclopaedia Britannica Article, The Amsterdam Lectures 'Phenomenology and Anthropology' and Husserl's Marginal Note in Being and Time, and Kant on the Problem of Metaphysics*, trans. T. Sheehan and R. E. Palmer, Husserl Collected Works Vol. VI (Dordrecht: Kluwer, 1997), p. 221; Hua IX 311. Hereafter referred to as '*Trans. Phen.*', followed by the page number and the Husserliana volume and page number.

whatever has immediate 'self-givenness' in the realm of self-conscious intuitive experience. One is focusing exclusively on what is given in the stream of one's own first-personal conscious experiencing, and on the manner of givenness of whatever is encountered within that stream of experiencing. All other forms of experiencing – including that of other actual subjects – have to be constituted from out of my own resources. This requires the ego coming to understand the essential nature of the ego in general and thereby modifying its own nature to include the possibility of other, different natures.

Husserl was deeply worried, however, that, on this version of constitution of the other from self-experience, one would never really encounter the other subject *as other*, as a truly distinct foreign consciousness, but only as some modification or projection of one-self. It is precisely this Cartesian 'solipsistic' approach to phenomenology that Husserl will seek to augment and to correct in his *Crisis*, although it is certainly true that he already signals this problematic in the *Cartesian Meditations* themselves. Phenomenology must come to grips with the phenomena of intersubjectivity. In the *Crisis*, however, Husserl will focus on the nature of communal experience and how community comes to be constituted, how 'communalization' occurs. It cannot be overemphasized that Husserl is by no means repudiating the approach of the *Cartesian Meditations*. Self-experience is always a necessary starting-point for phenomenological reflection. But he enlarges phenomenology in the *Crisis* by suggesting new approaches and specifically the approach '*by inquiring back from the life-world*' which is, of course, also the social and communal world. It is precisely the experience of intersubjectivity and the concept of a world as backdrop to all experience that requires a new kind of phenomenology of collective cultural experience.

THE *CRISIS* AS A DEFENCE OF THE ENLIGHTENMENT

In the *Crisis*, especially § 3, Husserl explicitly embraces a version of the Enlightenment project, especially in its Kantian sense, whereby enlightened humanity leaves behind enslavement to prejudice and enters the new realm of rational freedom by giving the law to itself, and freely undertakes to be bound by laws that are commanded by universal reason itself. Several times in the course of the main body of the *Crisis* (and in associated essays such as the 'Vienna Lecture'), Husserl emphasizes that the current crisis in the sciences and in European culture is a crisis of *reason*. Philosophy made a tremendous breakthrough in defining humans in terms of their potential to be rational, and the Renaissance and Enlightenment celebrated this rationality, but it has been distorted in a positivistic way by the natural sciences. Reason has been understood too narrowly, instrumentally, and in a 'one-sided' manner (C 291; K 338). Reason has been construed in terms of objectivism and naturalism. One cannot simply return to previous concepts of reason, either; the Enlightenment had too narrow a conception of reason (C 290; K 337). There is need to return to the 'genuine' sense of rationality as an ideal originally inaugurated by Greek philosophy in order to restore the true ideal of reason:

Rationality, in that high and genuine sense of which alone we are speaking, the primordial [*urtümlich*] Greek sense which in the classical period of Greek philosophy had become an ideal, still requires, to be sure, much clarification and self-reflection; but it is called in its mature form to guide [our] development. (C 290; K 337)

We shall explore this theme in subsequent chapters. Let us now introduce Edmund Husserl through a brief review of his life and thought.

CHAPTER I

Husserl's life and writings

I seek not to instruct but only to lead [*zu führen*], to point out
and to describe what I see. I claim no other right than that of
speaking according to my best lights, principally before myself
but in the same manner also before others, as one who has lived
in all its seriousness the fate of a philosophical existence.

(C 18; K 17)

EDMUND HUSSERL (1859–1938): THE EARLY YEARS

Edmund Husserl's life straddles the nineteenth and twentieth
centuries. His more or less exact contemporaries included Henri
Bergson (1859–1941), Sigmund Freud (1856–1939), John Dewey
(1859–1952), Heinrich Rickert (1863–1936), Josiah Royce (1855–1916),
Lucien Lévy-Bruhl (1857–1939) and J. G. Frazer (1854–1941). He was
born of middle-class assimilated Jews on 8 April 1859 in Prossnitz,
Moravia (now Prostejov, Czech Republic), then part of the Austro-
Hungarian empire. He studied in Gymnasium schools in Vienna
and in Olmütz (Olomouc, Czech Republic). In 1876 he entered the
University of Leipzig, where he studied mathematics, physics and
astronomy, and attended (but got little from) the philosophy lectures of Wilhelm Wundt (1832–1920). However, his friend Thomas
Masaryk (1850–1937) introduced him to the British empiricists. In
1878 he transferred to Berlin, where he studied mathematics with Karl
Weierstrass (1815–97) and Leopold Kronecker (1823–91). Weierstrass
had a formative influence on the young Husserl, awakening in him
the 'ethos for scientific striving', as he would later put it.[1]

---

[1] Malvine Husserl, 'Skizze eines Lebensbildes von Edmund Husserl', ed. Karl Schuhmann
Husserl Studies Vol. 5 (1988), 105–25, see esp. 112, records Husserl as saying: 'From Weierstrass
I got my ethos for scientific striving.'

In 1881 Husserl enrolled to study mathematics at the University of Vienna, and, in 1882, he received his doctorate with a dissertation on differential calculus. Following a period in Berlin as assistant to Weierstrass, in 1884 he moved back to Vienna to attend the lectures of Franz Brentano, one of the founders of experimental psychology. In his *Psychology from an Empirical Standpoint* (1874) Brentano aimed to found a new strict science, which, some years later, he termed 'descriptive psychology' (*deskriptive Psychologie*) and even 'phenomenology' (*Phänomenologie*).² This descriptive psychology was to be an a priori, classificatory science of mental acts and their contents based on the apodictic self-evidence of what Brentano termed 'inner perception'. Within this enquiry he identified intentionality as the chief characteristic of 'mental phenomena'. Intentionality means 'directedness to an object' (*die Richtung auf ein Objekt*, PES 88) and was for Brentano the one positive feature that uniquely characterized mental acts.

Husserl's two years (1884 to 1886) with Brentano inspired him to move from mathematics to become a philosopher. He invoked Brentano's descriptive psychology in his first publication, *Philosophy of Arithmetic* (1891),³ which aimed at the philosophical clarification of arithmetical concepts elucidating their 'psychological origin' (understood here in terms of descriptive psychology). Husserl became increasingly dissatisfied with Brentano's narrow commitment to a kind of representative theory of mental acts, and in his next book, *Logical Investigations* (1900–1), he offered a number of criticisms of Brentano's overall approach to psychic phenomena. In this groundbreaking book Husserl developed intentionality as a distinctive way of investigating all aspects of consciousness, meaning and knowledge. Much later, in his *Formal and Transcendental Logic* (1929), Husserl claimed that Brentano had failed to recognize the true meaning of intentionality because he had not seen it as a 'complex

---

² Franz Brentano, *Psychologie vom empirischen Standpunkt*, 3 vols. (Hamburg: Felix Meiner Verlag, 1973), trans. A. C. Rancurello, D. B. Terrell and L. McAlister as *Psychology from an Empirical Standpoint*, 2nd edn. with a new Foreword by Peter Simons (London: Routledge, 1995). Hereafter 'PES'.

³ Edmund Husserl, *Philosophie der Arithmetik: Mit ergänzenden Texten (1890–1901)*, ed. L. Eley, Hua XII (The Hague: Nijhoff, 1970), trans. Dallas Willard as *The Philosophy of Arithmetic: Psychological and Logical Investigations with Supplementary Texts from 1887–1901*, Husserl Collected Works Vol. x (Dordrecht: Kluwer, 2003).

of performances' that end up being layered in such a way as to make up the complex unity of the intentional object: 'Brentano's discovery of intentionality never led to seeing in it a complex of performances [*Zusammenhang von Leistungen*], which are included as *sedimented history* in the currently constituted intentional unity and its current manners of givenness – a history *that one can always uncover following a strict method*'. (FTL § 97, p. 245; Hua XVII 252).

Recalling his philosophical development in the *Crisis*, Husserl claimed his philosophical breakthrough came in 1898 when he realized that there was a 'universal a priori of correlation between experienced object and manners of givenness' (C 166n.; K 169n.1). Anything that is – whatever its meaning and to whatever region it belongs – is 'an index of a subjective system of correlations' (C 165; K 168). Every object and every meaning must be understood not solely as it is 'in itself' but in relation to the subjective acts which disclose it.

Husserl's *Logical Investigations* was the remarkable result of ten intensive years of logical research, during which he read then-contemporary logicians such as Mill (1806–73), Boole (1815–64), Bolzano (1781–1848), Lotze (1817–81) and Frege (1848–1925). But the book was anything but a textbook in logic. The first volume, *Prolegomena to Pure Logic*, published separately in 1900, was a sustained critique of psychologism. The second volume, subtitled *Investigations in Phenomenology and the Theory of Knowledge*, and published in two parts in 1901, contained six philosophical investigations that mark the true beginnings of his phenomenological method. The six investigations consisted of extended, careful philosophical analyses and clarification of issues in semiotics, semantics, mereology (the study of wholes and parts), formal grammar (the a priori study of the parts of any language whatsoever in regard to their coherent combination into meaningful unities) and the nature of conscious acts, especially presentations and judgements. In fact, it was these detailed analyses of the essential structures of consciousness, in terms of intentional acts, their contents, objects and truth-grasping character, especially in the last two Investigations, which set the agenda for the emerging discipline Husserl fostered under the name *phenomenology*.

The *Prolegomena* was enthusiastically received by established German philosophers, including Wundt, Wilhelm Dilthey

(1833–1911), and Paul Natorp (1854–1924). The second volume, containing the six investigations themselves, went largely unnoticed among the wider philosophical public, but a number of students of Theodor Lipps (1851–1914) in Munich read it as a new way of practising philosophy, and several travelled to Göttingen to study with him. He was also invited to Munich to give lectures. Husserl's *Logical Investigations* seemed to these readers to be an entirely new way of doing philosophy. Instead of the analysis of problems in the history of philosophy, it offered epistemological clarification through the use of an intuitive method and a critique of the basic concepts required in the activity of knowing and in the understanding of the object of knowledge.

In September 1901 Husserl was appointed to Göttingen University, a renowned centre of mathematics. Husserl joined a circle of scientists that included the mathematicians Felix Klein (1848–1925) and David Hilbert (1862–1943). Hilbert, who had already formulated his axiom of completeness for arithmetic and had published his hugely influential *Grundlagen der Geometrie* (1899), which organized geometry as a formal axiomatic system, had envisaged Husserl as playing a vital role in advancing the cause of *formalism* in mathematics and logic, but Husserl himself already suspected that the imaginary numbers would prove an obstacle to such completeness. Hilbert's students attended Husserl's seminars, including Ernst Zermelo (1871–1953), who also worked on set theory, Paul Bernays (1888–1977), and the physicist Hermann Weyl (1885–1955), who later attempted to integrate phenomenology into mathematics and physics.[4]

THE DISCOVERY OF THE PHENOMENOLOGICAL
REDUCTION (SEEFELD 1905)

Husserl underwent a change of direction around 1905, a turn first publicly revealed in lectures given at Göttingen University in 1906–7 (*Briefwechsel* VI 277), but treated in the research manuscripts known as the 'Seefeld pages' (*Seefelder Blätter*), written during the summer of 1905. While on holiday in Seefeld in Austria, in 1905, he wrote a manuscript in which he used the term 'phenomenological reduction'

---

[4] See especially Hermann Weyl, *Space-Time-Matter* (New York: Dover, 1952).

(Hua x 237) for the first time. These concepts were probably first publicly announced in his 1906–7 lecture course on *Logic and the Theory of Knowledge*.[5] In April and May 1907 Husserl delivered five lectures at Göttingen, later published as *The Idea of Phenomenology* on the reduction as a way of moving from the psychological to the truly epistemological domain.[6] He now began to characterize his phenomenology in transcendental terms and embarked on a serious re-reading of Kant for his 1905–6 lectures. A whole series of problems emerge together in these notes, problems with which Husserl continued to wrestle for the rest of his life: problems concerning the constitution of temporal experiences in consciousness, the enduring unity of the I across different acts and experiences, and the nature of its 'sense-giving' or 'meaning bestowal' (*Sinngebung*), the problem of the recognition of the other person in empathy, and, perhaps most importantly, the intersubjective constitution of objectivity. Thereafter, Husserl insisted that phenomenology should not be understood as the naïve or straightforward, essential description of acts of consciousness and their correlated objects, but had to be understood in terms of the acts and objects as uncovered through the phenomenological reduction. In particular, the reduction was supposed to suspend naïve commitments to the actual reality of what is perceived and grasped. In his earliest public discussion of reduction, *The Idea of Phenomenology*, he speaks of a 'philosophical reduction' and a 'phenomenological reduction' (IP, p. 4; Hua II 5) to exclude everything posited as transcendently existing, but he goes on to speak of an 'epistemological reduction' (*erkenntnis-theoretische Reduktion*) as necessary in order to focus on the pure phenomena of conscious acts as what he calls, borrowing from Descartes, 'thoughts' (*cogitations*). In the reduction, one also has to avoid misleading assumptions about the nature and existence of the meditating ego, Descartes' 'I am

---

[5] Edmund Husserl, *Einleitung in die Logik und Erkenntnistheorie: Vorlesungen 1906/07*, Hua XXIV (Dordrecht: Kluwer, 1984), pp. 165ff and 212, trans. Claire Ortiz Hill as *Introduction to Logic and the Theory of Knowledge: Lectures 1906/07*, Husserl Collected Works Vol. XIII (Dordrecht: Springer, 2008).

[6] Edmund Husserl, *Die Idee der Phänomenologie: Fünf Vorlesungen*, first published 1950 as Hua II, ed. Walter Biemel, now 2nd edn (The Hague: Nijhoff, 1973), trans. W.P. Alston and G. Nakhnikian as *The Idea of Phenomenology* (The Hague: Nijhoff, 1964). These lectures were intended as a general introduction to his lectures on the thing, *Dingvorlesung*, now Hua XVI. Hereafter 'IP'.

thinking' (*sum cogitans*, IP, p. 33; Hua II 43). Husserl has in mind the specific *bracketing* of a psychological interpretation of what is given in the acts of knowing. At various stages in his writings he refers to a *psychological* reduction as well as to *phenomenological, eidetic* and *transcendental* reductions. In the *Crisis* Husserl specifically addresses several ways into phenomenology through the performance of various reductions. He often speaks in the plural of different forms of reduction, and a whole literature has grown up discussing the supposed forms of the reduction.[7] In the text of the *Crisis* itself at least three 'ways' of performing the reduction are identified: what Husserl himself calls the 'Cartesian way' (*Crisis* § 43), the proposed new 'way from psychology' (*Crisis* § 59) and the 'way from the pregiven lifeworld' (*Crisis* Part IIIA). But the prominence of the psychological reduction, especially towards the end of the *Crisis* text (Part IIIB), is due to the fact that, in natural life as in the positive sciences (and indeed even in the 'depth-psychology' of the unconsciousness), there is an assumption that psychic life is understood and available in a straightforward way. Putting this assumption in brackets allows the true functions of constituting subjectivity to come to light. We shall discuss the psychological reduction further in Chapter 4 and the reduction to the life-world in Chapter 6 below.

Husserl was invited by the leading Southwest Neo-Kantian Heinrich Rickert to contribute an essay to Rickert's new journal *Logos*. This programmatic essay, *Philosophie als strenge Wissenschaft* ('Philosophy as Rigorous Science', published 1910–11),[8] offered a sustained critique of naturalism and historicism (as leading to relativism) and set the stage for many of the themes that are prominent in the *Crisis*. Husserl here extended his critique of *psychologism* to include all varieties of *naturalism* (including the naturalistic psychology of Wilhelm Wundt). But he also found a new target in the

---

[7] See, for instance, John J. Drummond, 'Husserl on the Ways to the Performance of the Reduction', *Man and World* Vol. 8 No. 1 (February 1975), 47–69, reprinted in D. Moran and L. Embree, eds., *Phenomenology: Critical Concepts in Philosophy* (London, New York: Routledge, 2004), vol. 1, pp. 231–51.

[8] Edmund Husserl, *Philosophie als strenge Wissenschaft*, in Husserl, *Aufsätze und Vorträge (1911–1921)*, ed. H.-R. Sepp and T. Nenon, Hua XXV 3–62 (Dordrecht: Kluwer, 1986), trans. Marcus Brainard as 'Philosophy as Rigorous Science', *The New Yearbook for Phenomenology and Phenomenological Philosophy* Vol. 2 (2002), 249–95. Hereafter 'PRS'. For Walter Biemel's remarks, see his 'Editor's Introduction' (*Einleitung des Herausgebers*) to Hua IX xvi.

increasingly influential historical hermeneutics of Wilhelm Dilthey, which he viewed as a historicism leading to relativism and hence to the collapse of the mission for science. In particular, Husserl singled out Dilthey's philosophy of worldviews (*Weltanschauungsphilosophie*) as denying the objective validity of cultural formations. The elderly Dilthey was put out that he was the focus of Husserl's attacks and wrote to Husserl denying the charge of relativism. He died shortly afterwards in 1911, but, years later, in his 1925 lectures, Husserl made amends, acknowledging Dilthey's important contribution to descriptive psychology.[9] It is clear that Husserl continues to engage with Dilthey in the *Crisis*, and not just because of the Berlin philosopher's importance for Heidegger.

THE PUBLICATION OF *IDEAS* I (1913) AND THE MOVE TO FREIBURG (1916)

In 1913, some twelve years after LU, Husserl published the first book of his *Ideas*, subtitled *General Introduction to Pure Phenomenology*. This was the first of his many 'introductions' to phenomenology. Like most of his other published books, it was written in a single feverish burst, over eight weeks of the summer of 1912. *Ideas* I aims to introduce the 'general doctrine of phenomenological reductions' (*Ideas* I, p. xxi; Hua III/1 5) which give access to the domain of pure consciousness, and also to give a general account of the structures of pure consciousness. While it is to promote phenomenology as an a priori science of essences, Husserl says that he will avoid the term 'a priori' as much as possible and instead employ the Greek term *eidos* meaning 'essence'. Husserl is proposing to understand the a priori in terms of essence. *Ideas* I also offers a description of life in the 'natural attitude' (a concept Husserl had introduced around 1907 in his *Idea of Phenomenology* lectures, to refer to the unquestioned manner of accepting the existence and givenness of the world in its usual temporal course) and of normal sciences as carried out in this attitude and in its theoretical complement ('the natural theoretical attitude', *Ideas* I § 1). It is in this work that Husserl emphasizes the 'worldly'

---

[9] Edmund Husserl, *Phänomenologische Psychologie: Vorlesungen Sommersemester 1925*, ed. Walter Biemel (The Hague: Nijhoff, 1968), Hua IX, trans. J. Scanlon as *Phenomenological Psychology: Lectures, Summer Semester 1925* (The Hague: Nijhoff, 1977). Hereafter '*Phen. Psych.*'

nature of the sciences of the natural attitude and their dogmatic nature, which must now be confronted by a critical turn, activated by an *epochē* or 'suspension', which puts out of play all worldly positings of consciousness in order to grasp its very essence. This work is extraordinarily ambitious, in that it attempts to lay the groundwork for a phenomenology of reason, and it is clear that Husserl's *Crisis* is a late attempt to revisit many of the issues originally presented in *Ideas* I.

On 1 April 1916 Husserl took up the Chair of Philosophy at the Albert-Ludwigs Universität Freiburg, where he would remain until his retirement in 1928. After the end of the First World War, especially, Husserl began promoting the idea of the need for an ethical 'community of reason' (*Vernunftgemeinschaft*, see Hua XXIX xiii n.3) to overcome what he took to be a situation of cultural breakdown, weariness of spirit and disintegration. In 1923–4, for instance, he wrote a number of articles for a new Japanese journal, *Kaizo*, on the theme of 'renewal' (*Erneuerung*), a journal to which Heinrich Rickert and Bertrand Russell (1872–1970) had also contributed.[10] In the opening paragraph he writes: 'Renewal is the universal call in our present, sorrowful age, and throughout the entire domain of European culture.'[11]

Husserl says that modern people have lost their faith in culture and there is danger of a 'decline of the West'. Husserl says that European culture has lost its way and strayed from its inborn *telos* (Hua XXVII 118) of freely given autonomous reason. Echoing the mood of many Germans in the early 1920s (at a time of economic hardship), he bemoaned the appalling state of affairs in the Weimar Republic where 'psychological tortures' and economic humiliation had replaced war or continued it by other means. For him this war and its aftermath showed up the 'inner falsity and senselessness' of European culture (Hua XXVII 23). Husserl saw the only hope for overcoming *Realpolitik* and rebuilding the confidence of a people

---

[10] Husserl wrote four articles in total, reprinted in Husserl, *Aufsätze und Vorträge (1922–1937)*, ed. T. Nenon and H.-R. Sepp. Hua XXVII (Dordrecht: Kluwer, 1989). The first *Kaizo* article, 'Renewal: Its Problem and Method', has been translated in HSW, pp. 326–34. A new translation of the four lectures by Philip Buckley will appear in the Husserl Collected Works series. The first three articles were published in *Kaizo*.

[11] Husserl, 'Renewal: Its Problem and Method', HSW, p. 326.

was through a spiritual retrieval of the human sense of purpose, a renewal of the ideals of the European Enlightenment (which culture, in his opinion, Japan had recently joined). The much talked-about 'decline of the West' is not irreversible. The answer is to shape our lives freely according to a life of reason. Only rigorous science can help us, Husserl says, but the problem is to find such a science, one which will be a true science of humanity, 'a science that would establish a rationality in social and political activity and a national, political technique'.[12] An a priori science of humanity (akin to the a priori science of mathematical physics that prescribes and regulates how natural science is to be conducted) is needed, a science of the 'spirit' (*Geist*), 'the *mathesis* of spirit and of humanity'.[13] This new a priori science of human spirit, Husserl continues, will have to come to grips with the 'inwardness' of each individual consciousness; each human being is an 'ego-subject' in a relation of empathy with other humans establishing a community together through their intersubjective, social acts. None of this can be understood if consciousness and subjectivity are approached naturalistically, as in current experimental psychology, as activities belonging to animal organisms causally interacting in a natural world. Husserl believes that we criticize our culture from the standpoint of ideal norms based on our ideal concept of a true and genuine humanity.[14] Husserl's theme of the renewal of philosophy and science through the creation of a universal moral order, and through a surpassing of narrow nationalisms in order to found true community in shared interests, will come to full expression in the *Crisis*.

HUSSERL'S PARIS LECTURES (1929) AND *CARTESIAN MEDITATIONS* (1931)

Several of Husserl's students, including Roman Ingarden (1893–1970) and Edith Stein, followed him to Freiburg, but his most important collaborator there would be Martin Heidegger (1889–1976), whom he met soon after his arrival in Freiburg. Heidegger had just completed his Habilitation thesis under Heinrich Rickert in 1915 and, strictly speaking, was never a student of Husserl's, although Husserl

[12] Ibid., p. 328.   [13] Ibid.   [14] Ibid., p. 330.

assisted Heidegger in the publication of his thesis. Heidegger had to enlist in the army in 1917, but after his return to Freiburg in 1919 he began lecturing and assisting Husserl. For the next decade Husserl and Heidegger became very close, sharing long philosophical conversations, even holidaying together. As part of their cooperation, Heidegger published an edited version of Husserl's *Lectures on Internal Time Consciousness* in 1928. Heidegger and Husserl had also attempted to collaborate on an article, 'Phenomenology', commissioned for the fourteenth edition of the *Encyclopaedia Britannica*.[15] Although several drafts were produced between September 1927 and February 1928, it became evident that their views diverged radically, and, in the final submitted version, Husserl had excised much of Heidegger's contribution, especially the latter's introductory paragraph locating phenomenology within fundamental ontology.[16] This failed collaboration revealed the growing fissure between their positions, and their relationship with one another deteriorated. When Husserl finally sat down to read Heidegger's own work, he felt bitterly disappointed.

The philosophical success of Heidegger's *Being and Time* (1927) forced Husserl to go on the offensive to defend his life's work.[17] He travelled to Amsterdam in April 1928 to deliver two public lectures on 'Phenomenology and Psychology', a development of his views as outlined in the recently completed *Encyclopedia Britannica* article.[18] On 23 and 25 February 1929, in Paris, Husserl delivered two two-hour lectures entitled 'Introduction to Transcendental Phenomenology' (later published as the *Paris Lectures*) at the Descartes Amphitheatre of the Sorbonne. In attendance were Emmanuel Levinas (1906–95), Lucien Lévy Bruhl, Jean Cavaillès (1903–44), Jean Héring (1890–1960), Alexandre Koyré (1892–1964), Jan Patočka, Gabriel Marcel and

---

[15] English translations of the various drafts of Husserl's *Encyclopaedia Britannica* article, as well as the text of the final published version, can be found in *Trans. Phen.*, pp. 80–196; Hua IX 237–301.

[16] See Herbert Spiegelberg, 'On the Misfortunes of Edmund Husserl's *Encyclopaedia Britannica* Article "Phenomenology",' HSW, pp. 18–20. For a full discussion of the affair, see Thomas Sheehan, 'The History of the Redaction of the *Encyclopaedia Britannica* Article', *Trans. Phen.*, pp. 36–59.

[17] See Martin Heidegger, *Being and Time*, trans. John Macquarrie and E. Robinson (New York: Harper and Row, 1962). Hereafter 'SZ', followed by the page number of English translation and then German original.

[18] Hua IX 302–49; trans. *Trans. Phen.*, pp. 213–53.

Maurice Merleau-Ponty. In 1931 a French translation of these lectures was published, edited by Levinas and Gabrielle Peiffer, assisted by Alexandre Koyré, entitled *Méditations cartésiennes (Cartesian Meditations)*. Husserl held back the German edition for further revisions.[19] He saw the lectures as merely offering a sketch of the breadth of transcendental life, the domain of transcendental phenomenology, but, due to their broad circulation, they have been seen as a canonical expression of his mature transcendental philosophy. In this regard the *Cartesian Meditations* explore the so-called 'Cartesian way' into phenomenology. In collaboration with his new assistant, Eugen Fink, Husserl sought to develop a new, expanded version of this *Cartesian Meditations* for publication in his *Jahrbuch für Philosophie und phänomenologische Forschung* (see letter to Ingarden February 16 1931).[20] Fink also produced his own *Sixth Cartesian Meditation*, which laid down the conditions that made it possible to undertake transcendental enquiry in the first place and proposed Husserl's work as a continuation of Kant's transcendental philosophy, with both a 'transcendental aesthetic' and a 'transcendental doctrine of method'.[21] Fink's work takes Husserl's work in a Heideggerian direction, as such former students of Husserl as Edith Stein pointed out. Nevertheless, Fink became very important as Husserl's interlocutor in the 1930s and was particularly influential during the writing of the *Crisis* texts. Fink was a student in Freiburg between 1926 and 1928, and attended both Husserl's and Heidegger's seminars. The young Fink arrived at just the right time to help Husserl realize his plans for a systematic presentation of his philosophy. For Husserl's final decade (from 1928 to 1938), he and Fink were almost inseparable, regularly taking walks together on the Lorettoberg mountain above Freiburg, deep in discussion. Husserl saw Fink as his loyal disciple

---

[19] Although a German typescript of the lectures circulated among Husserl's students, the original manuscript from which Levinas translated got lost. A revised German version of the text was eventually published in 1950.

[20] See Edmund Husserl, letter to Roman Ingarden, 16 February 1931, in Husserl, *Briefe an Roman Ingarden mit Erläuterungen und Erinnerungen an Husserl*, ed. Roman Ingarden (The Hague: Nijhoff, 1968), pp. 66–7.

[21] E. Fink, *VI. Cartesianische Meditation. Teil 1: Die Idee einer transzendentalen Methodlehre*, ed. Hans Ebeling, Jann Holl and Guy Van Kerckhoven, Hua Documente I (Dordrecht: Kluwer, 1988), trans. with an Introduction by Ronald Bruzina as *Sixth Cartesian Meditation: The Idea of a Transcendental Theory of Method. With Textual Notations by Edmund Husserl* (Bloomington: Indiana University Press, 1995).

to whom he would entrust the task of completing transcendental phenomenology, thus securing his legacy after the 'betrayal' of his erstwhile protégé Martin Heidegger. Fink's task was to take over his *Nachlass* and give it literary shape; clarifying, ordering and refining it into a finished system.

HUSSERL'S FINAL DECADE (1928–38)

Following his retirement from Freiburg in 1928, Husserl was increasingly concerned to protect the reputation of his version of transcendental phenomenology, which was now being challenged by rising star Martin Heidegger, whose *Being and Time* had appeared in 1927. After a long period of silence (no major publication had appeared since 1913), new works appeared. He plunged into a hectic set of lecture tours (Amsterdam in 1928 and Paris in 1929) and furious writing. Two new books were published: *Formal and Transcendental Logic* (1929) and the *Cartesian Meditations* (1931), the French translation of his 1929 lectures in Paris. In these texts, as in his 'Author's Preface' to the first English translation of his *Ideas* I (by W. R. Boyce Gibson (1869–1935)), Husserl proclaimed and defended his steadfast adherence to transcendental phenomenology and to transcendental idealism.[22]

In 1930–1 Husserl was working with his assistant, Eugen Fink, on the German edition of the *Cartesian Meditations* as the new authoritative statement of his philosophy and was even engaged in trying to present his phenomenology as a coherent philosophical 'system'. In particular he was struggling to develop his phenomenological account of the experience of the other person in what he called 'empathy' (*Einfühlung*), to which he had devoted the Fifth Cartesian Meditation. He was also working on the problems of intersubjectivity (*Intersubjektivität*), i.e. the relation between subjects, and on the constitution of the sense of the shared common 'world'.

---

[22] See Edmund Husserl, 'Nachwort zu meinen *Ideen zu einer reinen Phänomenologie und phänomenologischen Philosophie*', *Jahrbuch für Philosophie und phänomenologische Forschung* Vol. 11 (1930), 549–70; reprinted Hua V 138–62; trans. R. Roycewicz and A. Schuwer as 'Epilogue', *Ideas Pertaining to a Pure Phenomenology and to a Phenomenological Philosophy, Second Book* (hereafter '*Ideas* 11'), Husserl Collected Works Vol. IV (Dordrecht: Kluwer, 1989), pp. 405–30.

Husserl's personal situation completely changed in 1933, however, when the National Socialist Party came to power in Germany that January. In April 1933, based on an official decree concerning 'the re-establishment of a permanent civil service' that excluded non-Aryans from holding positions in the state service, Husserl was officially banned from teaching and publishing in Germany. On 4 May 1933, reacting to new decrees banning those of Jewish descent from public service, Husserl wrote to his longtime friend Dietrich Mahnke (1884–1939):

Finally, in my old age, I had to experience something I had not deemed possible: the erection of a spiritual ghetto, into which I and my children … are to be driven … We are no longer to have the right to call ourselves German; our spiritual work is no longer to be included in German cultural history. (*Briefwechsel* III 491–2, my translation)

Husserl was denied participation in official delegations of German philosophers attending such conferences as the 1934 International Congress of Philosophy held in Prague, although he wrote a letter that was read out at the Congress and drafted a text, the so called 'Prague Treatise'. He was, however, able to make private lecture trips to Prague and Vienna in 1935. Husserl was invited by the Vienna Cultural Society to deliver a lecture, 'Philosophy in the Crisis of European Humanity' (*Die Philosophie in der Krisis der europäischen Menschheit*), in Vienna on 7th May, which, due to its popularity, was repeated on 10th May. Husserl was one of a number of distinguished intellectuals (Ernst Cassirer, Martin Buber, and Thomas Mann) invited to give lectures to that Viennese society. This lecture is included in the series of *Crisis* texts (generally referred to as the 'Vienna Lecture', C 269–99; K 314–48). In the 'Vienna Lecture', Husserl speaks of a 'burning need' for an 'understanding of the spirit' which has arisen (C 296; K 344). As he had already outlined in his 1934 Prague lecture, it is Greek philosophy which created the idea of Europe as a 'spiritual, self-enclosed, unified form of life' (Hua XXIX 207) rather than as a geographically defined place. This theme is repeated in the 'Vienna Lecture' where he states that the name 'Europe' refers to 'the unity of a spiritual life, activity, creation, with all its ends, interests, cares and endeavors, with its products of purposeful activity, institutions, organizations' (C 273; K 319).

Six months later, on 14 and 15 November 1935, at the invitation of the Philosophy Circle in Prague, Husserl delivered two lectures, entitled 'The Crisis of European Science and Psychology' (*Die Krisis der europäischen Wissenschaft und die Psychologie*). Landgrebe, Schutz, Felix Kaufmann (1895–1949), and Jan Patočka, among others, were in attendance. While these lectures focused on the revolution of modern philosophy and science, Alfred Schutz recalled that, at a separate invited seminar, Husserl talked of the importance of the Greek breakthrough in philosophy and the emergence of the purely theoretical attitude, themes Husserl had been developing since the 1920s.[23] During his Prague visit, on 18 November 1935, Husserl also addressed the Brentano society, and, on the invitation of Roman Jakobson (1896–1982), the *Cercle linguistique*. Husserl's Prague lectures mark the beginning of his actual writing of the *Crisis*, with which he was preoccupied until serious illness prevented him in late 1937, from further work.

Husserl's circumstances – and those of his family – worsened following the imposition by the Reichstag of the Nuremberg Laws of September 1935, which brought the full force of the penal code down on those deemed 'non-Aryans'. In April 1935, in a letter to Landgrebe, Husserl had expressed the hope that he might not after all be relegated to the 'non-Aryan dung heap' (*Briefwechsel* IV 328), but by September of that year a new law based on the Nuremberg Laws had been promulgated, and Husserl's teaching licence was withdrawn, and, eventually, his German citizenship revoked. In one letter Husserl alludes to the 'bomb' of 15 September 1935 (*Chronik*, p. 467), a reference to the Nuremburg Laws.[24] As Husserl became officially isolated in Germany, he hoped to relocate his papers to Czechoslovakia, with the support of his former assistant, Landgrebe. *Experience and Judgment* (1938), a volume of Husserl's meditations selectively organized and edited by Landgrebe, was published in Prague shortly after Husserl's death, but was immediately suppressed in the aftermath of the German invasion of Czechoslovakia and was not circulated until

---

[23] Alfred Schutz, in H.L. Van Breda and J. Taminiaux, eds., *Edmund Husserl 1859–1959* (The Hague: Nijhoff, 1959), p. 88.

[24] According to the Reich Citizenship Law (part of the Nuremberg Laws), citizenship was based on race. Jews could not be citizens.

after the Second World War.[25] The *Crisis* came, then, towards the end of a long and active career and is Husserl's final statement on many of the issues that preoccupied him over a life-time. Husserl died on 27 April 1938 and was buried outside Freiburg.

THE IDEA OF 'CRISIS' IN HUSSERL'S WORK

Husserl did not really begin writing the *Crisis* until after he had returned from his Prague lectures in November 1935. Husserl published the first part of his planned book (§§ 1–27 of the present edition of the *Crisis*) in Belgrade in the yearbook *Philosophia*, which was edited by Arthur Liebert, a German Neo-Kantian philosopher who, like Husserl, had lost his professorship on account of his being Jewish and who was living in exile in Belgrade.[26] Husserl envisaged the *Crisis* as a radical, historical, retrospective critique of his own philosophical contribution, as well as a definitive statement in a new form, an 'historical-material introduction' (*historisch-sachliche Einleitung*, Hua XXIX xxxiii) to his transcendental phenomenology.[27]

The idea of a 'crisis' of the European sciences is not new in Husserl's thought: it already appears in various guises in his lectures and other writings from the time of his 1910–11 essay 'Philosophy as Rigorous Science' (where he had criticized philosophy for failing to measure up to science), through the 1920s, e.g. in his essays on the need for a 'renewal' (*Erneuerung*) of human cultural values in his articles written for the Japanese journal *Kaizo* (now Hua XXVII, 3–42), and emerging finally in print in *Philosophia* in 1936. As the idea evolved, it became not only a *scientific* crisis of method, but also an *existential* crisis of humanity, culture and reason. Since the outbreak of the First World War, and intensifying during the 1920s, Husserl, along with

[25] Edmund Husserl, *Erfahrung und Urteil*, rev. and ed. L. Landgrebe, trans. J. S. Churchill and K. Ameriks as *Experience and Judgment: Investigations in a Genealogy of Logic* (London: Routledge and Kegan Paul, 1973). Ludwig Landgrebe edited and selected a number of Husserl's manuscripts to produce *Experience and Judgment*.

[26] *Philosophia* also contained an article by Jan Patočka: 'Der Geist und die zwei Grundschichten der Intentionalität' [The Spirit and the Two Fundamental Levels of Intentionality], *Philosophia* Vol. 1 No. 1 (1936), 67–76.

[27] The German *sachlich* means 'material' or 'factual' in the sense of addressing the material issues, the facts of the matter. Husserl's slogan for philosophy was *zu den Sachen selbst*, 'back to the things or matters themselves'.

many other German philosophers (including Natorp and Scheler (1874–1928)), had been reflecting on the nature of contemporary culture and the need for a revision of the task of philosophy and a 'renewal' (*Erneuerung*) of Western or 'European' values of humanity. Husserl is not alone in diagnosing the present age as an age of crisis. The theme of crisis was prominent among German intellectuals of the time. Nor is he alone is seeing part of the problem as arising from the domination of the natural and exact sciences which have overrun all human experience (hence psychology takes over the business of managing people, e.g. the 'human resources' skills supposedly developed to manage our 'welfare'). As Aron Gurwitsch (1901–73) has pointed out, Husserl's description of the crisis of Western science is reminiscent of that of Max Weber (1864–1920) in his 'Science as Vocation' essay, where Weber speaks of increasing specialization and the distance between science and the view of the common person.[28] Husserl indeed admits, at the beginning of the 'Vienna Lecture', that the theme of the European crisis has been much discussed (C 269; K 314). The need to address it has become more real and urgent.

The word *Krisis* features in the titles of several studies Husserl possibly knew, including *The Philosophical Crisis of the Present Age* of Karl Joël (1864–1934).[29] The editor of *Philosophia*, Arthur Liebert, had also written a number of books on this theme, including *The Present Spiritual Crisis* and *Towards a Critique of the Present*,[30] as well as publishing an article in the very same issue of *Philosophia* as Husserl's own piece.[31] In 1936 the young Jan Patočka published an

---

[28] Weber originally gave the lecture in 1917. See Max Weber, 'Wissenschaft als Beruf', in Weber, *Gesammelte Aufsätze zur Wissenschaftslehre* (Tübingen: Mohr, 1922), pp. 524–55, trans. by Rodney Livingstone as 'Science as a Vocation', in Weber, *The Vocation Lectures: Science as a Vocation, Politics as a Vocation*, ed. David Owen and Tracy Strong (Indianapolis: Hackett, 2004). See Aron Gurwitsch, 'The Last Work of Edmund Husserl', *Philosophy and Phenomenological Research* Vol. 16 No. 3 (March 1956), 380–99, esp. 383n.

[29] Karl Joël, *Die philosophische Krisis der Gegenwart* (Leipzig: Meiner, 1914). Joël sent Husserl a copy of this text, for which Husserl thanked him (on 11 March 1914), saying he had read the work several times (*Briefwechsel* VI 205). See also Rudolf Pannwitz, *Die Krisis der europäischen Kultur* (1917) and Ernst Troeltsch, 'Die Krisis des Historismus', *Die neue Rundschau* 33 (1922), 572–90.

[30] See Arthur Liebert, *Die geistige Krisis der Gegenwart* (Berlin: Pan-Verlag R. Heise, 1923) and his *Zur Kritik der Gegenwart* (Langensalza: Hermann Beyer & Söhne, 1927).

[31] Arthur Liebert, 'Das Problem der Kulturkritik und die Kulturkritik unserer Zeit' [The Problem of Cultural Critique and the Cultural Critique of Our Time], *Philosophia* Vol. 1 No. 1 (1936), 243–313.

article entitled 'Masaryk's and Husserl's Conception of the Spiritual Crisis of European humanity'.[32] Heidegger too had spoken of the crisis of the sciences in his lectures of 1925, and again in *Being and Time* § 3, where he speaks of 'crises of foundation' in the sciences when their fundamental concepts are found to be problematic. In this sense, physics, logic and mathematics had all undergone intellectual crises and revolutions in their basic concepts during the first decades of the twentieth century.

This crisis, of course, in Husserl's eyes is not confined to the theoretical sciences; there is also a crisis in human values. As Hans-Georg Gadamer has reminded us, after 1918 there was a strong sense among European intellectuals of Western culture being in a crisis. Inspired by Nietzsche (1844–1900), such intellectuals as Max Weber and Oswald Spengler (1880–1936) pronounced on the state of Western culture. Spengler's *The Decline of the West* is one such popular, two-volume work, the first volume of which was published in the summer of 1918.[33] Interestingly, Spengler also discusses the relation between classical civilization and European–American culture, and is moreover interested in mathematics. Spengler claims that Greek classical mathematics had no genuine understanding of limit or infinity, and, accordingly, for Spengler, even the Greeks had no idea of history. On the other hand, the European West, with its concepts of the zero, limit and the infinite, has the necessary tools to develop a truly historical worldview. Husserl has similar views on the importance of infinity for modern mathematical science.

---

[32] See Jan Patočka, 'Masaryk's and Husserl's Conception of the Spiritual Crisis of European Humanity', in Erazim Kohák, ed., *Jan Patočka: Philosophy and Selected Writings* (University of Chicago Press, 1989), pp. 145–55.

[33] See Oswald Spengler, *Der Untergang des Abendlandes – Umrisse einer Morphologie der Weltgeschichte*, Band I: *Gestalt und Wirklichkeit*; Band II: *Welthistorische Perspektiven*. Vol. I appeared in 1918, Vol. II in 1922. The two volumes were reprinted Munich: C. H. Beck, 1923. Now translated in abridged form by Charles F. Atkinson as *The Decline of the West* [1918], Vol. I: *Form and Actuality* (New York: Alfred A. Knopf, 1926), Vol. II, *Perspectives of World History* [1928], ed. Arthur Helps and Helmut Werner (New York: Oxford University Press, 1991). Spengler revised Vol. I in 1922 and published the second volume in 1923 (in part influenced by Goethe and Nietzsche, the book forecasts the decline/sunset of Western civilization and there is a critique of democracy as driven by monetary interests). Spengler argues that traditional European philosophy has been too localized and parochial, and there is need for a proper 'world-history' which calls for a new 'morphology' of cultural and historical forms. Husserl speaks of the theme of the 'decline of the West' as only the latest in a line of sceptical weakening of the philosophical spirit, see Hua XXVII 122. He also speaks of the 'collapse of the West' (Hua XXVII 243) in his letter to the 1934 Prague Congress.

Clearly, behind Husserl's conception of 'crisis' is Kant's conception of 'critique' (*Kritik*), and, in many ways, the *Crisis* is Husserl's response to Kant. Husserl, like Kant, is dissatisfied with modern ways of doing philosophy that are enmeshed with a distorted conception of the world, established by the modern natural scientific method. Philosophy must be practised in a new way, avoiding traditional inventing of new philosophies (*Crisis* § 7), making edifying speeches and discussing 'philosophemes' (a term Husserl uses in the *Logical Investigations* and again in C 73; K 74), that is, common philosophical problems, themes or tropes. A new kind of self-reflection attentive to human 'historicity' is required, one that approaches the history of philosophy from a different point of view, breaking up what Husserl terms 'the crust of the externalized "historical facts" of philosophical history' to find deep hidden motivations and an inner unity. This is what Husserl will term the third and highest level of historicity – the level of self-conscious subjectivity – the level at which transcendental phenomenology becomes operative as a form of self-conscious permanent vigilance (K 557).

Husserl makes clear, especially in the *Crisis* Part II (§§ 25–7), that he follows the revolutionary breakthrough of Hume and Kant in understanding all objectivity as a constituted result of subjective activity. 'Transcendental', for Husserl as for Kant, means that the conditions for the possibility of objectivity have to be understood. To speak of an 'objective world' existing in itself is naïve objectivism. Modern science's embrace of that naïve objectivism has led to a crisis in the sciences, as he explains in the *Crisis* Part I (§§ 9–14) especially. Husserl, however, believes that although Kant recognized the essential correlation between the objective world and constituting subjectivity, in the end it took a naturalized view both of the objective world (which Kant construed as the world of Newtonian space, time and causality) and of subjectivity (which was understood in a psychologistic manner – especially by the Neo-Kantians). The true answer to this crisis of the sciences (the foundational crisis which Kant had already recognized) is only hinted at, initially, at the beginning of *Crisis* § 13, where Husserl introduces, but does not discuss in great detail, the notion of 'functioning subjectivity' (*leistende Subjektivität*, C 67; K 68), which he describes as operating everywhere 'in hiddenness'. It is one of the most important features of the *Crisis* that it introduces the notion of 'functioning subjectivity' (especially *Crisis* § 54), which is taken up by Fink and later by Merleau-Ponty in his *Phenomenology of Perception*, where he speaks of 'functioning intentionality (*fungierende Intentionalität*).[34] Functioning subjectivity, according to Husserl, is the collective and anonymous intentionality that gives us our sense of world, with its horizons of future and past. This subjectivity has been misconstrued in modern philosophy from Descartes to Kant as an internal or *psychological* subjectivity.[35] The problem of the relation of the objective world to this psychological subjectivity becomes the central problem in the turn to epistemology in Kant. The traditional transcendental objectivism is replaced in Kant's work by what Husserl calls 'transcendental subjectivism' (C 68; K 69). To understand the true relationships between subjectivity and objectivity, however, a radical enquiry into origins is required. This, for Husserl, is transcendental phenomenology, as we shall explore in Chapter 7 below.

One of Husserl's specifically philosophical motivations for writing the *Crisis* had to be to challenge the interpretation of his work being promulgated by more popular authors such as Martin Heidegger and Max Scheler. In part, the *Crisis* aims to offer a restatement and defence of his particular form of transcendental phenomenology against misunderstandings which he attributed to former followers – specifically Scheler and Heidegger (see K 439).

In particular, a new hermeneutic and existential phenomenology was being popularized in Germany due to the influence of Martin Heidegger's *Being and Time* (1927). When Husserl eventually read *Being and Time*, he was disturbed by its 'anthropological' tendency, as he saw it, and he was also particularly put out by a book, *Life-Philosophy and Phenomenology*, by Georg Misch (1878–1965),[36]

---

[34] Maurice Merleau-Ponty, *Phénoménologie de la perception* (Paris: Gallimard, 1945), trans. Colin Smith as *Phenomenology of Perception* (London: Routledge & Kegan Paul, 1962). Henceforth 'PP', with pagination of the English translation and then the pagination of the French edition.

[35] See Edmund Husserl, 'Kant and the Idea of Transcendental Philosophy', trans. Ted E. Klein and William E. Pohl, *Southwestern Journal of Philosophy* Vol. 5 (Fall 1974), 9–56; Hua VII 230–87. Hereafter 'KITP', with pagination of the English translation and the Husserliana volume and page number.

[36] Georg Misch, *Lebensphilosophie und Phänomenologie: Eine Auseinandersetzung der Diltheyschen Richtung mit Heidegger und Husserl* [Life-Philosophy and Phenomenology: A Dispute Concerning the Diltheyan Tendency in Heidegger and Husserl] (Bonn: Cohen, 1930; 3rd

a follower of Wilhelm Dilthey, which cast his phenomenology in a poor light in contrast to Heidegger's more existential and hermeneutical turn. The deeply wounded Husserl, anxious to establish the validity and intrinsic rationality and scientific rigour of his own approach over against what he took to be a certain ungroundedness, irrationalism and decisionism in contemporary life-philosophy (in which category he included Dilthey and Heidegger, as well as Nietzsche and Simmel (1858–1918)), began in the early 1930s to focus particularly on the themes of human life, the experience of the 'flowing, living present' (*strömend lebendige Gegenwart*), intersubjectivity and historicity (Hua xv xliv–xlv). Husserl even went so far as to say, in his *Nature and Spirit* lectures, that phenomenology was a truly *scientific* life-philosophy. In other words, Husserl claims to have been completely misunderstood when phenomenology as a more or less Cartesian philosophy of consciousness was contrasted with the supposedly more 'concrete' conceptions of life espoused by Heidegger, Scheler and others. Husserl's transcendental phenomenology explores the true meaning of intentional life.

THE ON-GOING INFLUENCE OF THE *CRISIS*

Husserl's *Crisis* continues to be relevant because it challenges philosophers and scientists to think about the nature of the present age with its dominant scientific and technological worldview, a view that has led, as Husserl believed, to universalization but at the same time to a kind of flattening-out of reason which has left many core human values unsupported and threatened. In his analyses of the current state and hegemony of the scientific-technological attitude, Husserl predicted the rise of naturalism, relativism and irrationalism in the face of the dominant instrumental reason. Somewhat in the spirit of Nietzsche, Spengler and others, Husserl is also attentive to the general mood of *weariness* sweeping through Western culture in this

---

edn Stuttgart: Teubner, 1964). For a discussion of Misch's impact, see Theodore Kisiel, *The Genesis of Heidegger's Being and Time* (Berkeley: University of California Press, 1993), pp. 454–8. Husserl himself wrote to Misch in 1929 to clarify what he meant by phenomenology and to explain that the 'relativity of nature' meant not the interrelation between things in nature, but rather the dependence of the concept of nature on the intersubjective community of researchers who define it. See Husserl, *Briefwechsel* Vol. vi. 276–7.

crucial period of the 1930s. As he saw it, 'Europe's greatest danger is weariness' (C 299; K 348). There is a danger of 'despair', of loss of sense of values, leading to estrangement, collapse and, ultimately, to 'barbarism'. However, Husserl is also, based precisely on his belief in the redeeming universality of philosophy, an optimist with regard to the teleology of European history. He writes: 'from the ashes of great weariness, will rise up the phoenix of a new life-inwardness [*Lebensinnerlichkeit*] and spiritualization as the pledge of a great and distant future for man, for the spirit alone is immortal' (C 299; K 348).[37] Husserl is certain of the future of the human spirit, because, he believes, transcendental phenomenology is the science that grasps the intrinsic meaning and inner rationality of the *accomplishment of spiritual life* in all its forms.

With old age and increasing frailty, Husserl is aware that the *Crisis* will be his last will and testament, and therefore he is speaking, as he puts it, 'as one who has lived in all seriousness the fate of a philo-sophical existence' (*das Schicksal eines philosophischen Daseins*, C 18; K 17). We shall have to consider in the course of this work whether Husserl's vision of philosophy's role in its relation to the crises of con-temporary culture offers the necessary challenge needed to address the situation, or whether it remains a merely rhetorical call to arms on behalf of a universal rationality which remains ungrounded. Let us now turn to examine the *Crisis* in more detail.

---

[37] Husserl frequently invokes this notion of human 'innerness' (*Innerlichkeit*), a concept that has a long history in German mystical thought going back to Meister Eckhart. Husserl means it in the sense of restoring a life of self-critical conscious rational subjectivity.

CHAPTER 2

Husserl's Crisis: *an unfinished masterpiece*

THE *CRISIS*: GENESIS AND STRUCTURE

Husserl's *Crisis* is not easy to summarize. Its themes and philosophical analyses are deceptively difficult. Due to the unique circumstances of its composition – written, as we have seen, during Husserl's last years and during the rise to power of the Nazi regime, under which, as a Jew, he personally suffered victimization – the *Crisis* cannot be seen as a unified book in the usual sense. It is, rather, a 'projected' book. In fact, it consists of a number of systematic parts – two were published in 1936 and a third exists as a typescript, collected with a loose assembly of partial segments and sketches for further parts, along with essays, reflections and public lectures – written over a period of years, more or less from 1934 to 1937, around a central theme, namely the crises of the mathematical and the human sciences, the consequences of these crises for Western culture and the role of phenomenological philosophy in addressing these crises.

The *Crisis*, especially in the Husserliana version (1954) edited by Walter Biemel, introduced the philosophical public to a hitherto unknown Husserl – the Husserl who had been lecturing in Freiburg in the 1920s, without significant publications. New themes included embodiment, empathy, the intuitively experienced life-world, normality, the experience of otherness, the encounter with the stranger, transcendental intersubjectivity and so on, all topics that would become prominent in post-Husserlian phenomenology. In part, Husserl is attempting to answer critics – including the Neo-Kantians and the life-philosophers – who maintained that his phenomenology of consciousness was outmoded. Thus, in his 'Foreword to the Continuation of the *Crisis*' (K 435–45, not translated in Carr), dating from early 1937, Husserl expresses regret that many of his readers have taken him to be an old conservative, sclerotically stuck in his ways, and merely regurgitating his old themes rather than facing up to the new criticisms (K 439–40). The reverse is true, he insists: he is thinking through the meaning of philosophy and phenomenology with renewed radicality.

The *Crisis,* in its present form, presents fragments of a vast, ambitious but unfinished project. According to Eugen Fink's brief outline (c. 1936) for the continuation of the *Crisis*, the work was to have five parts (C 397–400; K 514–17). The first two parts were published in the year book *Philosophia.* Husserl held back a much-reworked typescript of *Crisis* Part III, also intended for publication in *Philosophia*, but he kept on reworking it and never sent it back to the publisher.[1] The existing typescript is overlaid with Husserl's notes and emendations. In his 'Foreword to the Continuation of the *Crisis*' he writes: 'Insurmountable complications, as a result of my fluctuating health, had forced me to leave aside some of the already prepared drafts' (K 435, my translation). As a result, Husserl records, the published parts should be regarded as the mere 'overture' to the main work. It is to be understood as a self-reflection on the recent aims and methods of philosophy. The proposed critique of Kant is postponed, in part because the idea of a self-justifying philosophy (as conceived by Kant) is actually already articulated in Descartes. Husserl insists on the importance of performing the radical *epochē* as that which genuinely brings about the 'Copernican revolution' spoken of by Kant, and of developing 'a critique of Kant that refers back to the Cartesian primary establishment of the whole of philosophical modernity' (K 438, my translation).

Husserl's 'Foreword to the Continuation of the *Crisis*', written in early 1937, then outlines his plans for continuing the work – and unsurprisingly he places most emphasis on developing a 'teleological-historical way' that is to serve as the 'royal road' (*Emporleitung*) into transcendental phenomenology. Clearly, the reflection on the history of modern philosophy in the *Crisis*, then, is not an ancillary part of

---

[1] Walter Biemel claims that the text 'breaks off' (*bricht ab*) after Section 72, but see Philip Bossert, 'A Common Misunderstanding Concerning Husserl's *Crisis* Text', *Philosophy and Phenomenological Research* Vol. 35 No. 1 (1974), 20–33, who maintains that Part IIIB naturally ends with Section 72.

transcendental phenomenology, but is supposed to reveal its deepest meaning.

Husserl left behind a large collection of draft research manuscripts, written in shorthand and sorted into bundles (called 'convolutes') tied with string or ribbon. The manuscripts associated with the *Crisis* are labelled the 'K-series' ('K' for '*Krisis*'). These manuscripts are essentially working notes that Husserl's then assistant Eugen Fink had assembled in consultation with Husserl himself. The *Crisis*, then, in the Husserliana edition (1954), consists of the two published *Philosophia* articles (§§ 1–27 of the present expanded text), together with 'Part III' (§§ 28–72, prepared for publication but not published), along with the related research manuscripts, selected and edited by Walter Biemel. Biemel's interpretation and ordering of the texts is necessarily a work of reasoned judgement and surmise. Some of his editorial decisions have been questioned. Biemel included a Section 73, which Carr disputes as a proper concluding section and demotes to an appendix. Certainly, Biemel's choice of the assembled material and its ordering must be understood as speculative, based on hints given both by Husserl and by Fink.[2]

The Biemel edition contains a number of supplemental texts, including three 'essays' or 'treatises' (*Abhandlungen*), the most significant of which is Husserl's 'Vienna Lecture' (written in April and delivered in May 1935) – controversial because of its claim that 'Europe' stands as the name for the idea of universal humanity, and for its allegedly ethnocentric remarks about non-European cultures. The 'Vienna Lecture' introduces new material not found in the main body of the text. According to the draft plan for the *Crisis*, Part V was to cover 'The indispensable task of philosophy: humanity's responsibility for itself', and one can find elements of this theme in

---

[2] Biemel's master document for *Crisis* Parts I to III (§§ 28–71) is Husserl's own typescript, prepared originally by Fink but greatly overwritten with Husserl's own comments. Regrettably, Husserl's original shorthand manuscript for this typescript is not extant, as Biemel confirms (K 519). This typed draft includes not just interlinear comments, crossings-out, marginal comments and additions by Husserl, but also some by Fink and indeed by Ludwig Landgrebe; see Ron Bruzina, *Edmund Husserl and Eugen Fink: Beginnings and Ends in Phenomenology 1928–1938* (New Haven: Yale University Press, 2004), p. 215. Bruzina suggests Fink was particularly concerned to elaborate on 'horizon-consciousness' and on 'wakefulness', especially in *Crisis* § 37. Fink is implicitly criticizing Husserl for his focus on the world as primarily given in terms of physical objects, whereas Fink wants to show that 'horizon-consciousness' involves an essentially different kind of intentionality.

the 'Vienna Lecture', as well as in supplementary texts (collected in Hua XXIX).

Following these three *Abhandlungen*, Biemel has included twenty-nine associated supplementary texts. Carr has translated only six of these twenty-nine texts. The most important of them is a fragmentary essay on 'The Origin of Geometry' (the title was supplied by Fink),[3] which has been the subject of a long and influential commentary by the French philosopher Jacques Derrida because of the status Husserl attributes to the written sign in the fixing of ideal meanings for the transmission of knowledge.[4] We shall discuss 'The Origin of Geometry' in Chapter 3 below.

Soon after the *Crisis* appeared in *Philosophia* in January 1937, a few of Husserl's later short texts were published. Marvin Farber (1901–1980) arranged for the publication of several texts on the constitution of space, including the crucially important text usually known as 'The Earth Does Not Move', which we shall discuss in Chapter 3.[5] This text is, strictly speaking, not part of the *Crisis* texts, but, written in 1934 and published in 1940, it was quickly associated with the *Crisis* texts by Merleau-Ponty and others. To speak of the *Crisis*, then,

[3] Edmund Husserl, 'Die Frage nach dem Ursprung der Geometrie als intentional-historisches Problem', *Revue Internationale de Philosophie* Vol. 1 No. 2 (1939), 203–35. This text was edited by Eugen Fink and published in an issue of the journal in memoriam of Husserl, who had died the previous year. It is likely that Fink added the title, which translates as 'The Origin of Geometry as an Intentional-Historical Problem'. In his introductory preface Fink claims that Husserl had offered a regressive enquiry into the foundations of logic in his 1929 *Formal and Transcendental Logic*, and that now he was turning to a similar analysis of mathematics. Husserl's text was given an extensive review by Dorion Cairns in *Philosophy and Phenomenological Research* Vol. 1 (1940), pp. 98–109. Cairns focuses on Husserl's insistence that geometrical truths (e.g. the Pythagorean theorem) are ideal entities that are essentially the same unique entities in all contexts in which they appear. They can be shared intersubjectively but 'writing is what makes possible the permanent objectivatedness of ideal sense-formations' (Cairns, ibid., 102).

[4] Jacques Derrida, *Edmund Husserl's Origin of Geometry: An Introduction*, trans. J.P. Leavey Jr., ed. D. B. Allison (Sussex, NY: Harvester Press/Nicolas Hays, 1978).

[5] Edmund Husserl, '*Umsturz der kopernikanischen Lehre* in der gewöhnlichen weltanschaulichen Interpretation. Die Ur-Arche Erde bewegt sich nicht. Grundlegende Untersuchungen zum phänomenologischen *Ursprung der Körperlichkeit der Räumlichkeit der Natur* im ersten naturwissenschaftlichen Sinne. Alles notwendige Anfangsuntersuchungen', in Marvin Farber, ed. *Philosophical Essays in Memory of Edmund Husserl* (Cambridge, MA: Harvard U.P., 1940), pp. 307–25, trans. Fred Karsten as 'Foundational Investigations of the Phenomenological Origin of the Spatiality of Nature. The Originary Ark. The Earth Does Not Move', rev. by Len Lawlor, in Maurice Merleau-Ponty, *Husserl at the Limits of Phenomenology*, ed. L. Lawlor and B. Bergo (Evanston, IL: Northwestern University Press, 2002), pp. 117–31.

is not just to speak of a loosely connected series of manuscripts and research writings that Husserl wrote from, roughly, 1934 until he was forced through ill-health to abandon writing in the autumn of 1937.

THE *CRISIS*: AN UNFINISHED PROJECT

A crisis in science, as Husserl defines it, means that its scientific method has become questionable (C 3; K 1). He begins with an analysis of the significance of the modern revolution in the natural sciences (as exemplified by Galileo), with its 'mathematization of nature' (an idea explored earlier in Husserl's work), idealization of space and application of the new concept of infinity (see especially *Crisis* § 9). In this regard, Husserl's student, the Czech philosopher Jan Patočka (1907–77), aptly summarizes Husserl's leading question as follows:

The mathematization of nature assumes that the geometrically articulated characteristics of bodies have an intersubjective significance, and thus that they are *objective* in the proper sense of the word, in contrast to those aspects of our experience of the world about which we know even from our everyday experience that they are relative to a person or to a position. What does this truth, tacitly assumed by mathematization, imply?[6]

Husserl is precisely interested in how the scientific application of formal mathematics had the effect of changing the very conception of modernity.

Part II of the *Crisis* analyses the opposition between objectivity and subjectivity as it emerged both in modern science and in modern philosophy from Descartes to Kant. This leads, in Part III, to a discussion of the pregiven, always-taken-for-granted 'life-world', which had never before become a topic of enquiry, even for Kant, who did talk about the need for an overall sense of completeness in human life. Husserl then embarks on a renewal of the task of transcendental philosophy, involving a radicalization of Kant's project (or perhaps, more accurately, a clarification of Kant's original intention through the removal of naturalizing accretions), to take into account the working of anonymous *functioning subjectivity*. Functioning subjectivity is

---

[6] See Jan Patočka, Review of E. Husserl's *Crisis* articles in *Philosophia* (1936), published in *Česká Mysl* Vol. 33 Nos. 1–2 (1937), 98–107. My thanks to Lubica Učnik for providing this translation.

a key term in the *Crisis*, as we shall see. It is to be understood as the anonymous, collective intentionality that constitutes the sense of the *world* as such, as opposed to the active intentionality that individual minds consciously initiate (see Chapter 4 below). This interrogation of Kant leads Husserl to address the supreme paradox of transcendental philosophy, namely that humans are both natural objects that appear within the sphere of nature and are also 'subjects for the world', cooperating subjects who together *constitute* the world as such. In Part IIIB, Husserl also offers an extended analysis of the problematic status of psychology and claims that what can be discovered in psychology needs to be given a transcendental grounding in phenomenology.

Husserl's aim is to secure philosophy as a genuine form of intellectual practice 'in times of danger' (C 392; K 510) and to set it on its task in a secure way. He believes it is no longer possible to proceed in a straightforward or what he will call 'naïve' manner, as in the past: 'Reflection is required in every sense in order to right ourselves' (C 392; K 510). But such attuned critical reflection needs to be carried out in a careful, methodical manner. This meditation or self-reflection will unfold in the *Crisis* as a sustained critique of the inevitable development of philosophy from Descartes through Kant and German Idealism to the rise of positivism and the problematic emergence of psychology as a science.

Husserl's overall aim, then, is somewhat grandiose, nothing less than the 'rebirth [*Wiedergeburt*] of Europe from the spirit of philosophy', as he puts it in the 'Vienna Lecture' (C 299; K 347). Coming to terms with the spiritual culture of this 'universal' European humanity involves reflection on the 'original meaning' (*Ursprungssinn*, K 59) of the new sciences that burst onto and transformed the world in the seventeenth century. Husserl's opening move in the *Crisis* is to claim that, despite the undeniable progress of the natural sciences, there was a critical disorder and distortion at the heart of the modern scientific enterprise itself. We shall address Husserl's critique of the natural sciences in detail in Chapter 3. Furthermore, and parallel to this scientific crisis, there was a growing crisis in modern philosophy and in the human sciences generally. Philosophy also needs *self-reflection*, a reflection that includes thinking seriously about the meaning both of its Greek origins and its ultimate directedness towards its goal, what Husserl calls its 'teleology'. It is quite surprising to find Husserl talking about the 'inner sense' of history and attempting to trace the teleology of the modern philosophical tradition, for instance. But Husserl thinks of the field of the transcendental as a field of *life*, and individual lives are oriented towards goals and unified in terms of their overall goal or purpose. Husserl claims that 'being human is teleological being and an ought-to-be, and that this teleology holds sway in each and every activity and project of an ego' (C 341; K 275–6).

THE THEME OF HISTORY AND GENETIC PHENOMENOLOGY

In previous works, Husserl's main approach to phenomenology had employed a more static form of constitutional analysis, examining the 'levels and strata' (C 168; K 170) of meaning involved in the constitution of perceptual or other objects, but not particularly addressing issues of temporal and historical development. Husserl now introduces what he elsewhere explicitly calls 'genetic' phenomenology as a new approach that specifically addresses historical and temporal development. In fact, he had been discussing the concept of a genetic phenomenology in his lectures and research manuscripts from around 1917 onwards, but the *Crisis* is the first work to introduce the specific themes of *history* and the development of culture from a phenomenological perspective that seeks to understand its meaning-constitution.[7] 'The Origin of Geometry', for instance, makes mention of the need to understand the 'genetic origin' (*genetische Ursprung*, C 370; K 379) of concepts.

Primarily in the associated essays, especially the Supplements (e.g. 'Vienna Lecture', 'The Origin of Geometry'), rather than in Parts I to III, Husserl addresses larger topics, including the shift from mythic thought to rationality brought about by philosophy, the meaning of human temporality and 'historicity', cultural development (the 'shapes

---

[7] For a discussion of Husserl's genetic – and indeed 'generative' – phenomenology, see Anthony J. Steinbock, *Home and Beyond: Generative Phenomenology after Husserl* (Evanston, IL: Northwestern University Press, 1995), pp. 37–42 and also Donn Welton, 'The Systematicity of Husserl's Transcendental Philosophy: From Static to Genetic Method', in Welton, ed., *The New Husserl: A Critical Reader* (Bloomington: Indiana University Press, 2003), pp. 255–88.

of the spiritual world', C 7; K 4) and intercultural understanding,[8] the concept of nationality, internationality and 'supranationality' (*Übernationalität*, C 270; K 315),[9] the inbuilt teleology of Western civilization towards universal rationality and the threats facing it, and so on. At the outset Husserl raises the question as to whether history teaches us nothing but the contingency of human events, a meaningless cycle of progress and disappointment (C 7; K 4–5) or whether there is meaning and reason in history (C 9; K 7). To address these pressing questions, Husserl describes a methodological approach of 'questioning back' (*Rückfragen*) or 'backwards reflection' (*Rückbesinnung*) that he believes will allow him to penetrate through to the essential meaning at the heart of various forms of historically evolving cultural institution.

This new focus on history has inevitably led to comparison between Husserl's conception of history and that of Heidegger as already explicated in the latter's *Being and Time*, which had appeared some ten years earlier, in 1927. As we shall discuss in Chapter 5, many readers of the *Crisis* thought that Husserl was somewhat belatedly turning to address the problem of history because of Heidegger's radical accounts of human historicity and his proposed 'destruction of the history of philosophy'. As we shall see, however, Husserl had been addressing the themes of the meaning of history, tradition and what he broadly called 'generativity' (*Generativität*, the manner in which cultural meanings become established, laid down in sedimentations, and then handed on from one generation to another) from around 1911 onwards, and specifically in reaction to Dilthey, as well as to the Neo-Kantian discussion of the appropriate methodology for the human sciences. Husserl,

---

[8] In the *Crisis*, Husserl employs the term 'spirit' (*Geist*) in the usual German sense to mean broadly 'mind', 'soul', but especially human cultural achievements, understood as the products of collective human conscious or mental activity. He is concerned with the distinction between the natural and the cultural or human sciences (*Geisteswissenschaften*) as discussed by the Neo-Kantians (e.g. Rickert). In the 'Vienna Lecture' he speaks of the 'spirituality' (*Geistigkeit*) of animals as well as humans, meaning thereby something like the cultural world and behaviour of animals thought as a complex unified whole (see C 271; K 316).

[9] Husserl speaks of the notion of an 'over-nationality' or 'supranationality' also in his March 1935 letter to Lévy-Bruhl, written shortly before the 'Vienna Lecture', where he speaks of each national and supranational grouping having its own representation of the world. See 'Edmund Husserl's Letter to Lucien Lévy-Bruhl, 11 March 1935', trans. Dermot Moran and Lukas Steinacher, *New Yearbook for Phenomenology and Phenomenological Philosophy* Vol. 8 (2008), 325–48.

too, has his own version of the 'destruction' – or 'reconstruction' – of the history of philosophy from Descartes to Kant. In many ways, Husserl's *Crisis* parallels investigations carried out by Heidegger, but Husserl always insists his goal is to communicate the meaning and achievement of his transcendental phenomenology.

THE *CRISIS* AS AN INTRODUCTION TO TRANSCENDENTAL PHENOMENOLOGY

According to its subtitle, the *Crisis* aims to be *An Introduction to Phenomenological Philosophy.*[10] In fact, Husserl intended it to be the definitive introduction to his mature *transcendental* phenomenology, i.e. elaborating on the particular phenomenological approach that he had adopted subsequent to his 'discovery' of the procedure of the *epochē* (suspension, bracketing) and reduction (*Reduktion*) around 1905. In this regard, the *Crisis* was intended to replace his *Cartesian Meditations*, which has appeared only in French. With his assistant, Fink, he reworked the German version of the latter text during the early 1930s, but he remained dissatisfied with it because he could not properly accommodate the experience of others and intersubjective life generally. The *Cartesian Meditations* introduced the transcendental ego too suddenly – 'in one blow' (*mit einem Schlage*, C 77; K 78, C 150; K 153 and C 239; K 242) – and, as a result, its complex intentional content was not properly displayed. Husserl eventually abandoned his plan to produce an expanded German version of the *Meditations* and instead pinned his hopes on the *Crisis*. At the same time, Husserl saw the *Crisis* as an opportunity to correct what he regarded as misinterpretations of his position, so at times his presentation is polemical and the tone self-justificatory (as in his remark that some would rather accept Heidegger's and Scheler's account of his work rather than read his own writings, see K 439).

Husserl introduces his phenomenology in terms of some central concepts: self-reflection, sense-bestowal, intentionality and the theoretical attitude. We shall now discuss these concepts in turn.

---

[10] Husserl uses various German terms for 'introduction' to signify the notions of 'induction' or 'initiation' into phenomenology: *Einleitung, Einführung* and even *Emporleitung* ('initiation' or 'royal road').

SELF-REFLECTION (*SELBSTBESINNUNG*)

'Reflection' (*Besinnung*) and 'self-reflection' (*Selbstbesinnung*) are key terms for Husserl. Husserl intends the *Crisis* as a work of critical and historical reflection that looks backwards over the cultural development of modern science and culture since its Greek origins. He speaks of the need for 'self-understanding' (*Selbstverständigung*, K 435) or 'self-reflection' (*Selbstbesinnung*, K 437, a term repeatedly used of his work).[11] Thus, in Section 9, effectively summarizing the project of the *Crisis* as a whole, he speaks of the 'task of self-reflection which grows out of the "breakdown" situation of our time' (C 58; K 59). *Besinnung* means contemplative consideration specifically of an existential kind.[12] Husserl distinguishes between *Besinnung* and *Reflexion* ('reflection'):

The reflection [*Besinnung*] in question is a particular case of that self-reflection [*Selbstbesinnung*] in which man as a person seeks to reflect upon the ultimate sense of his existence. We must distinguish between a broader and a narrower sense of self-reflection: pure ego-reflection [*Ich-Reflexion*] and reflection upon the whole life of the ego as ego; and reflection [*Besinnung*] in the pregnant sense of enquiring back into the sense or teleological essence of the ego. (C 392n; K 510–11n.1)

Husserl, then, understands *Besinnung* more as a kind of existential self-meditation rather than as a Cartesian-style introspection, even one reflecting on one's life as a whole.[13] For Husserl, 'self-reflection' is exemplified by Descartes' *Meditations* (see CM § 1. p. 1; Hua I 43). Thus, in his 1934 Letter to the Prague Congress, he says his 'self-reflection' is in the radical spirit of Descartes (Hua XXVII 244). This requires performance of a suspension of commitment or *epochē* towards all existing tradition and all naïve thoughts concerning

---

[11] James Dodd sees reflection as a central theme of the work in his *Crisis and Reflection: An Essay on Edmund Husserl's Crisis of the European Sciences*, Phaenomenologica 174 (Dordrecht: Kluwer, 2004).

[12] See David Carr, *Phenomenology and the Problem of History: A study of Husserl's Transcendental Philosophy* (Evanston, IL: Northwestern University Press, 1974), p. 59. Paul Ricoeur translates *Besinnung* as *prise de conscience*.

[13] For this reason, Husserl also frequently employs the term 'consideration' or 'investigation' (*Betrachtung*, see e.g. C 70; K 71), e.g. 'historical considerations' (*historische Betrachtungen*, C 391; K 510) alongside 'historical reflection' (*historische Besinnung*, cf. C 17; K 16; and again C 392; K 510).

philosophical ideas and positions. Husserl uses several variations on the notion of 'reflection'. He frequently characterizes his reflection as a 'backwards reflection' (*Rückbesinnung*, C 17; K 16) or 'questioning back' (*Rückfragen*, or *Zurückfragen*, cf. C 56; K 57, C 69; K 70; see also K 185), a regressive enquiry into the 'original motivation' (*Ursprungsmotivation*, C 57; K 58) that gave rise to modernity. This concept of reflecting or questioning back is central to what he calls 'genetic' or 'genetic-historical' enquiry.

In the early 1920s Husserl became aware that his constitutive phenomenology had primarily been 'static', in that it examined the manner in which, for instance, perception of an object is established in the present. But besides this static enquiry, a *genetic* enquiry is required, one that understands how meanings and cultural forms gain their historical sense. Personal identity, cultural forms and ideas, are all products of historical and temporal constitution. In this sense the *Crisis* is an essay in genetic phenomenology. We shall now say more about the project of phenomenology as a 'making sense' of experience.

'SENSE-BESTOWAL' (*SINNGEBUNG*) AND 'SENSE' (*SINN*)

The notions of 'sense' (*Sinn*) and 'meaning' (*Bedeutung*) are central to phenomenology. Phenomenology is concerned with *meaning*, but one must be careful here not to think solely of linguistic meaning. Husserl tends not to distinguish sharply 'sense' (*Sinn*) from 'meaning' (*Bedeutung*), although he is aware of Frege's distinction. Insofar as he does make a distinction, he tends to employ 'meaning' primarily for linguistic meaning. The term 'sense', for Husserl, carries wider connotations, in that non-linguistic activities, such as perceiving, remembering and so on, also involve 'sense', i.e. we perceive the paper lying on the desk as having its own existence, self-identity, spatio-temporal continuity, objecthood, and relation to and distinctness from other objects, but also its own history, cultural meaning, significance and so on.

The central focus of phenomenology, it can even be said, then, is the problem of *sense*, of *meaning*.[14] Husserl often couples together the concepts of 'sense' and 'validity' (*Sinn und Geltung*, e.g. C 76; K 78)

---

[14] See Steven Galt Crowell, *Husserl, Heidegger, and the Space of Meaning: Paths toward Transcendental Phenomenology* (Evanston, IL: Northwestern University Press, 2001), pp. 3–18.

that things, people, situations, social actions and so on have for us as experiencing subjects in the world. From the standpoint of phenomenology, a thing's ontological status cannot be distinguished from its sense or meaning. Something can be a religious icon in one cultural context and a cultural adornment in another (e.g. a tattoo). Hence Husserl speaks of 'being-sense' (*Seinssinn*), or 'ontic sense' (Carr's translation, see C 122; K 124), or 'ontic meaning' (C 100; K 103), referring to this interwovenness of ontological standing and significance. He also regularly speaks of something's 'validity of being' or 'ontic validity' (*Seinsgeltung*, C 77; K 79).

All experiences, no matter how vague and apparently inconsequential (even illusions, hallucinations, dreams, reveries), make sense in some form, and the kind of sense an experience conveys has its own particular mode of 'givenness', its own peculiar way of coming to prominence, its own temporal duration, its structural form, implied connection with other experiences and so on. To perceive something as a physical, material thing, for instance, involves many levels of constitution of sense, but to see it as also a picture or *artwork* is to grasp it in a further and quite distinct mode of meaning disclosure, and distinct again from a tool used for a practical purpose, or a relic approached through religious veneration, a souvenir and so on. Language articulates this rich differentiation of kinds of object, but our rich perception already intuitively makes these discriminations, and it is phenomenology's task to document them and grasp their essential character.

Moreover, sense – and this is crucial for Husserl's phenomenology – is essentially 'two-sided', including both subjective and objective dimensions, or what Husserl calls a necessary 'correlation'. Husserl even uses the term 'correlation research' as shorthand for phenomenological investigation. The object as intended is termed 'noema' by Husserl (from *Ideas* I onwards, although, interestingly, the term does not appear at all in the *Crisis*); whereas the correlated intentional act is referred to as the 'noesis' (Husserl does mention 'noetic' modes of consciousness at C 74; K 75). Husserl talks of the noetic–noematic correlation in other writings, whereas in the *Crisis* he tends to simply use the shorthand of 'correlation'.[15] On the one

---

[15] It is likely that Husserl, in his mature years, had abandoned his earlier attempt to explicate the precise meaning of the noema. An entire critical literature has grown up around the

hand, it is an objective fact that a newspaper, for instance, has the sense *newspaper*, recognized at least in all those historical worlds that have a print culture. But there is also an act of collective establishing of that 'sense' in our culture. In order to grasp 'sense' phenomenologically, Husserl believes one has to step back from or bracket the existential status of the object. Even an imaginary object has an essential character, and it is the essence that Husserl is after (hence he separates essences from existence).

For Husserl, sense is not simply something outside us that we apprehend, it is something that is 'constituted' or put together by us due to our particular attitudes, presuppositions, background beliefs, values, historical horizons and so on. In short, phenomenology is a reflection on the manner in which things come to gain the kind of *sense* they have for us. 'Constitution' (*Konstitution*, see *Crisis* § 49), a term Husserl took over from the Neo-Kantians, refers to the manner in which an intended object is put together out of various layers of intentional acts to be grasped as the object we apprehend it to be. Constitution is involved even in the most passive acts of apprehending, as well as in the more active and creative forms of conscious act. Things not only have meaning, but their whole manner of *being* is an outcome of subjective and intersubjective (many cooperating subjects) constitution. As Husserl asserts: '[A]ll real, mundane objectivity is constituted accomplishment' (C 204; K 208). He writes in a crucial passage that sums up his understanding of intentional constitution:

In this regard we speak of the 'intersubjective constitution' [*intersubjektiven Konstitution*] of the world, meaning by this the total system of manners of givenness, however hidden, and also of modes of validity [*Geltungsmodi*] for egos; through this constitution, if we systematically uncover it, the world as it is for us becomes understandable as a structure of meaning [*Sinngebilde*] formed out of elementary intentionalities ... Intentionality is the title which stands for the only actual and genuine way of explaining, making intelligible. (C 168; K 171)

In his *Cartesian Meditations*, Husserl had already clearly articulated the basic insight of phenomenology as maintaining 'that every sense that any existent whatever has or can have for me – in respect of its

interpretation of Husserl's noema, but, given that the concept does not appear in the *Crisis*, we can ignore that discussion here.

"what" and its "it exists and actually is" – is a sense *in* and arising *from* my intentional life' (CM § 43, p. 91; Hua I 123). For Husserl, as he repeatedly stresses, the most usual sense of being is that an object exists 'in itself'. This sense of being, however, is an intrinsic part of the outlook of the natural attitude. How this *sense* of being is constituted remains Husserl's central focus. Let us now turn to the key concept of intentionality, which, as we have seen, Husserl inherited from Brentano.

INTENTIONALITY

Phenomenology begins from the intentional relation between constituting subjectivity and its correlated constituted object. Intentionality points to the intrinsic correlation between the object as meant and the subjective act which apprehends or means ('intends') it. As we saw above, in the *Crisis* Husserl says: 'And meaning is never anything but meaning in modes of validity, that is, as related to intending ego-subjects which effect validity' (C 168; K 171). The key to the phenomenological approach to 'meaning and validity' (*Sinn und Geltung*) is to see them as constituted by various activities of subjectivity. The general title for this approach is, for Husserl, 'intentionality'. He always highlights the importance of the discovery of intentionality. For instance, in *Phenomenological Psychology* (1925) he writes: 'the most universal essential characteristic of psychic being and living is exposed: intentionality. Psychic being is the life of consciousness; consciousness is consciousness of something' (*Phen. Psych.* § 4, p. 34; Hua IX 47). Similarly, in the *Crisis*, he emphasizes that intentionality is the key to philosophical understanding: 'Intentionality is the title which stands for the only actual and genuine way of explaining, making intelligible' (C 168; K 171).

Husserl speaks of the need to go back to the 'intentional origins' and attempt to follow the build-up of 'sense-formations' which we eventually experience in a completely immediate way as the whole intuited life-world, understood as an 'integrated framework of meaning' (*Sinnzusammenhang*, C 284; K 331) or 'meaning formation' (*Sinnbildung*, C 378; K 386). Husserl took his concept of intentionality from Brentano: 'Brentano had already made intentionality central for empirical human psychology' (CM § 40, p. 82; Hua I 115).

In *Crisis* § 68 Husserl says Brentano opened his eyes to the phenomenon of intentionality:

This is the place to recall the extraordinary debt we owe to Brentano for the fact that he began his attempt to reform psychology with an investigation of the peculiar characteristics of the psychic (in contrast to the physical) and showed intentionality to be one of these characteristics; the science of 'psychic phenomena' then has to do everywhere with conscious experiences. (C 233–4; K 236)

In his groundbreaking *Psychology from an Empirical Standpoint* (1874), Brentano had resurrected the medieval Scholastic concept of intention in order to define mental phenomena. He wrote in a passage that has since become classic:

Every mental phenomenon is characterized by what the Scholastics of the Middle Ages called the intentional (or mental) inexistence of an object, and what we might call, though not wholly unambiguously, reference to a content, direction towards an object (which is not to be understood here as meaning a thing), or immanent objectivity. Every mental phenomenon includes something as object within itself, although they do not all do so in the same way. In presentation something is presented, in judgment something is affirmed or denied, in love loved, in hate hated, in desire desired and so on. (PES 88)

Physical 'phenomena' occupy positions in space and time and have causal relations with one another, but psychic or mental phenomena, on the other hand, are uniquely defined by the fact that they are 'about' something, which may or may not exist. If I am *dreaming of the pot of gold at the end of the rainbow*, my act of dreaming is an intentional act directed at an object which does not exist, but nevertheless my mental act is genuine and genuinely takes this dreamt 'pot of gold' as its object.

Husserl took over Brentano's conception of intentionality but greatly expanded and clarified it. He felt that Brentano's own conception was too deeply embedded in an internalist and introspectionist outlook.[16] Brentano maintained (at least in his earlier years) that psychological states revealed themselves directly and immediately to

---

[16] See Dermot Moran, 'The Inaugural Address: Brentano's Thesis', Inaugural Address to the Joint Session of the Aristotelian Society and the Mind Association, *Proceedings of the Aristotelian Society Supplementary* Vol. 70 (1996), 1–27, and Moran, 'Husserl's Critique of Brentano in the *Logical Investigations*', *Manuscrito: Revista International de Filosofia*, Special Husserl Issue, Vol. 23 No. 2 (2000), 163–205.

consciousness (their *esse* is *percipi*) and that they were exactly as they presented themselves, whereas the external world was known only indirectly. Mental phenomena are best understood as composed of certain acts (presentations, judgements, emotional states of loving or hating) which are directed at what he called indifferently 'objects' or 'contents', which may or may not exist.

Already in his Fifth Logical Investigation, Husserl rejected almost all of Brentano's key assumptions but retained the central conception of intentionality now characterized as 'correlation research', that is, every mental act or lived experience is intentionally related to an object which is given precisely in the manner determined by the mental act or lived experience. In his mature works after *Ideas* I (1913), Husserl refers to this as the 'noetic–noematic' correlation. In the *Crisis*, Husserl reiterates his criticisms of Brentano as being entrenched in naturalism and not grasping the true character of intentionality (C 234; K 236).

Husserl records that Brentano never accepted the analyses in the *Logical Investigations* as a development of descriptive psychology and the 'mature execution' of Brentano's idea (*Phen. Psych.* § 3, p. 24; Hua IX 34). Husserl, then, must present intentionality in an entirely new context, stripped of the misleading apparatus of modern representationalist philosophy. For Husserl, intentionality properly construed made visible the manner in which things present themselves to consciousness in their various modes of meaningfulness. Thus, Husserl writes in the *Crisis*:

The world as it is for us becomes understandable as a structure of meaning formed out of elementary intentionalities. The being of these intentionalities themselves is nothing but one meaning formation operating together with another, 'constituting' new meaning through synthesis. And meaning is never anything but meaning in modes of validity, that is, as related to intending ego-subjects which effect validity. Intentionality is the title which stands for the only actual and genuine way of explaining, making intelligible. (C 168; K 171)

In the *Crisis*, intentionality is used to illuminate not just the essential structures of consciousness, perception, memory and so on, but also embodiment, the experience of others (empathy) and the vague but still genuine experiences of the horizon of the world.

THE THEORETICAL ATTITUDE (*DIE THEORETISCHE EINSTELLUNG*)

In the late 1930s Husserl frequently reflected on the 'ingress' or 'breakthrough into' (*Einbruch*, C 283; K 330) philosophy and the life of reason in ancient Greece. He believes that this spiritual Europe has a birthplace in ancient Greece, ushered in by a 'few Greek eccentrics' who singlehandedly developed 'a *new sort of attitude*' (C 276; K 321) – the theoretical attitude – towards life and the surrounding world, thereby inaugurating philosophy and, with it, science (C 276; K 321). Husserl makes a similar point in his earlier 1934 letter to Emanuel Rádl, President of the Eighth International Congress of Philosophy:[17]

Philosophy is the organ of a modern, historical existence of humanity, existence from out of the spirit of autonomy. The primordial form [*Urgestalt*] of autonomy is that of the scientific self-responsibility ... Philosophical self-responsibility necessarily gets itself involved in the philosophizing community. ... Herewith the specific sense of European humanity and culture is designated. (Hua XXVII 240; my translation)

In a tract written for the Congress, he speaks of the inseparable intertwining of science and philosophy: 'Where genuine science lives in practice, there lives philosophy; and where philosophy, there science: an inseparable one-inside-the-other' (Hua XXVII 185, my translation). Building on this Greek foundation, the West has a 'mission' (*Sendung*) to accomplish nothing less than the development of 'humanity' (*Menschheit*) itself (C 299; K 348).

Husserl's conception of this 'spiritual Europe' and its destiny, characterized by its theoretical attitude with its inherent universality and commitment to the ideal of infinite enquiry, leads him to distinguish the true shapers of Europe from certain cultural forms (he calls them 'empirical types'), even within geographical Europe, that, however, do not promote the ideal of universality. Most notoriously, in his 'Vienna Lecture', he singles out the Roma Gypsies (*die Zigeuner*) who constantly 'wander around' or 'vagabond' (*herumvagabondieren*, C 273; K 319) as not contributing to this ideal. Other 'types' of humanity, such as the age-old civilizations in China and India,

---

[17] This letter is published in Edmund Husserl, *Aufsätze und Vorträge (1922–1937)*, ed. T. Nenon and H.-R. Sepp, Hua XXVII (Dordrecht: Kluwer, 1989), pp. 240–4.

also lack this 'absolute idea' of European universality and remain 'empirical anthropological types' (C 16; K 14). Husserl predicts global Europeanization of the world but is concerned about its narrow, technicized nature due to the distortions inherent in European rationalistic scientific culture as it has developed.

TRANSCENDENTAL SUBJECTIVITY AND INTERSUBJECTIVITY

Husserl's *Crisis*, as we have emphasized, introduces transcendental phenomenology from a new, primarily historical perspective emphasizing human participation in the communally shared life-world. He wants deliberately to complement the methodological solipsist approach of 'egological self-reflection' (as he calls it in C 259; K 262) of the earlier *Cartesian Meditations*. In the *Crisis*, therefore, he explicitly begins from the standpoint of the 'pregiven' (*vorgegeben*) public world experienced in the natural attitude rather than from the inner consciousness of the solitary meditating subject.[18] Thereby the *Crisis* is in a position to open up phenomenology beyond its usual concerns with individual acts of perception and cognition to engage with the meaning of different and broader phenomena, including the modern scientific revolution, the meaning of 'nature' as defined by the exact natural sciences (especially physics), the meaning of culture and historical tradition, and the nature of the relation of European cultures to non-European cultures, raising problems of interculturality, as well as raising penetrating questions concerning the nature and vitality of philosophy and psychology (as a misconstrual of the true nature of subjectivity). In the *Crisis*, moreover, Husserl expressly links the theoretical crises besetting the natural and human sciences to the deep spiritual and intellectual crises affecting Western culture generally. In his view, these crises had in part been brought about by the spectacular success of the modern, exact sciences, whose overly naïve acceptance of the *objectivist* approach has ended up ignoring or sidelining urgent issues of human value.

---

[18] Already, on 11 June 1932, Husserl wrote to Roman Ingarden that he had come to the conclusion that transcendental phenomenology needed to begin from the 'natural possession of the world and of being', quoted in Bruzina, *Edmund Husserl and Eugen Fink*, p. 214.

To overcome this naïveté, Husserl offers an intellectual reconstruction and critical evaluation of the scientific transformation of
European culture that has been taking place since the seventeenth
century and that was, according to Husserl, occasioned by Galileo's
'mathematization of nature' (*Mathematisierung der Natur* – the
phrase appears in the very title of *Crisis* § 9). He is challenging the
cultural dominance of *scientism* (with its commitment to what he
calls 'objectivism') and *naturalism*, which he sees as having also led
to the acceptance of varieties of cultural relativism and ultimately to
skepticism. As a result, European intellectual culture in its highest
achievement (i.e. the sciences) is threatened by a profound and growing *irrationalism*. Husserl's proposed solution involves first and foremost 'clarification', bringing to *clarity* (*Klärung, Klarheit* – favourite
Husserlian terms) what exactly has happened through a reflection on
the meaning of the modern scientific achievement (and its implications for the development of modern philosophy).

Husserl wants to propose a meditative return to the ineliminable
roles of human subjectivity and intersubjectivity, hitherto neglected
in this pursuit of objectivity, not just to set the newly emerged science of psychology on a proper footing, but also to address issues of
central relevance to human existence. Subjectivity must be recognized as a transcendental condition for the possibility of objectivity
(and hence a condition for the very possibility of there being anything like a *world* as such). Husserl writes:

> Only a radical enquiry back into subjectivity – and specifically the subject-
> ivity which *ultimately* brings about all world-validity, with its content and
> in all its prescientific and scientific modes, and into the 'what' and the 'how'
> of the rational accomplishments – can make objective truth comprehensible
> and arrive at the ultimate ontic meaning [*Seinssinn*] of the world. Thus it is
> not the being of the world as unquestioned, taken for granted, which is pri-
> mary in itself … rather what is primary in itself is subjectivity, understood
> as that which naïvely pregives the being of the world and then rationalizes
> or (what is the same thing) objectifies it. (C 69; K 70)

But the problem of understanding subjectivity also raises the issue of
the relation between subjects. How can my ego also belong to what
Husserl calls 'transcendental intersubjectivity'? Husserl states that
the 'consciousness of intersubjectivity, then, must become a transcendental problem' (C 202; K 206). Transcendental subjectivity, for

Husserl, means the manner in which human subjects combine to constitute objectivity and to produce a common cultural and historical world.[19] In the *Cartesian Meditations*, Husserl admits that the phenomenological method initially appears solipsistic, but in truth phenomenology has to address transcendental intersubjectivity (CM §13, p. 30; Hua I 69). The concept of intersubjectivity (a term originally found in Fichte (1762–1814)) is introduced in the *Crisis* initially and primarily in terms of the manner in which the objectivity of the experienced world is achieved through intersubjective confirmation and validation (see C 128; K 130).[20] But Husserl also raises the issue of how subjects (what he often calls 'ego subjects') come to communicate and agree with one another and form larger communities united with common purpose (see e.g. C 163; K 166). The phenomenon of cooperating intersubjectivity is read back from the experience of a common world 'for all': 'Constantly functioning in wakeful life, we also function together, in the manifold ways of considering, together, valuing, planning, acting together' (C 109; K 111). This is the domain of what Husserl calls 'we-subjectivity' (*Wir-Subjektivität*, C 109; K 111) and which he regards as inaccessible to traditional psychological reflection since it is always presumed by the psychological approach (*Crisis* § 59). We shall return to discuss transcendental intersubjectivity in Chapter 7.

In Part III of the *Crisis*, Husserl offers a deep and important analysis of what he calls the 'paradox' or 'enigma' (*Rätsel*) of subjectivity (e.g. C 5; K 3), according to which human subjects must be considered both as transcendental subjects 'for the world' as well as embodied subjects objectified 'in the world'. Husserl's struggle to articulate and resolve this paradox is one of the most significant philosophical achievements of the *Crisis*. In fact, this discussion leads Husserl to a consideration of Kant's philosophy and to reflect on the meaning of transcendental philosophy in general. We shall discuss this in further detail in Chapter 7. Husserl's solution is to propose that the given world be understood not as world in itself but as the world as

[19] Husserl had already discussed transcendental intersubjectivity in *Formal and Transcendental Logic, Cartesian Meditations* and in the unpublished research notes collected in Hua XIII, XIV and XV.
[20] See Dan Zahavi, *Husserl and Transcendental Intersubjectivity*, trans. Elizabeth A. Behnke (Athens, OH: Ohio University Press, 2001).

correlated to the *natural attitude*. The natural attitude is a complex constellation of attitudes which presents the world as pregiven and simply there for me, spread out in space and time, and so on. All sciences take place within the natural attitude; they simply *assume* the existence of the world. These sciences are 'naïve', as Husserl puts it, precisely because they accept the world as 'present' or 'on-hand' (*vorhanden*) and 'actual' (*wirklich*). But how should this actuality be understood? To meditate on this means to transcend the natural attitude and to raise a transcendental question concerning the being of the world. This is Husserl's version of the question made canonical by Heidegger – the question of the meaning of being. But Husserl's answer is that being is always correlated with subjectivity, and hence that philosophy as such is necessarily transcendental.

Traditionally philosophy has attempted to supply a total explanation of the world as a whole, but it proceeded in naïveté that is no longer tenable and must now be grounded by transcendental philosophy. It is only the transcendental attitude (an attitude Husserl particularly characterizes in the *Crisis* and in the associated 'Vienna Lecture' as the attitude of the 'disinterested' or 'disengaged spectator') that highlights the true nature of the natural attitude. The natural attitude is, as it were, unknown to itself, until one applies the transcendental *epochē* (bracketing, or exclusion), whose very function it is to break with the world and transcend the natural attitude (C 176; K 179).

True philosophy, operating with a transcendental vigilance provided by the *epochē*, is necessary to prevent relapse into objectivism, naturalism and naïveté and to offer a true meaning-clarification of the nature of the world as an achievement of subjectivity. Thus, Husserl insists that the 'interest' of the phenomenologist cannot be aimed at the *ready-made world* (*die fertige Welt*, C 177; K 180) – a term picked up later by Hilary Putnam – but rather at explicating the nature of our intentional life as 'accomplishing life' (C 177; K 181) to which we are simply 'blind' (C 205; K 209) in the natural attitude.

PHILOSOPHY AND THE PROJECT FOR
A NEW HUMANITY

For Husserl, it is the task of philosophy, once the source of the sciences themselves, to take responsibility for restoring faith in reason.

Reason, *logos*, is the enduring legacy of the Greek philosophical tradition. Reason and science are what the Greeks have bequeathed to the West. Husserl's mission, then, is to save Western values and restore them to their original power. He confidently reasserts his faith in a transformed and expanded version of what were traditional Enlightenment values, and even invokes Beethoven's *Hymn to Joy*.[21] The naïve rationalism of the Enlightenment contained an inner absurdity, nevertheless: 'true and genuine philosophy or science and true and genuine rationalism are one' (C 197; K 200). Husserl maintains that the current crisis has been brought about because, since the Enlightenment, we have lost faith in this reason (C 10; K 8).

Husserl's defence of so-called 'European' values has been criticized, by the French deconstructionist Jacques Derrida and others, as a form of 'Eurocentrism'.[22] Husserl insists, however, that what he means by 'Europe' is not a geographically or politically defined place but rather a certain constellation of intellectual and spiritual achievements, outlooks and values, ones, moreover, that have universal significance and set 'infinite tasks'. For him, 'Europe' signifies the commitment to rational life as first discovered in the 'breakthrough' (*Durchbruch*) of ancient Greek philosophy by the labours of a 'few Greek eccentrics' (C 289; K 336). Husserl is reflecting on the nature of philosophy's origin and formation from the Greeks to the modern period (Descartes to Kant). For him, the 'primal establishment' (*Urstiftung*) of philosophy is at the same time, the primal establishment of modern European humanity (C 12; K 10).[23] As Robert

---

[21] Beethoven's 'To Joy' (*An die Freude*), also known as the 'Hymn' or 'Ode to Joy', is taken from the fourth and final movement of his Ninth Symphony in G Major, completed in 1824. Originally written in 1785 by Friedrich Schiller, it celebrates notions of brotherly universal love and reconciliation. *The Ode to Joy* was adopted as Europe's anthem by the Council of Europe in 1972.

[22] See, for instance, Ram Adhar Mall, *Intercultural Philosophy* (Lanham, MD: Rowman & Littlefield, 2000), esp. ch. 10 'Europe in the Mirror of World Cultures – On the Myth of the Europeanization of Humanity: A Non-European Discovery of Europe', pp. 109–22. See also Jacques Derrida, *The Problem of Genesis in Husserl's Philosophy*, trans. Marian Hobson (University of Chicago Press, 2003), pp. 154–7, and Robert Bernasconi and Sybol Cook, eds., *Race and Racism in Continental Philosophy* (Bloomington: Indiana University Press, 2003), esp. pp. 13–14.

[23] Husserl thinks of 'origin' (*Ursprung*) in terms of a process of origination or institution for which he uses the term 'primal establishment' (*Urstiftung*), which Aron Gurwitsch translates as 'institutive inception'. See Gurwitsch, 'The Last Work of Edmund Husserl', *Philosophy and Phenomenological Research* Vol. 16 No. 3 (March 1956), 380–99, esp. p. 386. In the *Crisis*, Husserl will also speak about 'ultimate or final establishment' (*Endstiftung*).

Bernasconi (b. 1950) puts it, for Husserl, Europe is 'the name of a humanity oriented to and motivated by a Greek destiny, a humanity written in history'.[24] I believe that Husserl is not claiming that there is anything racially superior about Western culture that marked it out for global domination. It is not because Europeans have bigger brains or are biologically more suited to science. Rather, he believes that ancient Greek philosophy made an extraordinary breakthrough with its discovery of the *logos*, the infinite and the detached, theoretical attitude which eventually, with Galileo, unleashed the monster that is modern mathematical science. No other culture that defined itself in terms of finite ends was capable of making this breakthrough. The fact that it happened in the West is part of the mysterious facticity of history.

The charge that Husserl is an ethnocentric chauvinist sits somewhat uneasily with the recognition that he himself was explicitly struggling against the appeals to race, 'blood and soil' (*Blut und Boden*) being propagated by the National Socialists and their fellow-travellers during the 1930s.[25] It is undoubtedly true that Husserl's careless remarks about Gypsies 'vagabonding' around Europe and not contributing to the ideal of universal humanity, and his condescending remarks about the humanity of Papuan natives, sound remarkable for someone who as a Jew was himself subjected to abuse in similar terms. The itinerant position of the Roma Gypsies surely occupies the role here of the 'wandering Jew'. On the other hand, Husserl was by no means alone in emphasizing the uniqueness and universality of European culture; such views were commonplace among German academics, especially in the writings of Max Weber, for instance.[26] Furthermore,

---

[24] See Alain David's essay in Bernasconi and Cook, eds., *Race and Racism in Continental Philosophy*, p. 13.

[25] The concept of 'blood and soil' emerged in nineteenth-century Romantic nationalism but was promoted by German National Socialism, especially by Richard Walther Darré, *Neuadel aus Blut und Boden* [A New Nobility of Blood and Soil] (Munich: Lehmann, 1930). The German people were rooted in a homeland (unlike the 'wandering' Jew).

[26] Seyla Benhabib has drawn attention to Max Weber's remarks in *The Protestant Ethic and the Spirit of Capitalism*, trans. Talcott Parsons (London: Unwin, 1930), p. 13, which emphasize the peculiar 'universal significance and validity' of Western culture. See Benhabib, 'Another Universalism: On the Unity and Diversity of Human Rights', Presidential Address to the Eastern Division of the APA, *Proceeding and Addresses of the American Philosophical Association* Vol. 81 No. 2 (November 2007), 7–32, esp. 25. Weber acknowledges the great developments in Indian and Chinese civilizations but claims that 'The Indian geometry had

he himself was attacked and ridiculed by Nazi ideologues for his supposed 'Jewish universalism'. Thus, the German philosopher and Nietzsche scholar Friedrich Würzbach (1886–1961) aligned himself wholeheartedly with the National Socialist cause and repeatedly attacked Husserl in his writings throughout the 1930s.[27] Würzbach wrote a series of populist articles on the importance of race and blood (one 1934 tract is entitled 'The Rebirth of Spirit out of Blood').[28] In his 1932 *Knowing and Experiencing*, Würzbach accuses Husserl of foolishness for not recognizing that culture is based on blood and inheritance. In opposition to the particularist claims of the National Socialists, Husserl was struggling to defend a certain universalist version of culture. Husserl's assertion in the 'Vienna Lecture' that 'there is, for essential reasons, no zoology of peoples' (C 275; K 320) is clearly a repudiation of race-based doctrines. Husserl is sharply aware of the complex relationships, both dependencies and separations, between different cultures and traditions. There are, in his terms, different 'historicities' (*Geschichtlichkeiten*, C 274; K 320), and indeed there are, as Husserl indicates in his 1935 letter to Lucien Lévy-Bruhl, even cultures that are self-enclosed unities, knowing no history. But he is also acutely aware of the new kind of universality and globalization brought about by the modern scientific and technological attitudes. This has been a 'revolution', brought about by the breakthrough to ideality, in the historicity of European culture (C 279; K 325). The effects of this revolutionary transformation have not completely worked themselves out, but by no means have they been understood.

---

no rational proof – this was another product of the Greek intellect' (*The Protestant Ethic*, p. 13) – and that a 'rational, systematic, and specialized pursuit of science' existed only in the West (pp. 15–16).

[27] See Würzbach, *Erkennen und Erleben: Der große Kopf und der Günstling der Natur* [Knowing and Experiencing: The Great Head and Nature's Minion] (Berlin: Wegweiser-Verlag, 1932). Würzbach bizarrely claims that a mystical energy called 'seed-energy' (*Keimplasma*) flows through human beings, transmitting culture through blood, with each race having its own *Keimplasma*. According to Würzbach, *Keimplasma* is what the pure 'minions of nature', such as Goethe, Kant, Nietzsche and Hitler, harness to lead the masses. Those who deny *Keimplasma* and think that rational argument can explain and ground cognitive thought and experience are *Gehirntiere* ('brain animals'), 'intellectuals', 'cripples' or 'big heads' (*große Köpfe*) – all terms Würzbach applies to Husserl. Würzbach considers Husserl's call for philosophy to be a rigorous science as 'un-German' (*undeutsch*) and 'Jewish' (*jüdisch*). After the war Würzbach, who was part-Jewish, claimed to have been a victim of the Nazis.

[28] F. Würzbach, 'Wiedergeburt des Geistes aus dem Blute', *Völkischer Beobachter* Vol. 14 (January 1934).

The turn to history, then, is an inevitable part of any phenomenology that seeks to understand humanity as such.

REASON IN HISTORY AND LIFE IN TRADITION

As we shall discuss in Chapter 5, history and culture are rarely encountered topics in Husserl's published works before the *Crisis* (apart from the *Kaizo* article). Indeed, Husserl had often been accused of largely neglecting history and culture in his attempt to establish an a priori, 'static' phenomenology of ahistorical essences, discovered on the basis of the single meditating subject's reflections (the so-called 'methodological solipsism'). But his encounter with Dilthey in 1910–11, and indeed his engagement with the question of the distinctive methodologies of the natural and cultural sciences in his *Nature and Spirit* lectures (1917),[29] sharpened Husserl's awareness of the need to deal with life and its specific organic processes of development and change. Moreover, Heidegger, in *Being and Time* §§ 72–7, with reference to Dilthey and others, had emphasized the primacy and centrality of the *historicity* (*Historizität*) or *historicality* (*Geschichtlichkeit*) of human existence understood as a connectedness of life lived with others in a world. In the course of his discussion, Heidegger emphasizes that it is human existence (*Dasein*) which is primarily historical, and other events are 'historical' precisely because they belong to the world opened up by the 'historizing' or 'happening' (*geschehen*) of Dasein.

Husserl, especially after his reading of Dilthey in 1910–11, was preoccupied with the problem of the relations between the natural and human or cultural sciences, and also the evolution of the history of philosophy. For instance, his *First Philosophy* lecture series of 1923–4 (Hua VII) dwells at length on the legacy of philosophy from Socrates to Kant. The *Crisis*, by taking an explicitly *historical* orientation and offering a narrative about the evolution of modernity, is an exception, as commentators including Gadamer and Ricoeur have recognized.[30] Both Dilthey and Husserl were concerned with the manner

---

[29] Edmund Husserl, *Natur und Geist: Vorlesungen Sommersemester 1927*, ed. Michael Weiler, Husserl Materialen (Dordrecht: Springes, 2002), Vol. IV.

[30] See Paul Ricoeur, 'Husserl and the Sense of History', in Ricoeur, *Husserl: An Analysis of His Phenomenology*, trans. Edward G. Ballard and L. Embree (Evanston, IL: Northwestern University Press, 1967), pp. 143–74.

in which an ego establishes itself as a living unity across time, and, already in the *Cartesian Meditations*, Husserl had written that the ego 'constitutes itself for itself, so to speak, in the unity of a history' (*Geschichte,* CM § 37, p. 75; Hua I 109).

In the *Crisis*, Husserl offers a sustained meditation on the concept of 'tradition', how past philosophy achieves a continuation in present thinking, and what the meaning of modernity itself is, themes that were also important for Heidegger,[31] Hannah Arendt (1906–75), Hans-Georg Gadamer, Hans Blumenberg (1920–96), and others. Husserl makes no reference to Heidegger, but he does talk about how, in developing a history, we are acting creatively, in the manner of poets. He even speaks of history as a kind of 'poetic invention' or 'poeticizing' (*Dichtung,* C 394; K 512), which might be understood as a kind of narrative reconstruction of the story of history to address current concerns.

Husserl never claims to be doing the history of philosophy in any straightforward sense. As he puts it, history is not a 'storehouse' of items that lie before one; rather, one picks and chooses depending on one's motivation. He sees himself, rather, as seeking the 'inner meaning and hidden teleology' of history:

> We shall attempt to strike through the crust of the externalized 'historical facts' of philosophical history, interrogating, exhibiting, and testing their inner meaning and hidden teleology. Questions never before asked will arise … In the end they will require that the total sense of philosophy, accepted as 'obvious' throughout all its historical forms, be basically and essentially transformed. (C 18; K 16)

Let us now turn to Husserl's 'historical-teleological' analysis of the birth of the modern mathematical sciences that have dominated Western modernity.

---

[31] See, for instance, Martin Heidegger's 1938 essay 'The Age of the World Picture', in Heidegger, *Off The Beaten Track*, trans. and ed. Julian Young and Kenneth Haynes (Cambridge University Press, 2002), pp. 57–85.

CHAPTER 3

Galileo's revolution and the origins of modern science

GALILEO: DISCOVERER OF MODERNITY

In the *Crisis*, Husserl offers an original and still provocative reading of the modern (what he broadly calls 'Galilean') scientific-technological revolution with its 'mathematization of nature' (*Mathematisierung der Natur*, C 61; K 61).[1] Husserl was not a trained historian of science and therefore cannot be expected to provide an accurate, detailed, historical assessment such as would measure up to current standards in the history of science – a discipline which was only in its earliest stages when Husserl was writing. Rather, he is a philosopher who is offering a creative, meditative re-reading of Galileo's achievement. He presents it as having a *unified sense* or meaning. Husserl summarizes his task on intellectual reconstruction as follows: '*What is the meaning of this mathematization of nature?* How do we reconstruct [*rekonstruieren*] the train of thought [*Gedankengang*] that motivated it?' (C 23; K 20).

The meaning of modern science can only be understood when a 'regressive enquiry' is carried out into how this new conception of nature and scientific knowledge came about. Husserl's study of Galileo, in *Crisis* § 9, then, has to be situated within his broader 'historical reflections' (*geschichtliche Besinnungen*, C 57; K 58) concerning the philosophical and cultural situation of his day. His general aim is to arrive at a 'reflective form of knowledge' (C 59; K 60) concerning the 'primal establishment' (*Urstiftung*) of modern science (C 73; K 75) that has shaped subsequent culture in the West. Husserl even speaks of the 'historical a priori' of modern physics (C 374; K 383), i.e. the a

---

[1] Husserl employs the name 'Galileo' to characterize the whole 'bestowal of meaning' (*Sinngebung*, C 58; K 58) that makes up 'natural science'.

priori conditions that made this scientific achievement possible. We shall have more to say about the nature of this historical a priori in Chapter 5 below.

Husserl – in line with other historians of scientific revolution of the time, e.g. Pierre Duhem, Ernst Cassirer, Alexandre Koyré and Jacob Klein (1899–1978) – sees Galileo as inspiring *both* modern science *and* modern philosophy (including Descartes). It should be stressed from the outset that, strictly speaking, Husserl is not concerned with Galileo as an historical person but rather as a figure standing for the origins of the modern scientific worldview. As Jacques Derrida puts it, Husserl's Galileo is 'an exemplary index of an attitude and a moment, rather than a proper name'.[2] 'Galileo', then, stands as shorthand for a crucial stage in modern scientific development: the moment nature becomes manifest as the idealized, mathematical complex. Similarly, in 'The Origin of Geometry', the term 'geometry' does not refer solely to the specific mathematical discipline of that name but is rather, for Husserl, a shorthand for the 'whole mathematics of space-time' (C 27; K 24), i.e. mathematical physics as applied to nature. In this sense, geometry is understood not just as a branch of pure mathematics but as the 'foundation of meaning' (*Sinnesfundament*, C 24; K 21) for the science of physics and the natural sciences. Galileo founded or established the science of *physics* in its modern form. He is one of the 'great discoverers of modernity' (C 53; K 53), albeit, as we shall see, what he founded was for Husserl a technique, an art (understood in the Greek sense of *technē*), a technology (*Technik*), rather than a true theoretical science.

Husserl links Descartes and Galileo together as co-founders of modernity. Already, in *Formal and Transcendental Logic* (1929), Husserl names both Galileo and Descartes as participants in the 'reshaping' of modern science and philosophy through the establishment of a 'new logic' (FTL, p. 2; Hua XVII 6). For Husserl, modernity in one sense may be said to have begun with the 'breakthrough' of Descartes, 'the primary founding genius of all modern philosophy' (C 73; K 75), who revolutionized philosophy with his discovery of transcendental subjectivity in the *ego cogito* (see *Crisis* § 16). But

---

[2] See Jacques Derrida, *Edmund Husserl's Origin of Geometry: An Introduction*, trans. J.P. Leavey Jr., ed. D. B. Allison (Sussex, NY: Harvester Press/Nicolas Hays, 1978), p. 35.

modernity had more properly been inaugurated through the 'primal establishment of the new natural science' (C 73; K 75), for which Galileo is the emblematic figure. Of course, Descartes himself, as Husserl acknowledges, was an early admirer of Galileo, and his entire *œuvre* can be seen as an attempt to prepare the intellectual mindset of his generation for the Galilean revolution.[3] Indeed, Husserl portrays Galileo as one of the founders of modern *philosophy* through his abstract theorization of nature.

Critics have long recognized that Husserl's account emphasizes Galileo's theoretical accomplishments as a mathematical Platonist rather than his experiments, empirical observations and technological achievements.[4] As Jan Patočka points out, however, empiricist interpretations of Galileo miss what is central to his task, namely that he is seeking the *essence* of motion. Galileo understands the components of motion as essentially mathematical (e.g. speed), unlike Aristotle.[5] Galileo's accomplishment, for Husserl, consists not in the development of experiments but in his discovery of a new and particular kind of *idealization* or 'co-idealization' (*Mitidealisierung*, C 38; K 37).[6] This mathematization of nature is captured through the novel application of an already existing geometry.[7] Indeed, Husserl in the *Crisis* offers an original characterization of modern mathematical

---

[3] Descartes learned of Galileo's condemnation in 1633 and wrote to Mersenne that if Galileo's view was false, so too were the 'entire foundations' of his own philosophy; see Stephen Gaukroger, *Descartes: An Intellectual Biography* (Oxford: Clarendon Press, 1995), pp. 290–2. Fearing retribution, Descartes withdrew from publication his own work on physics, *De Mundo*, and instead embarked on a project of preparing minds to receive the new scientific wisdom, beginning with the *Discourse on Method* (1637). See Michael Friedman, 'Descartes and Galileo: Copernicanism and the Metaphysical Foundations of Physics', in Janet Broughton and John Carriero, eds., *A Companion to Descartes* (Oxford: Blackwell, 2008), pp. 69–83.

[4] See Jürgen Renn's Introduction to his *Galileo in Context* (New York: Cambridge University Press, 2001), which points out that Alexandre Koyré, among other early twentieth-century Galilean scholars, ignored Galileo's Aristotelian background.

[5] See Jan Patočka, 'Galileo Galilei and the End of the Cosmos', in his *Aristotle: His Forerunners and His Heirs*, trans. Martin Pokorný and Erika Abrams (Prague: NČSAV, 1964), pp. 302–310.

[6] Husserl characterizes this idealization in several ways, including the idea of ideal exactitude, the taking of the exemplary individual instance as representative of the totality, the conception of the 'over and over again' (*immer wieder*), going beyond the existent actuality to the ideal possibility, the infinite idea of a thing as existing through its properties (K 359), and so on.

[7] See James W. Garrison, 'Husserl, Galileo, and the Processes of Idealization', *Synthese* Vol. 66 (February 1986), 329–38.

scientific method in terms of specific procedures and concepts such as abstraction, formalization, idealization, universalization and, finally, the emergence of the concept of *infinity*.

In order to understand idealization (*Idealisierung*), Husserl's distinction (first articulated in print in *Ideas* 1 § 13) between the procedures of *generalization* and *formalization* needs to be explained. Formalization (*Formalisierung*), for Husserl, is different from generalization. Generalization is the process whereby one moves from the individual to the species and the genus. Beginning with an individual physical object (e.g. a stone), one moves to the species 'spatial, material thing'. Formalization, on the other hand, abstracts from the material properties of a given entity and focuses on the object in terms of pure, empty, categorical forms. Thus, for example, a physical material object will be formalized as 'an entity'. Logic and mathematics employ formalization. Galileo 'formalizes' nature by seeing it in terms of an abstract grid of mathematical quantities. Husserl is one of the first to recognize that the 'abstractive closure' (*Geschlossenheit*, K 351) of the natural sciences is based on an abstraction and formalization away from the concrete individual occurrences. For Husserl (as, indeed, also for Heidegger), modern scientific research involves a particular 'formalization' of experience which should never be substituted for the fullness of that experience itself in its lived 'concretion'. Modern mathematical science imposes a particular kind of technical grid on everything that it seeks to explain. It cloaks everything, in Husserl's famous phrase, in a 'garb of ideas' (*Ideenkleid*, C 51; K 52), and the greatest danger is to substitute this ideal entity for the concrete experiential world that he terms the 'life-world', the 'original ground' (*Urboden*, C 49; K 49) for human life.

As part of the mathematization of nature Husserl also singles out Galileo's fateful separation of primary from secondary qualities, along with his radically new conception of nature as a closed sphere of universal causality. As Husserl writes: 'One can truly say that the idea of nature as a self-enclosed world of bodies [*Körperwelt*] first emerges with Galileo' (C 60; K 61). Galileo's scientific formulae are not just, or even primarily, expressions of relations between quantities; rather, they articulate ideal laws of nature. As a result of these striking innovations, Galileo, according to Husserl, transformed forever the way modern humanity thinks about the physical 'world of bodies' (*Körperwelt*, C 32; K 30), about 'nature' and indeed about the very meaning of *rationality* as such (including systematic knowledge, i.e. science and philosophy). With the success of Galileo, Husserl writes that, 'the world and, correlatively, philosophy, take on a completely new appearance' (C 61; K 62), and the nature of knowledge of the world is also radically transformed, as is the conception of the human knower.

Husserl believes that modern science has projected an idealized version of what the 'world in itself' is supposed to be like. In this regard, Husserl rejects what would now be termed a 'metaphysical realist' interpretation of modern mathematical science as uncovering the 'true' world as it really exists 'in itself', as opposed to describing 'merely aspects of the appearances' (C 117; K 119) available to the human senses – the domain of what Husserl calls the 'subjectively relative' (see C 32; K 30).[8] Furthermore, the idealized concept of the 'true world' (*die wahre Welt*), or 'true being' or the 'in itself' (*An-sich*, C 55; K 55), is given a very specific and peculiar determination in modern science. Modern science is committed to the notion of an unending process of investigation and self-correction as belonging to the very essence of enquiry, which has the sense of permanently getting closer to 'true being'.

Husserl's real target is the then current *positivist* and *neo-positivist* interpretations of modern science (*Crisis* § 3) associated with Auguste Comte (1798–1857), Mach and the Vienna Circle (Husserl was familiar with Schlick and Carnap). The nineteenth century had been the great age of *positivism*, the doctrine that rejected all forms of speculation and restricted knowledge to the contents of sensory experience. Auguste Comte (1798–1857), for instance, championed modern science against religious-mythic and metaphysical thought.[9] For the positivists, science was objective, inductive and experimental. Husserl regarded the positivists as holding an essentially mistaken conception

---

[8] See Hilary Putnam, *Representation and Reality* (Cambridge, MA: MIT, 1988). Putnam writes: 'What the metaphysical realist holds is that we can think and talk about things as they are, independently of our minds, and that we can do this by virtue of a "correspondence" relation between the terms in our language and some sorts of mind-independent entities.' See also Putnam, *Realism and Reason*, Philosophical Papers (Cambridge University Press, 1983), Vol. III, p. 205.

[9] See Auguste Comte's *Course of Positive Philosophy*, trans. by Harriet Martineau in *The Positive Philosophy of Auguste Comte* (London: Chapman, 1853).

of science owing to their deliberate narrowing of the concept of reason: they denied the essential contribution of subjectivity and as a consequence had 'decapitated' philosophy (C 9; K 7). For Husserl, on the other hand – as indeed for the German historian of ideas Hans Blumenberg – the real nature of modern science does not lie in the accumulation of data but in the creation of an all-consuming methodology.

Husserl was a critic not just of the positivist approach to science, but also of the outlook of the Neo-Kantians. The Neo-Kantians, following Kant, were also deeply interested in the formal sciences and in the reasons for the a priori applicability of mathematics to nature.[10] However, Kant had treated Newtonian science as simply a 'given' or as 'fact' (*Faktum*).[11] Indeed, Kant had assumed naïvely that precisely Newtonian space and time were encapsulated in the a priori forms of human sensible intuition. Husserl, on the other hand, always thinks of Newtonian science as a formal construction that does not map directly onto human, embodied, lived, intuitive space and time. Indeed, it is necessary to reflect on how the scientific account of the world (with its conceptions of space, time, causality and so on) has come to replace the thick world of everyday lived experience (the 'life-world') with its own formalized versions of space, time and causality.

THE GENESIS OF THE *CRISIS* GALILEO SECTION 9: HUSSERL, KOYRÉ AND KLEIN

Husserl's discussion of Galileo in Section 9 of the *Crisis* is undoubtedly one of the most influential and most discussed chapters in the book, so it is somewhat surprising to discover that it was a relatively late addition to the text of Part I as published in the yearbook *Philosophia* early in 1937. Husserl had originally submitted a very much shorter chapter – only three or four pages long – on Galileo as

---

[10] See especially Hermann Cohen, *Kant's Theorie der Erfahrung* [Kant's Theory of Experience] (Berlin: Bruno Cassirer, 1871; 2nd edn., 1885), which is often regarded as the foundational text of Neo-Kantianism.

[11] In general the Neo-Kantians presupposed the existence or 'fact of science' (*Faktum der Wissenschaft*), i.e. they accepted the validity of scientific knowledge, but they viewed the philosophical task as explaining how science is possible.

part of the original typescript of Part I. In September 1936 he wrote to Arthur Liebert, the editor of *Philosophia*, asking that publication be delayed while he continued to work on the Galileo section. This longer section, now expanded to almost forty pages, was eventually inserted into the printer's proofs as § 9, a huge addition that unbalances the overall narrative of Part I.

Husserl had already been addressing this question of the meaning of the modern scientific approach to nature in the late 1920s (see the supplement entitled 'Idealization and the Science of Reality – The Mathematization of Nature', C 301–14; K 278–93, which, according to Biemel, was written before 1928). His discussion of Galilean natural science and its impact occurs early in the *Crisis*, primarily in the extensive Section 9, but there are associated supplementary texts, e.g. Supplement 1 (K 349–56, not translated by Carr), and, most notably, the important and influential draft now known as 'The Origin of Geometry' (C 353–78; K 365–78). In fact, Husserl had been interested in Galileo's use of geometry from early in his career, when he was attempting to write the (subsequently abandoned) second volume of the *Philosophy of Arithmetic* (1891). Thereafter references to Galileo appear scattered through Husserl's work (e.g. EU § 10).

Various theories have been adduced to explain what occasioned the interest in Galileo. David Carr has suggested that visits by Alexandre Koyré, then an emerging Galileo scholar, sparked Husserl's interest and influenced his interpretation.[12] On the other hand, Reinhold Smid has shown (Hua XXIX il n.2) that Koyré's last visit with Husserl was in July 1932,[13] prior to the appearance of Koyré's studies on Galileo that began to appear in article form from 1935 on.[14] Furthermore, in 1937, Koyré himself remarked to Ludwig Landgrebe that he agreed with Husserl's Galileo interpretation (see Hua XXIX il), suggesting that Koyré was influenced by Husserl, rather than the other way round. In fact, Husserl's interest in Galileo's use of geometry was most probably

---

[12] Karl Schuhmann endorses Carr's claim; see his 'Koyré et les phénoménologues allemands', *History and Technology* Vol. 4 (1987), 152.

[13] *Chronik*, p. 413.

[14] These articles are collected in Alexandre Koyré, *Études galiléennes* (Paris: Hermann, 1939), trans. John Mepham as *Galileo Studies* (Atlantic Highlands, NJ: Humanities Press, 1978).

influenced by Jacob Klein, who had published a number of works on the origins of Greek geometry between 1934 and 1936.[15]

Historians of science (from Newton (1643–1727) to Koyré) are in agreement with Husserl in locating Galileo at the centre of the scientific revolution of the modern era. According to Koyré, for instance, it is Galileo's principle of inertial motion (that a body remains at rest or in uniform motion unless acted on by another body) that marks the modern breakthrough. This principle of mechanics may appear 'obvious' to us, Koyré writes, but it would not have appeared such to the ancient Greeks: 'In fact, the "evidence" and the "naturalness" which these concepts and considerations are enjoying are very young: we owe them to Galileo and Descartes, whereas to the Greeks, as well as to the Middle Ages, they would appear as "evidently" false, and even absurd.'[16] Koyré goes on to say that the Galilean concept of motion appears so natural to modern readers that we believe we can derive it from observation, whereas its 'establishment' actually required very difficult decisions and adjustments. In this respect Koyré follows Husserl in emphasizing the boldness of Galileo's concept of the 'mathematization of nature', the application of geometry to mechanics, and the emphasis on the ideal as opposed to what is sensibly apprehensible in experience (the basis of Aristotelian science). As Koyré puts it: 'Aristotelian physics does not admit the right, nor even the possibility, of identifying the concrete world-space of its well-ordered and finite Cosmos with the "space" of geometry.'[17] Koyré's point (repeated in other articles and essentially echoing Husserl's analysis) is that modern science took an abstract, ideal concept of space as a homogeneous infinite space and treated it as if it were the 'real' space that humans encounter in experience.[18] Koyré

---

[15] See Jacob Klein, 'Die griechische Logistik und die Entstehung der Algebra', *Quellen und Studien zur Geschichte der Mathematik, Astronomie und Physik*, Abteilung B: *Studien* Vol. III, No. 1 (1934), 18–105 (Part I), and No. 2 (1936), 122–235 (Part II); trans. Eva Brann as *Greek Mathematical Thought and the Origin of Algebra* (Cambridge, MA.: MIT, 1969; reprinted New York: Dover, 1992).

[16] See Alexandre Koyré, 'Galileo and the Scientific Revolution of the Seventeenth Century', *The Philosophical Review* Vol. 52 No. 4 (July 1943), 333–48, esp. 335.

[17] Ibid., 338.

[18] See Alexandre Koyré, 'The Significance of the Newtonian Synthesis', (1948), reprinted in Koyré, *Newtonian Studies* (Cambridge, MA: Harvard University Press, 1965), pp. 3–24.

portrays Galileo as going beyond Copernicus (1473–1543) and Kepler (1571–1630) in this respect, overcoming not just entrenched tradition and authority, but also what was up to then taken as 'common sense'.[19] Galileo counters the Aristotelian approach not by performing experiments, but by showing that it must be so and not otherwise. In this sense, physics is made to be an a priori discipline of necessary truths.[20] Koyré sums it up as follows: 'The Galilean revolution can be boiled down … to the discovery of the fact that mathematics is the grammar of science. It is this discovery of the rational structure of Nature which gave the a priori foundations to the modern *experimental* science and made its constitution possible.'[21] Koyré's view of Galileo in these remarks essentially conforms to Husserl's own bold reading of him as an a priori mathematical physicist.

HUSSERL'S 'HERMENEUTICAL' APPROPRIATION OF GALILEO

According to Husserl, there was a 'transformation' (*Verwandlung*, C 56; K 57) of the 'meaning-form' of nature in modern physics. Furthermore, this revolutionary transformation essentially went unnoticed and un-interrogated. It now stands in need of 'clarification' (*Klärung, Aufklärung*, C 56; K 57) in order to grasp the 'modern spirit' (C 57; K 58). In particular, Husserl seeks to uncover the concealed thought-formations and intentions that led to the 'construction' of the idea of *nature* as understood by modern science that has now become so thoroughly implanted in our culture that we somehow think of this scientific nature as if it were the 'natural' or common-sense view of modern humanity.

To bring the foundational moments of modern science to light, Husserl engages in an intellectual 'reconstruction' or 'interpretation' (*Deutung, Interpretation*). Husserl's intellectual *reconstruction* involves recovering the scientist's own motivations and, indeed, also revealing what other forces were at work on him, even those forces of which the scientist himself was unaware. This procedure is intuitive – seeking essential insight. Husserl's assistant, Eugen Fink, calls this procedure

---

[19] Koyré, 'Galileo and the Scientific Revolution of the Seventeenth Century', 345.
[20] Ibid., 347. [21] Ibid., 347n.6a.

of intentional reconstruction 'intentional history': an account which exhibits the coming to be of a particular meaning-formation. Husserl writes: 'In order to clarify the formation of Galileo's thought we must accordingly reconstruct [*rekonstruieren*] not only what consciously motivated him' (C 24–5; K 21–2).

In general terms, Husserl may be said to be offering a *hermeneutic* approach. His aim, as we have already mentioned, is to expose presuppositions – not just what consciously motivated the scientist (C 24–5; K 21), but what would have appeared 'obvious' or 'taken for granted' (*selbstverständlich*, C 24; K 21). This involves examining Galileo's conception or 'guiding model' (*Leitbild*, C 25; K 22) of mathematics, something effectively closed off from Galileo himself because of the different direction of his interest, but which naturally would have entered into his conception of physics. This intellectual reconstruction is, for Husserl, not history of ideas in the usual sense. It belongs to what Husserl will understand as seeking out the 'a priori of history', involving the identification of the formal features that make possible such an event of meaning, which we shall discuss further in Chapter 5 below.

Husserl recognizes that working scientists 'sure of the method' will be unhappy with the absence of scientific jargon (C 58; K 59) in his account. They will regard his approach as a kind of dilettantism. But he defends his approach. He is applying a phenomenological method of understanding which values 'original intuiting' (*ursprüngliche Anschauung*, C 59; K 59–60), seeking what is self-evident to intuitive inspection. His analysis necessarily involves a degree of simplification and idealization, but it aims at what is essentially true; he is not doing history in any strict chronological manner. He makes 'historical leaps' (C 58; K 59). Nevertheless, he claims to be basing his account on Galileo's 'known pronouncements' (C 58; K 58). Husserl acknowledges that more exact history would presumably show Galileo to be closer to his own predecessors, but he also invites his readers to perform their own 'reflections'. Husserl will stress that all scientific achievement takes place against the background of the kind of 'thick', sensuous intuiting of the life-world. He knows scientists will not be comfortable with this, but his approach is necessary in order to force them to meditate on the nature of their own methodology and how scientific ways of thinking build on ordinary life-situations.

Husserl begins by cautioning against attributing to Galileo an anachronistic, modern conception of physics, one that proceeds purely in 'the sphere of symbolism, far removed from intuition' (C 24; K 21). Galileo was most emphatically *not* a modern physicist operating in the world of pure symbols. Galileo's conception of mathematics still retained some naïve intuitive foundations – a certain inbuilt 'hidden presupposition of meaning' (*als verborgene Sinnesvoraussetzung*, C 25; K 22). Galileo's conception of motion and of bodies, for instance, remained entrenched in a more material conception inherited from the Middle Ages. Nevertheless, he does offer a new way of conceiving of nature.

GALILEO'S MATHEMATIZATION OF NATURE

As we saw above, Husserl (akin to Alexandre Koyré somewhat later) approaches Galileo from the standpoint of his Platonist idealization and mathematization of nature. Husserl writes: 'through Galileo's *mathematization of nature, nature itself* is idealized under the guidance of the new mathematics; nature itself becomes – to express it in a modern way – a mathematical manifold [*Mannigfaltigkeit*]' (C 23; K 20).[22] Galileo is credited with conceiving of nature as entirely amenable to exact quantification. As Galileo famously wrote in his *The Assayer* (*Il Saggiatore*, 1623), in a passage not even cited by Husserl:

Philosophy is written in this grand book, the universe … It is written in the language of mathematics, and its characters are triangles, circles, and other geometric figures. Without such means, it is impossible for us humans to understand a word of it, and to be without them is to wander around in vain through a dark labyrinth.[23]

On Husserl's reading, this idea of nature appears 'full-blown' (*fertig*, C 57; K 58) for the first time in the work of Galileo – hence his archetypal importance.

The mature Husserl frequently, as he had already done in *Ideas* I § 40, distinguishes between the physical thing as the object of

---

[22] Husserl means by 'manifold' not just a set (a collection of members), but a set plus the relations which hold between the members, as well as the properties of the members of the set; see David Woodruff Smith, *Husserl* (London, New York: Routledge, 2007), pp. 103–9.

[23] Quotation taken from Galileo Galilei, *The Assayer* trans. Stillman Drake in Drake, ed., *Discoveries and opinions of Galileo* (New York: Anchor Books, 1957), pp. 237–8.

our sensuous perceptual encounter and the scientific conception of the thing as found in physics. Following the pattern set by Galileo, physics discards the 'subjective-relative' or 'secondary' properties of a thing to concentrate on the primary properties. However, we only know that a physical thing is there and that we have access to it through our sensory perceptions. Physics, however, treats this sensuously experienced thing as merely a sign or indicator, as the bearer of certain properties. Husserl speaks (echoing Kant) of an 'empty X' which is assumed beneath the properties. Yet physical things are first and foremost experienced not as in physics but rather as found in everyday sensory perception. Husserl proposes then, in *Ideas* I § 41, to put aside our conception of the physical thing as found in physics in order to focus on the manner in which the thing is given in perceptual experience and the specific kind of 'transcendence' which the object has relative to the experience (and the manner in which every perception is inadequate in relation to the thing; see *Ideas* I § 44).

Already in his *Logical Investigations* (1901) Husserl had criticized the modern philosophical outlook (found in Descartes, Locke (1632–1704)) that regarded perception not as the direct grasping of the perceived object itself, but rather as an indirect apprehending of the thing through some kind of representation. The extrapolation of this view in science leads to a disastrous split between the object as experienced and the scientific object. Descartes, for instance, in his *Meditations* contrasted two ideas of the sun: one gained through sense perception and the other constructed through mathematical calculation and astronomy.[24] For him, the true idea of the sun is that of the astronomers who make use of geometry and mathematical physics. Descartes maintains that the true idea of the sun is *constructed* out of innate ideas of motion, distance, etc., rather than from the sensory manifestations of these qualities in our sensory idea of the sun. Galileo, who inspired Descartes, is responsible for the modern scientific acceptance of a decisive split between the experienced object (in this instance the visible sun) and the object as encountered in science (the scientific account of the sun).

---

[24] John Cottingham, Robert Stoothoff and Dugald Murdoch, eds., *The Philosophical Writings of Descartes* (Cambridge University Press, 1985), Vol. II, p. 27.

The scientific account strips away everything that belongs to human perception, what Husserl calls 'the subjective-relative'. In a typical passage in his *Dialogue Concerning the Two Chief World Systems*, for instance, Galileo proclaimed, through his mouthpiece Salviati, that he deeply admired the acumen of those early advocates of Copernicanism who, without the benefit of the telescope, had 'through sheer force of intellect done such violence to their own senses as to prefer what reason told them over that which sensible experience plainly showed them to the contrary'.[25] In *The Assayer*, Galileo had already laid out an account of colour, taste, touch, etc. as secondary qualities not really present in the object. There he writes:

I think that tastes, odors, colors, and so on are no more than mere names so far as the object in which we place them is concerned, and that they reside only in the consciousness. Hence, if the living creature were removed, all these qualities would be wiped away and annihilated ... To excite in us tastes, odors, and sounds I believe that nothing is required in external bodies except shapes, numbers, and slow or rapid movements. I think that if ears, tongues, and noses were removed, shapes and numbers and motions would remain, but not odors or tastes or sounds.[26]

Before exploring Husserl's reading of Galileo in more detail, let us find out more about Galileo, as he is not a figure familiar to students of philosophy.

THE HISTORICAL GALILEO

Galileo Galilei (1564–1642) was an Italian mathematician, astronomer, physicist, philosopher and experimental scientist. He is best known for popularizing and defending the Copernican heliocentric system, for employing the newly invented telescope to examine the heavens, for inventing the microscope, and for carrying out practical experiments involving dropping stones from towers and masts (to challenge the Aristotelian view that heavy bodies fall faster than lighter ones), examining the regular movements of the pendulum. Through

[25] Galileo Galilei, *Dialogue Concerning the Two Chief World Systems*, trans. Stillman Drake (Berkeley: University of California Press, 1967), p. 328.
[26] Galileo, *The Assayer*, in Stillman Drake, trans. and ed., *Discoveries and Opinions of Galileo* (Garden City, NY: Doubleday, 1957), pp. 274–7.

his use of the telescope Galileo discovered mountains on the moon and spots on the surface of the sun, as well as observing Jupiter's satellite moons and the phases of Venus. Because of a lack of uniform standards of measure, he had to set up his own units and standards of measurement for length and time (he had to count intervals of time), and Husserl emphasizes this contribution. Through experiments involving objects moving along inclined planes, he discovered the law of free fall, according to which, in a vacuum, all bodies would fall with the same acceleration, expressed as proportionality to time squared. Because of the breadth of his activities, historians of science differ as to whether Galileo was primarily an a priori mathematical physicist (as Husserl claims) or the first modern experimental scientist. Clearly, he was both.

Galileo's espousal of Copernicanism aroused accusations of heresy, and he travelled to Rome to defend himself. In 1616 the Jesuit Cardinal Robert Bellarmine (1542–1621) summoned Galileo to his residence in the Vatican to inform the scientist of the Inquisition's prohibition on the teaching of Copernican theory and explicitly enjoined him to speak of it only hypothetically. In 1632 in Florence Galileo published his *Dialogue Concerning the Two Chief World Systems*, in which the Ptolemaic and Copernican theories are apparently presented without the author purporting to take sides, but readers were in no doubt that the Copernican account was favoured. In October 1632 Galileo was ordered to appear before the Holy Office in Rome.[27] He was placed under house arrest but continued working, even after he went blind.

The historical Galileo continues to be interpreted in diverse and often conflicting ways. Husserl, Patočka and Koyré all see him as a mathematical Platonist who developed an a priori conception of nature; none emphasizes his empirical side. The Husserl–Patočka–Koyré interpretation has been challenged, however, by Stillmann Drake, Ernan McMullin, and others.[28] Furthermore, several recent scholars have attempted to replicate Galileo's original experiments, and these studies shed new light on Galileo's success

---

[27] For a detailed analysis of the events leading up to Galileo's trial, see Maurice A. Finocchiaro, *Retrying Galileo, 1633–1992* (Berkeley: University of California Press, 2005).

[28] See Ernan McMullin, 'Galilean Idealization', *Studies in the History and Philosophy of Science* Vol. 16 No. 3 (September 1985), 247–73.

as an experimental scientist.[29] There is also increased recognition (following Duhem's lead) that Galileo continued to work within the broad tradition of Aristotelian science; others emphasize Galileo's indebtedness to the artisan tradition of practical engineering,[30] or his debt to ancient Greek atomism.[31] Husserl of course also acknowledges that Galileo had not completely shaken off the prevailing scientific tradition.

Despite these readings of Galileo as a practical scientist, some historians continue to emphasize the importance of mathematics in Galileo's breakthroughs. Paulo Palmieri, for instance, has explored Galileo's use of mathematics,[32] and he has also attempted to reconstruct his empirical experiments.[33] It is clear that Galileo advanced science in many ways: constructing his own instruments, developing systems of measurement, performing experiments, questioning received wisdom and generating new theories. But it is also clear that he had a transformative effect on the science of his day and pursued his 'Pythagorean' interpretation with a conviction that went beyond the available empirical evidence. Galileo himself, as Husserl notes, operated with a confused distinction between 'pure' and 'applied' mathematics.

---

[29] Thomas B. Settle, 'Experimental Research and Galilean Mechanics', in Milla Baldo Ceolin, ed., *Galileo Scientist: His Years at Padua and Venice* (Padua: Istituto Nazionale di Fisica Nucleare; Venice: Istituto Veneto di Scienze, Lettere ed Arti; Padua: Dipartimento di Fisica, 1992), pp. 39–57, and Settle, 'Galileo and Early Experimentation', in Rutherford Aris, H. Ted Davis, and Roger H. Stuewer, eds., *Springs of Scientific Creativity: Essays on Founders of Modern Science* (Minneapolis: University of Minnesota Press, 1983), pp. 3–20. See also Stillman Drake, *Galileo at Work* (University of Chicago Press, 1978) and his three-volume co-edited collection of papers in *Essays on Galileo and the History and Philosophy of Science,* Stillman Drake, Noel M. Swerdlow and Trevor Harvey Levere, eds., (University of Toronto Press, 1999).

[30] Paul Rossi, *Philosophy, Technology and the Arts in the Early Modern Era*, trans. S. Attanasio (New York: Harper, 1970). There is no doubt that Galileo built on the technological insights of his day. He also made use of traditional Aristotelian impetus theory when it suited him; see Dudley Shapere, *Galileo: A Philosophical Study* (University of Chicago Press, 1974).

[31] See Pietro Redondi, *Galileo: Heretic*, trans. Raymond Rosenthal (Princeton University Press, 1987), pp. 10, 14 and passim. Galileo thinks of light in terms of corpuscles.

[32] See Paulo Palmieri, 'Mental Models in Galileo's Early Mathematization of Nature', *Studies in History and Philosophy of Science* Vol. 34 (2003), 229–64; and Palmieri, 'A New Look at Galileo's Search for Mathematical Proofs', *Archive for History of Exact Sciences* Vol. 60 (2006), 285–317.

[33] See Paulo Palmieri, *Reenacting Galileo's Experiments: Rediscovering the Techniques of Seventeenth-Century Science* (New York: The Mellen Press, 2008).

HUSSERL'S READING OF GALILEO AS A PLATONIST

Husserl presents Galileo as a Pythagorean Platonist mathematician, who perfected the ideal of exact measurement (and applied it to the recalcitrant area of motion), but who was aware that nature only imperfectly lives up to that ideal. Husserl's primary claim is that Galileo, in order to make nature more responsive to mathematics, had to *idealize* nature itself. Husserl does not comment on Galileo's use of the telescope or his other technological achievements. Instead, he stresses *idealization* and *mathematization*, but he also emphasizes the importance of Galileo's distinction between primary and secondary qualities. Galileo himself, of course, did not reflect on this idealization – nor could he have. He – like all discoverers, according to Husserl – was using 'a mixture of instinct and method' (*eine Mischung von Instinkt und Methode*, C 40; K 39). As a result, in Husserl's characterization, Galileo is both discoverer and concealer of the new science: 'a discovering and concealing genius' (*entdeckender und verdeckender Genius*, C 52; K 53).

Husserl credits Galileo with founding modern mathematical physics and with realizing the a priori nature of this discipline, which can never be fully confirmed by experience. In this respect Husserl offers an interesting characterization of the specific idea of a science of nature as progressing infinitely: 'It is the peculiar essence [*das eigene Wesen*] of natural science, it is a priori its way of being, to be hypothesis in infinity and verification in infinity' (C 42; K 41; translation modified). Husserl explains Newton's claim 'I do not invent hypotheses' (*hypotheses non fingo*) as meaning that science must be unerringly exact and methodical. To explain the manner in which mathematics applied to nature, as understood by Galileo, Husserl has the arresting term 'garb of ideas' (*Ideenkleid*, C 51; K 52). Mathematics 'dresses up' the life-world and represents it in terms of its own ideas: 'It is through the garb of ideas that we take for *true being* [*für wahres Sein*] what is actually a *method*' (C 51; K 52). What sort of a disguise is this 'garb of ideas'? How did it mask the method?

Husserl is particularly interested in Galileo's use of idealization to go *beyond* what is observable. Indeed, it is evident that a degree of idealization is required even to impose consistency on experimental results that can be quite varied. Galileo's experiments with falling bodies illustrate what is involved. In his unpublished *On Motion* (*De motu*), Galileo had theorized that bodies dropped in free fall from a height (e.g. a tower) will fall with a uniform speed which is not determined by their weight, but rather by what is now known as density or 'specific gravity' (not his term). When Galileo actually dropped bodies from heights, he found his results did not confirm his theory. In fact, the lighter body (i.e. that of the lower specific gravity) regularly moved ahead of the heavier body at the start of the fall, and it took some time for the heavier body to eventually overtake it. But Galileo did not let empirical non-verification affect the success of his theory. Instead he *idealized* to the law of falling bodies, which states that in a vacuum all bodies, regardless of their weight, shape or specific gravity, are uniformly accelerated in exactly the same way, and that the distance fallen is proportional to the square of the time taken.

Husserl completely plays down empirical discovery, the experimental method and induction. For him, the real breakthrough is that nature conforms to purely a priori ideal rules. Husserl emphasizes Galileo's 'accomplishment of idealization' or 'idealizing achievement' (*die idealisierende Leistung*, C 29; K 26). Nature actually operates only with a sub-set of these ideal rules. Husserl emphasizes the a priori deductive aspect of science, but, of course, this is indeed the role of modern mathematical physics as pursued by Stephen Hawking and others. They are not in a laboratory making observations but working solely with advanced mathematical models.

Husserl believes that a genuine science of the world requires identifying not only the most empty general laws for the universal 'style of the world' (*Weltstil*), e.g. every experience must be causally determined), but it must set up in advance and 'construct' all the possibilities of causal regulation – the 'infinitude of causalities' (*die Unendlichkeit ihrer Kausalitäten*, C 32; K 29). In this regard Husserl explicitly refers to scientific theory as a 'construction' (*Konstruktion*, C 32; K 30). Indeed, objectivity as such is a product of such mathematical idealization of the world (C 32; K 30). According to this construction 'subjective-relative' properties are transcended, and objects are thought a priori in an objective manner.

At the beginning of *Crisis* § 9, Husserl invokes the world of ordinary experience which is always given to experience in a 'subjectively relative' way (*subjektiv-relativ*, C 23; K 20). Husserl usually describes this changing realm in terms of Heraclitean change and Protagorean relativism: 'Each of us has his own appearances [*Erscheinungen*]; and for each of us they count as that which actually is [*als das wirklich Seiende*]' (C 23; K 20). In other words, in ordinary life, what appears manifests itself as what has being, yet we are aware of discrepancies between our experiences and our being-validations on the inter-subjective level. But we still assume a single world: 'Necessarily, we believe in *the* world' (C 23; K 20). For Husserl, there is an unquestioned, a priori, necessary presupposition of experience, namely that we all share a *single* world, albeit one that appears differently to each. All worlds are considered to be parts of the *one world* common to all. Husserl repeatedly stresses this point.

In Husserl's compressed description, he is saying that the 'sense' that there is a single world in itself is given along with the experience of subjective-relative variation, and in his 'pre-scientific' experience this is how it would have appeared to Galileo. In other words, there cannot really be a sense of variation unless there is already a sense of *the same* or identity. The 'world' is experienced as a kind of stable background of sameness and continuity against which subjective experience varies. Furthermore, Husserl emphasizes not just the unity, uniqueness and sameness of the phenomenon of world as experienced, but also points to the inherent *infinity* involved in the very idea of world as such. World as the horizon of experience necessarily shades off in a way that supports an infinite investigation.

In other words, mathematics creates the notion of the 'world in itself' with absolutely univocally determinable properties:

Thus mathematics showed for the first time that an infinity of objects that are subjectively relative and are thought only in a vague general representation [*Allgemeinvorstellung*] is, through an a priori all-encompassing method, *objectively determinable and can actually be thought as determined in itself*, or, more exactly, as an infinity which is determined, decided in advance, in itself, in respect to all its objects and all their properties and relations. (C 32; K 30).

The mathematical world can be constructed as something that has 'being in itself' (*An-sich-sein*, C 32; K 30). But mathematics can also show new properties of the intuited world in a kind of 'descending' (*herabsteigend*, C 30; K 32). This is a very Platonic way of speaking.

As a result, according to Husserl, Galileo not only developed a new ideal of scientific method involving idealization, but also generated a new conception of nature as the object studied by science.

In thinking about the natural world as approached in terms of geometry, Husserl says, Galileo abstracts from 'all that is in any way spiritual, from all cultural properties [*Kultureigenschaften*] which are attached to things in human praxis' (C 60; K 60). As a result of this 'abstraction', the world of corporeal bodies becomes 'a really self-enclosed world of bodies' (C 60; K 61), accompanied by the idea of a similarly self-enclosed natural causality. Nature understood as a region of self-enclosed causal laws as set forth by Galileo will henceforth be the very meaning of nature for philosophers and physicists such as Descartes and Newton.

Indeed, for Husserl, in Galilean science the very concept of 'world' itself undergoes a complete 'transformation of sense' (*Sinnverwandlung*, C 60; K 61), since it is now split into 'world of nature' and 'psychic world' (*seelische Welt*, C 60; K 61). This concept of a self-enclosed material world is new and not the same as that found in the ancients, even the ancient Materialists (e.g. Democritus). The basis of the conception is of a 'co-existence of the infinite totality' of bodies in space-time, understood and treated as having a 'mathematical rationale' (C 61; K 61). While knowledge of this nature is inductive and finite, nature-in-itself is infinite and mathematically ordered:

Out of the undetermined universal form of the life-world, space and time, and the manifold of empirical intuitable shapes that can be imagined into it, it [modern mathematics] made for the first time an objective world in the true sense – i.e., an infinite totality of ideal objects which are determinable univocally, methodically, and quite universally for everyone. (C 32; K 30)

According to this new conception, everything found in the intuitively experienced world is now given the 'world-style' (*Weltstil*) of 'corporeality' (*Körperlichkeit*, K 30), which Husserl equates with Descartes' extended substance (*res extensa*). Ideal geometry becomes applied geometry. But the world-style and its flow are already experienced as a unity, and that unity has its origins in the life-world. Husserl speaks of the 'style' (*Stil*) in which the world presents itself, i.e. things in the intuited life-world have a certain *habitual regularity*, the stream of experience is harmonious and constantly self-confirming but not in the manner of universal scientific lawfulness. For instance, water 'boils' (i.e. goes into an agitated state with bubbles, etc.) at different temperatures depending on how far above the ocean one is. The universal scientific statement 'water boils at 100 degrees Celsius' has to be qualified with respect to atmospheric pressure. Human lived experience adjusts to this 'world-style' (C 31; K 28). This follows on from Husserl's discussion of the world in *Ideas* I, where he sees it as a harmonious flow of experiences that confirm one another in an orderly way. Husserl claims that our experience presents the world as having a harmonious uniformity, and no matter how we imagine it differently, there will be some overall totality of unity which we have to assume. In contrast to the world of mathematical science, this intuited world, however, has the character of generality and typicality, not strict universality: 'In the life of prescientific knowing, we remain, however, in the sphere of the approximate, the typical' (C 31; K 29). In the *Crisis*, demonstrating his knowledge of contemporary physics, Husserl clearly distinguishes between early modern (Newtonian) and twentieth-century (Einsteinian) physics. Early modern physics conceived nature as composed of a set of ultimately indivisible elements (either continuous or discrete) in space-time that admit of only a single description. Classical physics was atomistic, mechanistic and determinist. For contemporary, post-Einsteinian physics, on the other hand, what is real is not uniquely determinable in advance (K 387). Nature can only be determined according to groups and types, and not as individuals. The new physics conceives of the world as a hierarchy of typicalities, not as a universe of atoms (K 390). Husserl speaks of a 'construction of type' (*Aufbautypik*, K 390). Physics has become a most powerful way of knowing nature, generating a 'physicalist technique' (K 390–1).

At the beginning of *Crisis* § 9, Husserl outlines the transformation of the old mathematics and science of nature in modernity, such that the finite space/place of Aristotelian science was replaced by infinite, homogeneous space, and haphazard discovery of objects was replaced by a single encompassing method, such that finite tasks are replaced by infinite tasks. He finds it remarkable that Galileo seems to have simply taken for granted the 'universal applicability of pure mathematics' (C 38; K 37). Husserl remarks on the 'strangeness' (C 37;

K 35) of Galileo's basic conception at least in relation to the accepted scientific situation of his time. According to Husserl, Galileo assumed 'that everything that manifests itself as real through the specific sense-qualities must have its *mathematical index* in events belonging to the sphere of shapes [*Gestaltsphäre*] – which is, of course, already thought of as idealized – and that there must arise from this the possibility of an *indirect* mathematization' (C 37; K 35–6). This leads Husserl to summarize Galileo: 'The whole of infinite nature, taken as a concrete universe of causality – for that was inherent in that strange conception – became [the object of] a *peculiarly applied mathematics*' (C 37; K 36). This universal causality, according to Husserl, was not arrived at inductively by generalizing from specific individual cases of causality but in fact preceded all induction. The assumption of universal causality came first. All possible changes have to take place according to laws laid down in advance (see C 308; K 286).

In his *Crisis*, Husserl believes he – unlike Galileo – must occupy himself with questions concerning 'the origin of apodictic, mathematical self-evidence' (*nach dem Ursprung der apodiktischen mathematischen Evidenz*, C 29; K 26). It never occurred to Galileo to question the 'how' of geometry's applicability to nature, 'to make geometrical self-evidence – the "how" of its origin [*das "Wie" ihres Ursprungs*] – into a problem' (C 29; K 26). 'Origin' (*Ursprung*) here, for Husserl, does not mean empirical, historical starting-point; rather he means geometry's 'original institution', what gave it the *sense* that it now has.[34]

Here (as in the 'Vienna Lecture') Husserl is interested in how a new 'attitude' (*Einstellung*) gets installed in human culture; he is interested in how a transformed concept of nature comes to replace the traditional intuited one. His account involves a 'shift of the direction of focus' (*Umkehrung der Blickrichtung*, C 29; K 26). Husserl is hinting at an 'intentional history' of mathematics. He acknowledges the 'mythic' foundation of geometry by a lost genius – the

---

[34] Compare Heidegger's more or less contemporaneous comments on the meaning of 'origin' in his 'Der Ursprung des Kunstwerkes (1935/1936)', *Holzwege*, GA 5, pp. 1–74, esp. p. 1; trans. as 'The Origin of the Work of Art (1935/1936)', in Julian Young and Kenneth Haynes, eds., *Off the Beaten Track* (New York: Cambridge University Press, 2002), where see esp. p. 1: 'Origin means here that from where and through which a thing is what it is and how it is.'

'Anaximander' of geometry. He speaks of the 'beginnings' (*Anfänge*, C 22; K 20) of algebra and of the development of geometry within the Platonic Academy (Euclid was, after all, at least according to the testimony of Proclus, a member of the Platonic school). But in the *Crisis* texts themselves Husserl does little more than sketch out how such an intentional history of mathematics might proceed. We shall return to discuss Husserl's 'The Origin of Geometry' fragment later in this chapter.

Let us now examine a particularly salient feature of Husserl's analysis of Galilean science – his conception of the discovery of *infinity*.

THE EMERGENCE OF THE CONCEPT OF INFINITY IN MODERNITY

For Husserl (as for Koyré and subsequently for Hans Blumenberg),[35] 'infinity' is an idea that shapes modernity. Husserl refers to the 'breakthrough' to the infinite in *Crisis* § 9, although, curiously, in the rest of the *Crisis* main text Husserl has little to say about the role of the discovery of infinity in the breakthrough to modernity. In the appended 1935 'Vienna Lecture', however, great stress is placed on this concept. Here he is arguing that philosophy is at the very essence of European rationality because it was Greek philosophy which originally gave humanity a 'revolutionary' change of attitude and 're-orientation' (*Umstellung*) – or 'transformation' (*Verwandlung*) – through the promotion of the ideas of *idealization* and *infinity*: 'But with the appearance of Greek philosophy and its first formulation, through consistent idealization, of the new sense of infinity, there is accomplished in this respect a thoroughgoing transformation [*Umwandlung*] which finally draws all ideas of finitude and with them all spiritual culture and [its concept of] mankind into its sphere' (C 279; K 325, translation modified).

Traditionally, Greek philosophy (e.g. Aristotle) did not accept the idea of an *actual* infinite. The infinite or 'limitless' (*apeiron*) as such was incomplete and hence not actual or real. Infinity as a positive notion is

[35] See Hans Blumenberg, *The Genesis of the Copernican World*, trans. Robert M. Wallace (Cambridge, MA: MIT, 1987) and Elizabeth Brient, *The Immanence of the Infinite: Hans Blumenberg and the Threshhold of Modernity* (Washington, DC: Catholic University of America Press, 2002).

largely a product of medieval Christian theology, itself expanding on
the development of the infinite One of the Neoplatonists.[36] Indeed,
even in 1831, the mathematician Carl Friedrich Gauss (1777–1855)
had written, following the Greeks, that the infinite is at best a *façon
de parler* in which one properly speaks of limits. Galileo shared this
traditional intuition that one cannot comprehend the infinite, and
he explicitly ruled out comparing different infinities as greater or less
than one another. In the late nineteenth century, however, mathematicians became especially interested in the idea of infinity, and
among them in particular, Husserl's colleague Georg Cantor (1845–
1918), a mathematician and committed Lutheran Christian. For
Cantor, transfinite numbers were infinite but somehow also defined
or completed sets. The integers (1, 2, 3, …), for example, could be
thought of as forming a complete albeit infinite set. Cantor was particularly inspired by St Augustine's dictum in the *City of God* Book
12, Chapter 18, which Cantor frequently cited, that every infinity is
in some ineffable way made finite to God, since it is comprehended
by Him. Cantor went on to show that these transfinite numbers,
though infinite, could actually be bigger or smaller than one another.
They had different 'cardinality'. For instance, the infinite set of even
numbers does not correspond to the infinite set of cardinal numbers.
Cantor believed the study of transfinite numbers also supported his
religious faith. In a letter to a Dominican priest in 1896, he even
wrote that he wanted to offer Christian philosophy 'for the first time
the true theory of the infinite'.[37]

According to Husserl, the emergence of the idea of infinity through
idealization is revolutionary and cuts off scientific culture from all
pre-scientific culture and sets it on an infinite road of discovery:

> Scientific culture under the guidance of ideas of infinity means, then, a
> revolutionization [*Revolutionierung*] of the whole culture, a revolutioniza-
> tion of the whole manner in which mankind creates culture. It also means
> a revolutionization of historicity [*Revolutionierung der Geschichtlichkeit*],
> which is now the history of the cutting off [*Entwerden*] of finite mankind's
> development as it becomes mankind with infinite tasks. (C 279; K 325)

---

[36] See Leo Sweeney, *Divine Infinity in Greek and Medieval Thought*, 2nd edn. (New York: Peter
Lang Verlag, 1998).

[37] See Joseph Warren Dauben, *Georg Cantor: His Mathematics and Philosophy of the Infinite*
(Cambridge, MA: Harvard University Press, 1979).

Idealization brings with it a consciousness of infinity, and, with that, reason breaks through to its own proper domain, freed from limits imposed by practical interests, and philosophy is set on the road to infinite tasks.

'THE ORIGIN OF GEOMETRY': EXPERIENCED SPACE AND SCIENTIFIC SPACE

Closely connected to Husserl's discussion of Galileo in *Crisis* § 9 is the so-called 'The Origin of Geometry' supplement. The title 'The Origin of Geometry' is somewhat misleading, as the text is really concerned with the problem of the transmission of ideal 'cultural acquisitions' (*Kulturerwerbe*) such as, in Husserl's favourite example, the Pythagorean theorem. 'The Origin of Geometry' is also important for its discussion of how space scientifically conceived is an idealization of concrete *lived* space (which is a correlate or 'embodiment', *Leiblichkeit*). As Husserl says in *Crisis* § 9(a), geometry is a world of ideal shapes, but we have become so familiar with moving from the world of experience to these shapes that we do not feel any particular tension between the space of geometry and lived space (C 24; K 21). The experience of corporeal bodies in intuitively lived space is different from the account of these bodies in the idealized version of the exact sciences. No flight of fancy can transform the lived shapes into the ideal shapes of geometry: geometrical space, Husserl insists, is not anything like imagined space (C 25; K 22). Bodies in real space fluctuate, and their self-sameness and likenesses to other bodies are merely approximate. Our accounts of these bodies suit 'practical interests'. Geometrical space, on the other hand, is formalized and idealized.

In 'The Origin of Geometry', Husserl is explicitly conducting a 'regressive enquiry' (C 354; K 366) looking back behind the taken-for-granted tradition of geometry to see how its 'ideal constructions' (*Idealgebilde*, C 49; K 49) were constituted. The essay does, however, briefly sketch the emergence of formal science from practical methods evolved by the Egyptians (associated with material in C 24–8; K 21–5). For Husserl, geometry emerged in surveying and measuring the intuitively given world (C 27; K 24), based on the 'essential form of the surrounding world' (*in der Wesensform dieser Umwelt*, C 27;

K 24–5). Such geometry arose from practical concerns, like the equal division of irregular land areas, measuring distances, journeys, building construction and so on. An 'art of measuring' (*Messkunst*, C 27; K 25) was required. As a start to this system, certain empirical shapes had to be taken as basic. The intuitive-surrounding world involves the 'typical' and the approximate.[38] These experientially intuited shapes cannot be communicated; hence they are not intersubjectively validated and made objective unless measurement is introduced (C 27; K 25).

Husserl's 'The Origin of Geometry' text returns to issues which he had been addressing since the beginning of his career, i.e. how objective (in this case, geometrical) knowledge is produced by temporally bound, individual acts of thinking. How does the ideal emerge out of the real and be preserved such that it can be returned to in thought? From the *Logical Investigations* onwards, Husserl had been concerned to defend the ideal objectivity of certain kinds of entities. Besides 'real' or 'actual' existent things, such as stones, animals and even conscious episodes (temporal slices of thinking), with their causal powers and interactions, there is, Husserl maintains, another domain of 'ideal' objectivities, such as the 'Pythagorean theorem' or 'the number 4', which must be understood as abstract unities of a peculiar kind. These ideal objects, moreover, are *not* psychological entities or their parts. The domain of objects is far wider than traditional empiricism envisaged. As Husserl writes in the *First Logical Investigation*: 'In sober truth, the seven regular solids are, logically speaking, seven objects precisely as the seven sages are: the principle of the parallelogram of forces is as much a single object as the city of Paris' (LU I **I** § 31 231; Hua XIX/1 106).

In 'The Origin of Geometry', Husserl continues to defend this ideality as sui generis and not reducible to psychic existence: 'Geometrical existence is not psychic existence; it does not exist as something personal within the personal sphere of consciousness; it is the existence of what is objectively there for everyone (for actual and possible geometers, or those who understand geometry)' (C 356; K 367).

Husserl's question now is: how do objective, invariant, self-contained, timeless truths (e.g. the Pythagorean theorem) get

---

[38] Husserl has more to say about the nature of intuitive 'types' in *Experience and Judgement* § 83.

constituted as the *same* across the living, historical context of changing, intersubjective human culture? Husserl writes: 'Our problem now concerns precisely the ideal objects which are thematic in geometry: how does geometrical ideality (just like that of all sciences) proceed from its primary intrapersonal origin, where it is a structure within the conscious space of the first inventor's soul, to its ideal objectivity?' (C 357–8; K 368–9). His answer is that geometrical discoveries become objectified in written forms. In being written down as symbols, what is written down becomes a 'sedimentation', detached from the original thinker, which can be reactivated by new acts of understanding, open to any possible reader. Husserl identifies written language as that which functions to preserve the ideality and iterability of meanings. The objectivity of geometry is made possible, Husserl says, through the 'body of language' (*Sprachleib*, C 358; K 369), precisely written language. It is Husserl's emphasis on the role of *written* language in preserving scientific insights that provided the main inspiration for Derrida's claim that Western culture has, since Plato's *Phaedrus*, prioritized speech over writing. Derrida's long commentary on 'The Origin of Geometry' is a wide-ranging, immanent critique of Husserl, concentrating on an account of signs and writing, and on Husserl's assumptions concerning historicity. Derrida highlights ambiguities and difficulties latent in Husserl's notions of ideal history, ideal origins and the 'historical a priori'. Whereas Husserl had believed that the very essence of the historical could be understood through an a priori essential insight, Derrida argues that phenomenological imagination is never rich enough to reconstruct the intellectual lives of people of radically different cultures. Husserl is forced to admit 'an irreducible, enriching, and always renascent equivocity into pure historicity'.[39] Derrida also criticizes Husserl's view of an absolute emerging in history, claiming instead that 'the absolute is present only in being *différant*'.[40]

Part of Husserl's story concerns how the ideal emerges from the flow of variations experienced in the life-world. Things are more or less straight, flat or round. There is, however, a limit to what can be done through this 'normal technical capacity of perfecting' (*das*

---

[39] Derrida, *Edmund Husserl's Origin of Geometry*, p. 103.
[40] Ibid., p. 153. Derrida coins the neologism '*différance*' to express the idea of both difference and deferral of significance.

normale technische Vermögen der Vervollkommnung, C 25; K 22). The ideal of perfection can get pushed further and further until we arrive at 'limit shapes' (*Limesgestalten*) which have for us the character of invariant and never-attainable limit 'poles' (C 26; K 23).

Things of the naturally sensuously intuited world have their own peculiar 'habits'. There is a certain 'belonging together' (*Zusammengehörigkeit*, C 30; K 28) that makes them out, as well as a certain 'typicality' or 'habit' (*Gewohnheit*, C 31; K 28), such that the empirical world has a 'general' or 'over-all style' (*Gesamtstil*).[41] Husserl's argument here is that even if we imaginatively vary the world, we continue to vary it according to the lines of this style. There is also an *invariance* to the empirically intuited world (e.g. experience is continuous, causation runs in a certain course, identity over time and so on). There is a 'universal causal style' to the life-world (C 31; K 29) which is not the same as scientific exact causation. The aim of science, for Galileo, is to overcome the subjective-relative which is a necessary, essential part of the 'empirically intuited world' (*die empirisch-anschauliche Welt*, C 29; K 27).

Indeed, in order to be used by the mathematical sciences of nature, the science of geometry itself required a change of attitude, 'a change [*Umstellung*] from the practical to the pure theoretical interest' (C 28; K 25). Shapes are now understood as 'universally available', from which other shapes can be 'constructed' in a univocal manner. This process of identifying 'limit shapes' Husserl calls 'idealization' (*Idealisierung*, C 26; K 23) and 'construction' (*Konstruktion*, C 26; K 23), allowing limit shapes to become acquired tools, 'cultural acquisitions' (*Kulturerwerbe*) that can be likened to other cultural products or objects (*Kulturobjekte*) such as 'tongs' or 'drills', except that their meanings are always one and the same across time (e.g. Husserl never tires of insisting that there can be but one 'Pythagorean theorem' and that its meaning remains unchanged). Cultural tools, on the other hand, can present themselves in many different exemplars.

The meaning of written ideal entities can be read off them instantly without having to re-intuit their meaning again. The preservation of

---

[41] James Dodd makes the point that 'world-style' is a concept intimately connected with 'surrounding world' (*Umwelt*) in Husserl's account; see his *Crisis and Reflection: An Essay on Edmund Husserl's* Crisis of the European Sciences, Phaenomenologica 174 (Dordrecht: Kluwer, 2004), pp. 89–90.

these cultural acquisitions becomes their 'embodiment' (*Verkörperung*) 'through speech and writing' (C 26; K 23), thereby reinforcing the theme developed in his 'Origin of Geometry', which is clearly directly related to the discussion in *Crisis* § 9(a), subtitled 'Pure Geometry'.

Geometry, the first form of idealization, became applied to the world of nature, but a second form of idealization took place which re-envisioned the very nature of sensuous reality itself. Husserl speaks of this as the indirect mathematization of the world of the sensory 'filling' or 'plenum' (*die Fülle*) involving different forms of abstraction and idealization. For Husserl, Galileo – and by implication modern science as such – is concerned not with the unique individual but with the universal. The individual is understood only as an example (*Exempel*): 'the individual fact is rather an example' (C 41; K 40). These sensory experiences have also to be recognized as extensively and intensively infinite: 'The whole concrete world of bodies *Körperwelt* is thus charged with infinities not only of shape but also of plena' (C 38; K 37). But for Husserl this experience of the infinity of the filling does not yet bring us to 'indirect mathematicizability' (C 38; K 37). Husserl sees a precise development from the geometry of shapes to constructive quantification and on to 'analytical geometry' (C 39; K 38).

Husserl's position is more complicated and subtle (and more ambiguous) than many have appreciated. Husserl does not think that 'nature' as something regulated by laws is idealized in exactly the same way in which numbers are idealized (hence Galileo is not simply repeating Plato). A particular bifurcation of experience took place in the constitution of scientific nature. He is thinking explicitly of the manner in which Galileo (and subsequently Hobbes (1588–1679)) treated certain properties as 'subjective' and as caused by other properties actually in nature, properties that were fully mathematicizable. This ultimately leads, in Husserl's view, to Kant's confused discussion of synthetic a priori. Why should certain properties be singled out as not subject to exact quantification, and why should they then be treated as 'merely subjective' (C 54; K 54)? Why was the sensory domain not seen as equally mathematicizable? Why was the underlying assumption that nature was mathematicizable not interrogated by scientists? Instead, they became brilliant but narrow technicians.

'THE EARTH DOES NOT MOVE' (1934)

Although not contained in the *Crisis* texts as published in Hua vi, 'The Earth Does Not Move' is an associated text from 1934 (published for the first time in 1940), which was an important influence on Merleau-Ponty and others. This fragmentary text (MS D 17), dated early May 1934 and often referred to as 'The Earth Does Not Move', claims that the life-world incorporates the outlook of pre-Copernican philosophy and science, namely a world in which the earth literally may be said not to move.[42] Here, Husserl is interested in the phenomenological origins of spatiality, tracking the development of the conception of the world as an infinite space in modern science. 'We Copernicans, we moderns', as he puts it, consider the earth as just one of the stars in infinite space (HSW, p. 222). He contrasts the pre-scientific experience of the 'openness', incompleteness and unlimitedness of the horizonality of the world with the scientific conception of infinity. Husserl writes:

The idea of the earth comes about as a synthetic unity in a manner analogous to the way in which the experiential fields of a single person are unified in continuous and combined experience. Except that, analogously, I appropriate to myself the reports of others, their descriptions and ascertainments, and frame all-inclusive ideas. (HSW, p. 222).

The concept of a horizon always has to be correlated with a reference point (e.g. the horizon is relative to where I am standing now). I have a sense of the horizon of my experience, and I can expand it to think of the border of Germany, and so on, until I conceive of the whole earth as a horizon. As Husserl says: 'Its horizon consists of the fact that I go about on the earth-basis (*Erdboden*), and going from it and to everything on it I can always experience more' (HSW pp. 224–35). In the pre-scientific outlook the world is the measure of all rest and movement and hence cannot itself be in motion. One cannot also speak of it being at rest, since it provides the frame for rest and

---

[42] The German text was first published as 'Notizen zur Raumkonstitution' [Notes on the Constitution of Space], *Philosophy and Phenomenological Research* Vol. 1 No. 1 (September 1940), 21–37 and is there mentioned as an extension of the text, 'Grundlegende Untersuchungen zur phänomenologischen Ursprung der Räumlichkeit der Natur', in Marvin Farber, ed., *Philosophical Essays in Memory of Edmund Husserl* (Cambridge, MA: Harvard University Press, 1940), pp. 305–25. This text is translated by Fred Karsten as 'Foundational Investigations of the Phenomenological Origin of the Spatiality of Nature' in HSW, pp. 222–33.

motion: 'In conformity with its original idea, the earth itself does not move and does not rest; only in relation to it are movement and rest given as having their sense of movement and rest' (HSW, p. 223).

In fact, as a whole, the earth cannot be considered a 'body' at all; rather, it is a 'ground' or 'ground-body' (*Erdboden*), a backdrop against which the very notion of corporeal body and its qualities has to be conceived. Is the notion of corporeality even meaningful in relation to the earth as a whole? For Husserl, the earth as a whole is conceived (in modern science and in the 'modern' attitude that has absorbed this scientific outlook) as a large body (akin to other bodies), deracinated from any fixed point of reference, but it is first and foremost the nexus for the possibility of certain confirmations and harmonious streams of experience. Husserl writes in his dense way how the life-world prefigures certain possibilities and encapsulates certain horizons that led to nature and being as a whole being viewed in a certain way.

For Husserl, our intuitions of the world, of corporeal bodies, space, time, causality and movement, are all given together in an interrelated way. They are experienced as such on the basis of my lived-bodily insertion in the world. It is primarily my body that gives a sense of orientation in space. But how do we get a specific sense of movement? Everything is experienced as at rest or in movement. We have to take the world as at rest and movements as relative to it. Thereby the concept of 'absolute rest' is arrived at. The starting-point must be the experience of being at rest (including the temporal sense of 'resting' in the present). But there are different ways of being at rest. Husserl gives the example of sitting in a railway carriage and experiencing the carriage around one as not moving or at rest but then looking out the window and seeing in fact that the train is moving. Motion and rest are experienced as relative, and the 'absolute' conception of rest and motion requires a special act of the mind to conceive.

Another associated text, 'Notes on the Constitution of Space', written in 1934 but published in 1940, offers the late Husserl's meditations on the constitution of space through our embodied experience.[43] In this text, Husserl discusses the manner in which experienced movement and rest are developed from our kinesthetic

---

[43] E. Husserl, 'Notizen zur Raumkonstitution', 21–37.

bodily movements (eye movements and touch, primarily) and eventually formalized as the scientific concept of absolute rest and motion (as found in Newtonian physics). Each organ (hand, foot, eyes) has its own range of distinctive movements that constitute the particular experience of spatiality of that organ; each organ has its 'zero-point' and has its own sense of place (*Ort*).[44] Each organ also has a corresponding set of specific sensory experiences, what Husserl calls 'hyletic data', corresponding to it – the touch sensations, visual sensations – that are taken for granted. The experience of the body moving is constituted in a very complex way out of these interconnected sensory chains of experiencing. Husserl is here taking up again the issue of embodiment that he had already explored in *Ideas* II. For Husserl, the scientific picture of the world has to be understood in relation to this primarily intuited embodied world of experience, one that has been 'forgotten' (*Crisis* § 9(h)) in our scientific explorations.

CONCLUSION

Husserl's remarkable *Crisis* § 9 on Galileo and on the nature of modern science, combined with his late associated essays on geometry, on the pre-Copernican world-picture and on the constitution of space through embodiment, amount to a complex and sophisticated account of the constitution of the contemporary scientific worldview. It is a tour de force of intellectual reconstruction and philosophical insight. Husserl ends Section 9 with a discussion of his method – anxious to explain the nature of the 'historical reflections' he is carrying out. His intellectual reconstruction of the breakthrough of Galileo identifies a number of theoretical moves that brought about the new scientific world-picture. These include:

1 'substitution' (*Unterschiebung*, C 50; K 50): Galileo substitutes the 'mathematically substructed world of idealities for the only real world' (C 48; K 49). This substitution was passed on to his successors – physicists of subsequent generations – and now threatens the foundations of the scientific achievement.

---

44 In 'Notizen zur Raumkonstitution', Husserl distinguishes between 'place' (*Ort*) and 'space' (*Raum*) as an open continuous system of places; see ibid., 27.

2 *omission*: Galileo did not enquire back into the 'original meaning-giving achievement' (*die ursprünglich sinngebende Leistung*) whereby a pure geometry emerged from practices in the life-world (C 49; K 49)

3 *abstraction*: Galileo abstracts from everything spiritual, from the human being as a person, etc., so his concept of what is included in the very idea of 'world' is too reductionistic (C 60; K 60). The result is that 'nature' is treated purely as a world of spatio-temporal bodies in a self-enclosed causal nexus. Problems concerning the status of the human sciences, and indeed of the very human as such, are the inevitable result.

What this Galilean mathematization of nature accomplished was the idea of the universe and of knowledge as one vast, indeed infinite, rational, closed system: 'The world is in itself a rational systematic unity… in which each and every singular detail must be rationally determined' (C 65; K 66). Inbuilt in this idea is the notion of infinite progress in knowledge (and also control of nature) towards the goal of omniscience.

Finally, as we shall explore further in Chapter 4, a crucial outcome of Galilean science in its impact on modern philosophy is a certain kind of *dualism*, a 'splitting' (*Zerspaltung*, C 60; K 61) of the world into that which is deemed to belong to 'nature' and has 'being in itself' and another world, which is the world of the *psychic*, which is deemed to be the 'subjective-relative'. For Husserl, this 'splitting off of the psychical' (*die Abscheidung des Psychischen*, C 62; K 62) is deeply problematic. Indeed, for Husserl, it gave rise to the whole set of worries about the mind and its powers that are evident in the Kantian critique of reason. A naturalization of the soul was inevitable and is initiated by Hobbes and fully developed in Locke (C 63; K 64).

Husserl's view of the origins of modern science has been subjected to many criticisms, specifically because it downplays Galileo's role as an experimental scientist. As Husserl himself concedes, he is of course simply offering a sketch that would need to be filled out with much more historical detail. Husserl's reading of Galileo was in fact further elaborated in greater historical detail, but without evident contradiction, by Koyré and indeed by Jan Patočka. Both defend Husserl's effort to portray Galilean science as seeking *essence*. The historian of mathematics Jacob Klein further fleshed out Husserl's account while at the same time offering significant criticisms.[45] In particular Klein gives more prominence to the geometer Franciscus Vieta (1540–1603), who developed modern algebraic notation – mentioned only once by Husserl in relation to the algebraic method (C 44; K 43).[46] Klein suggests that the Arabic number-system was primarily influential in leading to the indirect understanding of numbers and 'ultimately to the substitution of the ideal numerical entities, as intended in all Greek arithmetic, by their symbolic expression'.[47] Thus, for Klein, the technique of operating with symbols replaces the science of numbers.[48] According to Klein, the symbolic approach of modern algebra involves two main traits. It identifies the object with the means of its representation, and it replaces the real determinateness of an object with the mere possibility of making it determinate.[49] This form of abstraction distinguishes modern algebra from previous mathematics and explains its purely formal reference to an indeterminate 'empty something'. It is true that Vieta developed the modern symbolism used in algebra (where letters stand for unknown quantities), but he did not project this onto nature, as did Galileo. Notwithstanding Vieta's accomplishment (and Husserl acknowledges Vieta came before Galileo), Husserl's claim for the breakthrough character of Galileo remains intact. Far more important than the factual discussion of Galileo is Husserl's account of the manner in which modern science has developed its distinctive character and is now perpetuating itself as a kind of blind technique since its peculiarly idealized concept of nature is now simply taken for granted and substituted for lived-intuited nature. This substitution of the mathematically ideal for the intuited-real is precisely why science is in a crisis and why phenomenology is peculiarly well suited to address this crisis. In the next two chapters we shall examine Husserl's evaluation of the crisis in the human sciences, specifically psychology and history.

[45] Jacob Klein, 'Phenomenology and the History of Science', in Farber., ed., *Philosophical Essays in Memory of Edmund Husserl*, pp. 143–63; reprinted in Klein, *Lectures and Essays*, ed. Robert B. Williamson and Elliott Zuckerman (Annapolis, MD: St John's Press, 1985).
[46] However, Morris Kline, in his *Mathematical Thought from Ancient to Modern Times* (Oxford University Press, 1990), sees Vieta as a transitional figure. Prior to Vieta, algebra tended to be justified through geometrical proofs; Vieta and Descartes reversed this approach.
[47] See Klein, 'Phenomenology and the History of Science', in Klein, *Lectures and Essays*, p. 83.
[48] Ibid., p. 81.   [49] Ibid., p. 123.

CHAPTER 4

The crisis in psychology

PSYCHOLOGY AS THE SUPPOSEDLY EXEMPLARY SCIENCE OF SUBJECTIVITY

Husserl's critique of the sciences in the *Crisis* is not limited to the exact natural sciences but is even more concerned with the fate of the human sciences (*Geisteswissenschaften* – literally, 'sciences of spirit'), since these are centrally concerned with the values of human existence. In the *Crisis*, besides philosophy, which is treated throughout, he specifically discusses two human sciences: psychology and history. In this chapter I shall focus exclusively on Husserl's treatment of psychology and shall address his treatment of history in Chapter 5.

Husserl's preoccupation with psychology is evident from the opening pages of the *Crisis* Part I, which itself grew out of Husserl's Prague lectures of November 1935 (Hua XXIX 103–39 (there is no corresponding English translation)). These lectures were entitled 'Psychology in the Crisis of European Science' (Hua XXIX 103). Primarily because it claims to be *the* science of human subjectivity, Husserl regards psychology as an exemplary and privileged science of our current age (already in the *Logical Investigations* he speaks of this 'psychologically obsessed age', LU *Prol.* § 28). Psychology's problems, moreover, are symptomatic of the crisis in the human sciences generally, and, indeed, psychological issues are often entangled with issues even in the mathematical sciences (*Crisis* § 2). For Husserl, as we have seen, a science is in crisis when its task and method become questionable (see Hua XXIX 103). He believes that the foundations of psychology as a theoretical discipline have been flawed from the outset. The discipline is in permanent crisis, not just because of its 'retardation of method' (C 4; K 2), due to its late arrival as a science, but because its specific domain has been carved out in a confused manner from material deliberately excluded by the natural sciences. He writes that 'the history of psychology is actually only a history of crises' (C 203; K 207) and that it cannot be considered a genuine science (C 250; K 253).

Part IIIB of the *Crisis*, entitled 'The Way into Phenomenological Transcendental Philosophy from Psychology' (§§ 56–72), is a sustained critical meditation on the problematic nature and status of modern scientific or experimental psychology, examining the evolution of modern psychology (stemming from Descartes and Locke) and its inherent failure to become a true science. He also considers the possibility of a new, genuine science of subjectivity.

Psychology is in permanent crisis. It is in the grip of a reductive *naturalism* and *objectivism* and, through its aping of the methods of the natural sciences, it misconstrues the essential character and meaning of human subjective and intersubjective intentional life. Husserl, then, is proposing a radical rethink concerning the most basic concepts and procedures of psychology as a science of 'inner life' (*Innenleben*, C 243; K 246, see also K 297). He wants to strip it of naturalistic prejudices and ground it in a new phenomenological psychology, which he also calls 'pure' psychology (see C 238; K 240). Husserl's claim will be that his new phenomenological psychology offers an entirely new way of describing subjectivity in terms of its intentional acts, meaning-constitution, syntheses and intentional implicated horizons, and essential structures in their living interconnection, an account on a completely different level from anything achievable by scientific psychology, trapped as it is in its naturalistic and sensualist paradigm. However, even pure phenomenological psychology is itself, as we shall see in Chapter 7, in need of a further transformation, through the application of what he calls a 'universal *epochē*', into transcendental phenomenology.

The analysis of psychology provides Husserl with a new way to introduce (a new 'reduction' to) the *transcendental viewpoint* and a way into the phenomenology of intentional subjective and intersubjective life. As he puts it in the *Crisis*, psychology and transcendental philosophy are 'allied with each other in a peculiar and inseparable way' owing to the complex relations between the psychological, 'worldly' or 'mundane' ego and the transcendental ego

(C 205; K 209). Psychology and transcendental philosophy share an interest in the ego, intentional consciousness, self-consciousnes, and empathy, all considered within the constant backdrop of a universal world-horizon. There is, for Husserl, a strict *parallelism* between the psychological and transcendental approaches to subjectivity. Through a change in 'nuance' or register one can be transmuted into the other; phenomenological psychological insights can be transformed into transcendental insights. Husserl also repeatedly stresses that transcendental insights can be misconstrued (and indeed were misconstrued in the tradition of Hume and Kant) as psychological insights in a naturalistic setting. While translation is possible, so also is misunderstanding, and, to date, philosophy has not properly understood the transcendental domain.

In the *Crisis*, then – developing a theme expressed in his *Encyclopaedia Britannica* article on 'Phenomenology' as well as in his 1928 *Amsterdam Lectures* (Hua ix) – Husserl is seeking to found a radical, new science, transcendental phenomenology, which will finally put the primary science of subjectivity, i.e. psychology, on a secure footing. Thus Husserl writes:

Part of transcendental philosophy's own meaning was that it arose out of reflections on conscious subjectivity through which the world, the scientific as well as the everyday intuitive world, comes to be known or achieves its ontic validity [*Seinssinn*] for us; thus transcendental philosophy recognized the necessity of developing a purely spiritual [*geistige*] approach to the world. (C 201; K 205, translation modified)

Ultimately, transcendental phenomenology will completely revolutionize psychology. Negotiating the correct relationship between what he often calls 'inner' psychology and transcendental phenomenology, in terms of their understanding of subjectivity, is a major concern of Part III of the *Crisis*. While psychology claims to be the science of subjectivity *par excellence*, it has remained embedded within *the natural attitude* with its naïve assumption of the existence of the world. The natural attitude, moreover, carries within it the danger that it can deteriorate into what Husserl terms *the naturalistic attitude*, which both *reifies* and *absolutizes* this world. This reification means that the true nature of intentional subjectivity is obscured. A breakthrough is required to understand the transcendental ego, its role in the constitution of the world-horizon and its cooperation with other transcendental egos in what Husserl terms the transcendental field of 'total and universal subjectivity' (C 264; K 267) or 'transcendental intersubjectivity' (C 184; K 188; cf. Hua xxix 84). As Husserl writes:

> The consciousness of intersubjectivity, then, must become a transcendental problem; but again, it is not apparent how it can become that except through an interrogation of myself, [one that appeals to] inner experience, i.e., in order to discover the manners of consciousness through which I attain and have others and a fellow mankind in general, and in order to understand the fact that I can distinguish, in myself, between myself and others, and can confer upon them the sense of being 'of my kind'. Can psychology be indifferent here? (C 202; K 206)

Intersubjectivity requires that subjectivity and its own stream of 'inner experience' be thoroughly understood. Conversely, subjectivity itself cannot be understood if its interrelation with others is not recognized as intrinsic to it. One of psychology's great failures has been, for Husserl, that it has never made the constitution of the commonly shared public world into a problem. It has completely failed to identify the role of what Husserl calls anonymous 'functioning subjectivity'.

For Husserl, moreover, this genuine transcendental exploration of subjectivity must grasp the peculiar nature of human *lived embodiment* (*Leiblichkeit*), as well as the operation of the *personalistic* and *social* attitudes, and, indeed, what Husserl calls generally 'the life of spirit' or 'we-subjectivity' (*Wir-Subjektivität*, C 109; K 111). This broader conception of the human psychical and spiritual is initially developed in Husserl's *Ideas* ii and *Ideas* iii (texts that remained unpublished during his life), in his Freiburg lecture courses on *Nature and Spirit* (delivered between 1917 and 1928) and in *Phenomenological Psychology* (1925), but it receives its strongest and most concentrated expression in the *Crisis*. He writes there, for instance:

> What the person does and suffers, what happens within him, how he stands in relation to his surrounding world, what angers him, what depresses him, what makes him cheerful or upset – these are questions relating to persons; and so are questions of a similar sort relating to communities of every level: marriages, friendships, clubs, civic communities, communities of peoples, etc. (C 322; K 301)

I shall discuss further Husserl's concept of the person in Chapter 5, here, I shall focus on his phenomenological psychology, including his conception of *lived embodiment* (*Leiblichkeit* – he criticizes Kant for neglecting this dimension, *Crisis* § 28) and *empathy* (*Einfühlung*), as the basis for the experience of the subjective lives of others with whom we share the communal life-world. To counteract the deficiencies in empirical psychology, Husserl develops what he variously calls 'pure' or 'phenomenological' psychology, a theme with which he became increasingly preoccupied during the late 1920s.[1] This psychology proposed to disregard everything 'psychophysical' (i.e. the neurophysiological basis of the psychic) and develop a new way of describing accurately inner experience, based on a rigorous application of the *epochē*. Eventually, however, Husserl maintains, even this phenomenological psychology needs to be radically transformed through a further radical 'universal *epochē*' into a genuine, transcendental science of subjectivity and intersubjectivity. Only a genuine transcendental philosophy can offer a truly clarified account of what Husserl calls 'the psychic' (*das Psychische*) in its own terms rather than in the terms of naturalistic science. At the end of *Crisis* Part IIIB § 72, he writes:

The surprising result of our investigation can also, it seems, be expressed as follows: a pure psychology as positive science, a psychology which would investigate universally the human beings living in the world as real facts in the world, similar to other positive sciences (both sciences of nature and humanistic disciplines), does not exist. There is only transcendental psychology, which is identical with transcendental philosophy. (C 257; K 261)

Husserl does not deny that genuine advances have been made in the acquisition of psychological data, observations and so on, but he thinks that the philosophical underpinning essential to the interpretation of these data is inherently flawed. He maintains that discoveries can only be contextualized in a science if the nature of 'psychic being' (*seelisches Sein*, C 258; K 261) has itself already been understood. Psychology must become a genuine science of spirit.

---

[1] Husserl lectured on *Phenomenological Psychology* in 1925 (Hua IX). See also his *Encylopaedia Britannica* article (1927) and 'The Amsterdam Lectures on Phenomenological Psychology', *Trans. Phen.*, pp. 213–53; Hua IX 302–49. See also CM §§ 14 and 35, where Husserl discusses a pure, intentional, eidetic psychology that is distinct from experimental psychology.

A NOTE ON HUSSERL'S ANTIQUATED TERMINOLOGY: SOUL, PSYCHE, EGO, LIFE

Before proceeding, it is important to note that, in the *Crisis*, as in his mature writings generally, Husserl employs a broad set of terms inherited from traditional philosophy, and from the psychology of Brentano, Wundt and others, in respect of human subjectivity, such as 'soul', 'ego', 'psyche', 'spirit' and so on. Husserl is content to characterize psychology as the science of the 'soul' (*die Seele*) and to speak generally of 'ego-life' (*Ichleben*, C 245; K 248) or the 'ego subject' (*Ichsubjekt*, C 254; K 257), and its inner life. This is already evident in *Ideas* II, where he is struggling to express the nature of a science that can approach, appreciate and understand human life in the appropriate, non-reductionistic manner and yet continue to speak of soul and of the life of the 'person'. He even invokes the idea of 'spirit' and of 'objective spirit' (i.e. culture), taking over a term from German Idealism. These terms are metaphysically loaded, and, as a result, the radical nature of Husserl's proposals regarding phenomenological psychology is easily overlooked. But here is a clear instance of new wine in old bottles. Husserl is proposing a radically new way of approaching embodied subjectivity.

HUSSERL'S FAMILIARITY WITH EMPIRICAL SCIENTIFIC PSYCHOLOGY

It is not clear exactly how up to date Husserl was concerning the rapidly developing empirical science of psychology in the 1930s, but he had, from the beginning, a deep familiarity with Austrian, German and English psychology of the nineteenth century. Given his advanced age and deteriorating eyesight at the time of writing the *Crisis*, it is unlikely that he could have maintained his familiarity with then contemporary psychology (apart from some books by the social anthropologist Lucien Lévy-Bruhl on the collective psychology of primitive peoples that he read in 1935). In the *Crisis*, therefore, he primarily refers to an earlier generation of psychologists – Mill, Brentano, Wundt and Dilthey, all of whom worked with the contrast between descriptive and explanatory psychology. Although Husserl began as a mathematician, he was very early on attracted to the new science of psychology, deliberately choosing to study with Franz Brentano in Vienna, who was pioneering descriptive psychology. Indeed, the subtitle of Husserl's first book *Philosophy of Arithmetic* (1891), is *Psychological and Logical Investigations*, where the 'psychological' investigations involve identifying the mental acts required for performing elementary mathematical operations (e.g. counting). Subsequently, at Halle, he became familiar with the most renowned psychologists of the age, including Carl Stumpf ((1848–1936) teacher of several of the Gestalt psychologists, including Max Wertheimer (1880–1943), Köhler (1887–1967) and Koffka (1886–1941), and friend of William James (1842–1910)). Husserl read James' *Principles of Psychology* and, in the *Crisis*, invokes his notion of 'fringes', which he compares with his own concept of 'horizons' (C 264; K 267). He also had considerable interactions with three philosophers who were also active in psychology, namely Wilhelm Wundt, Paul Natorp and Theodor Lipps.

In his Göttingen years (1901–16), Husserl's research ran in parallel with the experimental psychology of the renowned psychologist Georg Elias Müller (1850–1934), with whom he shared students, e.g. David Katz (1884–1953), who wrote his dissertation on colour with Husserl.[2] Katz later developed a psychology of colour and touch that strongly influenced Merleau-Ponty and the 'ecological theory of perception' of James J. Gibson (1904–79).[3] Indeed, Husserl's phenomenology was closely associated with then current psychological explorations of sense perception and the constitution of space.[4] Husserl both anticipated and influenced the Gestalt psychologists (e.g. Max Wertheimer and Adhemar Gelb (1887–1934)).[5]

In his *Phenomenological Psychology* lectures of 1925, Husserl speaks of the enormous impetus given to the nascent science of psychology by the work of German physicists and physiologists (among them the 'psychophysicists') such as Johannes Müller (1801–58), Ernst Heinrich Weber (1795–1878), Heinrich Ewald Hering (1834–1918), Hermann

---

[2] See David Katz, *The World of Color*, trans. R. B. McLeod and C. W. Fox (London: Kegan, Paul, Trench, Trubner and Co., 1935; reprinted London: Routledge, 1999).
[3] See J. J. Gibson, *The Perception of the Visual World* (Boston: Houghton Mifflin, 1950).
[4] See Carl Stumpf, *Über den psychologischen Ursprung der Raumvorstellung* [On the Psychological Origin of the Representation of Space] (Leipzig: Hirzel, 1873).
[5] See Mitchell G. Ash, *Gestalt Psychology in German Culture 1890–1967: Holism and the Quest for Objectivity* (New York: Cambridge University Press, 1998).

von Helmholtz (1821–94) – whose concept of two dimensional 'plane beings' is mentioned in the *Crisis* – Gustav Theodor Fechner (1801–87) and others. This physiological psychology led to significant empirical discoveries. However, physiological psychology is theoretically deeply flawed, and psychology, insofar as it is genuine, must really be a 'descriptive' or 'pure' psychology, and indeed 'phenomenology'. Of course, Husserl had even less time for the attempt of the newly emerging psychological behaviourism (Ivan Pavlov (1849–1936), John Watson (1878–1958)) – he speaks of the 'exaggerations of the behaviourists' (employing the term *'Behavioristen'*, the English word 'behaviour' is crossed out, see C 247n.4; K 541; elsewhere he talks of the 'behaviourists') to establish a completely objective science of behaviour that eliminated the subjective altogether. As we shall see, he sided with the German Gestalt psychologists in rejecting behaviourism as a crude atomistic sensationalism that can monitor only the 'external sides of modes of behaviour' (*Aussenseite der Verhaltungen*, C 247n; K 251n.1).

Husserl also occasionally acknowledges 'depth psychology' (*Tiefenpsychologie*, C 386; K 473), by which he meant psychoanalysis as developed by Freud and Adler (in which his assistant Eugen Fink had a particular interest; see C 385–7; K 473–5). Husserl offers his own account of drives, tendencies and habitualities, to which we shall return.

GESTALT OR HOLISTIC PSYCHOLOGY

Although it does not feature prominently in the *Crisis*, Husserl was also quite familiar with Gestalt or with what he terms, in line with the custom of the day, 'holistic psychology' (*Ganzheitspsychologie*, a term associated with Felix Krueger (1874–1948) and invoked in the *Crisis*, C 297; K 344) through Stumpf, who was in Berlin, and especially through his Freiburg assistant Aron Gurwitsch, who had studied with the psychologists Kurt Goldstein and Adhémar Gelb at Frankfurt.[6] Indeed, Husserl had been a very early admirer of the

---

[6] See Aron Gurwitsch, 'Some Aspects and Developments of Gestalt Psychology', in Gurwitsch, *Studies in Phenomenology and Psychology* (Evanston, IL: Northwestern University Press, 1966), pp. 1–61.

work on Gestalt qualities of his exact contemporary, the Austrian Christian von Ehrenfels (1859–1932), one of the founders of Gestalt, and, of course, his Göttingen student David Katz was also closely associated with the Gestalt movement.[7] In general, Husserl was not convinced that Gestalt psychology provided much improvement over the 'sensualism' and 'atomism' (of the kind espoused, for instance, by Bertrand Russell in the early 1920s) of early twentieth-century empirical psychology. For him, even 'Gestalt' or 'holistic' psychology, although it opposed sense-datum atomism, remained attached to naturalism and objectivism (see also *Trans. Psych.*, p. 220; Hua IX 310). Gestalt psychology maintained that there were structures, patterns or forms that could be apprehended in experience and indeed in nature. Husserl's early defense of categorial intuition was precisely seen as a kind of Gestalt-apprehension. Thus, in 1936 Gurwitsch could comment on Husserl's influence on the development of Wertheimer's Gestalt psychology:

Among the factors which have contributed most to bringing the problem of Gestalt to the fore, one must count Husserl's discovery of the double meaning of categorial terms such as identity, similarity, unity, and the like ... The question of possibly apprehending at a glance the collective character of any multiplicity – without having the need, or the time, to go systematically through all the members composing such a collection – led Husserl to establish a distinction between two kinds of unity: one which is conceptual, categorial, and in this sense brought about; the other is immediately experienced and given alongside and at once with the sensory data, which, owing to it, appear as forming a unitary group not constituted by any categorial thought ... It is the particular merit of Wertheimer to have seen the specific nature of these facts and to have given them their place in psychology.[8]

Husserl's conception of psychology was quite broad and included the work of social thinkers such as Wilhelm Dilthey. After the publication of Heidegger's *Being and Time* in 1927, Dilthey's star was again on the rise. Slightly earlier, in his 1925 *Phenomenological Psychology* lectures, Husserl admits that he had earlier been blind to the achievement of Wilhelm Dilthey in the area of descriptive psychology because of the influential critique by the renowned psychologist Hermann

---

[7] See David Katz, *Gestalt Psychology: Its Nature and Significance* (New York: The Ronald Press Co., 1950).
[8] Gurwitsch, 'Some Aspects and Developments of Gestalt Psychology', p. 54.

Ebbinghaus (1850–1909) (see *Phen. Psych.* § 2). But he came to revise his opinion of Dilthey, especially the latter's essay on *Descriptive and Analytic Psychology* (1895),[9] and in the *Crisis* Husserl calls him 'one of the greatest humanists' (C 296; K 344), who was the first to recognize that a genuine science of the human as spirit had to be different from naturalistic psychology (cf. *Ideas* II, p. 376; Hua IV 365). At the same time, for Husserl, Dilthey – like Windelband (1848–1915) and Rickert – in the end remained bound up in objectivism and did not develop a true science of the spirit.

EMPIRICAL PSYCHOLOGY AS A SCIENCE OF FACTS

While Husserl's knowledge of contemporary psychology may not have been up to date at the time of writing the *Crisis*, his overall diagnosis of the nature of psychology continues to be relevant, especially his critique of its unquestioned commitment to naturalism and its lack of a true account of inner life (in terms of motivation, reason, instinct, empathy and so on).

Despite his early admiration for Brentano's a priori descriptive psychology, Husserl was never a great admirer of empirical psychology. He held that empirical psychology was a 'science of facts', facts about the 'psychic states' of human beings considered as animals embedded in nature. In the *Logical Investigations*, for instance, psychology is characterized as a factual, empirical science of consciousness, an empirical, causal science of physical organisms and their psychophysical states, the science that studies 'the real states of animal organisms in a real natural order' (LU *Intro.* § 6, 176; Hua XIX/1 23). Psychological laws (e.g. the 'law' of association of ideas) are merely inductions from experience (LU *Intro.* I § 6, p. 176; Hua XIX/123), expressible only as probabilities, at best mere approximations to the ideal laws found in physics and natural science generally.

Almost thirty years later, in his 1928 *Amsterdam Lectures* (Hua IX), Husserl reiterates this understanding of psychology as a study of animal (including human) mental 'behaviour' in the context of the real

---

[9] See Wilhelm Dilthey, 'Ideas Concerning a Descriptive and Analytical Psychology', in *Dilthey's Descriptive Psychology and Historical Understanding*, trans. Richard Zaner and K. L. Heiges (The Hague: Nijhoff, 1977), pp. 23–120.

world of nature (*Trans. Phen.*, p. 214; Hua IX 303). Psychology in this sense is theoretically dependent on more fundamental sciences such as physics, zoology and anthropology (i.e. physical anthropology). Psychological discussion, since it concerns real people, must make reference to the real spatio-temporal world and to embodied individual subjects in their causal interactions with nature. Empirical psychology, accordingly, must remain a form of psychophysics or, as Husserl prefers to say (see *Ideas* II, p. 368; Hua IV 357) a form of 'physico-psychology' (since physical nature must be given priority according to the very meaning of the method). Indeed, Husserl uses the older term psychophysics quite generally for scientific accounts that, for instance, explain perception in terms of brain processes.[10] Thus, he writes:

The task set for modern psychology, and taken over by it, was to be a science of psychophysical realities, of men and animals as unitary beings, though divided into two real strata [i.e. body and soul] (C 204; K 208).

This psycho-physical psychology usually assumes a certain atomistic sensationalism at its core (see *Crisis* § 67) and also wants to connect psychological laws to natural causal laws.

THE ERRANT HISTORY OF MODERN PSYCHOLOGY FROM DESCARTES TO DILTHEY

The *Crisis* sketches the evolution of modern psychology from Descartes, Hobbes and especially Locke, who conceived of psychology as a science based explicitly on the mechanical physics of Newton. Psychology received two different tendencies from the legacy of Descartes: on the one hand, 'treating souls in the same way as bodies and as being connected with bodies as spatio-temporal realities' (C 214; K 218) and, on the other, treating psychic events as *inner experiences*. One led to *psychophysics* and the other to *descriptive psychology*. Psychic faculties (or 'dispositions' as they became in Hume and others) were interpreted by analogy with physical forces. Both begin from a naturalistic presupposition. Both assume that

---

[10] The term 'psychophysics', associated with Fechner, is used in a general sense by Husserl to mean any psychology which depends on physiological explanation.

'souls' are dependent on bodies and that inner and outer experience can be distinguished from each other. Even Brentanian descriptive psychology was based on an entirely misleading conception of inner experience (which Husserl criticized in his Appendix to the *Sixth Logical Investigation*).[11]

As we saw in Chapter 3, Husserl's starting-point is the *dualism* introduced by the modern sciences with their abstractively idealized mathematization of nature that left the realm of the 'subjective-relative' out of account and focused solely on the physical world as a world of causally interacting bodies in space and time: 'The natural science of the modern period, establishing itself as physics, has its roots in the consistent abstraction through which it wants to see, in the life-world, only corporeity' (C 227; K 230). The legacy of Descartes' metaphysics and Galileo's physics was a 'dualistic world of bodies and spirits' (C 192; K 195), where the realm of the subjective was treated as something left over after the domain of nature had been defined as the area of study of the exact sciences: 'Once the bodily "side" has become part of the general task of natural science and has found its theoretically idealizing treatment there, the task of psychology is characterized as the "complementary" task, i.e., that of subjecting the psychic side to a corresponding theoretical treatment with a corresponding universality' (C 228; K 231). Psychology, at best, could only be a subsidiary science dependent on physics and physiology. Furthermore, psychology could never be a pure science of the psychical, in the way in which physics is a pure science that excludes everything psychical through a deliberate methodological performance of an abstraction. In the *Crisis*, Husserl therefore explicitly talks of the *failure* of psychology because in its 'primal establishment' (*Urstiftung*) it let its method be determined by natural science (C 203; K 207).

Husserl believes it is not enough to reject this dualism (*Crisis* § 65) – which he regarded as falsifying human experience that encounters a seamless single world of nature and culture – since it had been integrated into the sciences themselves. Scientists already

---

[11] Although Husserl criticizes the inbuilt assumption of the distinction between inner and outer experience, he himself uses this terminology, as well as describing inner experience as 'immanent'. However, he believes his account of intentionality means that these terms are invested with a wholly different significance.

approached experience in a dualist manner (disregarding subjective elements, feelings, values, emotions and so on). Dualism is thereby assumed to be not a 'metaphysical substruction', but grounded in our very experience of the life-world (which we shall discuss in Chapter 6). Yet, in the actually experienced life-world, the two opposed kinds of entities – natural and spiritual – are not experienced as distinct from one another. The psychological distinction between 'outer' and 'inner', an assumption at the very heart of scientific psychology, is itself the product of this assumed dualism (*Crisis* § 67) – it must be admitted Husserl himself employs this distinction (although he attempts to refine it). Psychology, then, insofar as it is based on a certain conception of the inner life and the manner of exploring it through 'inner perception', has been deeply misled.

Furthermore, Husserl claims that the resulting naturalistic psychology, since it begins from individual embodiment, could only be a science of *individual* selves or, as he puts it, 'souls' (*Seelen*, C 228; K 231), and this has an atomistic and individualizing effect on the other social and human sciences (C 228; K 232). This might seem surprising coming from Husserl, whose *Cartesian Meditations* has often been characterized as assuming a certain 'methodological individualism', but, in fact, Husserl is deeply aware that a science of social life, of culture, of spirit, requires a conception of cooperative intersubjectivity that cannot be built up beginning from the individualist assumptions of modern empirical psychology. Dilthey had criticized the prevailing explanatory psychology and had ingeniously recognized the importance of the interconnected 'nexus of life' (*Lebenszusammenhang*, a term Husserl also uses), but he had failed to provide a full phenomenology of flowing, intersubjective life with its intentional syntheses, implications, sedimentations, habitualities and horizons.

OBJECTIVISM IN PSYCHOLOGY

It is one of the main themes of the *Crisis* that naïve 'objectivism' in natural science, aided by the modern scientific concentration on quantifiable 'primary' qualities, has meant that subjectivity has also been misconceived by modern scientific psychology. Psychology, as it emerged in the naturalistic context between the seventeenth and nineteenth centuries ('from Hobbes to Wundt', C 230; K 233), had been set up to explore a domain that by its own definition can never be more than 'epiphenomenal'; since reality has already been characterized in terms of naïve objectivism as that which is exactly quantifiable. Psychology, then, ends up either as a dualistic or monistic naturalism (*Crisis* § 67).

In the tradition from Locke and Hobbes in particular, psychology was also committed to what Husserl calls sensationalism. The soul was thought of as a sealed-off domain in which sensations or sense data were reified (C 231; K 234). Husserl insists that, contrary to the sense-data theorists (he is thinking of the Vienna positivists such as Ernst Mach, but he could just as easily have mentioned Bertrand Russell), we are never first and foremost in contact with sensations or sense data: 'Here, in immediate givenness, one finds anything but color data, tone data, other "sense" data or data of feeling, will, etc.; that is, one finds none of those things which appear in traditional psychology' (C 233; K 236). Sensationalism is a kind of atomism to which Dilthey's holistic account of the interconnectedness of life was a justified and necessary reaction. For Husserl too, as we shall see, humans live and act in a holistically experienced world of intentions and values.

THE LEGACY OF BRENTANO'S DESCRIPTIVE PSYCHOLOGY

For Husserl, the true mode of psychic life becomes visible when its intrinsic intentionality is made manifest through the reduction. Here he acknowledges Brentano's discovery of intentionality as a decisive step forwards for psychology, even if Brentano himself had failed to grasp its significance. As we have seen, Husserl's fascination with psychology came from his early exposure to his teachers Franz Brentano and Carl Stumpf, both of whom were advocates of descriptive psychology. In his *Psychology from an Empirical Standpoint* (1874), Brentano had explicitly contrasted a descriptive 'empirical' psychology with physiologically based psychology (or 'genetic psychology'). Between 1887 and 1891 Brentano developed a programmatic 'descriptive psychology' (also termed 'psychognosy' and 'phenomenology') as an a priori, descriptive and apodictic science (i.e. its findings were necessary truths) that was theoretically more basic than genetic psychology.[12] Descriptive psychology was an a priori *exact* science, independent of and indeed providing a basis for 'genetic' or physiological psychology.

Husserl was initially enthusiastic about the possibilities of this descriptive psychology as a way of clarifying the mental operations (presentations, judgements) employed in mathematics and logic. In the first edition (1901) of the *Logical Investigations*, he initially characterized phenomenology as descriptive psychology: 'Phenomenology is descriptive psychology. Epistemological criticism is therefore in essence psychology, or at least capable of being built on a psychological basis' (LU I, *Intro.*, § 6, p. 176; Hua XIX/1 24). But in his early years in Göttingen (after 1902), he redefined phenomenology as an a priori essential (eidetic) science of consciousness in sharp contrast to empirical psychology, understood as the empirical study of the real mental states of humans and higher-order animals in the natural-scientific context.[13] Husserl is now more emphatic that phenomenology operates entirely on the evidence of pure intuition, within the 'sphere of immanence', i.e. bracketing all concerns with worldly existence and real psychological processes. From 1905 onwards, the phenomenological reduction is applied to purify insights of existential assumptions.

In his important *Phenomenological Psychology* lectures (1925), Husserl attempts once again to explicate the complex relationships between eidetic phenomenological psychology and empirical psychology as different approaches to subjectivity and first-person conscious life. It is here that he re-evaluates the descriptive psychology of Wilhelm Dilthey, which he had earlier dismissed. Almost a decade later, in the *Crisis*, Husserl again offers a sustained critique of psychology, this time telling a 'genetic' story of its emergence as a result of modern philosophy's turn to the cognizing subject (especially in Locke). Here Husserl again reiterates the inherent conceptual flaws of psychology, but he also revisits the descriptive psychology of

---

[12] Franz Brentano, *Descriptive Psychology*, trans. Benito Müller (London: Routledge, 1995). Hereafter 'DP' followed by the page number of the English translation.
[13] See Dermot Moran, 'Husserl's Critique of Brentano in the *Logical Investigations*', *Manuscrito: Revista International de Filosofia*, Special Husserl Issue, Vol. 23 No. 2 (2000), 163–205.

Brentano in particular, as we discussed in Chapter 2. Despite his criticisms of Brentano's naturalism and representationalism, Husserl built on Brentano's groundbreaking discovery of intentionality to develop a genuine intentional or phenomenological psychology which was in sharp opposition to the naturalistic misconstruction of psychology as an inductive science of facts about animal and human behaviour. To have a pure psychology that accurately describes human being-in-the-world, it is necessary, he maintained, to put aside psychological 'fictions' (i.e. theoretical postulates not grounded in actual experiencing) such as 'sense data'. Instead, one must begin from the genuine psychological realities which are more holistic: I see a tree, I hear the rustling of its leaves and so on (see *Crisis* § 68). As Husserl says, 'In straightforward world-experience we find human beings intentionally related to certain things – animals, houses, fields, etc.' (C 235; K 238). This is where a genuine psychology must begin – with concrete experience in its fullness.

In later works, Husserl uses a much more expansive notion of intentionality, according to which consciousness is not just intentionally directed at things in the world, but also co-constitutes horizons of intentional implication and, indeed, the entire worldly context in which such intentional objects are apprehended and made meaningful. Husserl tries to explain the constitution of the world in terms of intentionality, both individual and collective, as we shall see.

PSYCHOLOGISM AND THE STATUS OF IDEAL ENTITIES

One of Husserl's most persistent criticisms of experimental psychology as a science of subjectivity is that it failed to acknowledge the essential role of ideal senses and ideal objects in the constitution of objectivity, leaving it open to the charge of psychologism, the claim that logical and mathematical ideal truths (e.g. $2 + 2 = 4$) are reducible to psychological laws, i.e. are explainable in terms of how humans actually think or ought to think, rather than expressing necessary relations between purely ideal concepts. The first volume of his *Logical Investigations*, *Prolegomena to Pure Logic*, defended the ideality of logical and mathematical objects against 'psychologistic empiricism' (*Prol.* § 26). Husserl considered psychologism to be self-refuting: 'it is only inconsistency that keeps psychologism alive: to think it out to the end is already to have given it up' (LU *Prol.* I § 25, p. 56; Hua xvIII 88). Logic, Husserl insisted, as an a priori science of idealities, makes no assumptions about the existence or nature of mental states; it knows nothing of actual presentations or judgements (LU *Prol.* I § 23), or the 'facticities of mental life' (LU *Prol.* I § 23, p. 51; Hua xvIII 81). From the outset, the logical concern with meaning must be distinguished from the psychological approach: 'The pure logician is not primarily or properly interested in the psychological judgement, i.e., the concrete mental phenomenon, but in the logical judgement, i.e., the identical asserted meaning, which is one over against manifold, descriptively very different judgement-experiences' (LU I *Intro.* § 2, I p. 166, translation modified; Hua xIx/1 8). The varying psychological content of judgements has nothing to do with their ideal logical content: 'Multiplication of persons and acts does not multiply the propositional meaning [*Satzbedeutung*]; the judgement in the ideal logical sense remains single' (LU I § 31, 229; Hua xIx/1 105).

In his early writings Husserl sharply distinguished logic from psychology. Throughout his career he defends a strongly realist position concerning the ideal existence, unity and timelessness or omnitemporality of ideal objects (such as 'the number 4', 'the Pythagorean theorem', etc.). However, he became more interested, as in 'The Origin of Geometry' fragment, in the *subjective operations* (carefully construed in a non-psychological sense) that constitute these ideal objects and allow us to reiterate them without their identities being threatened. He became increasingly interested in developing a non-psychological account of the essential nature of this subjectivity that intuits idealities.

Husserl also began to acknowledge more and more the temporal and *historical* elements that went into the genesis or institution of these ideal concepts and their preservation across time (a preservation that calls for their *inscription* in some material form). He is now more aware that the ideal products of science have an inauguration and history just like any cultural product, even though they lay claim to a timeless validity. A genuine science of psychology would have to articulate this subjective relation with idealities, something that empirical psychology had singularly failed to do.

Husserl never altered his view of psychology as an *empirical* science of spatio-temporal realities. Psychology deals with human beings in a worldly context. Thus, in *Formal and Transcendental Logic*, he writes that psychology is a positive science, a branch of anthropology, and that it has mistaken transcendental interiority for psychological interiority:

It must never be lost sight of … that in psychology, psychic phenomena – more precisely, psychological data: the mental processes and dispositions (abilities) – are data within the already-given world … and that it is a falsifying dislocation [*eine verfälschende Verschiebung*] if one mistakes this psychological internal experience for the internal experience relied on transcendentally as an evidential experiencing of *ego cogito*. (FTL § 99, p. 253; Hua XVII 259–60)

It is, ultimately, transcendental phenomenology which clarifies the true nature and status of psychology as a science. As Husserl asserts: 'Once productive intentionality [*leistende Intentionalität*] has been discovered, everything, being as well as illusion, becomes understandable in its essential objective possibility; the subjectiveness of anything is then for us its constitutedness' (FTL § 100, p. 256; Hua XVII 263). Phenomenological psychology, based on intentionality, will be free of all reference to psychophysicality (see *Trans. Phen.*, p. 218; Hua IX 308) and to factors external to the purely psychological domain of intention and motivation.

Husserl proposes that a 'pure' psychological phenomenology, as a pure a priori science of the psychical, can provide a grounding for psychology just in the same way as mathematical physics is an a priori science underlying experimental physics. Pure phenomenological psychology will be an a priori, self-contained science based not on induction, but on individual instances which, understood according to free variation and purified of accidental elements, function as exemplars for essential truths. It will not be a science of facts (see *Trans. Phen.*, p. 230; Hua IX 322,) but of eidetic necessities, i.e. it will seek to understand the essences involved in the psychic as such, beginning from the factual self or ego and penetrating into the essence of the ego, its 'egohood' or 'I-ness' (*Ichheit*), and thence to the constitution of other egos. Phenomenological psychology uncovers the world of intentional correlation (objects presenting through their modes of givenness) but does not yet fully grasp the working of transcendental subjectivity. It needs a further transmutation through the application of a 'universal *epochē*' into *transcendental* phenomenology, which takes up all its discoveries but sees them in the new light of transcendental subjectivity.

FROM NAÏVE TO TRANSCENDENTAL SCIENCE: THE PSYCHOLOGICAL *EPOCHĒ*

From the phenomenological point of view, Husserl maintains, empirical psychology is 'naïve' in that it always presupposes human beings as natural beings in the 'pregiven' world as a world of material, physical entities causally interacting in objective space and time. As Eugen Fink puts it in his 'Outline for the Continuation of the Crisis': 'Psychology begins as a special science alongside others on the ground of the pregiven world' (C 398; K 514). Psychology proceeds by describing the behaviour of these beings through the employment of a grid of concepts derived from its pre-delimited scientific presuppositions. It draws on a network of empirical 'types' with regard to the classification of the psychic. At best these empirical findings offer surface facts which demand theoretical clarification.

A 'universal *epochē*' (*universale Epochē*, C 258; K 261) must be applied under which psychology can no longer appeal to the real world of humans and animals and their supposed 'ways of behaving' (*Verhaltungsweisen*, C 246; K 249). This psychological concept of *behaviour* is saturated with presuppositions that must be annulled. Husserl speaks of overcoming 'behaviouristic reductions' (C 247; K 251). This 'universal' *epochē* must apply to *all* position-takings towards the psychic, in contrast with the provisional or partial *epochē* found, for instance, in the professional stance of the psychologist who wants to isolate psychical events, abstracting them from the physical world.

As a result of this 'universal' *epochē*, with its 'Copernican 180-degree turn', as Husserl puts it elsewhere (see *Trans. Phen.*, p. 235; Hua IX 327), scientific positivity with its presumed commitments to reality is put entirely out of play. Psychology, in fact – and Husserl constantly speaks of this as a 'surprising result' – becomes transformed into the 'science of transcendental subjectivity' (C 258; K 261). This new science has to put aside all natural scientific and 'folk' concepts of the psychic and aims to confront genuine concrete experience. As Husserl writes: 'The first thing we must do, and first of all in immediate reflective self-experience, is to take the conscious life, completely without prejudice, just as what it quite immediately gives itself, as itself, to be' (C 233; K 236). It is precisely the manifestness ('phenomenality', *Trans. Psych.*, p. 218; Hua IX 307) of consciousness and its *modes* of manifestation that must be understood and, not as psychic occurrences paralleling physical events, but as meaningful experiential engagements in their own right that take place in the context of a world of intentional implications and motivations. Genuine psychology would study not just 'ways of behaving', memories, perceptions and so on, 'but also all acts of empathy … all associations and also the variations of acts … sedimentations – and also all instincts and drives [*Instinkte und Triebe*], not to mention "the horizons"' (C 246; K 249).

This genuine intentional psychology will be attentive to the intentional *syntheses* that are constantly being performed by consciousness and are missed by empirical psychology:

The genuine intentional synthesis is discovered in the synthesis of several acts into one act, such that in a unique manner on binding one meaning to another, there emerges not merely a whole, an amalgam whose parts are meanings, but rather a single meaning in which these meanings themselves are contained, but in a meaningful way (C 234; K 237).

This is a very good description of the complexities of synthesis, that is, the manner in which the experienced world is presented in a unified and seamless way through a myriad interlocking intentional acts. For instance, I am presently sitting in the room and am aware of its furniture, objects, lights and so on, but I also have a sense of its space behind my back, and I can gaze out the window to the trees and leaves and distant grey sky, and daydream of it being summer and remember the warmth of the garden then, and so on. All these experiences flow together in the one stream of consciousness. This is a genuine 'psychological' sphere, and it contains none of the immanent data beloved of the sensationalists and psychological sense-data theorists. Indeed, quite the opposite, intentional relations are experienced from the naïve point of view as 'real' relations (*Crisis* § 69).

Intentionality has to be understood in terms of the essential correlation between intentional act and intentional object (Husserl reaffirms his account of the noema – without using the term – as originally given in *Ideas* i, namely that the real tree can burn up but the noema tree, the perceived tree as perceived, cannot burn, cannot be affected by real-world causality; see *Crisis* § 70). It is this complex world of interconnected intentional objectivities that psychology – once it has accomplished its own *epoché* and reduction – has now to understand and to 'explicate' (see C 177; K 181). Life has to be understood as *intentional, 'accomplishing' life*, with its potentially infinite horizons of intentional implication, uniting together into the collective experience known as *spirit*.

Indeed, in this context – commenting on the need for a true psychology, and acknowledging Wilhelm Dilthey's imperfect contribution in this area – Husserl makes his most Hegelian of statements concerning the need for a new 'objective science of spirit' in his 'Vienna Lecture': 'The spirit, and indeed only the spirit, exists in itself and for itself, is self-sufficient [*eigenständig*]; and in its self-sufficiency, and only in this way, it can be treated truly rationally, truly and from the ground up scientifically' (C 297; K 345). Instead of relying on the theoretically compromised conceptions of empirical and descriptive psychology, an entirely new science of subjectivity must be conceived. This science must begin from the unified flow of conscious life which is already a manifestation of the life-world and must employ such phenomenological concepts as sedimentation, association, horizon, empathy, instincts and drives, thereby replacing naïve accounts of behaviour as understood in empirical psychology (see C 246; K 249).

As we have seen, in order to gain a genuine and unobstructed access to the world of the intentionalities proper to the psychological in the purified sense, a 'psychological *epoché*' has to be effected, which Husserl also calls the 'phenomenological-psychological *epoché*' (C 244; K 247) or the 'phenomenological-psychological reduction' (C 236; K 238). This is only one of the many forms of reduction discussed by Husserl, but, in his later works especially, he accords it a particular prominence and even priority. In the last sections of the *Crisis* Part IIIB (beginning from § 69), he engages in a complicated account of the nature of this 'phenomenological-psychological reduction'. Indeed, he explicitly states that he will leave it an open question how this phenomenological-psychological reduction relates to the transcendental reduction (C 236; K 239).

Of course, Husserl had always insisted on the importance of the correct understanding and performance of the *epochē* and the phenomenological reduction as the key to phenomenology. To illustrate what happens in the *epochē* that brackets the assumption of positivity, we can take the concept of temporality in psychology as an example. One of the greatest problems with modern naturalistic psychology, for Husserl, is that it understands the flow of psychic processes as a stream of real events unfolding in objective time, whereas the sense of temporality intrinsically involved in intentional psychic life is radically different and more complex (see *Trans. Psych.*, p. 220; Hua IX 310). The 'real' present acts of consciousness are always accompanied by 'unreal' or 'ideal' horizons of assumptions, meanings and psychic acts that point back to the past or forwards to the future. The present is always embedded in a horizon of meanings and assumptions that are not truly present.

Empirical psychology, furthermore, does not understand the nature of the noetic-noematic character of our intentional acts. It takes, for instance, *the person I married* to be a real, extant person in the world, whereas this person is actually an intentionally constituted entity. Thus, I could marry *the same person* again and again (albeit it psychoanalysis might be in a better position to identify this meaning-cluster). The psychological *epochē* steps back from and no longer endorses the naïve validating of everyday experience in the natural attitude that treats experiences and their objects as 'real', i.e. taking place in the actual world. Perceptions and other lived experiences continue to be experienced, but now are no longer believed to be real (what Husserl calls the 'co-performance of a validity', C 237; K 240).

This abstaining from the endorsement of the validity of experience is, Husserl says, 'within our freedom'. We can simply withdraw our doxastic commitments while still continuing to live on in the experience. This 'universal' *epochē* Husserl insists, goes further than the professional psychologist's *epochē*, which is an abstractive *epochē* that leaves out of account the world of the physical and focuses solely on the 'inner' world of immanent experiences: 'The psychologist establishes in himself the "disinterested spectator" and investigator of himself as well as of all others, and that once and for all, i.e., for all "vocational periods" of his psychological work' (C 239; K 242). It is clear that the psychologist in his or her professional capacity takes the position of the 'disinterested spectator' (which Husserl associates with the transcendental attitude), but this professional stance of the scientific psychologist is strictly limited and remains caught up in naïve 'position-taking' (in other words, actions which assert existence or confirm certain kinds of validity on intentional performances, the 'professional manner', 'the assumption of care' and so on). But *pure* psychology, in the special Husserlian sense, requires a further *epochē* that abstains from all position-taking: 'But the psychologist as such in his enquiry must … take and have no position: he must neither concur nor refuse, nor remain in problematic suspense, as if he had some say in the validities of the persons who are his subjects' (C 240; K 243). It is difficult to see how this can be done without the psychological attitude itself being transformed into the transcendental phenomenological attitude.

Psychology above all needs to carry out a specific *epochē* and reduction on its naïve conception of the psychical. Traditional psychology, moreover, is individualistic, in that it presupposes the isolated ego and its experiences as the starting-point, and this 'naïveté' also needs to be overcome. Husserl's new science – phenomenological psychology – must uncover the life of intentionality as the basis for understanding other persons and their intertwining intentionalities. This is the task of uncovering the 'intentional depths' that are the true subject matter for a psychology that has purified itself of presumptions about the human being. The intentional act becomes revealed in terms of its horizon of intentional implications and the implied contexts which surround it. We discover an entire interwoven 'nexus' (*Zusammenhang*) – a key term found also in Dilthey – of intersubjectivity: 'But each soul also stands in community [*Vergemeinschaftung*] with others which are intentionally interrelated, that is, in a purely intentional, internally and essentially closed nexus [*Zusammenhang*], that of intersubjectivity' (C 238; K 241).

In order to address how the manner in which other people enter into our subjective horizons must be understood, Husserl now speaks, in terms also taken up by his assistant, Eugen Fink, of a kind of '*epochē* within the *epochē*' (C 259; K 262). This *epochē* goes beyond the initial bracketing of the commitment to the world and asks about the constitution of the subjectivity of others. In particular, this second *epochē* aims to expose how the essential structures of the subjectivity of others can be constituted from *within* the individual's own ego, now taken as having absolute validity in the sense that it provides a paradigm for any ego whatsoever.

The *epochē*, as Husserl characterizes it, has two components. It must stop thinking of intentional objects as objects in the natural world, and it must stop endorsing the naïve belief-commitment, belief in being, that characterizes experience. Suspending both elements makes visible the intentional correlation, i.e. the noetic-noematic relation. Husserl also acknowledges a third effect of the *epochē*, namely that the nature of the ego is put in question. The ego is now exposed in its intentional structures and operations, freed from everything human. It is dehumanized, 'it is no longer the concrete, material, creaturely ego we normally speak of, that is, the human ego' (see 'Amsterdam Lectures', *Trans. Phen.*, p. 224; Hua IX 314). The ego is now uncovered as what Husserl calls (without ever quite elucidating what he means here) an 'ego-pole' (*Ichpol*) from which experiences stream or into which they enter. The nature of its syntheses now comes to the fore, including its own self-synthesis into a continuous acting ego-self. In the exploration of the ego in this deeper *epochē* certain *horizons* of empty, absent or possible experiences are now revealed as the context within which the ego operates, and these, of course, include the very deep layers of temporal horizons including past and future. Husserl acknowledges that horizons are especially complicated intentional products correlated with the subjective intentionality of the constituting ego. Horizons in themselves are not objects in the usual sense, and they are not fully real, yet they are presumed in all constitution of objectivity. We shall have more to say about horizon-consciousness in relation to history in our discussion of the life-world in Chapter 6.

Consciousness always includes both a degree of self-consciousness as well as an implicit consciousness of a surrounding world (C 251; K 255). The ego is never just an isolated subjectivity of inner experiences, a conception that is inherited from a certain reading of the Cartesian tradition. There is always the accompanying experience of the 'world horizon', a concomitant 'world-consciousness' (*Weltbewusstsein*, C 251; K 255, which Husserl often invokes, e.g. K 395, K 457, K 494 and K 514) attached to all supposedly psychological acts. The 'real' psychological world which is first encountered has to be given a radical shift using the 'universal *epochē*' (C 239; K 242). How this world-consciousness comes about is the real mystery for pure psychology, and this question is what transforms it into transcendental philosophy. Husserl's radical new psychology must be able to confront this world-givenness or manifestation straight on. In other words, scientific psychology, as constituted within twentieth-century science, has failed by taking too inward a route and not recognizing that the phenomenon of the manifestation of the world in consciousness is itself the primary phenomenon.

It is now clear what the subject matter and tools of phenomenological psychology are. They are intentionalities, syntheses, drives, horizons, intentional implications, habitualities and their correlated ego- and object-poles. One of the most important intentional performances, and one that is crucial for the new pure psychology, is *empathy*, the experience through which we recognize and understand the intentional lives of other subjects.

EMPATHY (*EINFÜHLUNG*) AND THE UNDERSTANDING OF OTHERS

The understanding of others requires what Husserl calls – borrowing from the Munich philosopher and psychologist Theodor Lipps – empathy (*Einfühlung*), which itself has to be analyzed in terms of its constitution in one's experience of oneself. From the beginning, Husserl had great difficulties even in *formulating* the problem of inter-subjectivity, which he generally covers under the topic of 'empathy', even though he expresses his dissatisfaction with that expression. Other subjects have to be understood through an 'empathetic understanding' (*Nachverstehen*, e.g. C 236; K 239). For instance, Husserl describes the manner in which one person understands the other by a kind of co-constitution of the other's intention in the listener in 'The Origin of Geometry', where he writes:

In the contact of reciprocal linguistic understanding, the original production [*Erzeugung*] and the product of one subject can be *actively* understood by the others. In this full understanding [*Nachverstehen*] of what is produced by the other, as in the case of recollection, a present coaccomplishment [*Mitvollzug*] on one's own part of the presentified activity necessarily takes place; but at the same time there is also the self-evident consciousness of the identity of the mental structure in the productions of both the receiver of the communication and the communicator; and this occurs reciprocally. (C 360; K 371)

Husserl frequently uses the term *nachverstehen* ('re-understanding' or, as Carr variously translates it, 'sympathetic understanding' or 'empathetic understanding') as his version of the hermeneutic task to comprehend the other. *Nachverstehen* involves a kind of openness to others, the intention to grasp their intention (see C 177; K 180 and C 236; K 239).

Husserl emphasizes the inescapably intersubjective character of human experience and always criticizes the individualism from which empirical psychology springs. Nevertheless, he begins from the first-person experience of the self or 'egoic subjectivity'. He accepts the Cartesian breakthrough insight that all experience – including the experience of others – is channelled through oneself as a first-person subject, or what he calls, following Descartes, an *ego cogito*. For Husserl, despite the fact that we live in an intersubjective and plural world (what he calls the 'with-world', *Mitwelt*, *Crisis* K 482 – similar to Heidegger's 'being-with', *Mitsein*), there is an absolute priority that must be accorded to 'self-experience' (*Selbsterfahrung*, *Crisis* § 22; see also K 395, K 486), i.e. the first-person manner in which one's own conscious experience unfolds. Husserl accepted the Cartesian starting-point that begins with self-experience. Husserl even characterizes this self-experience as 'inner' or 'immanent' (see *Trans. Psych.*, p. 221; Hua ix 311), although he is aware of the misleading Cartesian overtones in this term. This ego intends objects and also cooperates in the constitution of objectivity and worldhood with other egos in complicated but chartable forms of 'intentional implication' (C 258; K 261–2). There is a network of interacting egos adding up to a 'we-subjectivity' and 'we-community' (*Wir-Gemeinschaft*, K 416). In the Fifth Cartesian Meditation, Husserl had tried to reduce the egoic subject back to its original sphere of ownness (for which Husserl has several terms, e.g. *Eigenssphäre*, CM; § 44, p. 93; Hua i 125 and *Eigenheitssphäre*, CM § S4, p.119; Hua i 148; 'primordial sphere',

Primordialsphäre, CM § 44, p. 93; Hua I 125), with everything foreign excluded, but found even there that empathy was co-instituted. In the *Crisis*, Husserl begins in the concrete intersubjective world but continues to emphasize the constituting role of the ego. The topic of the constitution of the other subject in empathy is briefly mentioned in *Ideas* I § 1 and treated in detail in Husserl's private research manuscripts, but it receives its most public, published discussion in the *Cartesian Meditations* (1931), especially the Fifth Meditation. In fact Husserl wrote a great deal about this in his meditations on intersubjectivity in the unpublished manuscripts (Hua XIII, XIV and XV) that supplement the very sketchy outline in the *Crisis*.

Husserl contrasts this 'originary' (*originär*) or primordial manner of self-givenness in self-experience with what he calls 'other experience' (*Fremderfahrung*), which he regards as 'non-originary' (*nicht originär*), in the sense that one can never do more than reproduce the first-person life of the other which he or she experiences in a first-person, originary way.

Traditional psychology had primarily focused on the individual ego and its inner life, but Husserl believes that the domain of the *other subject*, as well as the whole domain of *intersubjectivity* and *socialization* (produced through harmonizing and cooperating subjects), are equally deserving of psychological attention, but proper access to these phenomena had been blocked due to the inadequacies of the individualist psychological method that accepted the various abstractions imposed by the natural sciences. Indeed, the subject's access to the other subject (the other 'ego' or 'alter ego', *alter ego*, C 258; K 262) is one of the major phenomenological problems that preoccupied Husserl from around 1905 to the end of his career. He had been working on the topic of 'the experience of the other' (*Fremderfahrung*) in private, beginning with a critique of the existing theories of empathy found in the German psychologists Theodor Lipps, Hugo Münsterberg (1863–1916) and others.

Although Husserl's position in the *Crisis* is often contrasted with that of the *Cartesian Meditations*, in the *Crisis* too Husserl does not do away with the notion of starting from the 'sphere of ownness', although that term does not appear as such. In the *Crisis* he does speak of 'my original sphere' (*meine originale Sphäre*) or 'primordial sphere (*Primordialsphäre*, C 185; K 189) or, generally, of the domain of 'primordiality' (*Primordialität*, C 185; K 189 and C 259; K 262). The 'always singular' transcendental ego first constitutes its own sphere, its own domain of consciousness, and with that 'a first sphere of objects, the "primordial" sphere' (C 185; K 189). Repeating claims also made in the *Cartesian Meditations*, Husserl insists in *Crisis* § 54(b) that the phenomenologist must begin from his or her own 'original sphere', i.e. from those conscious experiences that are experienced in a first-person, 'original' manner. I begin within the 'primordial sphere' or 'sphere of ownness' and, through empathy, which is not just an imaginative envisaging of a possible other mind but rather a quasi-perceptual apprehension based on analogization, I develop an essential account of the structures of human 'co-subjectivity' (*Mitsubjektivität*, C 255; K 258), even discovering the essential forms belonging to any kind of community, family, social institution or nation. This constitutive phenomenological account leads eventually to what he calls the 'essential structures of absolute historicity' (*Geschichtlichkeit*, C 259; K 262) of a transcendental community of subjects, which we shall discuss in more detail in Chapter 5. Indeed, for Husserl, the whole of transcendental philosophy, as we shall see in Chapter 7, is precisely nothing other than the transcendental subject reflecting on its own structures (C 259; K 263).

Husserl's concept of the primordial or original sphere is difficult and challenging. It receives its greatest elaboration in the *Cartesian Meditations*, but there it has often been misunderstood as a retreat into solipsism, whereas Husserl's main aim is to use various forms of methodological exclusion to expose the subjective structures whereby the singular subject constitutes both itself as a person, its world and the others with whom it shares the common world. But, even in the *Cartesian Meditations*, discussion of the original sphere is never meant to imply that the ego as such exists in an isolated or self-enclosed way. In fact, Husserl explicitly invokes the notion of the 'island of consciousness' (CM § 41, p. 83; Hua I 116) as an illusion of modern epistemology carried out in the natural attitude. Rather, the transcendental ego essentially includes and participates in the 'open plurality of other egos' (CM § 41). In the *Crisis*, similarly, Husserl is emphatic that all meaning and constitution must begin from the singular 'I' or ego, although one must recognize that this is the transcendental, not the factual, ego.

Husserl talks of the original, constituting 'singular I' that constitutes itself in its own kind of living through time, what Husserl calls 'self-temporalization' (*Selbstzeitigung*, C 185; K 189), a topic to which we shall return in Chapter 7), and which involves, according to a dense and obscure formulation that occurs only once in the *Crisis*, a 'de-presentation' (*Ent-Gegenwärtigung*) or absenting of oneself from oneself. Husserl sees the elaboration of self-experience – and the kind of synthesis whereby the self gains identity across different experiences – to be intimately related to its manner of living through time. The self constitutes its own tempo of experiencing time, its own peculiar sense of the present, past-for-it and future-for-it. In the present now, I apprehend myself immediately in a kind of *self-presence* (both present in the flesh and before myself right now), but I have also got to understand variations of myself as belonging to the past or projecting into the future. I can remember back certain distances with shadings of detail, e.g. *being* a 10-year-old schoolboy, even though I am no longer that child, and yet my ego is identical with his (through a peculiar form of synthesis that Husserl struggles to document). Regarding the relation of present to past ego, Husserl writes: 'Thus, the immediate "I" [*das aktuelle Ich*] performs an accomplishment [*Leistung*] through which it constitutes a variational mode [*Abwandlungsmodus*] of itself as existing (in the mode of having passed)' (C 185; K 189).

Husserl believes that the 'I' is primarily experienced in the present tense, in its immediate self-presence, and that, through a peculiar kind of synthesis, it identifies itself with the ego that intrinsically belongs to past experiences. I consciously take myself to be the same person as the child that I am now remembering I once was. This occurs through a kind of 'modalization' or 'variation' of myself that is governed by a priori essential laws that it is the business of phenomenology to identify. This *self-identification* over time gives Husserl a clue to how the other person is also constituted within my experience. The difference is that the other subject occupies the *same temporal present as* myself (rather than being a past modification), although I have no privileged access to his or her temporal stream. Thus, Husserl wants to clearly differentiate between me *imagining myself as another person* and my perceptual apprehension in empathy of the actual other person. At the same time, I cannot apprehend the other as a subject without attributing to him or her certain attributes I experience primarily in myself.

Husserl believes the experience of the other is a form of constitution which is based on a peculiar modal variation of self-experience: 'Only by starting from the ego and the system of its transcendental functions and accomplishments can we methodically exhibit transcendental intersubjectivity and its transcendental communalization [*Vergemeinschaftung*], through which, in the functioning system of ego-poles [*Ichpole*], the "world for all" and for each subject *as* world for all is constituted' (C 185–6; K 189). It is *through oneself* that one comes to experience the kind of processes that lead to the constitution of the other. Moreover, this other has to be constituted not just as an ego or self or subject like myself. The act of constituting the other has also got to constitute the 'other' character of the other, i.e. what makes the other person continue to be apart from and different from me, with his or her own constituting subjectivity. I have to apprehend the other's self-experience as presented to me in an empty manner, but I do genuinely experience the other *as a distinct other* 'ego' with his or her own identity and subjectivity. I apprehend the other 'in the mode of incomprehensibility', Husserl says (Hua xv 631).

Indeed, there are some passages in the late Husserl where he emphasizes the primacy of the other, and of the 'first other', i.e. the mother, in our own self-experience. Otherness is experienced primarily in the form of the human subjective other. For Husserl, at the same time, access to the other always comes *through oneself*. Paradoxically, it is I who constitute the other not just as an 'ego' (although never experienced in the same way) like my ego but precisely as an *other*. One could say that the late Husserl is moving towards the articulation of an 'intertwining' (*Verflechtung*; *Ineinander*, C 255; K 258) between myself and the other, where each is open to and dependent on the other. Indeed, in his research manuscripts, Husserl discusses different forms of what he explicitly calls the 'I–Thou' (*Ich–Du*) relation and even forms of the 'master–servant' relation (reminiscent of Hegel), as well as such reciprocal relations as are encountered in families, clubs, societies and so on, as we shall discuss further in Chapter 5.

EMBODIMENT (*LEIBLICHKEIT*)

We cannot leave the discussion of pure psychology without discussing the theme of lived *embodiment*, which is one of Husserl's great contributions. Despite being framed in the metaphysical language of the 'incarnation (*Verkörperung*) of souls', his thinking about embodiment or 'livedbodiliness' is strikingly original. The empirical psychological approach to the physical body does not capture correctly the living human body that mediates and informs human experience. Husserl distinguishes (see *Crisis* § 28) the lived or animate body (*Leib*) – the body as organism, the fleshly body as inhabited by an ego that holds sway over it – from the body (*Körper*) understood as a piece of physical nature. Thus, Husserl speaks of a 'living-embodied egoity' (*leibliche Ichlichkeit*, C 108; K 110), of an 'I-body' (*Ichleib*), a 'living corporeal body' (*Leibkörper,* CM § 51, p. 113; Hua I 143). Of course, it is evident that the human living body can behave exactly like any other physical body in nature, and this is the basis for the Cartesian treatment of the body as *res extensa*, whose parts are outside one another (*partes extra partes*). As an extended physical entity the body enters into causal relations with other bodies. In this sense, a human body can fall exactly as a stone does. It has volume, density, mass, weight, physical parts and so on (and, of course, these are identified as the 'primary properties' studied by the natural sciences). The main difference between *the body as physical entity* and the body as *animate* is that the animate body is always given as *my own* body (*Crisis* § 28) and is experienced as a *centre* from which I act, a *locus* of my incorporation in space, something over which I 'govern' or 'hold sway' (*walten*). I have an immediate sense of being able to change my position, shift my body in my chair and so on. Husserl, of course, does not mean to suggest that I have *complete* control over my body – there are many functions which are autonomous – rather, it is that I first and foremost experience my body as an organ of perception, willing and action. The entire world is mediated through my body.

Primarily Husserl emphasizes that the lived body is experienced in the first-person way, something over which I have control and which is a centre of spatial orientation:

Everyone experiences the embodiment of souls [*Die Verkörperung der Seelen*] in original fashion only in his own case. What properly and essentially makes up the character of a living body I experience only in my own living body, namely in my constant and immediate holding-sway [*Walten*] through my physical body alone. Only it is given to me originally and meaningfully as organ and as articulated into particular organs; each of its bodily members has its own features, such that I can hold sway immediately [*unmittelbar walten*] through it in a particular way – seeing with the eyes, touching with the fingers, etc. (C 217; K 220).

The lived body (*Leib*) is experienced, as Husserl puts it, as a series of 'I can's'. I am, as he puts it, an 'ego of abilities or capacities' (*Ich der Vermögen*, C 108; K 110). I can turn my head and look around, moving my eyes, shifting my upper body. All these bodily movements belong to and enable the perception to take place. The living body is both literally and figuratively the centre of my experiences and the means of my perceptual encounter with the world. It is an 'organ of perception'; it is experienced as a living, functioning tool, but one that, in normal situations, does not call attention to itself. It becomes obtrusiveness only if something goes wrong, e.g. I move my head but my neck is stiff; I touch something with a blister on my finger. All forms of ego-relatedness to the world are mediated through my body; even abstract thought (consider Rodin's sculpture *The Thinker*). I am always related to things as lifting, carrying, holding, reaching for, standing back from and so on (see *Crisis* § 28). The body is not a passive centre of experiences but a locus for action and self-directed movement. In this sense, the living body is never absent from the perceptual field (C 106; K 108) – a point which is later repeated by Merleau-Ponty – although it is not usually 'thematic' in the perception.

Each of us experiences our embodied 'soul' in our individual case in a primordial way (*Crisis* § 62). This involves sensuousness and 'kinestheses' (sensations of movement). Husserl maintains in *Ideas* II that the lived body is grasped primarily through touch and what he calls 'kinesthetic sensations', and he repeats this point in the *Crisis*, where he speaks of 'kinaestheses' (C 217; K 221). A body becomes a body in the lived sense not just by being seen (this would present merely a physical *Körper*), but by having touch, visual, pain and movement sensations localized within it (*Ideas* II § 37). For Husserl, there is a normal optimal situation for the body – upright, looking forward. He lists various characteristics of the lived body: it is a centre of orientation, the 'zero-point' of my space; it is also the centre of my 'now'; it is a unifying locus for all my sensory and kinesthetic experiences (vision, touch, taste, smell, sense of bodily movement); it is the 'organ of my will', and through my body I experience my capacities for free movement as a kind of immediate 'holding sway' (see *Crisis* § 62). In *Ideas* III (Hua V 118) he explains that the lived body (*Leib*) should not be thought of as a physical body with a consciousness added on (as in Descartes) rather it has to be thought of as a sensory field, a field of localization of sensation. The body, he says, forms an 'existential stratum'. The lived body, furthermore, is only an 'incompletely constituted thing', for Husserl, by which he means that it is experienced with 'gaps'. I have a sense of my back but do not see it, for example. There are absences that can be filled in; I can learn to move my fingers in the right way to play the piano, for instance.

This experienced and experiencing body, Husserl claims, as mediator of our experienced world, has never been the proper subject of any science before phenomenology. Husserl is surely right there is no one science that addresses the lived body as experienced – such a science would include all forms of bodily experience, what Husserl calls *somatology* in *Ideas* III. The anorexic's peculiar sense of her own body would have to come into play here, as well as the experiences of athletes or dancers. Empirical psychology, due to its method, has treated it in an objectivist and piecemeal manner. The manner in which a living body is spatio-temporally localized and is involved in a living relationship with causality differs greatly from the body understood purely as a physical entity. The ego that inhabits a body does not get its uniqueness from its causal relations with nature but rather already has a uniqueness for Husserl (*Crisis* § 62) that is not simply that of having spatial and temporal coordinates: 'For the ego, space and time are not principles of individuation; it knows no natural causality, the latter being, in accord with its meaning, inseparable from spatiotemporality' (C 218; K 222). Each embodied ego has its unique character, its 'style' and 'habits'. The ego lives inside its own web of motivations, meanings, drives, tendencies and its own inalienable free will, what generally speaking Husserl calls 'governing' or 'holding-sway' (*walten*): 'Only through my own originally experienced holding-sway, which is the sole original experience of lived-bodiliness as such, can I understand another physical body as a living body in which another "I" is embodied and holds sway' (C 217; K 221).

Other subjects – including some animals – turn or tilt their heads in order to see, reach out to touch, shrink in fear, and so on. Husserl does not address the limits of this apperceptive analogization. He does seem to think we could not understand a living organism without a sense of its self-movement as somehow – no matter how different physiologically – paralleling our movements. We can get a sense even of a jellyfish's propulsion through the water by watching its movements (for Husserl on jellyfish, see Hua XIV 113–15). (Husserl here does not seem to be far from the imitation theory of empathy of Lipps and others.) In the *Crisis*, Husserl only hints at the form such a science of embodiment could take.

Before we leave Husserl's treatment of psychology we should address two forms of psychology that were popular in the 1930s – on the one hand depth psychology or psychoanalysis (as practised by Freud, Jung (1875–1961), Adler and others), and, on the other, the race psychology (called at the time *Rassenseelenkunde*) promoted by National Socialists in Germany, which did gain a foothold in the academy during that decade (as promoted by Husserl's own former student Ludwig Ferdinand Clauss (1892–1974)). First let us turn to psychoanalysis.

HUSSERL AND PSYCHOANALYSIS OR 'DEPTH PSYCHOLOGY'

Already in the 1930s Husserlian phenomenology had been criticized from the point of view of 'depth psychology',[14] i.e. the various psychologies of the unconscious prevalent at that time, e.g., Bleuler (1857–1939), Freud, Jung, Adler. Phenomenology is accused of holding an idealist approach to consciousness that treats 'unconscious' processes as activities that can eventually be brought to consciousness. Fink, in defence of Husserl, returns the criticism and claims that depth psychology itself seems to take unconscious phenomena as self-evident in

---

[14] As Eugen Fink indicates in his short essay on the problem of the unconscious accompanying the *Crisis* (see C 385–7; K 473–5).

their own way. Fink writes: 'For the unconscious, too, as well as for consciousness, there exists the *illusion* of everyday, given immediacy: we are all familiar, after all, with the phenomena of sleep, of fainting, of being overtaken by obscure driving forces, creative states, and the like' (C 387; K 474). Fink claims, and here he is articulating Husserl's own views, that no philosophy of the unconscious can proceed until the nature of being-conscious in the world is truly understood, i.e. the nature of 'wakefulness' (*Wachheit*), consciousness in its various levels of alertness. Furthermore, the later Husserl was far from thinking that all aspects of our intentional life can be brought to the forefront of consciousness as if they were illuminated by a Cartesian ray of awareness and incorporated into the ego as part of its own intentional acts. Indeed, quite the reverse. For Husserl, generally, consciousness of the present is surrounded by horizons of consciousness of the past that is no longer, the projected and imagined future, the possible, the wished for, the feared. The person is made up of a conscious 'egoic centre' and what can be envisaged as a widening set of overlapping horizons that include fantasized selves and modifications of selves (dream personae and so on). As Rudolf Bernet has suggested, for Husserl the unconscious is best understood as a kind of consciousness of the non-present.[15] Intentional life is a life of implication, as Husserl insists. How can one separate whom one loves from whom one imagines one loves, for instance? For Husserl, as indeed for Freud, the unconscious becomes conscious in a peculiar way, protruding into conscious life in the form of dreams, slips of the tongue, and compulsive or regressive behaviour.[16] So Husserl is essentially at one with depth psychology in approaching the unconscious through multi-layered conscious experiences.

Husserl's genetic account of the evolution of conscious life recognized the complexity of the condition known as 'wakefulness', as well as the importance of pre-conscious 'drives' (*Triebe*) and 'instincts' (*Instinkte*) that may be experienced at a pre-egoic level, e.g. pangs of hunger, desire for warmth, the desire to smoke tobacco, but that

---

[15] See Rudolf Bernet, 'Unconscious Consciousness in Husserl and Freud', in Donn Welton, ed., *The New Husserl: A Critical Reader* (Bloomington: Indiana University Press, 2003), pp. 199–219.

[16] See also Aaron Mishara, 'Husserl and Freud: Time, Memory and the Unconscious', *Husserl Studies* vol. 7 (1990), 29–58.

eventually get taken up by the ego (either embraced or resisted). Husserl further acknowledged that the 'wakefulness' of adult consciousness evolved from and somehow contained in a sedimented way (as a 'trace') the experiences of the child, now overlaid with contemporary experiences. As Husserl remarked in the *Crisis*, consciousness consists not just of clear moments (such as perception, memory, etc.), but also of 'obscured forms [*Verdunkelungen*], sedimentations – and also all instincts and drives, not to mention the "horizons"' (C 246; K 249). Instincts and drives belong to what Husserl calls the 'underground' (*Untergrund*, C 149; K 152) of the self. They are experienced in complicated forms, and it is never a matter of straightforward causal or mechanical stimulation. Even instinctual drives are taken up by the free ego at a higher level. Thus, in *Ideas* ii Husserl writes:

> the personal Ego constitutes itself not only as a person determined by *drives* ... but *also as a higher, autonomous, freely acting* Ego, in particular one guided by *rational motives* ... Habits are necessarily formed, just as much with regard to originally instinctive behaviour ... as with regard to free behaviour. To yield to a drive establishes the drive to yield: habitually. (*Ideas* ii § 59, p. 267; Hua iv, 255, translation modified, emphases in original)

Already in his early writings on perception, imagination and image consciousness from around 1905, Husserl had developed very careful accounts of fantasy, dreams, wishes and other representational states. Indeed, he discussed, for instance, how real wishes (e.g. the desire to have a holiday) can emerge within flights of daydream fantasy or in a dream.[17] Fantasy can enfold real feelings and wishes as well as fantasy feelings and wishes. Watching a movie can produce a fantasy desire to kill, not a real desire, and so on. In this regard, Husserl is close to Scheler and Lipps, who also wrote about fantasy feelings.

In the *Crisis*, Husserl invokes but does not develop in any systematic manner the distinction between two fundamental modes of consciousness, namely being awake and being asleep (a puzzling form of consciousness but not complete lack of awareness). Of course, phenomenology must begin from 'wakefulness' (*Wachheit*), which Husserl defines in terms of the ego being active and responding to

---

[17] See Edmund Husserl, *Phantasy, Image Consciousness and Memory (1895–1925)*, trans. John Brough, Husserl Collected Works Vol. xi (Dordrecht: Springer, 2005), pp. 251–2.

stimuli and affections, being turned towards them. Sleep, on the other hand, is unresponsive to affection. The sleeping ego too may have experiences (not just dreams but bodily sensations) that often carry over into the waking state (one can talk about a good sleep or a restless one), but the ego does not lay claim to them as products of itself as it would with experiences in wakeful life. There is no doubt that as conscious wakeful subjects we are aware not only that we dream, but also of the contents of our dreams, and not just in the retelling (as Wittgenstein suggests), but as images and memories that are retained in wakefulness and haunt it. Husserl explores these dream and fantasy states in other writings, but in the *Crisis* he simply states that a full phenomenological psychology is needed to treat these phenomena in a non-naïve way, and he suggests a new way of understanding them in terms of horizons, sedimentations and habitualities.

RACE PSYCHOLOGY AND BIOLOGISM IN THE 1930S

Finally, let us turn here to Husserl's relationship with the racial biology and race psychology that was being promoted in the 1930s by the National Socialists in Germany. Husserl's 'Vienna Lecture' of 1935 may be seen as an explicit repudiation of such approaches. The political context of the coming to power of the National Socialists in the 1930s gave a particular urgency to Husserl's critique of psychology and the human sciences. Indeed, some commentators, e.g. De Gandt,[18] have claimed that Husserl was protesting against the racist, determinist biologism of peoples espoused by Nazi theorists and their philosophical fellow-travellers, among whom could be found some of Husserl's own students, such as Ludwig Ferdinand Clauss and Oskar Becker (1889–1964).[19] Husserl was undoubtedly interested in the collective psychology of social groups, peoples, nations and indeed even 'races' (see, for instance, Hua XXXIX 178, 606; Hua XV 613, 622).[20] He articulates in his 1935 letter to the French ethnologist Lucien

---

[18] See François De Gandt, *Husserl et Galilée: Sur la crise des sciences européennes* (Paris: Vrin, 2004), p. 29.

[19] See Dermot Moran, '"Even the Papuan is a Man and Not a Beast": Husserl on Universalism and the Relativity of Cultures', *Journal of the History of Philosophy* Vol. 49 No. 4 (October 2011), 463–94.

[20] Husserl speaks quite generally of different social groups, collectivities of humans, including those identified as a 'people' (*Volk*), a 'nation' (*Nation*) and a 'race' (*Rasse*), that can be

Lévy-Bruhl considerable appreciation for the latter's anthropological approaches to primitive mentality.[21] He was particularly interested in Lévy-Bruhl's claims that the primitive has different conceptions of time, space and causation from that of the scientifically informed modern European. But on the other hand, Husserl did not draw conclusions that ranked one race or human grouping as 'higher' or more advanced than another. Oskar Becker, however, did publish a number of articles on race, including a notorious one entitled 'Nordic Metaphysics' (1938), that drew on the racial characterizations of another of Husserl's former students, Ludwig Ferdinand Clauss.[22] Clauss was an anthropologist and popular travel writer who went on to have a chequered relationship with the Nazis (because he espoused racial theories but rejected the Nazi claim that races were biologically based). Clauss repudiated the narrow, physiologically based race theories of some of the other National Socialist ideologues and instead developed a theory as to how climate and terrain influenced psychology and led to certain racial characteristics emerging. His cultural anthropology claimed to employ phenomenological description (especially empathy) to understand and classify different cultural types (types of psyche) based on physical attributes and their interaction with their environments. A people's collective 'soul' is forged in its interaction with its own landscape. There are desert peoples and forest peoples, people for whom space is infinite and peoples who choose to live in more restricted horizons. Nordic peoples, on Clauss' view, had a sense of open expansiveness not available to Mediterranean peoples, for instance. The Nordic landscape has an openness that calls for space to be traversed; accordingly, it lies in the essence of the Nordic soul that it must penetrate and dominate the

---

identified by their adherence to social norms, use of language, sense of identity and also physical characteristics. Sometimes he puts the word 'race' in inverted commas (e.g. Hau XXXIX 178).

[21] See 'Edmund Husserl's Letter to Lucien Lévy-Bruhl, 11 March 1935', trans. Dermot Moran and Lukas Steinacher, *New Yearbook for Phenomenology and Phenomenological Philosophy* Vol. 8 (2008), 349–54.

[22] See Oskar Becker, 'Nordische Metaphysik', in *Rasse: Monatsschrift der Nordischen Bewegung* Vol. 5 (1938), 83–92. Becker criticizes Heidegger's *Being and Time* for not accommodating the crucial concept of 'race'.

whole world. Other cultures, Claus claimed, must necessarily accept this Nordic mode of dominating distances.

In opposition to these particularist racial theories, Husserl maintains that there is no 'zoology of peoples' (C 275; K 320), and that everything to do with the life of spirit is unique and unrepeatable. Hence, all science of culture or 'spirit' (*Geist*) must be open-ended and unfinished. Husserl advocated a kind of universalism that also promoted the possibility of individual peoples and races transcending their local outlooks and 'world representations' and developing a universal outlook (as the ancient Greeks did through the discovery of philosophy).

CONCLUSION

From his time as a student of Brentano and Stumpf, Husserl developed a deep interest in and familiarity with a priori descriptive psychology and also with the then nascent discipline of empirical scientific psychology. During his Göttingen years he interacted with some of the leading experimental psychologists of his day. He influenced Gestalt concepts through his own analyses of grasping collectivities, as well as through his students David Katz and Aron Gurwitsch.[23] However, Husserl consistently criticizes empirical psychology (especially positivism and behaviourism) for its naturalism and objectivism, for prioritizing 'external' natural, causal and conditioning factors (as determined by induction) and for making use of a concept of 'inner life' which derives from natural life. Because of its preoccupation with psycho-physical causality, so-called 'scientific' psychology does not know how to break with a certain naïveté in its view of subjective life (see C 243–4; K 246–8). The true intentional life, on the other hand, is a 'title for correlations' (C 245; K 248), and these correlations and intentional implications have not even been noticed, never mind understood. Husserl's phenomenological psychology offers the possibility of an account of human behaviour at the level of intentionality, passivity, syntheses, sedimentations, habitualities,

---

[23] See especially Aron Gurwitsch, *The Field of Consciousness* (Pittsburgh, PA: Dusquesne University Press, 1964) and his *Studies in Phenomenology and Psychology* (Evanston, IL: Northwestern University Press, 1966).

horizons and so on. Furthermore, Husserl prioritizes embodiment in a radical and field-challenging way. His studies of the lived body with its own functioning intentionality through which it constitutes the world in which it lives had an enormous influence on Merleau-Ponty. Husserl's later writings on instincts and drives are now a major source for those seeking a phenomenological way of grounding Freud's speculative accounts of the unconscious. Husserl developed a conception of the social world that he believed addressed problems in Dilthey's conception, and his pure phenomenological psychology offered a form of psychology that overcame what he perceived as the naturalistic limitations of Brentano's intentional psychology.

CHAPTER 5

Rethinking tradition: Husserl on history

HUSSERL ON THE MEANING OF HISTORY

In Part I of the *Crisis*, the natural sciences (especially mathematical physics) are treated in the figure of Galileo, as we saw in Chapter 3. In the *Crisis* Part III, as we saw in the last chapter, the status of psychology as a science is discussed critically. In this chapter, we shall examine Husserl's overall conception of *history* (variously *Historie*, *Geschichte*),[1] including his account of the development of Western (i.e. what he calls 'European') culture, which focuses specifically on the emergence of theoretical reflection, essential to scientific rationality, and the breakthrough to the very idea of philosophy itself with its conception of 'purposive life' (*Zweckleben*, K 502), a life lived according to reason (*Vernunftleben*, C 117; K 119). Understanding the meaning of history is central both to the *Crisis* project and to Husserl's mature conception of transcendental phenomenology. Husserl himself, in his Preface to the *Philosophia* articles, describes the *Crisis* as a 'teleological historical reflection' (C 3; K xiv n.3) involving an intellectual 'reconstruction' and 'backwards questioning' (*Rückfragen*) of the history of Western culture (specifically the development of modern philosophy and natural science). History is being deliberately explored as a way of understanding transcendental

---

[1] Unlike Heidegger (see SZ §§ 6 and 76), Husserl does sharply distinguish between history (*Geschichte* – which Heidegger relates to the verb *geschehen*, 'to happen') understood as historical factual occurrences and history (*Historie*) understood as the more formal imposition of an historical narrative, as in 'natural history' (*Naturhistorie*, K 304). Thus, at C 331; K 310, Husserl uses the word *Historie* instead of *Geschichte* for the course of human history (cf. C 333; K 312). Husserl appears to use the words interchangeably at K 492. He speaks of 'world history' as *Weltgeschichte* at C 66; K 67 but uses the term *Welthistorie* at C 334; K 313. Similarly, he speaks of 'factual history' (*Tatsachenhistorie*) in 'The Origin of Geometry' (C 371; K 380 and C 378; K 386).

constitution, and thus, in his 'Foreword to the Continuation of the *Crisis*' (Supplement XIII, K 435–45 – not translated in Carr), Husserl refers to his approach as a 'teleological-historical way' to the idea of transcendental phenomenology. In this 'Foreword' he emphasizes that the historical mode of exposition is 'not chosen by chance' but rather is central to his task (*Crisis* K 441), since he wants to exhibit the whole history of philosophy as possessing a 'unitary teleological structure' (*eine einheitliche teleologische Struktur*, K 442).

From the beginning of the *Crisis* Husserl has been leading us to reflect on the inner meaning of history. In a related text from 1934, entitled 'The History of Philosophy in Connection with the Historical Science and with Culture', he defines history in the following somewhat dense manner: 'History [*Die Historie*] is the science of the genesis of humanity, understood in a personal sense, and its surrounding life-world [*Lebensumwelt*], as it has come to be in this genesis, in each present in actual praxis in the ongoing shaping of the standing cultural world' (Hua XXIX 53, my translation). Husserl wants to understand history in terms of the cultural evolution and shaping of personal and interpersonal existence with due recognition of the peculiar sense of time-consciousness. He is interested in how a sense of history comes to be established, how humans situate themselves in cultural contexts and traditions, and he is also interested in identifying the necessary a priori features that make such living in history possible.

Husserl is not interested in 'external' history; he wants to explore what he calls 'inner history' (*innere Historie*, C 378; K 386) with its 'inner historicity' (Hua XXIX 417) in contrast to 'factual history' (*Tatsachenhistorie*). What finally emerges then, is a reflective consideration or treatment of history (*Geschichtsbetrachtung*, C 58; K 59) which is at the same time a 'critique of history' (ibid.). The historical evolution of culture and science has to have a definite 'meaning-form', that is, it has to have an intelligible character to its development.

The meaning of history itself will be explored through the *history of philosophy*. Throughout the *Crisis*, this focus on 'teleology' or 'goal-directedness' (*Teleologie*, from the Greek *telos* meaning 'goal', 'aim', 'purpose' or 'end') primarily targets philosophy. He explicates the inner 'teleology' of modern philosophy from Descartes to Kant. Husserl, without reference to Hegel, but clearly following broadly in the German Idealist tradition, sees the history of philosophy as having exemplary significance. Husserl firmly believed that the history of philosophy (and by implication the history of 'European', i.e. Western culture in general) had to be understood as exhibiting an intelligible structure and trajectory.

Husserl understands history as part of the a priori structures that make meaning possible. History consists in the institution or constitution of meaning. His overall aim is to understand not just what history itself is (as an intentionally constituted 'complex of sense', *Sinneszusammenhang*), but also to understand what is *essential* or *invariant* to history as a form of human intentional instituting and constituting. History as mere blind facts will be incomprehensible unless the 'a priori of history' and its inner essence are understood. Husserl writes: 'All (merely) factual history [*Tatsachenhistorie*] remains incomprehensible because, always merely drawing its conclusions naïvely and straightforwardly from facts, it never makes thematic the general ground of meaning [*den allgemeinen Sinnboden*] upon which all such conclusions rest, has never investigated the immense structural a priori [*strukturelle Apriori*] which is proper to it' (C 371; K 380).

Husserl wants to chart 'essential' or 'eidetic history', including identifying its hidden goal (*telos*) and 'motivation' (C 11; K 9). This involves overcoming what he calls the 'naïve instinctive' approach to history (Hua XXIX 228), and instead seeing history (and paradigmatically the history of *philosophy*) as essential to temporal human existence and as a form of meaning-making or meaning instituting, and also as the manner in which tradition is passed along. The underlying essential a priori structures that govern the constitution of historical, communal life must be laid bare. In this regard he refers paradoxically to the 'essential structures of absolute historicity' (C 259; K 262) which seems to suggest that even 'historicity' has an invariable eidetic structure. He speaks of the 'history of essence' or 'essential history' (*Wesenshistorie*, C 350; K 362) and of a universal 'a priori of history' (C 349; K 362 and C 351; K 363), all terms that are problematic and raise the suspicions of those who deny a teleology to history. Husserl is struggling to resolve satisfactorily the inevitable tension between the concept of a purely static a priori (as found in Kant) and of an a priori that takes account of 'genesis' and is related to human

development and progress in history (Hegel). This clarification of the
a priori of history is, finally, for him, the key to unlocking the relation
between the natural and the human sciences (*Geisteswissenschaften*).

Husserl is primarily interested in how 'history' as such comes
about as a unified sense-complex, how it gains its unified significance, and how this sense of the meaning of the shared past goes on
to inform and direct present human life. How does history come
about? How is the historical world constituted by us? These are his
questions. Moreover, any attempt to understand history must recognize its double-sidedness. On the one hand, history (understood
in terms of chains of meaningful events and the unfolding of their
significance) is the sphere of the unique, the one-off, temporally
marked event, the domain of *facticity* (*Faktizität,* C 349; K 362 and
C 377; K 385) and *contingency*. On the other hand, as Husserl also
recognizes, history is the domain of habit, the sedimented, tradition,
the intersubjective, the social, the communal – life lived according to
settled norms and values. Human activities cohere together into traditions and shape specific cultures with their own particular ways of
developing and unfolding (which Husserl usually calls 'historicities').
Cultures, for Husserl, also aim at rational goals, as we shall see.

The question of history includes deep questions of how certain
things or events become invested with significance through some
kind of inauguration or 'primal foundation' (*Urstiftung*), of how
meanings become crystallized into 'habitualities' (*Habitualitäten*),
'sedimented' into traditions, transmitted across generations in the
process known as 'generativity' (*Generativität*). In 'The Origin of
Geometry', Husserl even offers a definition of history in his sense:
'We can now say that history [*Geschichte*] is from the start nothing
other than the vital movement [*die lebendige Bewegung*] of the being-
with-one-another [*Miteinander*] and the interweaving [*Ineinander*]
of the original formation of meaning [*Sinnbildung*] and sedimentation of meaning [*Sinnsedimentierung*]' (*Geschichte ist von vorn-
herein nichts anderes als die lebendige Bewegung des Miteinander und
Ineinander von ursprünglicher Sinnbildung und Sinnsedimentierung,* C
371; K 380; translation modified). Husserl's claim to be able to delin-
eate the essential 'a priori of history' is both attractive and deeply
problematic. How can an essentialist history cope with the contingent aspect of human life? Is there not a danger (to which, arguably,

Hegel succumbed) in attempting to impose a unified meaning on the course of history, when it might be merely irrational fact ('one damn thing after another', as Henry Ford is reputed to have put it)? In fact, as we shall see, Husserl clearly differentiates between events that merely succeed one another –'factual history' (*Tatsachenhistorie*) – and historical development in the genuine sense of a life unified and ordered to a goal, functioning in terms of what Husserl generally calls 'teleology' (*Teleologie*; see K 559).

THE MOTIVATIONS BEHIND HUSSERL'S TURN TO HISTORY

Prior to the *Crisis*, Husserl had largely ignored – at least in his published works (aside from the *Kaizo* articles, published in Japan in 1923–4 and therefore largely inaccessible to readers in Europe at that time (see Hua xxvii 3–43)) – the whole problematic of human collective living in community and society, i.e. how a unified sense or meaning can arise out of the multiple intentional actions of humans in the past. His major publications present the new science of phenomenology primarily from the standpoint of individual consciousness with its lived experiences (*Erlebnisse*) and rarely address the issue of historical, social and communal life (admittedly *Formal and Transcendental Logic* § 100 does briefly sketch the history of transcendental philosophy). The *Crisis* was therefore welcomed by Husserl's students because it offered Husserl's most sustained effort to develop a phenomenological approach to the issues of temporality, finitude, historicity, and cultural and generational development (the phenomenon Husserl calls 'generativity', *Generativität*, C 188; K 191, i.e. the manner in which meanings become sedimented in being passed from one generation to another).[2] These new themes transformed phenomenology.

---

[2] Husserl develops his own terminology for talking about history and tradition. His concept of 'generativity' is one such example. Carr translates it – somewhat misleadingly – as 'genesis'. For a discussion of the meaning of 'generativity' in Husserl, see Anthony Steinbock, *Home and Beyond: Generative Phenomenology after Husserl* (Evanston, IL: Northwestern University Press, 1995), esp. p. 3. Husserl discusses 'generativity' in greater detail in texts associated with the *Crisis* (see esp. the 1934 supplement, 'Different Forms of Historicity', Hua xxix 37–46).

There are several factors motivating Husserl to come to grips with the problematic of history, including the Neo-Kantian dispute over the proper methodology for the human sciences, the meaning of the history of modern philosophy, the challenge presented by Heidegger's hermeneutical phenomenology and the overall threat of a decline of the scientific spirit into irrationalism. We shall treat each of these issues in turn.

The Neo-Kantian Dispute over the Methodology for the Human Sciences

There had been a long-running discussion concerning the nature and status of the human sciences among German philosophers at the end of the nineteenth century, especially among the Neo-Kantians (including Windelband, Rickert, Cassirer) and the life philosophers (Simmel, Dilthey), as well as among the followers of French positivism (Comte, Durkheim). An issue of particular importance (at a time when psychology, sociology, economics and political science were just beginning to take the scientific forms that matured during the twentieth century into distinct disciplines with their own empirical – and often heavily quantitative – methods) was whether there was indeed a distinct method for the human sciences, as Windelband and Rickert insisted. For example, Wilhelm Windelband characterized the natural sciences as '*nomothetic*', explaining things in terms of a general lawfulness, whereas the human sciences were interested in the individual and in issues of value, which he called '*ideographic*'.[3] Similarly, Heinrich Rickert contrasted the urge for generalization found in the natural sciences with the sense of the specific and of individual value that was to be found in the human sciences.[4] Wilhelm Dilthey, furthermore, sought to contrast natural scientific *explanation* (*Erklärung*), which examines natural *causation*, with human scientific *description* (*Beschreibung*), which is interested in a different form of causation that Dilthey calls *motivation*. Indeed, Dilthey, as we saw in

---

[3] See Wilhelm Windelband, 'Rectorial Address on History and Natural Science' (1894), trans. Guy Oakes in *History and Theory* Vol. 19 No. 2 (February. 1980), 169–85.
[4] See, for instance, Heinrich Rickert, *The Limits of Concept Formation in Natural Science: A Logical Introduction to the Historical Sciences*, trans. and ed. Guy Oakes (New York: Cambridge University Press, 1962).

Chapter 4, had contrasted descriptive with explanatory psychology, a move which won Husserl's approval. Finally, Husserl had already been addressing the issue of the nature of the human sciences and their relation to the natural sciences in his Freiburg lectures on *Nature and Spirit* from 1917 to 1927 (Hua XXXII), where his focus is often on Rickert, and also in his *Phenomenological Psychology* lectures (1925), where his focus is Dilthey. Husserl acknowledges that Dilthey's conception of the 'connectedness of life' (*Lebenszusammenhang*, a term also used by Husserl, see C 149; K 152) is a powerful conception, which, however, needs more adequate theoretical grounding and clarification.

In line with the approach of Wilhelm Dilthey and the Neo-Kantians (Windelband and Rickert), Husserl too believes that the human sciences required a specific methodology distinct from the natural sciences. He maintained, however, that the entire natural/human sciences distinction needed a much deeper intellectual grounding. In the *Crisis*, then, he clearly intended to comprehend not just the methodology of the natural sciences (*Naturwissenschaften*), but also the status of the *human* or *cultural* sciences (*Geisteswissenschaften*). Indeed, according to Husserl's overall plans for the *Crisis*, he intended to add sections on the human sciences at the latter end of the book, but, in the texts selected by Biemel for Hua VI, he is mainly concerned with the relations between the scientific world and the life-world as the ground for all the sciences, both the natural and the human. It is important, then, to interpret the analysis of history in the *Crisis* and 'The Origin of Geometry' as in part a continuation of a meditation carried out in his *Nature and Spirit* lectures.

The Meaning of the History of Philosophy

A second motivation driving Husserl's concern with history was his overall attempt to comprehend the essence of *philosophy*. During the 1920s in Freiburg he was increasingly focused on the *history of philosophy*, especially in the modern period, as in his *First Philosophy* (*Erste Philosophie*) lectures of 1923–4, which he explicitly calls a 'critical history of ideas' (Hua VII 3), and in a short sketch of 'a history of transcendental philosophy' in his 1929 *Formal and Transcendental Logic* (see especially § 100), where he also speaks of the need for a 'critical consideration of history' (FTL, § 100, p. 261; Hua XVII 268). There he engages in a 'historico-critical digression' on modern philosophy (FTL, § 100, p. 266; Hua XVII 273) and interprets intentionality as a complex of performances whose 'sedimented history' (*sedimentierte Geschichte*, FTL, § 97, p. 245; Hua XVII 252) can be uncovered.

For Husserl, philosophy has an *essential*, integral relation to its history, unlike other sciences, for whom the history of the science plays no theoretical role or role in discovery (e.g. the history of chemistry does not have a role in the advancement of scientific discovery in chemistry). As Husserl writes in the *Crisis* Supplement XXIV (not translated in Carr), philosophers live in the present in their actual lives, but in their professional vocation they are in communicative interaction with philosophers of previous generations (constituting a unique form of philosophical 'generativity', K 489):

For philosophers of the present day the philosophical past is genuinely motivating. The peculiar modality of the horizon of the philosopher – generations and their works, their thoughts. Every philosopher has his historical horizon, encompassing all the philosophers, who have formed their thoughts in philosophical co-existence, and has worked on new philosophers as entering anew into this co-existence. (*Die philosophische Vergangenheit ist für den Philosophen der Gegenwart aktuell motivierend. Eigentümlicher Modus des Horizontes des Philosophen–Generationen und ihre Werke, ihre Gedanken. Jeder Philosoph hat seinen geschichtlichen Horizont, alle Philosophen befassend, die in philosophischer Koexistenz ihre Gedanken gebildet und auf neue Philosophen, als in diese Koexistenz neu eintretende, gewirkt haben*, K 488, my translation)

This poetical reconstruction consists of treating the past of philosophy not as a dead set of facts, but as a resource for current problems (see K 488). Husserl speaks about the need for a treatment of history as a critical appropriation of the past, in order to fully participate in the meaning of *philosophy*, to understand what it is and what it does (C 391; K 510). Radically, he maintains that philosophers engage with their history as poets do with their tradition, reconstituting it and refounding it through their own creative activity and engagement in a kind of poetic invention or 'poetizing' (*Dichtung*). Philosophy has its own 'philosophical generativity' (K 488), which can even lose its power over time and degenerate such that living ideas become merely texts and documents. But even here the sedimented documents and material remain to be re-awoken in subsequent generations. In this sense, in a unique way, living and dead are joined together, and the sense of the field or horizon of a problem or theme is greatly expanded. The past can be retrieved and reworked under new motivations. The dynamics of this intellectual process of philosophy with its past serves as a general model for history for understanding the nature of history in its relation to culture.

The Challenge of Heidegger's Being and Time

Another important factor motivating Husserl's turn to history, which cannot be overlooked but, at the same time, must not be overinterpreted, was the publication of Heidegger's *Being and Time* in 1927 (in contrast, Husserl had published nothing since *Ideas* I in 1913). Heidegger's work shone the spotlight on Husserl's silence and required him to articulate publicly his own understanding of time, history and finitude. Heidegger's importance grew in the early 1930s, especially after the publication of Georg Misch's *Life-Philosophy and Phenomenology*, which contrasted Husserl's work unfavourably with the new hermeneutics. Husserl felt compelled to defend his own approach to the essential a priori of history, including his own conception of historicity and lived tradition.

Inevitably, Husserl's *Crisis* was interpreted by many critics as his supposed riposte to Heidegger's hermeneutical phenomenology with its existential-ontological exposition of the historicity of Dasein (especially in *Being and Time* Part V §§ 72–7 on 'Temporality and Historicity').[5] Heidegger there talks about 'the problem of history' and even of the meaning of 'world history'. For Heidegger, all efforts to solve the problem of history (including those that compared its methodology to that of the natural sciences) already took for granted the intrinsic meaning of human historical happening, making history, what Heidegger calls *Geschehen* (historicizing): 'The specific movement in which Dasein *is stretched along and stretches itself along,* we call its "*historizing*"' (SZ § 72, p. 427; 375).

---

[5] Husserl found the term 'historicity' (*Geschichtlichkeit*) in Heidegger and in Dilthey, whose *Der Aufbau der historischen Welt in den Geisteswissenschaften* (1910), translated as *The Formation of the Historical World in the Human Sciences* by Rudolf Maakreel and John Scanlon (Princeton University Press, 2002) he had read in 1911.

For Heidegger, *being historical*, i.e. being the kind of entity who lives through history, and with historical consciousness, depends first and foremost on the intrinsic temporality of human existence, of human life stretched between birth and death. Furthermore, what is primarily historical are not the things from the past (ruins, monuments, documents and so on), but rather human existence (Dasein) itself (SZ § 73, p. 432; 380). In these sections of *Being and Time*, Heidegger discusses Dilthey in particular (and also Dilthey's friend and correspondent, Count Paul Yorck von Wartenburg (1835–97)).

With the publication of Husserl's research manuscripts on intersubjectivity (Hua XIII–XV) and his *Nature and Spirit* lectures (regularly delivered in Freiburg until 1927, now Hua XXXII), as well as Hua XXXIX on the life-world, we can now recognize that Husserl had been concerned with the problematic of communal living in history and the issue of 'historicity' (for which he employs two terms more or less indiscriminately (*Geschichtlichkeit, Historizität*)) for a much longer period and quite independently of Heidegger. Indeed, it is more likely that Husserl's conception of spontaneous, absorbed 'living-in' (*Dahinleben*) influenced Heidegger's conceptions of human collective living in the historical 'we-world' rather than the other way around.

The Threat of Irrationalism

The French hermeneutic philosopher Paul Ricoeur (1913–2005) wrote that the ageing Husserl – that most apolitical and non-historical of thinkers – was in his late years 'summoned by history to interpret himself historically'.[6] In other words, Husserl was forced by the political upheavals of his time to address explicitly the issue of the meaning of history. While it is absolutely correct that Husserl did recognize the urgency of engaging with the crisis of rationality exemplified by the rise of National Socialism in Germany and did challenge its race psychology (as we saw in Chapter 4), he was far more deeply preoccupied with the inherent irrationalism in philosophy

---

[6] See Paul Ricoeur, 'Husserl and the Sense of History', in Ricoeur, *Husserl: An Analysis of His Phenomenology*, trans. Edward G. Ballard and L. Embree (Evanston, IL: Northwestern University Press, 1967), p. 144.

and in the positive sciences. Husserl was never simply reacting to current political events; rather, his thinking reflects a long, inner gestation and self-reflection.

Husserl's explicit turn to history in the *Crisis*, then, is largely a matter of his own internal development. He was influenced here not so much by Heidegger or by the political turmoil of the 1930s as by his own concerns to develop phenomenology outwards from an egology, through his studies of empathy, to an intersubjective philosophy of collective spirit (as is evident from his discussion of the constitution of the intersubjective world and the need to overcome the 'illusion of transcendental solipsism' in *Formal and Transcendental Logic* § 96). Phenomenology begins with the ego but cannot be considered complete until it has addressed the nature of communal and historical living, and, accordingly, the manner of meaning constitution in the historical and social sciences.

GLIMPSES OF HISTORY IN HUSSERL'S EARLIER WORK

There is, at least at first blush, a certain superficial truth to the popular characterization of Husserl as lacking interest in history. A well-known anecdote records Heidegger and Husserl in an extended conversation, Husserl laying out his plans for a system of transcendental phenomenology, when Heidegger supposedly interrupts him with the question: 'And what about history?' Husserl allegedly answers: 'I had completely forgotten about that.'[7] This possibly apocryphal story lends credence to the common misconception that Husserl – in contrast to his successor, Martin Heidegger – was unconcerned with history, society or culture. Indeed, Heidegger expressed his own frustration with Husserl. In his *History of the Concept of Time* lectures (1925), for instance, he states that Husserl's position on history, as elaborated in his 'Philosophy as Rigorous Science' essay (1910–1911), 'must be described as impossible' and that it was rightly criticized by the ageing Wilhelm Dilthey.[8]

---

[7] See Heinrich Wiegand-Petzet, *Encounters and Dialogues with Martin Heidegger 1929–1976*, trans. Parvis Emad and Kenneth Maly (University of Chicago Press, 1993), p. 80.
[8] Martin Heidegger, *History of the Concept of Time: Prolegomena*, trans. Theodore Kisiel (Bloomington: Indiana University Press, 1985), § 13c, p. 119.

Husserl rarely made history 'thematic', i.e. he did not make it a specific target of his reflections, in his early and middle periods. On the other hand, in 'Philosophy as Rigorous Science' he was concerned with the human, social or cultural sciences (*Geisteswissenschaften*). In *Ideas* I § 60 (Hua III/I 115) he refers briefly to humans as 'subjects of history' and in *Ideas* II (especially Supplement XIV) he distinguishes between material beings that are 'history-less' (*geschichtlos*) and psychic beings that are conditioned by their past (*Ideas* II § 33). He also describes the manner in which humans come to think of themselves in terms of communal life and shared motivations within the context of a social and institutional world, all the while struggling to maintain their individuality even in their personal interconnections (see *Ideas* II § 34). Indeed, already in *Ideas* II Husserl declares (in a manner that will later find an echo in *Cartesian Meditations* § 37) that the ego has a history: 'The Ego, however, is not an empty pole but is the bearer of its habituality [*Träger seiner Habitualität*], and that implies that it has an individual history' (*Ideas* II § 64, p. 313; Hua IV 300). The ego is earlier treated as a kind of source from which experiences flowed; now it is understood as constituting its identity in an historical manner. In his *Kaizo* articles, and, of course, in his private reflections on history and on social and communal life in the Husserliana *Intersubjectivity* volumes, Husserl develops the discussion of human living and growing in community, as well as the emergence of communal norms and the living of life according to ideals. But it is in the *Crisis* that history is first given explicit treatment.

THE PHENOMENOLOGY OF THE COMMUNAL SPHERE

As the *Cartesian Meditations* makes clear, Husserl's phenomenology explicitly begins, in the spirit of Descartes' *Meditations*, from the individual ego's own self-reflection on his or her 'lived experiences' (*Erlebnisse*) as intentional performances. However – and this is already clearly stated in *Ideas* II – he also recognized that the ego itself has a history and constitutes its experiences in terms of an extended, flowing *life*, a concept usually more associated with Wilhelm Dilthey. Moreover, this life involves the experience of the world as the non-objectifiable horizon of all experience. As he writes in the *Cartesian Meditations*:

The ego constitutes himself for himself in, so to speak, the unity of a history. We said that the constitution of the ego contains all the constitutions of all the objectivities existing for him, whether these be immanent or transcendent, ideal or real ... That a Nature, a cultural world, a world of men with their social forms, and so forth, exist for me signifies that possibilities of corresponding experiences exist for me (CM § 37, pp. 75–6; Hua I 109–10).

As we can see from this passage, the entire cultural world (including history), as well as the world of *nature* (primarily construed as the world of physical, spatial things – which he calls 'thing-world', *Dingwelt*), must be constituted through the apprehending ego's own constituting acts and experiences. Nature and culture – or, to speak more accurately, the naïvely experienced world of intertwined 'nature' and 'culture' – are experienced by me in a constituted and inseparable manner. Husserl, however, gave primacy in his earlier research to an account of this constitution as primarily 'static', i.e. descriptive of what is actually given as it is given. Thus, in the *Cartesian Meditations*, Husserl explains that phenomenology must initially be 'static': 'The phenomenology developed at first is merely "static"; its descriptions are analogous to those of natural history, which concern particular types, and, at best, arrange them in their systematic order. Questions of universal genesis and of the genetic structure of the ego ... are still far away' (CM § 37, p. 76; Hua I 110).

Static phenomenology, then, documents the existing strata of the experienced world, but Husserl will elaborate on the need for a *genetic* phenomenology in his *Crisis* (although he does not explicitly use that terminology in the text). This genetic phenomenology must tell a dynamic story that recognizes origins and *genesis*, coming into being, the evolution of meaning forms, both active and passive. Passive genesis – as Husserl explains in CM § 38 – accounts for the manner in which the ego always already finds itself in a constituted meaningful world of 'ready-made' objects. Thus, in 'The Origin of Geometry', Husserl speaks of the need for geometry and epistemology generally to perform a 'historical backward reference' (*historische Rückbeziehung*, C 370; K 379). He claims that the ruling 'dogma' (presumably the Neo-Kantian approach) has sharply distinguished epistemological elucidation from historical and 'humanistic-psychological' explanation. Matters of 'genesis' had been ignored in previous philosophy.

For the mature Husserl there is the need – and here Husserl is, possibly under the influence of Fink, finally beginning to recognize the groundbreaking contribution of Hegel – for a genetic story of the history of consciousness in its evolution. Phenomenology has to have a tale of origins – not actual temporal origins (there are no 'first' human beings, Husserl says, Hua XXIX 37), but events of meaning institution or 'originary foundation' (*Urstiftung*). Already in *Philosophy of Arithmetic*, Husserl has been concerned with the 'origin' (*Ursprung, Entstehung*) of numbers. The history of consciousness is also the history of *origination* ('genesis') and *constitution*, that is, of *sense-making*. Furthermore, history, as Husserl makes clear, is a difficult subject matter for science, because it does not exist *external* to persons; it cannot be completely objectified. It consists of the intentional achievements of humans individually and collectively, in which human beings are both *agents* (the sphere of active genesis, CM § 38) and also passive carriers of sedimented traditions.

Philosophy, for Husserl, as we saw above, cannot escape its history; philosophers are 'heirs to the past' in respect of the very goal set for philosophy (C 17; K 16). Indeed, philosophers have a duty to carry through a historical self-reflection in order to articulate the needs of the time. Philosophers are mediators of the meaning of their culture more or less as public servants are responsible for shepherding the state:

In *our* philosophizing then – how can we avoid it? – we are *functionaries of mankind* [*Funktionäre der Menschheit*]. The quite personal responsibility of our own true being as philosophers, our inner personal vocation, bears within itself at the same time the responsibility for the true being of mankind; the latter is, necessarily, being toward a *telos* and can only come to realization, *if at all*, through philosophy – through *us*, *if* we are philosophers in all seriousness. (C 17; K 15)

Elsewhere Husserl sees 'functionaries' not merely as passive bearers or conveyors of tradition, but as actively and creatively *constituting* (filtering, validating, suppressing, affirming, maintaining, renewing) our sense of belonging to institutions through our participation and endorsement of them, with 'our tasks, our duties, our responsibilities' (Hua XXIX 229; cf *Crisis* Supplement XXIV K 489). Philosophers have a *telos*; they seek truth (Hua XXIX 229). They also carry the burden of interpreting the historicity of their people. Thus, he speaks of mathematicians as 'functionaries of knowledge of the world' in his Prague Treatise of 1934 (Hua XXVII 185). As he explains (Hua XIV 183), the functionary exercises not just his personal will, but also the will of the public service. He becomes more than an individual: he participates in and ratifies the public process. Hence, also the philosopher preserves, communicates and validates ideas.

The essential relation of philosophy to its history is, however, by no means straightforward, but rather is essentially creative. Indeed, Husserl has a very subtle appreciation of the peculiar manner in which philosophy approaches its own history. He speaks of historical continuity in philosophy as involving a kind of 'poeticizing' (*Dichtung* – a term that more usually means poetry or fiction, literature) of the history of philosophy. By that he means that philosophers identify their historical predecessors not by some factual documenting of the external facts of the history of philosophy, but through a kind of inner alignment or harmony, an 'interweaving' (*Ineinander*) of intention, rather in the manner in which poets choose those whom they have decided have influenced them. Poetry and philosophy make their own traditions through taking up the poems or thoughts of earlier generations and revivifying them (see C 392–5; K 511–13). Philosophy is unique (in comparison with the natural sciences) in recruiting past philosophers into its present concerns. Philosophers of the past are joined with those of the present into a single 'community of philosophers' (*Philosophengemeinschaft*, K 444), a 'community of thinkers' (*Denkergemeinschaft*, K 444). The continuity of philosophical problems and discussions from generation to generation leads to a very particular 'generativity' in the history of philosophy itself (K 444).

As we have seen, Husserl employs the term 'generativity' (*Generativität* – a term that appears extremely rarely in his published works but is found in C 188; K 191) to summarize the different ways and processes through which meaning is passed on from one human generation to another. Anthony Steinbock explains this term as signifying both the process of becoming a generation and a process that occurs over generations.[9] History as such cannot be understood until one recognizes how this generativity operates. Generativity functions in lots of complex and hidden ways, e.g. children's games pass from

---

[9] Steinbock, *Home and Beyond*, p. 3.

one generation of children to another, while the adults have often forgotten them. Meanings can be preserved, encoded with further meanings, or be distorted, obliterated or repressed. What is transmitted can remain dormant and then suddenly be re-awoken. Languages are transmitted from one generation to another, and at the same time linguistic shifts slowly and inevitably take place. The cultural, human world is the outcome of successive acts of constitution by human beings over generations in history, but these constitutions include what is passively carried along in a sedimented manner.

COMMUNALIZATION AND HISTORICITY

In the *Crisis* Husserl often speaks of the process of 'communalization' (*Vergemeinschaftung*, C 262; K 265, cf. C 277; K 322 and K 357), whereby humans become socialized into various groupings. Indeed, his concept of 'with-one-another' (*Miteinander*) parallels Heidegger's 'being-with-others' (*Mitsein*, SZ § 26). Thus, in *Crisis* § 47, he speaks of the human character of 'living-with-one-another' (*Miteinanderleben*, C 163; K166; see also C 108; K 110) and of cooperating as 'co-subjects' (*Mitsubjekte*, C 164; K 167) who belong together in a 'co-humanity' (*Mitmenschheit*, C 165; K 168). He speaks more generally of a collective, shared intentionality or 'we-subjectivity' (*Wir-subjektivität*, C 109; K 111). This collective intentionality and the action of subjectivity in the plural has become a matter of interest in the philosophy of mind only in recent decades.

In the *Crisis*, Husserl investigates the interpersonal, intersubjective, communal world, the world of what he calls 'socialities' (*Sozialitäten*), families, peoples, nations (he sometimes speaks of the Greeks as a 'nation', *Crisis* K 322), and even 'super-nations' (*Übernationen*, C 270; K 315, C 275; K 320, C 276; K 322 and C 280; K 326), by which he means larger groupings of nations or peoples united by a common purpose, e.g. the idea of 'Europe' (see Hua XXIX 229), 'India' or 'China'. Humans are members of families, clubs, groups, linguistic communities, religious or political institutions, states and so on. These belongings are subject to norms. Thus, he speaks of Germans as 'good Europeans' participating in the culture of Europe (see Hua XXIX 229).

Human communities or 'socialities' have their own historical orientation and trajectories, their own outlooks, horizons, paths and destinies in history, which Husserl loosely terms 'historicities' (*Historizitäten, Geschichtlichkeiten*). These can be more or less narrow or broad, and interweave with one another in complex ways; cultural groupings can even lack history and be self-enclosed. *Historicity*, for Husserl, does not have quite the same technical sense that it has in Heidegger. For Husserl, it means the way in which human groupings constitute and live out, across the interchanges and transmissions of the generations (what, as we have seen, Husserl terms 'generativity'), a common history. A historicity is a 'unity of becoming'. He writes in a supplementary text entitled 'Levels of Historicity: First Historicity' (not translated in Carr):

Historicity [*Geschichtlichkeit*] in the most general sense has always already been in progress [*in Gang*], and in this progress it is rightly a universal, which belongs to human existence. It is a unified becoming [*ein einheitliches Werden*] according to persons, in persons, and, as an environment, according to the plurality of forms of the environment, which can be seen as the unity of an organism. (K 502, my translation)

For Husserl, every social grouping has its own 'historicity' or structural way of evolving its history: 'Each kind of cultural formation has its historicity, has its character of having become [*Charakter der Gewordenheit*] and its relation to the future and, indeed, in reference to its historical, living, productive and utilizing humanity' (K 504, my translation). Moreover, different historicities can be grouped into various stages of development: there are different 'levels' (*Stufen*) of historicity, although these should not be understood simply as temporal stages. Rather, they indicate different levels of sophistication in the overall organization and outlook of a society.

Elsewhere Husserl speaks of 'transcendental historicity' (Hua XXIX 80), meaning thereby the a priori conditions that make possible living historically. Note here that Husserl characterizes historicity as a universal and necessary property belonging to human existence. As we shall see below, Heidegger makes historicity into an existential characteristic of Dasein. Husserl also speaks in this text of 'original generative historicity' (K 501) and of the historicity of the natural world and of the cultural, intersubjective domain. For Husserl, nature itself (as a cultural product) has a *history* in the very same way that the cultural world, which is more usually considered to be historical, does. Indeed, Husserl insists that the 'spiritual surrounding world' (*geistige Umwelt*) of peoples is just as important a matter of study as the natural world (see K 548–9). Husserl prefers to speak of the fusion of nature and culture as the 'culture-things-surrounding world' (*Die Kultur-Sachen-Umwelt*, K 501), emphasizing that the human world encounters both cultural and natural objects in an interwoven unity.

That Husserl is interested in the existential structures of human culture is evident at the beginning of *Crisis* § 2, where he speaks of human beings 'in their spiritual existence' and of the 'shapes of the spiritual world' (C 7; K 4). In another text associated with the investigations that became the *Crisis*, albeit written prior to 1930, Husserl raises the question of the methodology of the natural sciences and asks whether there can be such a methodology, and also whether there can be one for the human sciences and for history: 'Is there a method for encompassing the realm of the "spirit", of history, in all its essential possibilities, so that one can arrive at "exact" truths through exact concepts for this realm' (C 322n.; K 301n.).

As we saw in Chapter 4, Husserl wants nothing less than a 'science of spirit' (*Geisteswissenschaft*), what he calls, in the 'Vienna Lecture', 'an objective science of the spirit' (C 297; K 345). But such an 'objective' science has to recognize that spirit itself is constituted by interwoven subjective and intersubjective intentionalities. Thus, for instance, in the same lecture Husserl speaks of the 'spirituality' (*Geistigkeit*) of animals as well as humans, meaning thereby something like the cultural world and behaviour of animals thought of as a complex, unified whole (see C 271; K 316).

In emphasizing the importance of history, Husserl frequently contrasts groups who live historically and have a 'living historicity' (Hua XXVII 187) with those who lack history or are 'history-less' (*geschicht-los*; see his letter to Lévy-Bruhl).[10] In a supplementary text to the *Crisis* (Supplement XXVI, K 502–3, not translated in Carr), Husserl

---

[10] See 'Edmund Husserl's Letter to Lucien Lévy-Bruhl, 11 March 1935', trans. Dermot Moran and Lukas Steinache, *New Yearbook for Phenomenology and Phenomenological Philosophy* Vol. 8 (2008), 352.

refs to the different 'levels of historicity', and in an associated text on the naiveté of science (Hua xxix No. 3) from the autumn of 1934, he reflects on the levels of historicity and the manner in which human beings live in history with a sense of past, present and future. Different histories relate to their past in fundamentally different ways. At the lowest level of this historicity is the stagnant world of the primitive which 'lacks history' (Hua xxix 39) and is immersed in a mythical cosmology: 'The first surrounding world is the in-between-realm between earth and heaven' (Hua xxix 38). Different national groupings have their distinct myths of their place on earth and locate themselves relative to what is above and below. Each myth furthermore conceives its people in relation to what is for them earth *as a whole*. Hence, there is already a kind of intrinsic and shared *universality* (Hua xxix 44) in mythic story-telling.

The mythical outlook, moreover, exhibits a natural 'animism' (Hua xxix 4, 38) whereby nature itself is experienced as a living person. Physical things in nature are not experienced as mere objects: they are thought to participate in life. The dead, for instance, are considered to continue to inhabit the world (Husserl is echoing similar claims to be found in Lévy-Bruhl). Thus, in a 1934 fragment entitled 'Human Life in Historicity' associated with the *Crisis*, Husserl had written:

The original animism. Man lives his spiritual life not in a spiritless world, in a world [understood] as matter, but rather as a spirit among spirits, among human and super-human, and this world-totality [*Weltall*] is, for him, the all of existing living, in the way of spirit, of the I-being, of the I-living among others as I-subjects, life in the form of a universal I-community [*Ich-Gemeinschaft*]. (Hua xxix 3, my translation).

The key point – and Husserl emphasizes this in his 'Vienna Lecture' – is that myth offers a comprehensive account of the world as a whole. It is a way of envisaging the *universal world*, albeit construed in terms specific to that people. It possesses universality but has not conceived of the infinite tasks that would set it on the pathway to genuine theoretical science.

There are lower and higher groupings, less complex and more complex social forms, from small family groupings to multinational civilizations. Humans live in families, groups, communities, nations and even certain supra-national unities (cf. 'Vienna Lecture'). Strictly speaking, furthermore, Husserl writes, there are no 'first' humans (Hua XXIX 37); rather, families give rise to families, generations to generations. Nations live in a 'homeland' (*Heimat*, Hua XXIX 9) or 'home-world' (*Heimwelt*),[11] or 'near-world' (*Nahwelt*, K 303), that is familiar to them; each group has its own specific sense of what is familiar and what is unfamiliar or foreign. Each nation has its opposing nation (Hua XXIX 38–9, 41) and so on.

Husserl's concern with the constitution of the social, public sphere out of the intentional acts of individuals and social groupings is made clear in his famous 1935 letter to the French anthropologist Lucien Lévy-Bruhl, written when he was preparing his forthcoming Vienna lectures. In this letter, Husserl speaks of the need for a new kind of social-scientific anthropology which treats of persons on the personal level, understanding their forms of interaction as sense-giving and evaluative.[12]

We now have a clearer insight into the kind of communal psychology which Husserl sought to develop. It is a psychology or anthropology that recognizes persons *as persons*. Let us now examine Husserl's concept of personhood more closely.

PERSONS AND THE PERSONALISTIC ATTITUDE

The concept of the person is the key concept for Husserl's thoughts on community, on the process of communalization, and on the meaning of history. As Husserl proclaims in the *Crisis*: 'A particularly privileged position in the surrounding world is occupied by its persons' (C 328; K 307). From *Ideas* II on, Husserl frequently speaks about the specifically personal approach adopted by humans, what he calls the 'personalistic attitude' (*die personalistische Einstellung*, *Ideas* II § 49), according to which subjects recognize each other as subjects interested in reasoning and valuing. Persons relate to one another in complex intentional ways, according to their *motivations*,

---

[11] Husserl frequently uses the term 'homeworld' (*Heimwelt*, e.g. K 303 and Hua XXXIX 335] to express the manner the world always appears within a familiar context (the world as *die normale Lebenswelt*, Hua XV 210). The world is constituted according to normality and abnormality (Hua XXXIX 385–91) and unfolds necessarily within relations of proximity and remoteness.

[12] See 'Edmund Husserl's Letter to Lucien Lévy-Bruhl, 11 March 1935', p. 350.

sedimented traditions, values, beliefs and desires, and so on. These cannot be accounted for in the natural scientific approach. According to Husserl, moreover, this personal attitude is supported by the underlying sense of a shared, common world in which we act and suffer together: 'We could not be persons for others if there were not over against us a common surrounding world. The one is constituted together with the other' (*Ideas* II, p. 387; Hua IV 377).

For Husserl, being a person is a relational concept. He – following Kant – singles out the way humans use personal pronouns: saying 'I' and 'We'. To be an 'I' is always to be an 'I' over against a 'you', a 'he', a 'she'. An 'I' recognizes others as also being 'I's in their own right (as being literally alter egos).[13] Husserl, for instance, speaks of the 'I–you synthesis' (*Ich–Du Synthesis*, C 172; K 175) and the even more complicated 'we–synthesis' (*Wir–Synthesis*, ibid.), according to which we feel a common bond of fellowship with others. He speaks of people interacting in a personal, communal world, both acting on it and being affected by it, e.g.:

> What the person does and suffers, what happens within him, how he stands in relation to his surrounding world, what angers him, what depresses him, what makes him cheerful or upset – these are questions relating to persons; and so are questions of a similar sort relating to communities of every level: marriages, friendships, clubs, civic communities, communities of peoples, etc. (C 322; K 301)

Husserl's characterization of persons stresses not just the traditionally ascribed characteristics of freedom and rationality, but also their intentionality, self-consciousness, autonomy, emotions, rationality, sense of values, and ability to enter into normative social and moral relations. But most of all he stresses their capacity to weave meanings that are socially recognized. The recognition of and from others is crucial to personhood. Human life is lived in the plural such that even the Cartesian *cogito* needs to be reframed as a communal 'we think', *nos cogitamus* (Hua VIII 316).[14]

Husserl has also inherited from the school of Brentano and Meinong (1853–1920) the notion of 'personalities of a higher order'

---

[13] In the background is Hermann Cohen (1842–1918), who – prior to Martin Buber (1878–1965) – spoke of the importance of the 'I–thou relation' (*Ich–Du Beziehung*).

[14] See David Carr, 'Cogitamus Ergo Sumus: The Intentionality of the First-Person Plural', in Carr, *Interpreting Husserl* (Dordrecht: Kluwer, 1987), pp. 281–96.

(*Personalitäten höherer Ordnung, Crisis* § 55 – see also Hua XIV 183), i.e. social groups or institutions which act like persons writ large, a conception of social groups as old as Plato's *Republic*. According to this notion, collective identities are formed on the analogy of individual persons.[15] A social collectivity is a plurality that can also act as a unity (see Hua XIV 201). A club can announce 'we are joining the national league', thereby expressing the collective wish.

Persons grow and develop. They have a shared sense of a common world formed by *tradition* (even if that tradition consists entirely of erroneous beliefs, as Husserl remarks, C 326; K 305). A people lives in a world of tradition, a 'traditional world'. In his *Intersubjectivity* volumes Husserl declares in a note written around 1921–1922: 'Life in prejudgement, life in tradition. In the widest sense, it belongs to every ego-life [*Ichleben*] to be life in tradition' (Hua XIV 230, my translation).

Similarly, Husserl writes in *Crisis* Supplement XXIV (accompanying Section 73):

Each human being as a person stands in his or her generative interconnectivities [*generativen Zusammenhängen*], which, understood in a personal, spiritual manner, stand in the unity of a historicity; this is not just a sequence of past factualities [*Tatsachlichkeiten*], but it is implicated in each present, in its factuality, as a hidden spiritual acquisition, as the past, which has formed that specific person, and as such is intentionally implicated in him as his formation or upbringing [*Bildung*]. (K 488, my translation)

We have definite perceptual experiences of a common, shared world where our experiences are harmoniously confirmed by others. We have a sense of a shared past with others of our community or family. There is a particular manner in which a group relates to its past, preserves a memory of past achievements, grievances and so on. In the *Crisis*, Husserl begins his 'backward reflection' (*Rückbesinnung*, C 48; K 48; see also C 50; K 50 and C 72; K 73, etc.) from the conception of history as a Heraclitean stream of constant change, but he soon points out that the experience of the social and historical *world* is not the same as the experience of *nature* as given in the natural-scientific

---

[15] The concept of personalities of a higher order, already found in Hegel and later in Scheler, is discussed at greater length in Husserl's ethical writings; see James G. Hart, *The Person and the Common Life: Studies in Husserlian Social Ethics*, Phaenomenologica 126 (Dordrecht: Kluwer, 1992), pp. 255–81.

attitude. The world as understood from the personalistic attitude, or the attitude of engaged practical living, is a world of personal and social *interests* and involvements. What stands out is not *nature* in the natural-scientific sense, but rather things that matter to us, values, actions, feelings, motivations. The human being experiences himself or herself as acting and suffering in a world which is through and through a personal world, absolutely not the world of objective science.

Husserl speaks of an 'intersubjective harmony of validity' (*die intersubjective Einstimmigkeit der Geltung*, C 163; K 166). Indeed, as Husserl will insist, the very idea of *objectivity* as such, of a common objective world – including, and perhaps most especially, scientific objectivity – is not a given brute fact of experience but a very unique and particular achievement of subjects cooperating together. Naïve experience does not even raise the issue of objectivity. It simply lives in its experiences with an acceptance character (*Urglaube*). At the experiential and perceptual level, the sense of the objectivity of a physical object, for instance – its having a kind of 'being in itself' independent of us – is precisely based on the idea that there are other possible views of the object, ways that others have of perceiving the object, which I can envisage and understand even if I do not currently experience the object in this way. In the modern mathematical sciences, this 'objectivity' is established by results that can be replicated by others performing similar experiments, by peer review and so on, all activities that involve reference to others and forms of communal agreement and co-confirmability.

A community consciousness also engenders the sense of belonging to the *one, shared world* (and Husserl here recognizes the important contribution of a shared *language*). Of course, Husserl recognizes that in the course of our collective experience, there are also situations where our perceptual viewpoints are challenged or even negated by others; there can be 'disharmonies' or 'discrepancies' (*Uneinstimmigkeiten*). He thinks these extraordinary correlations between subjects' modes of experiencing the world and the unified open world as experienced have never before been explored (*Crisis* § 48), yet they form the basis for the very sense of the concept of 'world'. This 'correlation', furthermore, between our experiences and the world was a motive for classical scepticism but was never investigated in its own right.

Phenomenology, then, has a duty to enquire into the constitution of the natural and the intersubjective world.

To summarize, human life in the natural attitude is never primarily the singular life of the individual *cogito*, but rather a life lived in community, by persons who engage in personal relations with one another, who are members of families and communities across generations. This particular way of being immersed in history already makes us historical beings (see *Ideas* ii, Supplement XIV, p. 387; Hua iv 377) who interpret one another according to certain *intuitive* understandings and motivations.

TELEOLOGY AND GOAL-DIRECTED LIFE

As we have seen, Husserl's reflections on history begin from the fact that we, as temporal beings, live lives that are meaningful because of our communal engagement with others. Husserl also (in this respect very close to Aristotle) has a sense of our lives as being directed towards 'goals' (*Zwecke*) – either ones we explicitly set ourselves (as our 'life-vocation', *Lebensberuf*) or ones we simply drift into and accept unquestioningly (see C 379; K 459). These goals are determined by our horizon of interests, and the life-world overall encompasses and enables these purposive structures that belong to our active lives (C 382; K 462). The manner in which individuals and communities are oriented towards goals inevitably raises the question of the overall teleology of societies and of history in general. All communities come together and are unified around particular sets of values and purposes. To be human is to live under the 'ought' and is also to live purposively. As Husserl writes: '"that being human is teleological being and an ought to be" [*das Menschsein ein Teleologischsein und Sein-sollen ist*] and that this teleology holds sway in each and every activity and project of an ego' (C 341; K 275–6).

This teleology, moreover, has to become visible through a kind of 'self-understanding' that is achieved only in and through philosophy itself. There is no substitute for philosophy for making visible a culture's values and teleology; other life-forms do not give the same degree of self-understanding – 'self-understanding according to a priori principles' (C 341; K 276).

Frequently in the *Crisis* (specifically §§ 15, 16, 26, § 29 and 56), Husserl declares history – and more particularly the history of philosophy – to be guided by purposiveness or what he calls '*teleology*'. Thus, he speaks of a 'hidden teleology' in history and writes: 'Our task is to make comprehensible the teleology in the historical becoming [*in dem geschichtlichen Werden*] of philosophy, especially modern philosophy, and at the same time to achieve clarity about ourselves, who are the bearers [*Träger*] of this teleology, who take part in carrying it out through our personal attentions' (C 70; K 71).

According to Aristotle, both living and non-living things have particular ends (states) towards which they are directed, e.g. it belongs to the nature of water and earth to seek a lower place. Living beings, especially, consciously strive towards their ends, e.g. humans strive towards happiness (for Aristotle). It is one of the hallmarks of modern natural science, since Galileo and Descartes, that it has abandoned teleological explanations of natural events (in terms of 'ends' or 'final causes') and focuses exclusively on efficient or mechanical causation. Husserl, however, is not concerned with applying teleological explanations to nature but primarily uses the term 'teleology' to refer to the specific networks of ends which motivate human life and culture. Indeed, the core concept of intentionality as directedness has an inbuilt teleological character, for Husserl, since empty intentions necessarily aim at fulfilment.

Husserl believes that to regard history as a mere arbitrary domain of facticity is itself a symptom of modernity's loss of faith in rationality. At the outset of the *Crisis* he states that he will not accept that 'the shapes of the spiritual world' merely form and dissolve 'like fleeting waves' (C 7; K 4). One cannot live genuinely in a world where progress and disappointment are taken as mere arbitrary happenings. Husserl maintains that 'the whole historical process has a remarkable form, one which becomes visible only through an interpretation of its hidden, innermost motivation' (C 11; K 9). The exemplary history which Husserl will examine – as did Hegel – is the history of philosophy itself. It is not uniform progress. Indeed, it will be seen from within as a kind of continuous struggle between reason and unreason (C 13; K 11). History has a *telos* or goal. There must be '"meaning" or reason in history' (C 9; K 7).

In the *Crisis*, Husserl claims that what he calls 'European humanity', i.e. Western scientific culture founded on the ancient Greek revolution, has itself made a revolutionary transformation from an enclosed particular life to adopting a goal of universal rationality as its guiding ideal. There is, undoubtedly, Husserl insists, a *telos* which is 'inborn in European humanity at the birth of Greek philosophy' (C 15; K 13); it is the idea of people seeking to live by philosophical reason, and hence break with myth and tradition. Husserl raises the question whether this *telos* is illusory or merely an accidental accomplishment, one among many in the history of civilizations, or whether it is, as he himself clearly believes, 'the first breakthrough [*Durchbruch*] to what is essential to humanity as such, its *entelechy*' (C 15; K 13).

According to Husserl, moreover – and this has proved controversial – only Europe has a *teleology* in the strict sense, that is, a driving force aiming at a universal goal; in this case, the driving force is towards the theoretical life (see C 278; K 323 – and Husserl had already articulated this in his Prague Treatise of 1934; see Hua XXVII 207). This European absolute idea is one of *theoria*, the adoption of the purely theoretical attitude, breaking with its own cultural particularity and absorption in itself. This breakthrough involves the discovery of ideality and 'the idealizing accomplishment' (*die idealisierende Leistung*, C 346; K 359), the commitment to evidence and justification, the recognition of the universality of reason, and the commitment to the idea of infinite enquiry and 'infinite tasks' (albeit a concept not clearly specified by Husserl). As Husserl puts it, a new *telos* was opened up for all of humanity by the ancient Greeks: 'that of humanity which seeks to exist, and is only possible through philosophical reason, moving endlessly from latent to manifest reason and forever seeking its own norms through this, its truth and genuine human nature' (C 15; K 13). Europe in the spiritual sense is, for Husserl, essentially an 'international' and unified project (Hua XXVII 207).[16]

In contrast to this universal and breakthrough spiritual idea which drives 'European' scientific-philosophical culture, other world civilizations ('supernations') such as India and China represent what

---

[16] Husserl always emphasizes that it is its commitment to *philosophy* as a theoretical knowledge of the world (see Hua XXVII 208) that makes Europe a spiritual form open to infinite tasks.

Husserl calls 'empirical types', that is, loosely defined collectivities that lack a defined essence.[17] What can this mean? According to Husserl, what sets the European ideal of humanity apart is precisely its claim to *universality* and indeed a specific directedness towards *infinite* enquiry and infinite realization of the task of gaining knowledge (see *Crisis* § 15 and Hua XXIX 390). Furthermore, the teleology of Western humanity is expressed by and is precisely incarnated in the practice of philosophy itself as it emerged with the Greek enlightenment, and it has continued ever since.

Husserl maintains that the Indian and Chinese civilizations do exhibit a *universal* interest in the sense they have produced all-embracing, mythopoeic cosmologies, but they have done so from the standpoint of purely *practical* interests and have failed to develop a fully transcendent conception of universal reason and purely theoretical knowledge. Husserl is emphatic: 'But only in the Greeks do we have a universal ("cosmological") life-interest in the essentially new form of a purely "theoretical" attitude, and this as a communal form in which this interest works itself out for internal reasons, being the corresponding, essentially new (community) of philosophers, of scientists (mathematicians, astronomers, etc.)' (C 280; K 326). Husserl maintains that the Greeks broke through to a new form of life – the form of life of *theoria*, dominated by what Husserl calls 'the theoretical attitude' (see C 36; K 35). Only the Greeks made philosophy into a whole form of life, one breaking through mere finite world-views. The new theoretical attitude operates at a remove from the concerns of practical life. The theoretical attitude is precisely the attitude of detached contemplation, of the 'disinterested' or 'non-participating' spectator about which Husserl talks a great deal in his mature works. According to the 'Vienna Lecture' (and indeed the Prague lectures of 1935), the theoretical attitude is characterized by

---

[17] According to Husserl, perceptual experience, although primarily directed at individual entities, also identifies groups of individuals according to certain loose generalizations or 'types' based on similarity. In a 1925 letter to Landgrebe, Husserl says he is interested in the idea of 'type' as found in Dilthey and that of ideal type in Weber (*Briefwechsel* IV 247). In *Ideas* II § 60, Husserl claims personal life manifests a *typicality*. There is what is typical for human beings as such, but also what is typical for this individual. In EU (§§ 80–5), Husserl explains how empirical generalities (universals linked to individual objects) are based on types pre-constituted in passivity: 'The factual world of experience is experienced as a typified world' (EU § 83).

wonder or amazement at the world. The theoretical attitude does not merely live through epistemic states of believing and judging, but rather involves self-conscious attentiveness to these acts as they are being carried out. The theoretical attitude necessarily involves a shift of attention or focus away from practical engagements. It involves applying an *epochē* to all practical interests and focusing purely on the demand for truth, and in this way, Husserl believes, it prepares human subjects for the life of 'self-responsibility' (C 283; K 329). The theoretical attitude opens up a world of infinite tasks and unites humans together in the quest for rational 'self-responsibility' (*Selbstverantwortung*, C 197; K 200 and C 283; K 329). For Husserl, in the 'Vienna Lecture', philosophical life has ushered into history a new kind of praxis, 'that of the universal critique of all life and of all life-goals' (C 283; K 329). Henceforth, human life has to be lived as an absolutely self-critical constant re-evaluation of all its aims and achievements.

HISTORY IN RELATION TO REASON

The concept of history, Husserl insists, must be connected to the concept of 'reason' and the progress of universal instantiation of the ideals of a rational life. Husserl, following Kant, is deeply interested in understanding the meaning of reason as a normative ideal. Reason plays an important role in *Ideas* I (see 'Phenomenology of Reason', *Ideas* I §§ 136–45). Reason, on Husserl's account, has a number of levels (theoretical, axiological, practical). There is, furthermore, a dynamic element to reason. It is seeking to realize itself, come to self-actualization and also self-clarity, as Husserl writes:

> Thus philosophy is nothing other than (rationalism) through and through, but it is rationalism differentiated within itself according to the different stages of the movement of intention and fulfilment; it is *ratio in the constant movement of self-elucidation* [*Selbsterhellung*] begun with the first breakthrough [*Einbruch*] of philosophy into mankind, whose innate reason was previously in a state of concealment [*Verschlossenheit*], of nocturnal obscurity. (C 338; K 273)

Human culture is seen by Husserl as sustained by a dynamic tendency towards rationalization. Husserl's overall sense – here much stronger than Heidegger's – is that history exhibits purposiveness and inner rationality. Heidegger tends to characterize the history of a people in terms of something like 'fate' and 'destiny' which has either to be endured or embraced by a kind of deliberate decision. Husserl, on the other hand, seems to regard historical development as being driven by an impulse towards ever-inclusive rationality. The teleology of Western philosophy is the life of reason: 'Philosophy, science in all its forms, is rational – that is a tautology' (C 339; K 274).

Husserl invokes the image of the 'dawn' (*Bild des Morgenrots*) characterizing the Greek spirit. In the *Crisis*, he repeatedly invokes the ancient conception of philosophy as the systematic knowledge of everything. In *Crisis* § 8, for instance, he speaks of the 'idea of philosophy in general' as 'the science of the universe, of all that is' (C 23; K 20).[18] According to Husserl, the Greeks found a way to think of 'the All' or the universe as a *whole* united under specific principles. This 'breakthrough' challenged mythological conceptions of the world that were primarily concerned to provide an intelligible context for practical action but never challenged the finite limits of their world-conception and paved the way for the sciences through the conception of the world as infinite and open to infinite enquiry.[19] Husserl, then, sees the Greek scientific breakthrough to the universal as setting an entirely new 'second' level of human 'historicity' above the level of primitive, practical life (see K 557).

The Greeks had a particular theoretical approach in their discovery of 'the totality of what is' that led them to pay peculiar attention to the nature of humankind. Husserl speaks of the correlative 'discovery' (*Entdeckung*) of 'long-familiar man' (*des altbekannten Menschen*) as the 'subject of the world' (C 339; K 273). Modern humanity has a singular history that has brought it to its present point, but that history must be meaningful; there must be identifiable breakthroughs and transformations of sense that can be seen leading up to the present situation. There is even the possibility of a particular historical

---

[18] Elsewhere Husserl characterizes philosophy as 'a universal knowledge of what is' (C 29; K 26) and 'a scientific knowledge of the world' (C 31; K 29).

[19] The idea that Greek philosophy brought about the decisive shift from mythos to logos was a common theme among German classical philosophers of the period. See, for instance, Wilhelm Nestle, *Vom Mythos zum Logos: Die Selbstentfaltung des griechischen Denkens von Homer bis auf die Sophistik und Sokrates* (From Myth to Logos: The Self-Development of Greek Thought from Homer to the Sophists and Socrates) (Stuttgart: Kröner, 1940).

tradition (historicity) breaking out of its particularity and establishing a 'new humanity' (K 503).

From its origin in Greece, philosophy has had a driving aim or *telos*, its 'sense of a goal' or 'end' (*Zwecksinn*, C 394; K 512, cf. Hua XXIX 379). Philosophy, moreover, has an underlying unity of sense, apart from its obvious competing systems. There is a 'concealed unity of intentional interiority' (*verborgene Einheit intentionaler Innerlichkeit*) in philosophy, as Husserl makes clear in his long discussion of 'Teleology in the History of Philosophy' (Hua XXIX 362–420) written in 1936–7. In the modern period, Descartes was involved in the transformation and 'forming anew of the idea of philosophy' (*Neuformung der Idee der Philosophie*, Hua XXIX 397) and continued philosophy's mission in a radical way (*Crisis* § 56). But underneath the obvious diversity and plurality of philosophical ideas and methods, there is the unity of its trajectory towards its 'sense of purpose' (*Zwecksinn*, C 191; K 194).

History has a *teleology* because the projects that humans have set themselves transcend their immediate practical purposes. The Greeks, for instance, set themselves a particular task in terms of formulating systematic knowledge of the world that went beyond practical interests. These 'goals' bind people together for generations (*Crisis* § 15). Philosophers are charged with the task of continuing these reflections and making them transparent and so bringing them into 'the living present' (*lebendige Gegenwart*, C 15; K 73), a constant and very rich Husserlian theme.

THE *CRISIS* AS INTENTIONAL HISTORY

We have now come to appreciate something of the depth of Husserl's critical appropriation of the concept of history. The term 'intentional history' has frequently been used to describe Husserl's approach, although this phrase itself does not appear in the *Crisis*. Indeed, the term 'intentional-historical' was introduced by Eugen Fink in the subtitle he added to 'The Origin of Geometry'.[20] But what does 'intentional history' mean?

---

[20] See C 353n.1. This subtitle is missing from the text in Carr's translation.

As we saw, Husserl, in his 1936 Preface to the two parts of the *Crisis* published in *Philosophia*, says that he is carrying out a 'teleological historical reflection' (C 3; K xiv n.3) concerning the 'origins of our critical, scientific and philosophical situation'; a kind of intellectual 'reconstruction' or 'backwards questioning' (*Rückfragen*) of the history of Western culture (and philosophy) in order to produce an 'eidetic history' and identify its hidden goal (*telos*) and its 'hidden, innermost motivation' (C 11; K 9). Husserl uses the phrase 'historical reflection' (*historische Besinnung*, see C 17; K 16; see also C 392; K 510) many times to characterize the kind of transcendental philosophical reflection which is being carried out in the *Crisis* and which he believes is essentially different from other kinds of reflection within the sciences. For the first time, questions of origin, genesis and inner essence are coming to the fore. For Husserl, the 'hidden unity of intentional inwardness' (*Innerlichkeit*) makes possible the 'unity of history' (C 73; K 74), which has to be consciously embraced as 'our history' (C 71; K 72). On the other hand, this critical situation points to the necessity of carrying out a 'transcendental-phenomenological transformation [*Umwendung*] of philosophy' itself (see K xiv n.3). Philosophy has an essence and a teleology, but human willed resolve is necessary to take up this essence and realize it.

Husserl's critical reflection on the inner essence of historical becoming, then, is clearly not historical investigation or philosophical analysis in the usual sense, as indeed Husserl himself reminds us several times (see *Crisis* § 15). Thus, Husserl writes in his 'The Origin of Geometry' text: 'our investigations are historical in an unusual sense, namely, in virtue of a thematic direction which opens up depth-problems quite unknown to ordinary history, problems which in their own way [however] are undoubtedly historical problems' (C 354; K 365). He goes on to say that he is not interested in the 'philological problem' of who were the actual first initiators of geometry. His interest, rather, is in the 'original sense' which geometry acquired millennia ago and still preserves today. He is interested, then, in the origination and preservation of 'sense' (*Sinn*) or 'meaning' – how a certain form of idealization came to be identified and developed – one whose application to nature only came about in the age of Galileo. This sense has to be uncovered by a 'regressive enquiry' (*Rückfrage*, C 354; K 366). Husserl goes on to claim: 'Making geometry self-evident, then, whether one is clear about this or not, is the disclosure of its historical tradition … Carried out systematically, such self-evidences result in nothing other and nothing less than the universal a priori of history with all its highly abundant component elements' (C 371; K 380). To show how an essential form originates and to trace its intellectual lineage and transformation – this is precisely the disclosure of the working-out of history, its *Wirkungsgeschichte* (history of effects), as Gadamer will later call it. In the *Crisis*, a fundamentally new dimension has been added to phenomenology: a genetic dimension.

HUSSERL AND HEIDEGGER ON HUMAN HISTORICALITY

Husserl, in fundamental agreement with Heidegger and Dilthey, maintains that human beings are 'historical beings' through and through. To exist is to live temporally and generationally, and this demands being *historical*, to be a being whose self-meaning and self-understanding are intimately entwined with the evolution of one's personal and communal cultural life involving intentional inter-action with generations before and, indeed, to come. Moreover, for Husserl as for Heidegger, it is simply a brute contingent fact that one is inserted into history in this specific time and place, in this body, in this culture, speaking this language, holding this set of beliefs and so on. In this regard, Heidegger speaks of 'thrownness' (*Geworfenheit*, SZ § 38, p. 223; 178) and Husserl of the irrational 'fact' (*Faktum*) of our existence and, more generally, borrowing a word from the Neo-Kantians, of our 'facticity'. For Husserl, it is the task of transcendental philosophy, under the *epochē* to come to terms with the unavoidable facticity of human subjective living and to grasp its essential form (see C 178; K 181–2).

Heidegger's analytic of Dasein identifies a priori structures which enable human existence as such. One existential structure is that human beings are essentially temporal and also have 'historicity'. According to Heidegger in *Being and Time* § 72, human existence has a stretched-out connectedness between birth and death. The manner in which Dasein 'is stretched along and stretches itself along, we call its 'historizing' (*das Geschehen des Daseins*, SZ, § 72, p. 427; 375). Heidegger goes on to say: 'To lay bare the structure of historizing, and the existential-temporal conditions of its possibility, signifies that one has achieved an ontological understanding of historicality [*Geschichtlichkeit*]' (SZ, § 72, p. 427; 375). Heidegger speaks of the 'conditions for the possibility' of human existence's being historical, of gaining an ontological understanding of historicity. Heidegger also insists his enquiry has got nothing to do with history in the usual sense, and he too is interested in the 'essence of history' (SZ § 73, p. 429; 378). According to Heidegger, what is primarily historical is Dasein, and other entities (such as objects in a museum) are historical because they once belonged to a world constituted by Dasein (a world that is no longer). Heidegger also emphasizes the role of *repetition* (*Wiederholung*) in historical living: 'the authentic repetition of a possibility of existence' (SZ § 74, p. 437; 385). 'By repetition, Dasein first has its own history made manifest' (SZ § 74, p. 438; 386). But the key point for Heidegger is that repetition comes out of a decision, and this decision is being made with regard to the future. Dasein decisively takes over its history with an eye to the future or allows itself to be carried along. History, for Heidegger, is a project; it has its roots essentially in the future (SZ, § 74, p. 438; 386). For Heidegger, the phenomenon of the connectedness of life (as inadequately recognized by Dilthey) can be experienced authentically or inauthentically. Authentic existence has really to be understood as brought about by a kind of resoluteness, by what he calls 'a loyalty of existence to its self' (SZ § 75, p. 443; 391). Inauthentic experience of life's connectedness is oblivious to the moment of history and as such 'seeks the modern'.

Heidegger's account of history in *Being and Time* has many points in common with Husserl. Husserl too is concerned about moments of origin, acts of institution and their *repetition*. He is of course primarily concerned with the emergence of scientific idealities (such as the Pythagorean Theorem) and how they are handed down as 'the same' across repeated acts of scientific cognizing. Husserl emphasizes more than Heidegger the need for habituality and the sedimentation of meanings so that they become accepted 'common-sense'. He also reflects on the different stances we take towards tradition. In some senses we are entirely blind to it. We use roads that someone else built some time before us. We may be uninterested in the principles involved in establishing the text when we read Shakespeare. We have our own 'folk' sense of what happened before us. We have our more or less informed, more or less prejudiced partial sense of our family history, what our fathers did in the war and so on. This is somewhat parallel to the analysis of *das Man*, the anonymous 'one' or 'they self' discussed by Heidegger (see SZ § 75). For Heidegger, equipment, books and so on have their fates, institutions have histories, and even nature is historical in the sense that a landscape can be the site of a battle and so on. Husserl too speaks of the manner in which things are embedded in the horizon of history and tradition.

Husserl and Heidegger both emphasize the need to come to terms with the responsibility of taking up the task of history, but Heidegger makes this into a uniquely personal obligation, part of one's individual authenticity, whereas Husserl places this burden primarily on the philosopher as the mediator of the meaning of history and as its critical guardian.

GENESIS, UNIVERSAL HISTORY AND WORLD HISTORY

Husserl's view is that every spiritual accomplishment has an 'origin' (*Ursprung*) or 'genesis' (*Genesis*) (Hua XXIX 57) and needs a story of origin, an 'archaeology'. Furthermore, every effort at understanding is a kind of setting something into context. *Tradition* (discussed in 'The Origin of Geometry') has exactly this function. Earlier in the *Crisis*, Husserl assumes the essential and intrinsic rationality of history. Indeed, he believes we abandon reason itself if we abjure the notion of 'reason in history'. As we have seen, Husserl believes history must be understood as a kind of 'total unity' (*Gesamteinheit*, C 71; K 72), which is a 'unity of motivation' (understanding actions through reasons rather than causes). It has a kind of 'spiritual unity' because of the 'task' it is attempting to carry out. Philosophy has been assigned a task by history, and philosophers, as the 'functionaries of humankind' (C 71; K 72), have to carry out this task, make it vital again and rediscover its 'concealed historical meaning' (C 71; K 73). This involves the 're-establishment' (*Nachstiftung*) of the original 'primal establishment' (*Urstiftung*) of Greek philosophy (C 71; K 72). In Husserl's language, every original primal establishing has a state which stands as its *Endstiftung*, final establishment (C 72; K 73), that belongs to it 'essentially' (*wesensmässig*).

Husserl seems to think it is possible not just to find the origins and goals of individual cultures, but of humanity as a whole. In 'The Origin of Geometry' text, Husserl speaks of 'universal history' (C 353; K 365) in relation to his enquiries into 'the deepest problems of meaning' (ibid.).[21] In this text, which we have already examined in Chapter 3, Husserl takes the history of geometry to have 'exemplary significance' for the history of science and indeed for the history of European culture in general. He is interested in terms of the manner in which texts are interpreted and concepts are passed along by tradition. Moreover, these traditions take on different meanings as we contextualize them relative to our current concerns. For Husserl, as a philosopher one is philosophizing in one's own time, with one's own inherited stock of concepts and common opinions, with the scientific outlook of one's own day (K 492). Each philosopher's present is finite but stands in the context of an infinite horizon (K 494). How an infinite science is possible based on finite experiences is one of the key problems, Husserl acknowledges (K 499).

In this discussion of tradition, Husserl speaks both of 'universal history' and the idea of a 'universal a priori of history'. Universal history – as in Herder (1744–1803) and Kant – suggests the idea that there is a goal, at least as an ideal, of rational progress in the history of humanity. What could such an a priori mean? For Husserl, the universal a priori of history means the set of universal and necessary structures and procedures that make history as a unified meaning possible. These structures are related to human temporal existence. As Husserl writes in a *Crisis* supplementary text probably from 1936:

The a priori is related to the being of mankind and the surrounding world that is valid for it in experience, thinking and acting. But the a priori is something ideal and general, which on the one hand refers to men themselves as objects and on the other hand is a structure within men who form it. (C 349; K 362)

This captures very well the double-sidedness of the a priori for Husserl. The a priori specifies formal conditions that make meaningful experience possible, but on the other hand those very a priori

[21] On 'universal history', see Immanuel Kant, *Idea for a Universal History from a Cosmopolitan Point of View* (1784), trans. Lewis White Beck, in *Kant: On History* (Indianapolis: The Bobbs-Merrill Co., 1963).

forms have their source in transcendental subjectivity. Heidegger himself praised Husserl for giving a new sense to the a priori (understood as the eidetic), but in his late work he also reconnects it with subjectivity in its temporal flow. Husserl – and he will be followed here by Merleau-Ponty – is moving towards historizing the a priori. The meaningfulness of the historical world is due to the actions of human subjects who are necessarily incarnated in the world and have their own way of projecting meaning into the future and taking up the remembered past. We shall discuss this further in Chapter 7.

Besides 'universal history' Husserl also regularly invokes the idea of 'world history' – a concept familiar from Hegel.[22] In *Being and Time*, also, Heidegger had specifically defined 'world-history' where he speaks of it as the 'historizing of the world in its essential existent unity with Dasein' (SZ § 75, p. 440; 389). He stresses that history is not the product of a 'worldless subject' but that 'Dasein's historicality is essentially the historicality of the world'. At the end of the *Crisis*, Husserl too speaks of the 'history of the world' or 'world history' (*Weltgeschichte, Welthistorie*) as an infinite idea which guides reflections on history generally:[23]

World-history [*Weltgeschichte*] – its temporal concrete being as streaming present with its past and future – can be understood as the history of the world, [which is] valid for us, from out of myself, [the history] of our world perspective in its subjective temporality, in which our worldviews appear according to their content and validity for us. *The history of the world itself, in itself, that is world-history in the sense of an infinite Idea*: the idea of [world-history] which is similarly projected into the infinite, continuously thought of as correcting, across the infinity of factually valid worldviews. There belongs also to this the idea of an infinite historical past which could be corrected in all the past presents with respect to the totally determined present. What, however, does *future regarding to the infinite* mean? One has to earnestly face up to whether the thus supposed world in itself can have sense and what sense. (*Crisis*, Appendix XXV, K 501, my translation)

The idea of the history of the world is itself an infinite idea. Husserl believes that world-history offers a 'horizon of infinities' (C 390;

---

[22] See G. W. F. Hegel, *Lectures on the Philosophy of World History: Introduction*, trans. H. B. Nisbet (New York: Cambridge University Press, 1975).

[23] Husserl uses the term 'world history' (*Weltgeschichte, Welthistorie*) several times in the *Crisis*, e.g. C 66; K 67 and C 274; K 319.

K 509) which takes humans beyond their individual worldviews that limit them. All history, for Husserl, begins, from the constitution of the present as a shared present with others – a common present (*Mitgegenwart*, Hua XXIX 54). The constitution of world history requires projecting backwards a sense of a common past and, even more challenging, generating an ideal of an infinite future.

UNIVERSALITY AND EUROCENTRISM

Husserl's account, especially in his 'Vienna Lecture' and *Crisis* § 36 (as well as in Hua XXIX 386–92), of the Greek philosophical breakthrough to universal rationality has been criticized as 'Eurocentric'. Husserl speaks of the *universality* inherent in 'European' philosophical culture of the *logos* and contrasts it with other communal life-worlds, which are, in his view, merely 'empirical-anthropological' *types*, with their own peculiar 'historicities' and 'relativities'. Husserl often emphasizes that the most prominent feature of cultural plurality is precisely its relativity: 'relativity belongs to the normal course of life', he writes. Indeed, in this context, he regularly invokes the idea of the 'relativity of everything historical' (*die Relativität alles Historischen*, C 373; K 382).

In his research manuscripts of the 1920s and 1930s Husserl frequently discusses the complex relationships that exist between different cultures and traditions. Different cultures have their specific *historicities* (C 274; K 320; see also Hua XXIX 53). They follow different languages, norms, ways of life and so on. This is simply a matter of fact. In addition, there are a number of related texts, both those collected in the *Crisis* Supplementary Volume (Hua XXIX) and in the *Intersubjectivity* volumes (especially Hua XV), as well as in the recent volume on the life-world (Hua XXXIX), which discuss the empirical differences between peoples and also the layers and strata of social groups and nations, and even the idea of the larger international collectivity or 'supernations' or 'supranations' (*Übernationen*), such as 'Europe' or the League of Nations. Furthermore, there are, even as Husserl indicates in his 1935 letter to Lucien Lévy-Bruhl, cultures that are 'self-enclosed' (*abgeschlossene*) unities, knowing no history. The Papuan, for Husserl, can have no sense of history in any genuine sense.

According to Husserl, into this classical world of closed cultures, the ancient Greeks bring a new form of universality which leads them, through the grasp of *idealization* to *infinite* tasks, to break through the finite horizons of the environing world (*Umwelt*), which presents itself to them as a familiar or 'near-world' (*Nahwelt*, Hua XXVII 228), and to arrive at the highly refined concept of the 'true world' or the 'scientific world [which] is a purposeful structure [*Zweckgebilde*] extending to infinity' (C 382; K 461).

This claim to the uniqueness and inherent transcendent universality of European culture seems to strike a false note, given Husserl's overall efforts to renew the Enlightenment ideals of universal reason. However, Husserl is arguing essentially that the Greek self-critical philosophical culture, a reason that constantly seeks grounds, provides the only genuine form of self-critical universality that transcends all particular cultures and most especially its own.

CONCLUSION

Husserl's attempts to understand the a priori structures of human historizing parallel in many ways his efforts to understand psychology. He wants to uncover the very structural processes involved in the making of history itself, hence he generates his own technical terms such as 'living-with-one-another', 'communalization', 'generativity', 'historicity', 'habituation', 'sedimentation'. Life, in Husserl's language, is always life in tradition; there is a constant gathering-up and passing-on (as well as forgetting) of what went before. The paradigm for considering historical processes is, as it was for Hegel, the history of philosophy. For Husserl, present philosophy encompasses all previous philosophy within its horizon, in his 'living present' (*lebendige Gegenwart*, K 489).[24] The task of each philosopher is to renew and re-animate the tradition of philosophy, appropriating it and accommodating it into new horizons and new meanings. Husserl also emphasizes the responsibility of the philosopher charged with the task of creating the future through a re-animation of the past.

---

[24] The concept of the 'living present' is a central concept in Husserl's late work (C 71; K 73); see Klaus Held, *Lebendige Gegenwart: Die Frage nach der Seinsweise des transzendentalen Ich bei Edmund Husserl, entwickelt am Leitfaden der Zeitproblematik* (The Hague: Nijhoff, 1966).

Using the exemplary pattern of the history of philosophy enlivened and mediated by living philosophers, Husserl conceives of human history as a unified teleological structure, which is in a way supported by the living present, by contemporary actors in the social and communal world. History, as the movement of peoples in time, makes sense because it is appropriated and understood by the present generation who are the living agents in reconstituting the historical past as *their own time*.

Husserl's interpretation of the constitution of history and the manner in which humans are both formed by and are bearers of tradition anticipated and influenced Hans-Georg Gadamer's *Truth and Method*. Individual life is temporal, but temporality is also communal and historical. To live is to live historically. Indeed, in a late manuscript from the summer of 1937 Husserl sees the exploration of what he had in *Ideas* I called the 'natural concept of the world' and later the 'life-world' as precisely the exploration of the 'historical world' (Hua XXIX 426). It is time, therefore, to turn to Husserl's complex concept of the life-world.

CHAPTER 6

Husserl's problematical concept of the life-world

In Husserl's later work the magic word *Lebenswelt* (lifeworld) appears – one of those rare and wonderful artificial words (it does not appear before Husserl) that have found their way into the general linguistic consciousness, thus attesting to the fact that they bring an unrecognized or forgotten truth to language. So the word '*Lebenswelt*' has reminded us of all the presuppositions that underlie all scientific knowledge.

(Hans-Georg Gadamer)[1]

THE LIFE-WORLD AS UNIVERSAL PROBLEM

In this chapter I shall attempt to draw together Husserl's diffuse remarks about the life-world (primarily in *Crisis* §§ 33–8, 43 and 51) into a coherent exposition of this influential but ultimately problematic concept. The life-world, in Husserl's hands, is a rich, multi-faceted notion with some apparently paradoxical or even contradictory features that have puzzled even sympathetic commentators.

Husserl's *Crisis* became famous for its extensive yet somewhat formal treatment of the concept of the 'life-world' or 'world of life' (*Lebenswelt*) – at least in his main published works – life-world is mentioned briefly in *Cartesian Meditations* § 58.[2] It is in the *Crisis*

---

[1] Hans-Georg Gadamer, 'The Ideal of Practical Philosophy', in Gadamer, *Praise of Theory: Speeches and Essays*, trans. Chris Dawson (New Haven: Yale University Press, 1998), pp 50–61, esp. p. 55. Gadamer is wrong; the term *Lebenswelt* features in Grimm's *Deutsches Wörterbuch* of 1885 (see Hua XXXIX xlvi).

[2] The term 'life-world' appears four times in the *Cartesian Meditations* (CM § 58, pp. 133–6; Hua I 160–3) in regard to an I that lives in a plurality of other I's in an overall 'surrounding world' (*Umwelt*); see CM § 58, p. 133; Hua I 160, CM § 58, p. 135; Hua I 162 (twice) and CM § 58, p. 136; Hua I 163. The term is found in Husserl's manuscripts from around 1917 and in Heidegger's lectures from 1919.

that Husserl claims to have discovered the life-world as a fundamental and novel phenomenon previously invisible to the sciences and to have identified it for the first time as a 'universal problem' (*Crisis* § 34). Indeed, there is – as Husserl himself insists – a specific and entirely new science of the life-world itself (*Crisis* § 51) that would, among other things, offer a new basis for grounding the natural and human sciences. There has never been such an investigation of the 'life-world' as 'subsoil' (*Untergrund*) for all forms of theoretical truth (C 124; K 127).

Husserl claims that his enquiry needs a wholly new methodology and that his explorations in the *Crisis* are at best tentative and preparatory. The 'life-world' demands a different type of investigation that goes beyond the usual scientific treatment of the natural or human world. It must be descriptive of the life-world in its own terms, bracketing conceptions intruding from the natural and cultural sciences (this requires a special *epochē*, according to *Crisis* § 36), and identifying the 'types' (*Typen*) and 'levels' (*Stufen*) that belong to it. Accordingly, Husserl speaks of an 'ontology of the life-world' (*Ontologie der Lebenswelt*, *Crisis* § 51; Hua XXIX 140), although, in the *Crisis* itself, he certainly does not give the concept the full elaboration it demands, and many commentators feel his account falls short of the necessary 'thick' description of our cultural world. Furthermore, Husserl offers different characterizations of the life-world, raising questions of the consistency of his own approach.[3] Thus, David Carr speaks of 'many faults and confusions in his exposition' of the life-world.[4] For instance, Husserl speaks in the plural of 'life-worlds' but also stresses that ultimately there is only *one* overall 'world' for which a plural makes no sense. Furthermore, the problem of the life-world is discussed by Husserl in relation to a cluster of related notions, including 'horizon' (*Horizont*), 'surrounding world' (*Umwelt*),[5]

---

[3] There is a huge literature on Husserl's concept of the life-world, but see Gerd Brand, 'The Structure of the Life-World According to Husserl', *Man and World* Vol. 6 (1973), 143–62; and David Carr, 'Husserl's Problematic Concept of the Life-World', Fred Kersten, 'The Life-World Revisited' and Toru Tani, 'Life and the Life-World', in D. Moran and L. Embree, eds., *Phenomenology: Critical Concepts in Philosophy* (London, New York: Routledge, 2004), Vol. I, pp. 359–417. See also the entry on '*Lebenswelt*' in Joachim Ritte and K. Gründe, eds., *Historisches Wörterbuch der Philosophie* (Basle, Stuttgart: Schwabe, 1980), Vol. V, p. 152.

[4] David Carr, 'Husserl's Problematic Concept of the Life-World', p. 359.

[5] At times Husserl identifies 'life-world' and 'surrounding world' (*Umwelt*), but sometimes he differentiates between them. 'Surrounding world' (*Umwelt*) – Cairns' and Carr's translations

'environment' (*Umgebung*)[6] and 'generativity' (*Generativität*), i.e. the manner in which human lives intersect across generations, leading to the overall and complex problem of the constitution of 'tradition' and indeed the 'a priori of history'. All these concepts need to be carefully differentiated.

Its exploratory and provisional character notwithstanding, Husserl's conceptualization of the 'life-world' has been hugely influential in contemporary European philosophy and in the social and human sciences, and has been taken up in varying ways by Alfred Schutz, Jan Patočka, Martin Heidegger, Hans-Georg Gadamer, Hannah Arendt, Jürgen Habermas, Aron Gurwitsch and Bernhard Waldenfels (b. 1934), among many others. In this chapter, therefore, we shall retrieve and order Husserl's many formulations of this somewhat elusive and ambiguous concept.

HUSSERL'S MULTIPLE CHARACTERIZATIONS OF THE LIFE-WORLD

'Life-world' is, for Husserl, a term that has many significations, depending on the context. Antonio F. Aguirre has summarized Husserl's treatment of the life-world under a number of helpful headings in relation to the sections of the work in which they appear.[7] According to his analysis, the life-world is:

- 'the forgotten meaning-fundament of natural science' (*vergessenes Sinnesfundament der Naturwissenschaft*, C 48; K 48)
- the unexplored presupposition for Kant's philosophy (*Crisis* §§ 28–32)

---

to capture the '*Um-*', which means 'around' or 'surrounding' – is sometimes given a more restricted meaning, e.g. for the 'habitat' of an animal, whereas 'life-world' is treated as a more fundamental context in which all meaningful activity and passivity occur.

6 Husserl tends to use the word *Umgebung* (Cairns and Carr translate this primarily as 'environment') for the narrow background against which perceptual objects appear; see CM § 38, p. 79; Hua I 113 and C 260; K 264. See also K 480. At K 487, Husserl speaks of the 'I-environment' (*Ich-Umgebung*) and the 'environment of persons that surrounds each of us'. Overall, the term *Umgebung* has fewer than a dozen occurrences in the *Crisis* Hua VI edition. However, Husserl is not exact in his use of these terms and sometimes uses *Umgebung* in place of *Umwelt* for the habitat of animals and humans; see K 354.

7 See A. F. Aguirre, *Die Phänomenologie Husserls im Lichte ihrer gegenwärtigen Interpretation und Kritik* (Darmstadt: Wissenschaftliche Buchgesellschaft, 1982), p. 87.

- the pregiven world, the correlate of the natural attitude (*Crisis* § 38)
- the theme of historians who try to reconstruct the life-worlds of peoples (C 147; K 150)
- the theme of a non-transcendental ontology (*Crisis* § 37)
- the theme of a transcendental science (*Crisis* § 38)
- the unthematized horizon which never has been brought to explicit attention.

One could add further characterizations. Primarily, life-world connotes the 'world of experience' (*Erfahrungswelt*) as immediately given, already there, 'taken-for-granted' or 'obvious' (*selbstverständlich*). Husserl often contrasts the life-world as 'intuitive' (*anschaulich*), 'real' (*real*) and 'concrete' (*konkret*), with the world of science as 'objective', 'ideal' and 'abstract'.[8]

As pregiven, the life-world possesses a certain 'unsurpassability' (*Unhintergehbarkeit*). It cannot be transcended. Every kind of experience is based on a sense that things are already there. The world lies concretely at the heart of every natural conscious experience (KITP, p. 22n.; Hua VII 246n.1). The life-world is so intimately present that it is not even a 'presupposition' (*Voraussetzung*), since all presuppositions are already founded in this 'pregivenness'.

The life-world has an essentially *subjective* and intersubjective character such that it cannot be completely objectified. Husserl calls it the sphere of the 'merely subjective relative' (*bloss subjektiv relativ*), 'a realm of subjective phenomena' (*Crisis* § 29). In this sense, the concept of the life-world deliberately resists a purely objective description. Husserl's life-world is, then, not to be equated with the totality of beings (what Husserl calls the 'total world', *Allwelt*), nor the Kantian limit idea of a projected but inexperienceable whole. Rather, it connotes a thickly experienced context of embodied human acting and knowing that is not completely surveyable, not fully objectifiable, and which has an inescapably intersubjective and 'intertwined' (*Ineinander*) character. It is, following the ancient Greeks, the realm

---

[8] See Walter Biemel, 'Gedanken zur Genesis der Lebenswelt', in Gerhard Preyer, Georg Peter and Alexander Ulfig, eds., *Protosoziologie im Kontext 'Lebenswelt' und 'System' in Philosophie und Soziologie* (Frankfurt: Humanities Online, 2000), pp. 41–54. Compare *Phen. Psych.* § 25, p. 109; Hua IX 142–3.

of *doxa* ('belief' or commonly held 'opinion', see *Crisis* §§ 34 and 44), i.e. the Heraclitean 'subjective-relative' domain that remains constantly functioning for human beings even when they are absorbed in the practice of science. Husserl introduces the experienced world in this way in his discussion of Galileo, where he emphasizes the underlying conviction of *one* world:

> Pre-scientifically, in everyday sense-experience, the world is given in a subjectively relative way. Each of us has his own appearances; and for each of us they count as [*gelten als*] that which actually is. In dealing with one another, we have long since become aware of this discrepancy between our various ontic validities [*Seinsgeltungen*]. But we do not think that, because of this, there are many worlds. Necessarily, we believe in the world, whose things only appear to us differently but are the same. (C 23; K 20)

The fleeting character of the experienced world was also a prominent feature of the natural concept of the world in the work of Richard Avenarius, as we shall discuss below. Both Husserl and Avenarius recognize that there must be invariant structures running through the stream of variations. These allow the life-world to be characterized in terms of its a priori character – it has a certain conception of space, time, causality, and so on. Of course, the life-world is also lived through in a very specific, *temporal* way, as we saw in Chapter 5, it is through and through *cultural, traditional* and *historical*. In this chapter we shall emphasize its role as the ultimate *horizon* of all sense.

The term 'life-world' is introduced to supplement – or indeed sometimes replace – other conceptions, including the 'natural world' (*die natürliche Welt, Ideas* I § 27), 'the intuitively given surrounding world' (*die anschauliche Umwelt, Crisis* §§ 9a, 59), the 'straightforwardly intuited world' (*Crisis* § 33), the 'taken-for-granted, pregiven world of experience, the world of natural life' (C 204; K 208), the 'environment' (*Umgebung*), the 'world of experience' (*Erfahrungswelt*, C 346; K 360), the world of culture (*Kulturwelt*, Hua IX 113), 'worldlife' (*Weltleben*), the 'human world' and so on.[9] The primary meaning of the life-world is, for Husserl, the 'world of everyday experience'

---

[9] See Ernst Wolfgang Orth, *Edmund Husserls 'Krisis der europäischen Wissenschaften und die transzendentale Phänomenologie': Vernunft und Kultur* (Darmstadt: Wissenschaftliche Buchgesellschaft, 1999), pp. 132–6.

(*Alltagswelt*) or the 'pregiven' surrounding world (C 47; K 47). Husserl even speaks in *Crisis* § 72 of the 'subscientific everydayness of natural life' (C 260; K 264), using the term 'everydayness' (*Alltäglichkeit*) more usually associated with Heidegger (see SZ § 52). Both Husserl and Heidegger speak about spontaneous absorbed 'living along' (*dahinleben*, see SZ § 67, p. 396; 345 and *hineinleben*, 'to be happy-go-lucky',[10]) although Husserl stresses the naïve, 'taken-for-granted nature' of this attitude, whereas Heidegger stresses more the nature of everydayness as indifference and inauthenticity.

For Husserl, the life-world is the permanent 'background' (*Hintergrund*, C 189; K 192) of all experience, and as such it is rarely foregrounded for explicit scientific examination: 'Consciously we always live in the life-world; normally there is no reason to make it explicitly thematic for ourselves universally as world' (C 379; K 459). As a background concept, Husserl's concept of the 'life-world' is not just a new, additional, broad term for the *world as a whole*. Nor is it to be understood as 'the world in itself' (*Welt an sich*) or 'the true world' (*die wahre Welt*), which are scientific idealizations; rather, it is, as Bernhard Waldenfels puts it, a 'polemic counter-concept' that counteracts and counterbalances various modern scientific and philo-sophical tendencies of conceiving the world, including the Kantian conception of world.[11] In this sense, Husserl's conceptualization of the 'life-world' acts as a counterpoint to his analysis of the nature of formalized scientific knowledge. His argument is that any under-standing of scientific knowledge, and indeed our understanding of the *subjective* (as, for instance, misleadingly developed in modern psychology), needs to be corrected by taking into account the start-ing-point and 'ground' (*Grund, Boden* or indeed 'grounding soil', *der gründende Boden, Crisis* § 34e) of all knowledge in the life-world. In this sense, life-world is a concept whose ontological significance has been missed, since it escapes treatment in objectivist fashion.

---

[10] The German verb *hineinleben* means literally 'to live into', 'to immerse oneself into', but it is used in colloquial German expressions to mean 'to take each day as it comes' (*in den Tag hineinleben*). Similarly *dahinleben* has the colloquial sense of 'to go with the flow', 'to live along with life' and also, more rarely, 'to vegetate'.

[11] See Bernhard Waldenfels, 'Homeworld and Alienworld', in Ernst Wolfgang Orth and Chan-Fai Cheung, eds., *Phenomenology of Interculturality and Life-World, Phänomenologische Forschungen Sonderband* (Freiburg/Munich: Karl Alber, 1998), pp. 72–87, esp. p. 72, reprinted in Moran and Embree, eds., *Phenomenology* Vol. IV, pp. 280–91.

As Husserl insists, 'to live is always to live-in-certainty-of-the-world' (*Inweltgewissheitleben*, *Crisis* § 37); natural living is 'living in belief' (*Glaubensleben*), that means, living in a kind of blind acceptance of the givenness of the world in its objective and temporal appearance. It is so immediate that it is normally unnoticed and never 'thematized', i.e. explicitly made the object of reflection. Husserl sometimes characterizes this basic belief as an *Urglaube*, primordial belief, bedrock belief, that goes much deeper than anything that might be characterized as 'certainty'.

Husserl often stresses that the life-world (in contrast with the idealized world of the natural sciences – with endless space and time and exact causality) is a world understood as providing some kind of limit (*Limes* C 313; K 292). The ancients always understood their world as a finite world (see Hua xxix 141), for which he uses the Greek *peras* (πέρας Hua xxix 141), in contrast with the unlimited, (απειρον), that which escapes all rational measure. As we shall see, Husserl believes that ancient mythic thought and Greek philosophy initially described the life-world in intuitive ways. It was the Greek sceptics who questioned this presumed intuitive worldview and made the status of the world itself into a problem. This recognition of the distinction between world-for-me and world-for-all is a defining moment in human history, the breakthrough of Greek scepticism.

The life-world is always the intentional correlate or *counterpart* of human experiencing, acting and valuing, of life in the natural and personal attitudes. Husserl speaks, moreover, of the 'intertwining' (*Verflechtung*) or interpenetration between nature (as the object of the sciences and natural experience) and spirit (as culture) in the life-world (see *Phen. Psych.* § 16). The life-world, then, has to be understood as including the overlapping sets of objects which surround us in life as perceptual objects, instruments and tools, food, clothing, shelter, art objects, religious objects and so on. The life-world therefore encompasses both the world of 'nature' (as it presents itself to us *in our everyday dealings* with it, including mountains, sky, plants, animals, planets and so on) and the world of 'culture', including ourselves, other persons, animals, social institutions, artifacts, symbolic systems, languages and religions.

Furthermore, the life-world cannot be understood as a static context since it includes the idea of historical evolution and development; it somehow includes past, present and future.

THE 'PRE-SCIENTIFIC' INTUITIVE WORLD OF NAÏVE BELIEF

In his earliest discussion of the concept in *Crisis* § 9 (relating to the emergence of modern mathematical science), Husserl contrasts the 'pre-scientific' (*vorwissenschaftlich*) life-world with the world as conceived by the exact mathematical natural sciences. One should not conclude from this initial contrast that the life-world is to be construed solely in terms of the pre-scientific world, the world *before* it became transformed by technology – the world of raw nature, as it were. For Husserl, humans – no matter how technologically advanced – always live in a life-world; and our highly technological world always has its own character of 'taken-for-grantedness'. As Husserl's student Ludwig Landgrebe writes (summarizing Husserl): 'It is essentially impossible to find men in any "pre-worldly" state, because to be human, to be aware of oneself as a man and to exist as a human self, is precisely to live on the basis of a world.'[12] The contemporary worldview is precisely interwoven with sedimented scientific discoveries. We simply accept electricity as there, on hand, in the same way as water. Radio waves are 'in' the air.

This *interwovenness* (*Verflechtung*) between the experience of 'nature' and of our technological, cultural world makes the life-world more complex. If modern technological practice is an integral part of the life-world, how can one still maintain the distinction between world of experience and scientific world? How can Husserl maintain and exploit the contrast between the life-world and the scientific world in cultures where science and technology mediate the experience of world itself? The life-world, on the one hand, in Husserl's conception, grounds and supports the world of science (which is essentially different from it), and, on the other hand, it encompasses the world of science: all scientists are members of the life-world. The modern

---

[12] Ludwig Landgrebe, 'The World as a Phenomenological Problem', *Philosophy and Phenomenological Research* Vol. 1 No. 1 (September 1940), 38–58, esp. 53.

life-world is itself shaped by science: 'Now the scientific world ... like all other worlds [determined by particular] ends, itself "belongs" to the life-world; just as all men and all human communities generally, and their human ends both individual and communal, with all their corresponding working structures, belong to it' (C 380–1; K 460).

Husserl's answer is to understand life-world as a *horizonal* structure, one that includes contexts, possibilities, temporal distantiations which are intuitively experienced and can never be objectified in science. Rather than being an extant totality of things, the life-world is actually a 'horizon' that stretches from indefinite past to indefinite future and includes all actualities and possibilities of experience and meaningfulness. The life-world provides a living context or 'world-horizon' (*Welthorizont*) which precisely makes humans human.

Natural life is characterized by Husserl as 'mundane' or 'worldly'.[13] For Husserl, as for Heidegger (whose equivalent concept is 'being-in-the-world' (*In-der-Welt-sein*, SZ §§ 12–13)) human beings are beings who essentially live immersed (*Dahinleben*) in a *world* understood as a vaguely defined context of meaning and action. Heidegger himself states that it has become commonplace to say that humans require a 'surrounding world' or 'environment' (*Umwelt*), but the deeper ontological meaning of this statement is not appreciated – to be in a world is an a priori character of human existence (SZ § 12, p. 84; 57–8). Husserl's version of this claim is to speak of natural 'world-life' (*Weltleben*, C 51; K 51),[14] and indeed he characterizes humans as essentially belonging to the world, as being, in his phrase, 'children of the world' (*Weltkinder*), a term not used in the *Crisis* itself but frequently found in other works (see Hua VIII 169; *Phen. Psych.* § 43; Hua IX 216).

SOURCES OF THE LIFE-WORLD: AVENARIUS'S 'PREFOUND' WORLD

Contrary to Gadamer, the term *Lebenswelt* does not originate with Husserl but can be found in late nineteenth- and early

---

[13] Husserl uses both the German adjectives *weltlich* ('worldly', K 178, 180) and *mundane* ('mundane', K 208) to characterize life in the natural attitude.

[14] The term 'world-life' (*Weltleben*) appears in the *Crisis* at C 68; K 69, C 119; K 121, C 125; K 127, C 255; K 259 and C 284; K 331.

twentieth-century authors. The term features in Grimm's *Deutsches Wörterbuch* of 1885 (see Hua XXXIX xlvi) and is found in the poet Hugo von Hoffmannsthal (in a text dating from 1907–8) and in the life-philosophers Georg Simmel (in a 1913 text) and Rudolf Eucken (1846–1926).[15] Husserl also uses a similar word, *Lebewelt* ('world of living things', employed by geologists and palaeontologists, e.g. Karl Diener (1862–1928)), to refer to the world of flora and fauna.[16] Indeed, *Lebewelt* occurs in *Ideas* I (in all three editions published during Husserl's life, Hua III/1 115), but the editor of the Husserliana edition, Karl Schuhmann (1941–2003), corrected it to *Lebewesen* based on an occurrence of that word in a similar context in the *Crisis* (C 239; K 242).

The proximate source for Husserl's conception of life-world is Richard Avenarius' conception of the 'natural world', which Husserl discusses in some detail. In the late nineteenth century positivists such as Richard Avenarius[17] and Ernst Mach (1838–1916)[18] advocated an examination of the pre-scientific world of immediate experience as the basis on which to construct the scientific conception of the world (an idea taken up by the Vienna Circle in its *Manifesto*). Husserl was deeply influenced by both Avenarius and Mach, and, in his *Amsterdam Lectures* of 1928, he credits Mach with pursuing phenomenology *avant la lettre* (*Trans. Phen.*, p. 213; Hua IX 302). Indeed, in his 1910–11 *Basic Problems of Phenomenology*, Husserl explicitly associated his concept of a 'naturally experienced world' with Richard Avenarius' concept of the 'pregiven' world of experience.

Husserl's earliest characterization of life-world is that it is always 'pregiven' (*vorgegeben*), 'on hand' (*vorhanden*, BPP 107; Hua XIII 196), echoing Avenarius' notion of the 'prefound' (*das Vorgefundene*).

---

[15] It is not clear if Husserl knew of the use of the term *Lebenswelt* in Georg Simmel and others.

[16] See Ernst Wolfgang Orth, '"Lebenswelt" als eine unvermeidliche Illusion? Husserls Lebensweltbegriff und seine kulturpolitischen Weiterungen', in Preyer, Peter and Ulfig, eds., *Protosoziologie im Kontext 'Lebenswelt' und 'System' in Philosophie und Soziologie*, pp. 28–54.

[17] Avenarius advocated a scientific philosophy that eschewed both metaphysics and materialism and was grounded in experience; see his *Der menschliche Weltbegriff* (The Human Concept of the World) (Leipzig: O. R. Reisland, 1891; reprinted London: Elibron Classics, 2005).

[18] See Ernst Mach, *The Analysis of Sensations and the Relation between the Physical and the Psychical*, trans. C. M. Williams and Sydney Waterlow (New York: Dover, 1959).

Avenarius' 'natural concept of the world' (*natürlicher Weltbegriff*) captures human experiencing prior to explicit scientific theorizing and prior to the split between physical and psychical that emerged in modern science and philosophy. Our experience is of what is 'prefound' experience (*das Vorgefundene*), to which we attach significance (*Deutung*) or value. We experience others as having similar experiences to ourselves and similarly have an 'experience of our environment' (*Umgebungserfahrung*) in which we are involved and which develops alongside us as we develop.

According to Avenarius, the natural world-concept is the experience of the world as 'changing appearances' (*Variationserscheinungen*), but here is a 'principle of coordination' (*Prinzipialkoordination*) whereby we experience constancy in this world of fluctuating experiences. Husserl admires much of Avenarius' description but believes he does not recognize the need for the phenomenological *epochē* and for the specifically *phenomenological attitude* to bring this whole domain to light (BPP 110; Hua XIII 198). Despite Avenarius' efforts to avoid metaphysical constructions and materialism, he remains, for Husserl, a prisoner of naturalism.

FROM 'SURROUNDING WORLD' (*UMWELT*)
TO LIFE-WORLD

The vague concept of a 'world' as the backdrop for our perceptual experiences already occurs in the *Logical Investigations*, although not named as such (William James' concept of the 'halo', corresponding to the notion of 'horizon', is mentioned). Prior to settling on the term 'life-world' around 1917, Husserl spoke primarily of the 'natural surrounding world', the 'human cultural world', the 'world of immediate experience' (*Erfahrungswelt*), the 'world for me' (*Welt für mich*). The life-world, in one obvious sense, is the world of our surroundings, our 'surrounding world' (*Umwelt*), but – and this is important, in terms of our contemporary Western culture – our *Lebenswelt* is also permeated with scientific and technological determinations.

The concern with the *natural attitude* can be traced back to Husserl's transcendental turn (*c.* 1907 – the term appears in *The Idea of Phenomenology*) – and the idea of *nature* as the objective correlate of this attitude can be found in 'Philosophy as Rigorous Science'

(1910–1911). The term 'life-world' becomes current for Husserl after 1917 (prominent, for example, in *Phenomenological Psychology*, 1925) to capture the peculiar character of the pregiven environing world.[19] In the *Crisis*, the term *Lebenswelt* first appears in Section 9(h) on Galileo, where it is introduced as 'the forgotten meaning-fundament of science' (C 48; K 48). The life-world and its structures are precisely what get covered up by the 'cloak of ideas' of modern mathematical science. Husserl returns to give a much fuller exposition of the life-world in *Crisis* Part IIIA §§ 33–8, where he raises the question concerning the 'sense of being' or 'ontic meaning' (*Seinssinn*, C 123; K 125) and 'mode of being' (*Seinsweise*) of the life-world. In particular, *Crisis* § 34 'Exposition of the Problem of a Science of the Life-World' (which, like Section 9, is divided into sub-sections, indicating substantial revision and expansion) gives an extended treatment of the concept of 'life-world'. In these sections, he explicitly invokes life-world as a way of correcting Kant.

THE LIFE-WORLD AS ESSENTIALLY SUBJECTIVE AND NOT OBJECTIFIABLE

The life-world has to be understood as including everything that is experienceable, the horizon of all experience. In this regard, Husserl opposes Kant's view that the world is not experienceable in itself. Already in his *Phenomenological Psychology* (1925), he writes: 'Kant insists that the world is not an object of possible experience, whereas we continue to speak in all seriousness of the world precisely as the all-inclusive object of an experience expanded and to be expanded all-inclusively' (*Phen. Psych.* § 11, p. 71; Hua IX 95). For Husserl, there is a genuine if vague experience – an intuition – of the world as the background of our experiencing. The world is co-intended as a *horizon* of experiences, and there is a genuine 'world-consciousness' (*Weltbewusstsein*). There is a direct and immediate 'experience of the world' (*Welterfahrung*) as really *one*, *there*, in the *present* (Hua VIII

---

[19] The term 'life-world' appears in supplements to *Ideas* II (*c.* 1917), in the *Nature and Spirit* lectures of 1919 in E. Husserl, *Natur und Geist: Vorlesungen Sommersemeste* 1927, ed. Michael Weile, Husserl Materialen Vol. IV (Dordrecht: Springer, 2002), p. 187, in the Kant Society lecture of 1924 (Hua VII 232) and in *Phenomenological Psychology* (1925) (see Hua IX 240, 491, 496).

321). Husserl writes that only the life-world is experienceable whereas the 'true world' as an idealization is not:

The contrast between the subjectivity of the life-world and the objective, the 'true' world, lies in the fact that the latter is a theoretical-logical sub-struction [*Substruktion*], the substruction of something that is in principle not perceivable, in principle not experienceable in its own proper being, whereas the subjective, in the life-world [*das lebensweltlich Subjektive*], is distinguished in all respects precisely by its being actually experienceable (C 127; K 130)

Husserl speaks about this real but non-objectifiable experience of the world in *Crisis* § 71. I am not just conscious of entities within the world, but of the world itself, although it is not to be understood as another entity:

If I were not conscious of the world as world, without its being capable of becoming objective in the manner of an [individual] object, how could I survey the world reflectively and put knowledge of the world into play, thus lifting myself above the simple, straightforwardly directed life that always has to do with things? How is it that I, and each of us, constantly have world-consciousness [*Weltbewusstsein*] (C 251; K 254–5)

Against Kant, then, there is a genuine experience of 'world' which is different from the experience of individual things, events, persons in the world. Furthermore, Kant aligned the form of experience precisely with the framework of science, the world as known: for instance, framing sensuous intuition with the temporal and spatial forms exactly as they were found in Newtonian science.

In this most obvious sense, the life-world is the world as experienced by living subjects, both individually and collectively. In one of the earliest occurrences (*c.* 1917–18) of the term 'life-world', Husserl writes (and note the reference also to 'functioning subjects'): 'The life-world is the natural world – in the attitude of natural life [*Einstellung des natürlichen Dahinlebens*] we are living functioning subjects [*fungierende Subjekte*] together in an open circle of other functioning subjects. Everything objective about the life-world is subjective givenness, our possession, mine, the other's, and everyone's together' (*Ideas* II, Supplement XIII, p. 385; Hua IV 375). To live immersed in (*Dahinleben*) the life-world is to live the life of a functioning subject. *Functioning subjectivity* is also discussed in the

Crisis (e.g. C 261; K 265). 'Functioning' here means something that is going on in the background but that is not the object of conscious awareness or intention. Functioning subjectivity is, for Husserl, the kind of anonymous, practical, intentional life that is involved in the production of an intersubjective social world. Functioning subjectivity, of course, plays a major role in Maurice Merleau-Ponty's *Phenomenology of Perception*.[20] We shall discuss it further in Chapter 7.

In this sense of being a subjective and intersubjective world, the life-world has to be understood on its own 'spiritual terms'. In the same supplement to *Ideas* II, Husserl writes: 'The life-world of persons escapes natural science, even though the latter investigates the totality of realities' (*Ideas* II, p. 384; Hua IV 374). In *Ideas* II, Husserl sharply contrasts objects of nature in the scientific sense with everyday, natural-attitude objects of experience:

> In ordinary life [*im gewöhnlichen Leben*] we have nothing whatever to do with nature-objects [*Naturobjekten*]. What we take as things are pictures, statues, gardens, houses, tables, clothes, tools, etc. They are value-objects [*Wertobjekte*] of various kinds, use-objects [*Gebrauchsobjekte*], practical objects. They are not objects which can be found in natural science. (*Ideas* II § 11, p. 29; Hua IV 27)

Similar statements can be found in *Crisis* § 36 and elsewhere. Thus, in *Thing and Space* (1907), Husserl contrasts the scientific understanding of platinum (as an atomic complex, etc.) with the perceptually experienced object, a heavy lump of hard, cold metal in the hand (see DR, p. 4; Hua XVI 6). Husserl is insistent on this difference in the *Crisis*:

> The bodies familiar to us in the life-world are actual bodies, but not bodies in the sense of physics. The same is true of causality and of spatiotemporal infinity. These categorial features of the life-world have the same names but are not concerned, so to speak, with the theoretical idealizations and the hypothetical substructions of the geometrician and the physicist [*die theoretischen Idealisierungen und hypothetischen substruktionender Geometer und Physiker*] (C 139–40; K 142–3)

---

[20] Maurice Merleau-Ponty (PP, pp. xviii; xiii) contrasts 'operative intentionality' with 'act intentionality' (of the kind exercised in judgements). Operative intentionality is responsible for our pre-predicative experiences of ourselves and of the world. See also PP, pp. 418; 478.

Objects as they appear in the natural attitude, the everyday, naïve, straightforward, practical attitude, prior to science, are natural-world objects, and the context in which we experience them is the living, human world – the *life-world*.

THE LIFE-WORLD AS HISTORICAL AND THE CRADLE OF TRADITION

The life-world, for Husserl, stands not just for our *present* and 'co-present' (*Mitgegenwart*) surrounding environment, our possession or 'having' (*Habe*): it also has a temporal dimension stretching backwards into the indefinite past and pointing forwards into an indefinite future. The life-world is a world of cumulative tradition acquired through what Husserl calls *sedimentation* (*Sedimentierung*, C 362; K 372), according to which certain earlier experiences become passively enfolded in our ongoing experience, just as language retains earlier meanings in its etymologies. As Husserl says in 'The Origin of Geometry', 'cultural structures appear on the scene in the form of tradition; they claim, so to speak, to be "sedimentations" [*Sedimentierungen*] of a truth-meaning that can be made originally self-evident' (C 367; K 377). Indeed, Husserl speaks of 'sedimentation' as 'traditionalization' (C 52; K 52).[21] For every intentional act, there is a background of inactive presuppositions that are sedimented but still function implicitly (*Crisis* § 40).

The life-world is a world of 'living tradition' (C 366; K 376), our remembered pasts and our projected futures. These traditions are sedimented and layered into the context of the world itself. Wittgenstein in his *Philosophical Investigations* (§ 18) compares language to a city where the old centre has narrow, winding streets, but the new suburbs are laid out in geometrical grids, and later he remarks, 'language is a labyrinth of paths' (§ 203).[22] The life-world is similarly textured and layered and laid over or 'sedimented' with tradition in a labyrinthine manner which phenomenology must untangle and document.

---

[21] Husserl usually employs the verb 'to sediment' (*sedimentieren*) or the noun, that expresses a process 'sedimentation' (*Sedimentierung*); see e.g. C 149; K 152, C 246; K 249 and C 362; K 373.

[22] Ludwig Wittgenstein, *Philosophical Investigations*, trans. Elizabeth Anscombe (Oxford: Blackwell, 2001), p. 7.

In this regard, Aron Gurwitsch correctly captures this aspect of life-world when he writes that the term *Lebenswelt* '*has essentially a historico-social connotation: a Lebenswelt* is relative to a certain society at a given moment of its history'.[23] Hans-Georg Gadamer similarly writes: 'The concept of the life-world is the antithesis of all objectivism. It is an essentially historical concept, which does not refer to the universe of being, to the "existent world" ... the life-world means something else, namely the whole in which we live as historical creatures.'[24] This is an apt formulation: the life-world is the only world in which we live, and furthermore is one in which we live as historical and communal beings. It is the life-world as historical that is the subject matter of historians 'who must ... reconstruct the changing, surrounding life-worlds of the peoples and periods with which they deal' (C 147; K 150).

THE LIFE-WORLD AS HORIZON

The life-world is pregiven precisely as a 'universal *horizon*' (*Horizont*, C 281; K 327). Husserl's innovative concept of *horizon* presents complex difficulties.[25] Horizon generally expresses the idea of a certain indeterminate context. It has both spatial and temporal connotations, but its real sense for Husserl is as a 'context of meaning' which provides some kind of limit. The foundational meaning of the notion of 'horizon' is the co-perceived context within which a perceived object is perceived: literally, the limit of the visual scene. Husserl also speaks of humans living within the *horizons* of their historicity (*Crisis* § 2), horizon here providing an interpretive context. He explicates the concept of 'horizon' in his *Passive Synthesis* lectures, where he speaks of a 'horizon of references' built into the experience itself:

... everything that genuinely appears is an appearing thing only by virtue of being intertwined and permeated with an intentional empty horizon, that

[23] Aron Gurwitsch, 'The Last Work of Edmund Husserl: II. The *Lebenswelt*', *Philosophy and Phenomenological Research* Vol. 17 No. 3 (March. 1957), 376.

[24] Hans-Georg Gadamer, *Truth and Method*, 2nd rev. edn., trans. Joel Weinsheimer and Donald G. Marshall (London: Sheed and Ward, 1989), p. 247.

[25] On Husserl's concept of horizon, see Tze-Wan Kwan, 'Husserl's Concept of Horizon: An Attempt at Reappraisal', in Moran and Embree, eds., *Phenomenology* Vol. I, pp. 304–38 and Roberto Walton, 'The Worldhood of the World and the Worldly Character of Objects in Husserl', in Tom Nenon and Philip Blosser, eds., *Advancing Phenomenology: Essays in Honor of Lester Embree* (Dordrecht: Springer, 2010), pp. 139–55.

is, by virtue of being surrounded by a halo of emptiness with respect to appearance. It is an emptiness that is not a nothingness, but an emptiness to be filled out; it is a determinable indeterminacy (APS 42; Hua XI 5–6)

A horizon, no matter how vague and amorphous, is not nothing. Horizons by their very nature possess a certain openness, indefinability and a constantly shifting (withdrawing) character. We can never arrive at a horizon any more than we can arrive at the end of the rainbow.

Already in *Ideas* I, Husserl understands 'world' in general as 'collective horizon of possible investigations' (*Ideas* I § 1, see also § 27, where he speaks of the world as a 'never fully determinable horizon'). Every experienced thing is experienced with a horizon of 'determinable indeterminateness' (*Ideas* I § 44). All forms of knowing, believing, supposing, doubting, willing, acting and suffering presuppose the backdrop of this horizonal world (including the temporal horizon that fades off in two directions). In this regard, Husserl speaks of a peculiar 'horizon-consciousness' (*Crisis* § 47). The world is the ever-present context of our 'doings and undergoings' (*Tun und Leiden*); this horizonal character is essential to 'world' (*Ideas* I § 47). Horizons overlap and interpenetrate but point towards a single overall context, an ultimate horizon of horizons, i.e. the *world*.

However, it is not clear if the horizon of the *life*-world is precisely co-extensive with the horizon of *world* itself – what horizons could belong to the world which do not also belong to the life-world? Perhaps the horizons of mathematics, for instance, are artificial constructs that push beyond the life-world, although nothing outruns the 'world' as such. Husserl's account of the overlap between lifeworld and world is not at all clear. For Husserl, the world-horizon as such is 'constant' (C 251; K 255); it acts as an ultimate context both for historical life-worlds and for the specialist kinds of world (e.g. world of science) built on the foundations of the life-world. The apperception of 'world' (explicit or not) runs through all our experience. In *Crisis* § 37 the world is seen as the horizon for all our experience of entities. The 'world' in this sense is an ideal, a limit idea, an 'idea lying at infinity', as he says in 1924 (*eine im Unendlichen liegende Idee*, KITP, p. 45; Hua VII, 274). *World* is a 'universal field fixed in advance' (*Crisis* § 36), a correlate of the sense-bestowing functions of conscious life. As Ludwig Landgrebe explains, the world is intrinsic to all intentional experience: 'The world is the all-embracing doxic basis, the total horizon that includes every particular positing.'[26]

In this sense, Husserl believes the world *as phenomenon* emerges along with the *cogito* in the phenomenological reduction, although it was missed by Descartes. Everything experienced is originally experienced as part of this encompassing 'natural' *world*. It is first and foremost revealed as a 'world of things' (*Dingwelt*), i.e. physical material entities in space (stones, trees, water and so on), but it is also a *world of living things* (*Lebewelt*), animals and, most especially, other human subjects, with their cultural products and even scientific constructions. These are given within a 'perceptual field' with their internal and external horizons (*Crisis* § 47).

According to Husserl, the open horizon of the world includes, for example, my consciousness of other humans not actually known to me:

There need be no one in my perceptual field, but fellowmen [*Mitmenschen*] are necessary as actual, as known, and as an open horizon of those I might possibly meet. Factually I am within an interhuman present [*in einer mitmenschlichen Gegenwart*] and within an open horizon of mankind; I know myself to be factually within a generative framework [*in einem generativen Zusammenhang*], in the unitary flow of a historical development [*Geschichtlichkeit*] in which this present is mankind's present and the world of which it is conscious is a historical present with a historical past and a historical future. (C 253; K 256)

This open horizon, for Husserl – as for Heidegger (see SZ § 26) – has an a priori character. There is always 'world-consciousness' (*Weltbewusstsein*) implicated in our intentional acts. As horizon, furthermore, the life-world has an 'open', 'unending', 'infinite' character, although it was through Greek philosophy that its infinity was revealed.

LIFE-WORLD AS 'FUNDAMENT', 'GROUND' AND 'UNDERGROUND'

In contra-distinction to the characterization of life-world as horizon with its connotations of openness, Husserl also characterizes the 'life-world' as 'ground' (*Grund*) or 'soil' (*Boden*, see *Crisis*

---

[26] See Landgrebe, 'The World as a Phenomenological Problem', 38–58, esp. 41.

§ 7), 'fundament' (*Fundament*), or, indeed, as the 'underground' or 'subsoil' (*Untergrund*) for scientific inquiry (at *Crisis* §§ 9(b), 29 and 34(a)), the 'unspoken ground of cognitive accomplishments' (*Crisis* § 30), 'constant ground of validity, an ever available source of what is taken for granted' (*Crisis* § 33).

These two characteristics – ground and horizon – could be seen as being in tension: openness versus groundedness. In what sense can the life-world function both as *horizon* (an indefinite and vaguely delineated limit – from the Greek *horos*, meaning 'boundary') and as a *ground* (a self-evidence or validity that is incontrovertible, even apodictic)? As a horizon, the world is not objectifiable; it retreats as emptily co-intuited *behind* the directly presented objects of experience that are primarily intuited (for Husserl, in the first instance, primary physical things as perceived). On the other hand, a 'ground' normally is construed as a *reason*, something that gives the sense of legitimation, justification, entitlement, stability, security, a rational basis, a principle, on the basis of which true assertions can be made (Husserl speaks of seeking a truly apodictic 'ground' like the Cartesian *cogito* at *Crisis* § 30 and a 'universal apodictic ground' at *Crisis* § 7). Indeed, phenomenology itself aims at 'ultimate grounding' (*Letztbegründung*) – logic, for instance, can never be a secure science until it is grounded in the universal 'life-world' (*Crisis* § 36). But one should not attribute to Husserl a rigid sense of 'ground' in the form of a Cartesian, axiomatic, self-evident first principle from which evident truths are deduced. The concept of ground has to be understood as relational – for those on a ship, the ship is their ground, their ultimate reference point.

Husserl understands 'ground' as possessing an intrinsic openness and fertility. Thus he writes: 'The ground of experience [*Erfahrungsboden*], opened up in its infinity, will then become the fertile soil [*Ackerfeld*] of a methodical working philosophy, with the self-evidence, furthermore, that all conceivable philosophical and scientific problems of the past are to be posed and decided by starting from this ground [*Boden*]'(C 100; K 104). Indeed, to start from this ground is precisely to work from the outside in, as it were; to begin with the presupposed vague context of all experience and see how it is operative in the individual sciences.

Investigations into the life-world, Husserl claims, will provide a new ground for philosophy. In this sense pre-scientific life has to be the irremovable ground of scientific endeavour. Husserl talks about the life-world as the 'ground' of our 'human world-life' (*Crisis* § 44) as well as providing the ground for our scientific theorizing. In other words, the life-world is the ground not just of scientific, but of all possible *praxis*.

The way to reconcile the concept of life-world as horizon with life-world as ground is precisely to think of grounding in a new sense – not as rational justification, but as a contextualization whereby meaning itself is secured through its horizontal connections with meanings lived through and established in the non-objectifiable world of living and acting. It is this kind of non-rational grounding that appealed so much to Merleau-Ponty in his *Phenomenology of Perception*. Husserl himself is quite clear that the kind of grounding provided by the life-world is different from logical or epistemic grounding. Indeed, it is literally a pre-logical ground of the logical. Thus, he writes:

There has never been a scientific enquiry into the way in which the life-world constantly functions as subsoil [*Untergrund*], into how its manifold prelogical validities act as grounds for the logical ones, for theoretical truths. And perhaps the scientific discipline which this life-world as such, in its universality, requires is a peculiar one, one which is precisely not objective and logical but which, as the ultimately grounding one, is not inferior but superior in value. (C 124; K 127)

The life-world is not a principle of rational grounding. By its very nature, it cannot provide any kind of objective grounding at all, certainly not the kind of ultimate principle that traditional rationalism (e.g. Spinoza (1632–77) sought. The peculiarity of the grounding of the life-world is that it provides an ultimately subjective, pre-logical, pre-rational, temporally dispersed, never fully actual grounding. It provides a peculiar kind of evidencing. Indeed, the life-world is a 'realm of original self-evidences' (C 127; K 130), which itself provides the grounding for every conceivable type of evidencing. The life-world itself is an always available source of what is taken for granted (C 122; K 124), given in a 'primal self-evidence' (K 131). In this sense, the life-world is the ground of all 'accomplishing life' (*Crisis* § 34d), the 'constant ground of validity' and the continuing confirmation of evidence.

Husserl is insistent on the radicality of his proposal concerning the life-world as *ground*, but there are some difficulties involved in grasping what he means by 'ultimate grounding'. He is positing the life-world as an ultimate, living, evolving context of meaning, something that permits sense to be coherent, harmonious and continuous, an all-encompassing, living cocoon that enables human historical and communal life in its intentional syntheses and passivities. The life-world, paradoxically, then, is not opposed to the Husserlian notion of the transcendental ego but is precisely its correlative pole. There can be no ego without world and vice-versa. The nature of the transcendental ego shall be further discussed in Chapter 7.

THE LIFE-WORLD AS THE INTERSUBJECTIVE, COMMUNAL WORLD

Husserl insists that the world as the ultimate horizon of human experience must not be conceived solipsistically as just *my* world; rather, it is an inherently communal world, a world 'for others', a world potentially available 'for everyone' (*für jedermann*, C 296; K 343 and C 358; K 369). The life-world enables *communalization* (*Vergemeinschaftung*). It is given as being available 'for all', i.e. not just actual subjects, but for all possible subjects. In other words, the very idea of a world essentially involves the idea of infinitely many different possible ways of experiencing it and, equally, an open-ended and infinite plurality of possible 'co-subjects' (*Mitsubjekte*, C 164; K 167 and C 184; K 188) to experience it. The very idea of *world*, accordingly, has an a priori *universality*, which precisely accounts for the experience of objectivity and of intersubjective plurality. The world is pregiven as *communal*: 'Obviously, this is true not only for me, the individual ego; rather we, in living together [*in Miteinanderleben*], have the world pregiven in this "together," as the world valid as existing for us and to which we, together, belong, the world as world for all, pregiven with this ontic meaning [*Seinssinn*]' (C 109; K 111). Being given 'for all' (not just all present but all possible subjects) is part of the 'being-sense' or ontic meaning of the world. A world is what is in principle there for any subject whatsoever. What is visible is visible not just to me but to anyone with a similarly appropriate visual system located in my place. A genuine Robinson Crusoe experience is a priori impossible, Husserl insists. Each human implicitly includes other humans – our shared language as spoken by each of us offers an example here. The communal world is also a world of communication between communicating subjects. Husserl even employs the term 'communication community' (*Mitteilungsgemeinschaft* K 371) – later taken up by Jürgen Habermas. As a consequence of this essentially communal and intersubjective character, the world is never just an objectivity lying 'outside' us. It is precisely the world of our 'interests', purposeful activities, strivings, 'abilities' (*Vermögen*) and 'habitualities' (*Habitualitäten*, *Crisis* § 36). It is the world in which we live and move and have our being; the world in which we act and suffer. It is the world which pulsates according to our life interests (see K 500).

In the *Crisis*, the world is primarily oriented to 'waking' life (see C 281; K 327), given in a synthetically harmonious, unified manner, albeit incomplete and interminable. Husserl emphasizes the 'connectedness' (*Zusammenhang*), 'belongingness' (*Zugehörigkeit*) and 'harmony' (*Harmonie*) of human experience, in its seamless flow. In our lives, passive syntheses are performed that guarantee the ongoing continuity of our experience. In a manner strongly reminiscent of Dilthey (whose central concept is 'life', *Leben*), Husserl also speaks of the nexus or 'connectedness of life' (*Lebenszusammenhang*). The life-world forms a 'meaning-complex' (*Sinneszusammenhang*), a context of sensefulness. This world is always experienced as the 'one, existing world' (*die eine seiende Welt*, C 317; K 296). This intuition of *unity* is absolutely fundamental to the experience of world. As Husserl will discuss, this does not rule out that there can be discrepancies between one individual's experience and another's, or between one group and another.

Intersubjective agreement is itself based on what Husserl calls '*normality*' (*Normalität*, K 487; cf. *Phen. Psych.* § 20), an a priori structural characteristic of worldhood. The world is defined by what 'normal' subjects experience, e.g. those with sight and hearing, and not born blind or deaf. For Husserl, colour-blindness is an abnormality that is, of course, normal for the persons with that condition. There has to be a 'core of commonness' (see *Phen.*

Psych. § 20, p. 98; Hua IX 129) in our experience of the world. In this regard, traditions are important, as traditions set down and maintain across time what has been taken for granted as valid. 'Traditionalization' and holding on to tradition (*Überlieferung*) are forms of normalization. The highest level of 'normality' for humans is when they act in person-to-person relations within the context of a people (*Volk*, K 487) ordered as a state with relations of mastery and obedience (K 487). In *Crisis* Supplement XXIV (not translated in Carr), Husserl speaks of people finding their allotted roles within the social order. But in this instance, he claims philosophers have uniqueness. Philosophers stand in relations of motivation with past philosophers in a manner that is quite exceptional (K 488). In the 'Vienna Lecture', similarly, Husserl speaks of the advent of philosophy as challenging and disrupting traditionality (C 288; K 335). The ancient Greek philosophers challenged the accounts of the gods found in Homer and in the Greek folk tradition. But it requires a special motive to put the taken-for-granted world in question (C 281; K 327).

For Husserl the life-world has overall primacy and fundamentality with regard to 'being' (*Sein*), 'sense' (*Sinn*) and 'validity' (*Geltung*). Sciences grew through understanding and documenting the regularity of the world's pregivenness. Galileo, however, as we saw in Chapter 3, introduced a transformation which effectively cut off the life-world such that it became, as Husserl says, the 'forgotten meaning-fundament' of the sciences (*Crisis* § 9(h)). At this point Husserl writes:

It is this world [the pregiven world] that we find to be the world of all known and unknown realities. To it, the world of actually experiencing intuition, belongs the shape of space-time together with all bodily shapes incorporated in it; it is in the world that we ourselves live, in accord with our bodily [*leiblich*], personal way of being. But here we find nothing of geometrical idealities, no geometrical space or mathematical time with all their shapes (C 50; K 50)

There are different layers or levels to the experience of the life-world, and they form a hierarchy. For Husserl, what has primacy is the world according to external perception (the attitude of 'outer experience'; see Hua IX 494), whereby what is most prominent is the 'world of things' (*Dingwelt*), the 'universe of things' (*das All der Dinge*, C 142; K 147), physical entities distributed in space-time, the 'ontic universe' (*das ontische Universum*, § 37).[27] Husserl uses the Greek *ta onta,* meaning 'beings'. These spatio-temporal things appear to us in a special way, and indeed, Husserl insists (in *Crisis* § 34), we could develop an 'ontology of the life-world' which would document the different 'ways of being' (*Seinsweise*) of life-world entities understood as utensils, art-works, talismans, tokens, etc., i.e. things as they *mean* to us in their specific senses, as they have a certain 'value and validity' (*Geltung*) for us rather than as 'things of nature' (*Naturobjekte*) in the sense of science. The life-world contains physical things and cultural objects at the same time. We live in a 'culture-things-environment' (*Kultur-Sachen-Umwelt*). Nature is exhibited within culture – a 'nature reserve', for instance, is a cultural concept.

It is clear that Husserl thinks of the life-world as bodily and culturally experienced in a first-person way (both singular and plural) which is primarily attuned to meaning or sense (*Sinn*) and value (*Geltung*). The particular manner in which we encounter and experience space (as near/far, up/down, confining/comfortable, mine/alien), time (long, short, boring, interesting), causality, thinghood (solid, sticky, liquid) and so on is encapsulated in the term 'life-world' and is correlated to us as embodied living organisms, everything Husserl means by '*Leib*'. Husserl thinks that Kant is explicitly wrong in trying to apply the formal scientific (Newtonian) conceptions of space and time, and causality, to this world of experience. It has its own bodily way of being spatial and temporal. Everything in the life-world has its unique mode of appearing and it has a certain way of being incarnated: 'For everything that exhibits itself in the life-world as a concrete thing obviously has a bodily character, even if it is not a mere body, as, for example, an animal or a cultural object, i.e. even if it also has psychic or otherwise spiritual properties' (C 106; K 108). Let us return now to the complex question of the unity and plurality of life-worlds.

FORMS OF THE LIFE-WORLD

Husserl invokes the 'singularity' and indeclinability of the concept of world. On the other hand, he also speaks about 'life-worlds' in

---

[27] See Yu Chung-Chi, 'Schutz on Life-World and Cultural Difference', in Lester Embree, ed., *Schutzian Social Science* (Dordrecht: Kluwer, 1999), pp. 159–72, esp. p. 159. Husserl gives primacy to the perceptually experienced world, whereas Schutz gives primacy to the social world of action and working (which he calls *Wirkwelt*).

the plural as changing, being replaced by other life-worlds, and so on. Let us recall Husserl's student Aron Gurwitsch's comments cited earlier: 'a *Lebenswelt* is relative to a certain society at a given moment of its history; it must be taken as it is conceived by the historical community whose world it is.'[28]

In this respect, there must be a *plurality* of such 'worlds'. At the same time, Husserl insists on an overall universal, necessary or invariant structure that defines it. As Gurwitsch comments: 'Notwithstanding its relativity, the *Lebenswelt* exhibits an invariant structure, more precisely, an invariant structural framework within which the relative and changeable finds its place.'[29] Every *Lebenswelt* has a lived conception of space, place, corporeality, causation (which is not the causality of the formal sciences), action and so on. Things, practices and other cultural acquisitions in the life-world have their habitual character and 'styles'. In the *Crisis*, Husserl even speaks of a 'general science' of the *Lebenswelt* which will identify the lawful 'essential typicalities' (Husserl uses the term '*wesensgesetzliche Typik*') that correspond to it.[30]

Husserl contrasts various kinds of life-world in the *Crisis* and in his later writings – the world of the ancient Greeks, of Chinese peasants, natives of the Congo, the Papuans, Hindus, Bantu people and so on (see *Crisis* § 36).[31] Indeed, Husserl frequently speaks of the *relativity* of the life-world – different peoples simply inhabit different worlds. Some worlds (e.g. the European) have science as an essential part of their world; others have no sense of science. Some cultures are closed off in themselves with no sense of history; other cultures are essentially historical. Husserl tries to get to what is essential to the life-world by engaging in an imaginative free variation from existing worlds. Through this he claims to see that, for example, science is an essential possibility for human worlds, even if it is not factually realized (see Hua IX 492). As we shall see, both Merleau-Ponty

---

[28] See Gurwitsch, 'The Last Work of Edmund Husserl: II. The *Lebenswelt*)', 370–98, esp. 372.
[29] *Ibid.*, 376.
[30] Gurwitsch suggests that Aristotelian science is essentially a science of the *Lebenswelt*.
[31] In Supplement XXVII, written in 1925 and entitled 'Subjectivity and the Natural Conception of the World', to his *Phenomenological Psychology* lectures, Husserl speaks of the personal and historical worlds of human beings and of gaining the 'region human' through free eidetic variation starting from the world of actual human beings (he mentions Europeans, Papuans, Bantu, and so on); see Hua IX 487–507.

and Derrida seized on this issue in Husserl and questioned whether a genuine free variation is possible in terms of human culture and historicity or whether, as Merleau-Ponty believed, Husserl came to acknowledge the limits of free imaginative variation and turned instead to the factual plurality of life-worlds available through the anthropological studies of Lévy-Bruhl and others.

THE LIFE-WORLD AS A REGION OF EVIDENCES

The life-world is, for Husserl, as we saw earlier, 'a realm of original self-evidences' (*Crisis* § 34(d)). This is crucial. The life-world has to support both natural everyday human practices and the very special-ized forms of verification demanded by the sciences. It is the manner in which experiences are made meaningful, 'pre-delineated', contex-tualized, and confirmed in the life-world that ultimately motivates and justifies our use of those experiences to make further scientific claims that extend beyond the life-world. It is because, for instance, our perceptual experience synthesizes the different aspectual presen-tations of an object into views of the one, same object that we are justified in talking about *the* object, with its own identity conditions, and so on. There could be no scientific account of the rainbow if the rainbow was not actually seen by humans in their experiences. There has to be a set of transformations whereby we come to *see* the rain-bow in the full sense of visual perception and also 'understand' or construe it scientifically as a spectrum of light caused by the refrac-tion of sunlight through raindrops present in the atmosphere.

It must be borne in mind that Husserl was writing at the very time when the logical positivists of the Vienna Circle were advocating,[32] in opposition to everyday experience, a 'scientific conception of the world' (*eine wissenschaftliche Weltauffassung* – the term itself is found in the *Manifesto* of the Vienna Circle).[33] According to the *Manifesto*: 'The

[32] On the complex history of the Vienna Circle, see Thomas Uebel, 'On the Austrian Roots of Logical Empiricism: The Case of the First Vienna Circle', in Paolo Parrini, Wesley C. Salmon and Merrilee H. Salmon, eds., *Logical Empiricism: Historical and Contemporary Perspectives* (University of Pittsburgh Press, 2003), and Alan Richardson and Thomas Uebel, eds., *The Cambridge Companion to Logical Empiricism* (Cambridge University Press, 2007).

[33] For the text of the *Manifesto* of the Vienna Circle, see Sahotra Sarkar, *The Emergence of Logical Empiricism: From 1900 to the Vienna Circle* (New York: Garland Publishing, 1996), pp. 321–40.

scientific world conception is characterized not so much by theses of its own, but rather by its basic attitude, its points of view and direction of research. The goal ahead is unified science.'[34] Note that the Vienna Circle positivists see the scientific conception as a particular 'attitude' – correcting and replacing what Husserl had termed the natural attitude. The proposed methodology of the Vienna Circle was that of logical analysis – inspired by the logical atomism of Bertrand Russell. Indeed, Russell is quoted as saying his method is an extension of that used by Galileo: 'It [logical atomism] represents, I believe, the same kind of advance as was introduced into physics by Galileo: the substitution of piecemeal, detailed and verifiable results for large untested generalities recommended only by a certain appeal to imagination.'[35]

The Vienna Circle advocated evaluating statements on the basis of whether they were meaningful (i.e. verifiable) or simply meaningless. In opposition to this general kind of scientific positivism, Husserl strongly opposed the view that the 'natural conception' of the world (understood as 'naïve') can simply be replaced by the 'sophisticated' scientific conception. For Husserl, entirely different attitudes are involved – and the scientific attitude isolated and formalized only what was measurable in the larger world of the subjective-relative. Moreover, Husserl stressed that scientific research is carried out by natural-attitude humans and that scientific research generates its own peculiar kind of historicity – its products have a different kind of temporal existence in contrast with those of art-works, for instance (see K 506). The life-world operates with its own norms of evidencing.

THE LIFE-WORLD AS CORRELATE OF THE NATURAL ATTITUDE

Husserl's concept of the life-world has to be correlated with his notion of the 'natural attitude' (*die natürliche Einstellung*, K 300). Both concepts – 'natural attitude' and life-world as 'natural worldly life' (*Crisis* § 43) – emerged in his thinking during his Göttingen

---

[34] See 'The Scientific Conception of the World: The Vienna Circle', in Sahotra Sarkar, ed., *The Emergence of Logical Empiricism*.

[35] *Manifesto of the Vienna Circle*, quoting Bertrand Russell, *Our Knowledge of the External World* (London: George Allen & Unwin, 1914; reprinted 1922), p. 14.

period. Thus, in his 1907 *Thing and Space* lectures (DR, p. 2; Hua XVI 4), he already speaks of the natural attitude prior to science, contrasting, as we saw, the nature of platinum as described by the scientist (atomic complex, etc.) with what is grasped experientially, as a heavy lump in the hand (DR, p. 4; Hua XVI 6). Husserl offers a descriptive sketch of the naturally experienced world in *Ideas* I, but, in the early 1930s, he becomes particularly interested in the manner in which the world is given as one, common, communalized world for us, a world layered with natural things, living things (*Lebewelt*), animals, human communities and cultural establishments (Hua VII 243). The intersubjective, cultural and peculiarly temporal unfolding through history of this collective 'with-world' (*Mitwelt*, K 482) is now his particular focus.

All activities of consciousness, including all scientific activity and indeed all knowing, initially take place within the natural attitude (Hua XIII 112). The idea of the natural attitude first appears in print in *Ideas* I (1913), and it is extensively discussed in *Ideas* II (see especially § 49). In the essay 'Philosophy as Rigorous Science' (1910–11), it is linked with naturalism. But the correlate of the natural attitude, strictly speaking, is not nature. In *Ideas* I, Husserl portrays the natural attitude as the sphere of *doxa*,[36] correlated with 'world' (*die Welt*), initially understood as 'my natural surrounding world' (*meine natürliche Umwelt*, *Ideas* I § 28). This is the world in which I find myself all the time and which supplies the necessary background for all intentional acts. The true 'correlate' of the natural attitude is the *world* (*Ideas* I § 50), the horizon of possible investigations, the permanently present yet always receding background for all consciousness. Husserl elaborated on the basic structures of this 'surrounding world' (*Umwelt*) in *Ideas* II under the title 'The Constitution of the Spiritual [*geistige*] World'.

In our natural experience, we live spontaneously and naïvely in this world, 'swimming' with the flow of its givens, which have the character of being 'on hand' (*vorhanden*) and 'actual' (*wirklich*, *Ideas* I § 50). The natural world primarily has the character of actuality and presence; it is simply there. Furthermore, 'world', in this sense,

---

[36] Husserl uses many different phrases for this attitude including the 'natural theoretical attitude' (*Ideas* I, Hua III/1 94) and the 'natural-naïve attitude' (*Ideas* III, Hua V 148).

as we have seen, must not be understood as meaning what scientists now describe as the natural world *tout court* (i.e. the world of matter, energy, stellar systems and so on), nor simply the world of culture, but rather the world *precisely as experienced*, starting from the present and from ourselves, but including our pasts and projected futures and our cultural lives with other 'co-subjects' (*Mitsubjekte*, C 184; K 187; see also Hua IX 488). This is a *personal* and *interpersonal* world. I belong to a family, a 'people' (*Volk*), a cultural milieu (Husserl even uses the term *Volkgeist*), a generation, an historical period and so on. Philosophers today might speak of our 'folk' conception of the world. Husserl is conscious of the legacy of Dilthey, with his descriptions of the historical cultural world.

In his 1935 letter to the French anthropologist Lucien Lévy-Bruhl (and elsewhere), Husserl speaks of human living in this 'we-world':

Saying 'I' and 'we,' they find themselves as members of families, of associations, social units [*Sozialitäten*], as living 'together,' exerting an influence on and suffering from [*hineinwirkend in und leidend von*] *their* world – the world, which has sense and reality for them, through their intentional life, their experiencing, thinking, [and] valuing. Naturally, we have known for a long time that every human being has a 'world-representation' [*Weltvorstellung*],[37] that every nation, that every supranational [*übernationale*] cultural grouping lives, so to speak, in a distinct world as its own surrounding world, and so again every historical time in its [world].[38]

---

[37] Husserl does not use the more common term *Weltanschauung* ('worldview') here but the less usual *Weltvorstellung* (cf. 'The Vienna Lecture', C 272; K 317, where he writes: 'the historical surrounding world of the Greeks is not the objective world in our sense but rather their "world-representation", i.e. their own subjective validity with all the actualities that are valid for them within it, including, for example, gods, demons, etc.'). The term 'worldview' has a somewhat negative connotation for Husserl, given his documented stance against the 'worldview philosophy' (*Weltanschauungsphilosophie*) of Dilthey and others. In his 'Philosophy as Rigorous Science' (1910–11), the term 'worldview' means primarily an individual's approach to the world. Husserl writes:

Worldview is also an 'idea,' of course, but that of a goal lying in the finite, to be actualized principally in an individual life-time after the manner of steady approach, just like morality, which would certainly lose its sense if it were the idea of a principally transfinite infinite. The 'idea' of worldview is accordingly for each age a different one.

See PRS, p. 287; Hua XXV 52. In his correspondence in the 1930s, Husserl refers to National Socialism as a 'new worldview' (*neue Weltanschauung*), *Briefwechsel*, IV 313.

[38] 'Edmund Husserl's Letter to Lucien Lévy-Bruhl, 11 March 1935', trans. Dermot Moran and Lukas Steinacher, *New Yearbook for Phenomenology and Phenomenological Philosophy* Vol. 8 (2008), 349–54, esp. 350.

Husserl makes a similar statement in the *Crisis*, where he speaks of living personal life 'as "I," as "we" in action and passion [*in Tun und Leiden*]' (C 322; K 301).

Husserl himself has a tendency to speak of the natural attitude as a 'primitive' or fundamental attitude shared by all peoples. Thus, in his lecture to the Kant Society in 1924, the natural attitude is the 'original' attitude of humans living in the world: 'The natural attitude is the form in which the total life of humanity is realized in running its natural, practical course. It was the only form from millennium to millennium, until out of science and philosophy there developed unique motivations for a revolution.'[39] This suggests that, at least in terms of its essential character, there is only one natural attitude of humans over millennia, namely, the attitude of acceptance of the world, an unquestioning belief in the reality of the world, in its oneness, in its pregivenness as real, valid, constant and so on.

Husserl contrasts the 'natural attitude' with its corresponding world of 'normally experienced nature' (e.g. *Phenomenological Psychology* § 20, p. 98; Hua IX 128) with the 'objectively true' conception of nature found in the natural sciences.

The natural attitude itself, furthermore, while it pervades our consciousness, is not articulated; it is 'unthematic, unthought, unpredicated'. Indeed, it is – as an attitude – invisible, blind to the fact that it is an *attitude*, with 'blinkers' on. It does not know that it itself is an *achievement* (*Crisis* § 58) and that it is correlated with a specific kind of objectivity, namely the natural and cultural world as given in a certain temporal flow. The natural attitude is shot through with 'world-belief' (*Weltglaube*), naïve immediate confidence that the objects of perceptual experience are really there. Of course, the aim of the *epochē* is to overcome the natural attitude with its 'general thesis' of the world; all positing (*Setzung*) becomes, as Husserl says elsewhere, the 'phenomenon of positing' (Hua XXIV 212).

This conception of the natural attitude itself is not unproblematic. Clearly, the 'natural attitude' as an all-encompassing attitude must be shot through with prejudices of all kinds – religious, metaphysical, cultural, educational, technological and scientific. It is also, in the modern era, saturated with scientific, technological learning (e.g.

---

[39] See Husserl, KITP, p. 20; Hua VII 244.

we take it for granted that things like petroleum, electricity and gas belong to our world). At the same time, for Husserl, the life-world has been systematically *distorted* by post-Galilean science, as we discussed in Chapter 3. Therefore, in modernity, the natural attitude has been transmuted into the natural-scientific or 'naturalistic attitude'. Husserl addresses this problem specifically in *Crisis* Appendix III, 'The Attitude of Natural Science and the Attitude of Humanistic Science, Naturalism, Dualism, and Psychophysical Psychology' (C 315–34; K 294–313). Here he sees naturalism (as in his earlier *Philosophie als strenge Wissenschaft* (1910–11)) as understanding the world solely in terms of material extended objects in space and time, subject to causality: 'Naturalism looks at the world as filled-out extension and thus considers the world in general only as nature in a broader sense' (C 315; K 294). Naturalism further understands the duration of human experience merely as objective duration. At best it recognizes human subjectivity as some kind of supervenient entity on top of the physical constitution of bodies. In fact, human existence proceeds from a peculiar kind of inner temporality, and the structure of this 'immanent time' (C 316; K 295) needs to be carefully studied.

Over and against this 'scientific' (C 316; K 295) or 'naturalistic' attitude, the attitude which reveals persons and cultural artifacts is rather the 'personal attitude' (*die personale Einstellung*, C 317; K 206), which Husserl describes as follows:

> Interest is directed towards human beings as persons who, in personal actions and passions, are related to 'the' world, who, in the community of life [*im Miteinander des Lebens*], of personal interrelations, of activities and other ways of being, determined by and comporting oneself towards worldly things, have one and the same surrounding world, a world of which they are conscious [that it is] one and the same. (C 317; K 296)

This personal attitude is really the fully concrete, natural attitude of which the naturalistic attitude is a modern distortion.

ONE WORLD BUT RELATIVITY OF LIFE-WORLDS

As we have seen, Husserl always stresses the familiar world is always experienced as the 'one, existing world' (*die eine seiende Welt*, C 317; K 296). The very idea of a 'world' is the idea of a surrounding whole that acts as a unified horizon for experience. Husserl says that 'the plural makes no sense' when applied to the world (*Crisis* § 37); it is impossible to even conceive of a multiplicity of entirely distinct worlds. On the other hand, Husserl does also allow for a plurality of historical life-worlds and frequently speaks of life-worlds in the plural, e.g. *Lebensumwelten*, C 147; K 150; cf. CM § 58, p. 133; Hua I 160). How can these seemingly conflicting claims be reconciled? The question must also be raised as to whether and in what sense we moderns can be said to belong to the *same world* as the ancient Greeks. In one sense, as Jan Patočka points out, we can touch and see some of the cultural *products* (e.g. surviving temples, vases, statues, etc.) of other cultures and times, but, on the other hand, their cultural context – their *world* – of gods and customs and their significance escapes us. For Husserl (see *Crisis* § 36 and the 'Vienna Lecture'), different peoples and cultures can have very different, even competing, concepts of value, different 'historicities' (as we saw in the last chapter), amounting to different life-worlds to which they belong (the most obvious contrast is between *historical* and *history-less* life-worlds, and Husserl often references the Papuans as his example of a history-less, primitive, pre-technological culture). There is simply a profusion of different cultures, either contemporaneously or across history, which can be so self-enclosed as to constitute different life-worlds. Ludwig Landgrebe, indeed, speaks of Husserl's conception of 'self-enclosed worlds' (*geschlossene Welten*) – cultures closed in on themselves, lacking communication with other cultures – as a limit-concept, an idealization of what 'worldhood' or 'worldliness' (Husserl's *Weltlichkeit*, C 188; K 192) involves.[40] Landgrebe writes:

A closed home-world is indeed a limiting concept – a device for making the structure of a home-world particularly distinct – since, as a matter of fact, that would be a type nowhere to be found, certainly not in connection with any group now in existence. Everywhere the foreign projects into the home-world; the worlds surrounding different social groups are tied together by countless threads.[41]

---

[40] It would be interesting to compare Husserl's and Heidegger's conception of 'worldliness' or 'worldhood' (*Weltlichkeit*), see Heidegger, SZ § 14.
[41] See Landgrebe, 'The World as a Phenomenological Problem', 49.

Strictly speaking, in reality there is no completely isolated human group.

At the same time, while acknowledging the profusion of life-worlds, Husserl claims that the life-world as such (with its natural way of experiencing) has a universal, formal, a priori structure. How is this universal life-world, experienced as *one*, to be reconciled with the factual plurality of life-worlds and 'world-views' or 'world-representations' (*Weltvorstellungen*)? For Husserl, there is simply as a matter of fact an empirical 'relativity of the surrounding life-worlds of particular human beings, peoples, and periods' (C 147; K 150). Each person primarily understands his or her own life-world and surrounding culture, the historical period to which he or she belongs (*Crisis* § 71; cf. CM § 58). But these life-worlds can be understood as each parts of a larger whole – each life-world presupposes the 'general ground of the validity of the world' (C 147; K 151). One can understand worlds as standing in relations of horizonality to one another. One is a German first, but also a European, and so on.

For Husserl, moreover, attention to the life-world means attention must be paid to history, tradition and culture. If the life-world is constantly varying with culture and history, are there not wholly incommensurate life-worlds? Questions immediately arise about the relationship between the life-world and the natural attitude. Is there one common natural attitude for *all* humans, e.g. one underlying the conception of physical objects, spatio-temporal continuity, universal causality and so on, regardless of language and custom? This natural attitude would be called today the 'folk' attitude towards things, based on universal features of human embodiment and living (e.g. sleeping, eating, defecating, procreation, sign-use, and so on). Or are there many different natural attitudes (with different embedded conceptions of space, time and causality) corresponding to different cultures and societies? Husserl wants to establish a universal 'form' of the life-world, but also to allow for the diversity of life-worlds that are established across history.

Lucien Lévy-Bruhl, an almost exact contemporary of Edmund Husserl, was famous in his day for advocating a way of understanding so-called 'primitive' societies, which he claimed were characterized by a 'primitive mentality' embued with 'collective representations' (a conception he borrowed from Émile Durkheim (1858–1917)).

According to Lévy-Bruhl, 'a definite type of society, with its own institutions and customs will, therefore, necessarily have its own mentality'.[42] As Husserl himself attests in his letter to the anthropologist in March 1935, Lévy-Bruhl's speculations on the differences between the 'primitive mentality' and the Western or 'European' mind had a strong influence on him. Indeed, Lévy-Bruhl's speculations more or less paralleled Husserl's own thoughts about the correlations between attitudes and the 'worlds' correlated with them in his later writings (e.g the 'Vienna Lecture'). In his later works (especially in Hua xxxix), Husserl clearly distinguishes between two kinds of enquiry into the life-world: empirical and a priori. It is an empirical task to document the different life-worlds and their 'styles' (*Stile*) and 'habitualities' (*Habitualitäten*) as they occur through history. It is an a priori task to identify the essential form of any life-world whatsoever.

HOME WORLD AND ALIEN WORLD

A predominant emphasis in Husserl's treatment of the life-world is the manner in which it provides a basis of sense or 'meaning-fundament' for everything we do. The taken-for-granted nature of our world is such that it is only when we encounter another alien world that our own world is foregrounded. Husserl very frequently speaks of our 'familiar world' or 'near-world' (*Nahwelt*, C 324; K 303) as the 'home-world' (*Heimwelt*, C 324; K 303). It has the character of being accepted and familiar. The world is not a neutral objectivity but is something shared with others and, especially, with those who live in our proximity. Not just humans but certain species of animals (e.g. dogs) have a shared world in this sense (see K 482n.), a conception developed by Jakob Johann von Uexküll (1864–1944).

Each of us has our home-world with its own horizon of familiarity, beyond which things appear as strange, unfamiliar, foreign, alien. The world unfolds necessarily within relations of proximity and remoteness. The world is, Husserl states, a meaningful horizon that emerges continually in the unity of a history, and is inevitably lived

---

[42] See Lucien Lévy-Bruhl, *How Natives Think*, trans. Lilian A. Clare (London: George Allen & Unwin, 1926), p. 27.

through different perspectives and across distances. The home-world is experienced as encircled by this 'alien world' (*Fremdwelt*, C 324; K 303).

The home-world as the 'near-world' or familiar world can be quite enclosed and restricted in terms of our particular customs, dialects, habits, traditions, conceptions of past and future, and so on. The home-world in this sense is a kind of enveloping world, the communal equivalent of the individual 'sphere of ownness' (*Eigenssphäre*) which Husserl speaks of in his *Cartesian Meditations*. There is a process of 'normalization' whereby we appropriate our customs, habits and so on as *familiar* and normal, whereas others are treated as unfamiliar, strange and even 'abnormal'. The familiar is presented alongside the equally primordial unfamiliar (Hua xv 165) and, moreover, the unfamiliar must always be understood as having a kind of incompleteness. We are at home in the familiar (speaking our native language, for example), and we understand the unknown (e.g. a foreign language) on the basis of what is already known. There could never be a connection with the completely unfamiliar.

Indeed, every world has this structural bipolar tension of familiar and strange (Hua xv 43). There are, of course, degrees of familiarity and unfamiliarity. Even the totally strange (e.g. a completely foreign language) presents itself to us as familiar, *as a language*, and not just as senseless noise. Husserl frequently invokes the African or Chinese – or indeed the Papuan – worlds as *alien worlds*: 'But when we are thrown into an alien social sphere [*in einem fremden Verkehrskreis*], that of the Negroes in the Congo, Chinese peasants, etc., we discover that their truths, the facts that for them are fixed, generally verified and verifiable, are not the same as ours' (C 139; K 141). In order to truly understand them we need to put ourselves in their place. Ideally, we need to grow up in their world (see Hua xxxix 158). Alternatively, we can imagine ourselves in their worlds and grasp what is typical for us (trees, buildings, animals and so on), even though their typification is not available to us. Husserl writes in one manuscript:

The individual type [*Individualtypik*] is not completely known to me: a plant, but a strange sort, a field, but full of plants that are unfamiliar to me. The work on the field: I do not figure out their typical way to cultivate the land. A house is built in alien ways. Is it a temple, or is it a building of the government? I am in China, in the market trade and traffic, but in an alien way. I do know that they have their own typification [*Typik*], but I have no knowledge of them; somehow there are people there in the market. (Hua XXXIX, 159, my translation)

Something typical in one world is unfamiliar in another.

THE TRUTH OF THE PRE-COPERNICAN WORLD

The conception of familiar and strange worlds allows us to introduce and to frame the discussion concerning the late Husserl's contrast between the pre-Copernican world of experience and the post-Copernican, Galilean world of natural science. As we saw in Chapter 3, Husserl had long been reflecting on the impact of Galilean science on the pre-Copernican world of experience. His late essay on the truth of the pre-Copernican worldview is an important exploration of the notions of rest/motion that prevail in the life-world. According to the Ptolemaic conception of the world, the world did not move, and the sun and planets orbited around the earth. After Galileo, the situation is reversed and the earth is said to orbit around the sun. In a late text, Husserl explores the sense in which the earth may be said *not to move*; the pre-Copernican picture expresses a certain truth about life-world experience. Already in *Ideas* II, Husserl had asserted that the scientific idea of a thing as not changing without a cause is not in fact in line with intuitive experience (*Ideas* II § 16, p. 53; Hua IV 49). Naïve experience believes a thing *can* change on its own and finds nothing incoherent in that idea. Husserl writes:

It was the new science of nature which first grasped this idea of a strict identity in the absolutely determined and unequivocal dependencies of causality (an idea that has to be set off from any empirical apprehension) and which developed the demands implicit in this idea, demands which determine essentially the course of the scientific investigation into nature. (*Ideas* II § 16, p. 52; 49)

The life-world encapsulates a comprehensive way of experiencing that has its own truth (as in our everyday experience of the earth as motionless), even if it conflicts with science. Husserl never fully works out the implications of this clash between everyday intuition and scientific explanation. He is more concerned to write about the transformation that the scientific attitude, or indeed the theoretical attitude generally, has wrought on the natural attitude.

THE THEORETICAL ATTITUDE OF
THE DISINTERESTED SPECTATOR

Husserl's 'Vienna Lecture' is one of his most extensive explorations of the relations between various fundamental attitudes, including the 'natural primordial attitude' (C 281; K 327), the 'religious-mythical attitude' (C 282; K 328), the 'theoretical attitude' (C 280; K 326) and so on. In his later works, from the 1920s on, Husserl frequently speaks about the attitude of the 'detached', 'non-participating' spectator (*unbeteiligter Zuschauer*, Hua XXXIV 9), or 'disinterested spectator' (*uninteressierter Zuschauer*, see especially *Crisis* §§ 45 and 68 and the 'Vienna Lecture').[43] He also speaks of this as the theoretical attitude, or the attitude of 'theoretical praxis', or simply *theoria*, C 282; K 328, an historically late attitude in terms of the development of world culture that had its particular breakthrough in ancient Greece. In this new attitude, the human enquirer 'turns away from all practical interests and, within the closed sphere of its cognitive activity, in the times devoted to it, strives for and achieves nothing but pure *theoria*. In other words, man becomes a nonparticipating spectator, surveyor of the world; he becomes a philosopher' (C 285; K 331).

The disinterested spectator has broken free from the 'captivation' (*Befangenheit*) or bewitchment of the natural attitude and has initiated the transcendental *epochē* thereby to be free of practical engagements and interests. Rather than swimming with the stream of temporal, experienced life, the disinterested spectator is able to see the world as the harmonious unfolding of a stream of subjective appearances; in other words, he or she is able to see the world as the outcome of the process of constitution by the transcendental ego. The *uninterested* or *disinterested* spectator or observer is no longer captivated by the fundamental belief in the world or the general thesis of the natural attitude. Indeed, the disinterested spectator is in a position to identify the natural attitude in its working and understand it precisely *as a stance*. Furthermore, the disinterested spectator realizes that the

---

[43] The term 'disengaged' or 'disinterested spectator' does not appear in *Ideas* I.

concept of 'world in itself' and 'being in itself' that evolved in the theoretical attitude and became especially thematic in the scientific outlook is itself a constituted outcome of a specific attitude.

CONCLUSION: THE ENDURING INFLUENCE OF HUSSERL'S CONCEPT OF LIFE-WORLD

Although certain key aspects of Husserl's discussion of the life-world are extremely challenging, as we have seen, the life-world quickly established itself as a theme of discussion among his students and followers, including Landgrebe, Heidegger, Schutz, Patočka, Gurwitsch, Gadamer and others, and can now be said to be a concept which has established itself in contemporary philosophical discourse.

The young Martin Heidegger already invokes the concept of *Lebenswelt* in his early lecture courses in Freiburg (1919–23).[44] In his 1919–20 *Basic Problems of Phenomenology* lecture course, for instance, Heidegger speaks of a 'primordial science of life' (*Ursprungswissenschaft vom Leben*) and also explicitly discusses the concept of *Lebenswelt*.[45] In *Being and Time* (1927), he explores the 'world of everyday Dasein' (*die Welt des alltäglichen Daseins*), and indeed Merleau-Ponty claims, in his *Phenomenology of Perception* (1945), that 'the whole of *Sein und Zeit* springs from an indication given by Husserl and amounts to no more than an explicit account of the "*natürlicher Weltbegriff*" or the "*Lebenswelt*" which Husserl, towards the end of his life, identified as the central theme of phenomenology' (PP, pp. vii; i). Heidegger, however, is critical of the primacy given to the theoretical attitude in Husserl and instead advocates recognition of the pragmatic character of our world-engagement.

Alfred Schutz wrote on the topic of human natural and social experience in his *The Phenomenology of the Social World* (1932),[46] a

---

[44] The posthumous publication of Heidegger's early Freiburg lecture courses show that Heidegger started his lecturing career with reflections on Husserl's concept of the life-world and the nature of the shift towards the theoretical attitude (themes found in Husserl's *Ideas* II manuscripts).

[45] See Martin Heidegger, *Grundprobleme der Phänomenologie (Wintersemester 1919/20)*, ed. Hans-Helmuth Gander, GA 58, 2nd edn (Frankfurt: Klostermann, 2010) §§ 11, 13, and 14, pp. 69, 75, 83–5, 174f., 250 and 261.

[46] Alfred Schutz, *Der sinnhafte Aufbau der sozialen Welt* (The Meaningful Construction of the Social World) (Vienna: Springer, 1932; reprinted Frankfurt: Suhrkamp Taschenbuch, 1974),

work that was praised by Husserl, and that – significantly – appeared before Husserl's own *Crisis* (1936). Schutz distinguishes between different dimensions of world, including the 'world of contemporaries' (*soziale Mitwelt*), 'world of predecessors' (*Vorwelt*) and the 'world of one's successors' (*Folgewelt*), as well as the social world of the present, what he calls 'the realm of directly experienced social reality'.[47] Schutz emphasizes such features as the stratification of the life-world into zones, hierarchies and so on; the manner in which experience is 'typified' (organized around identifiable empirical types such as 'dog', 'tree' and so on);[48] and the manner in which a background has to have *relevance* to the issue on hand in order to motivate action. He also speaks explicitly of the 'environment' (with reference to Husserl's *Ideas* I § 41), which he defines as 'that part of the external world that I directly apprehend', including not just natural objects but social objects, languages and so on.[49] This is what Schutz calls 'the world of the we'.[50] Through Schutz's subsequent publications,[51] life-world became an important theme in sociology, especially in the United States.[52]

As early as 1936, prior even to the publication of Husserl's *Crisis* articles, the Czech philosopher Jan Patočka published his Habilitation thesis in Czech entitled *The Natural World as a Philosophical Problem*.[53] In this work, Patočka employed Husserl's concept of the life-world as a way of understanding communal human existence and applying it to Heideggerian problems connected to historicity and finitude. Patočka had been present at Husserl's Prague lectures and was in correspondence

trans. George Walsh and Frederick Lehnert as *Phenomenology of the Social World* (Evanston, IL: Northwestern University Press, 1967; London: Heinemann, 1972).

[47] Schutz, *Phenomenology of the Social World*, pp. 142–4. Schutz credits Schiller with the term *Folgewelt*.

[48] See Alfred Schutz, 'Type and Eidos in Husserl's Late Philosophy', in Schutz, *Collected Papers III: Studies in Phenomenological Philosophy*, ed. I. Schutz (The Hague: Martinus Nijhoff, 1966), pp. 92–115.

[49] Schutz, *Phenomenology of the Social World*, p. 170.

[50] Ibid., p. 171.

[51] See for instance, Alfred Schutz, 'Some Structures of the Life-World', trans. Aron Gurwitsch, in Schutz, *Collected Papers III*, pp. 116–32.

[52] See Alfred Schutz and Thomas Luckmann, *The Structures of the Life-World*, Vol. I, trans. Richard M. Zaner and H. Tristram Engelhardt, Jr. (Evanston, IL: Northwestern University Press, 1973).

[53] Jan Patočka, *Přirozený Svět Jako Filosofický Problém* (Prague: Československý Spisovatel, 1992). An English translation is currently in preparation.

with Husserl, but the *Philosophia* articles had not yet appeared when Husserl wrote his work. Patočka continued to write through his life about the life-world as a challenge to scientific technicity.[54] In his 'Epilogue to the French edition of *Natural World as a Philosophical Problem*' written many years later (1976), Patočka notes that his use of the term 'natural world' derived from Husserl's terms 'natural world', later *Lebenswelt*, or 'the world of our life' (*monde de vie*).

---

[54] See, for instance, Jan Patočka, 'Edmund Husserl's Philosophy of the Crisis of the Sciences and His Conception of a Phenomenology of the "Life-World"', trans. Erazim Kohák, in Erazim Kohák, ed., *Jan Patočka. Philosophy and Selected Writings* (Chicago, London: University of Chicago Press, 1989), pp. 223–38, and 'The "Natural" World and Phenomenology', trans. Erazim Kohák, in Kohák, ed., *Jan Patočka*, pp. 239–73.

CHAPTER 7

Phenomenology as transcendental philosophy

> Natural human understanding and the objectivism rooted in
> it will view every transcendental philosophy as a flighty eccen-
> tricity, its wisdom as useless foolishness; or it will interpret it
> as a psychology which seeks to convince itself that it is not
> psychology. (C 200; K 204)

PHENOMENOLOGY AS THE 'FINAL FORM' OF
TRANSCENDENTAL PHILOSOPHY

Having reviewed Husserl's critique of the natural and human
sciences (including psychology), his analysis of history and culture,
and his novel analysis of the life-world, it is now time to explicate the
nature of his transcendental phenomenology and, in particular, his
unwavering commitment to transcendental idealism. I shall primarily focus on Husserl's mature transcendental phenomenology and his
transcendental idealism as it is expressed throughout the *Crisis*, especially in Part III A and B, and in some of the important supplementary texts, but I shall also explain the background to his conversion
to transcendental idealism.

In his mature writings, especially after *Ideas* I, Husserl always
insists that phenomenology is possible only *as transcendental philosophy*, and that the correct understanding of the *epochē* and the reduction are essential for understanding the move to the transcendental
required by any genuine, ultimately grounded 'first philosophy'.[1] The

---

[1] Husserl adopted from Descartes (and of course originally from Aristotle) the idea of an
ultimate grounding science which is called *prima philosophia* or 'first philosophy'. Husserl
insists that fully clarified transcendental phenomenology (which includes even the 'phenomenology of phenomenology') is the ultimate first philosophy.

Crisis offers an extended and trenchant explication and defence of phenomenology as a form – the 'final form' (*Endform, Crisis* § 14) – of transcendental philosophy.[2] Indeed, the very title of the *Crisis* includes the phrase 'transcendental phenomenology', and in the course of the work he specifically identifies his position as 'transcendental idealism', albeit, he maintains, in an entirely new sense.

Husserl considers the domain of transcendental subjectivity not just to be a set of formal conditions for knowledge (as in Kant), categorial frameworks and formal rules for organizing experience, but to be a domain of *life*, of *living* (*Leben*), of genuine *experience* (*Erfahrung*), a domain that has never before been examined in philosophy. Husserl further insists that the *epochē* and reduction are necessary gateways to this transcendental 'field' (*Feld*), which is a field of *experience*, a field of direct *intuition*, and, moreover, one of unlimited extent. The transcendental domain is a domain of conscious experiences, albeit a domain of experience which cannot be entered from the natural attitude. There is a genuine experience of worldly consciousness, of the sense of the past, the future, horizons of possibility, impossibility and so on. In this regard, it is also important to understand that the 'life-world', discussed in depth in the previous chapter, is actually a *transcendental* concept.

Husserl wrote an important defence of his idealism in his 'Author's Preface to the English Edition' (1931) of *Ideas* translated by William R. Boyce Gibson (1869–1935),[3] but the *Crisis* offers a greatly expanded account. In his proposed Foreword to the Continuation of the *Crisis* (not translated by Carr) he writes:

I ask only one thing here at the outset, that in reference to these prejudices, one's intended knowing-in-advance [*sein vermeintliches Im-voraus-Wissen*], one keeps whatever is meant by the words phenomenology, transcendental, idealism (as transcendental-phenomenological idealism, etc.) locked tightly in one's breast, as I have fitted them out with completely new meanings. (K 440, my translation)

---

[2] Notice that Husserl says 'an' endform – he is not asserting that phenomenology is the future of all philosophy or that transcendental philosophy can only resolve itself in phenomenology.

[3] See Edmund Husserl, 'Author's Preface to the English Edition', *Ideas: General Introduction to Pure Phenomenology*, trans. W. R. Boyce Gibson (New York: Collier Books, 1962), pp. 5–22. Husserl's slightly different German text was originally published in *Jahrbuch für Philosophie und phänomenologische Forschung* Vol. 11 (1930), reprinted in Hua v 138–62; trans. R. Rojcewicz and A. Schuwer as 'Epilogue', *Ideas* 11, pp. 405–30.

Husserl thus insists that transcendental idealism, or – as he calls it here – 'transcendental-phenomenological idealism' is idealism in an entirely new sense, and that one must put to one side all previous conceptions of transcendental idealism as found within the European philosophical tradition and rethink the concept anew (see K 440). He also distances himself from those of his own followers who did not take the transcendental turn (he has in mind primarily the Munich philosophers, such as Hedwig Conrad-Martius, Moritz Geiger (1880–1937) and Alexander Phänder), but he will also criticize Max Scheler and Martin Heidegger for misunderstanding his transcendental stance. In the *Crisis*, he writes against the realist phenomenologists: 'in opposition to all those phenomenologies that were motivated by the *Logical Investigations* that form the so called "phenomenological school". It is thus called transcendental philosophy, even though it is not an advancement, a remodelling or an improvement or disimprovement of the Kantian' (K 431, my translation). Furthermore, this new transcendental idealism has to be understood in terms of the radical carrying-out of the transcendental reduction.

THE ORIGIN OF THE WORLD

In the *Crisis*, Husserl, rather than beginning from the standpoint of the meditating, isolated ego, as in the *Cartesian Meditations* (1931), now begins from the experience of the *world*, from the 'natural possession of the world'. Summarizing this new approach, Husserl wrote to his friend Roman Ingarden on 11 June 1932: 'I have come to the conclusion that only a really concrete explication [*Emporleitung*] that ascends from the natural possession of the world and of being [*Welt- und Seinshabe*] to the "transcendental"-phenomenological stance … can serve.'[4] The world in question, of course, is the 'pregiven life-world' (as discussed in Chapter 6) which is 'always already there' (*immer schon da*, C 142; K 145) and is experienced in 'simple' (*schlicht*), 'straightforward' (*geradehin*) 'ongoing life' (*Dahinleben*, C 150; K 153). The *Crisis* exposition of transcendental phenomenology, then, begins from this 'natural possession' (*Habe*) of the world in

---

[4] See Husserl, *Briefwechsel* III 285; trans. Bruzina, p. 214.

everyday experience. The life-world in which we live 'naïvely' will be, under the transcendental *epochē*, transformed into a 'transcendental phenomenon' (C 174; K 177).

Husserl's late phenomenology, then, is correctly characterized by his student Eugen Fink when he emphasizes, in his 1933 article,[5] that Husserl is primarily concerned with the constitution of *world*, with what Fink calls 'the origin of the world' (*Ursprung der Welt*). For Husserl, the central mystery of intentional experience is how it is that a *world* is given to us, how 'world-consciousness' (C 398; K 514) is possible. The horizonal phenomenon of *world* went unnoticed in previous philosophy; now it must be foregrounded. Husserl himself frequently underscores his mission to explore the consciousness of world. His new transcendental approach involves a 'radical reshaping [*Neugestaltung*] of our whole way of looking at the world' (C 175; K 178). Identifying this horizonal world and making it thematic means already to have disrupted the hold of its influence and to be already moving 'above' it to the *transcendental* attitude (C 152; K 155) that regards world as always correlated with a constituting subjectivity or intersubjectivity. The aim, as the very title of *Crisis* § 41 indicates, is the 'discovery and investigation of the transcendental correlation between world and world-consciousness' (*Weltbewusstsein*, C 151; K 154). In this section, Husserl says that the performance of the phenomenological *epochē* is precisely to make one free – 'free of the strongest and most universal, and at the same time most hidden internal, bond, namely, of the pregivenness of the world'. Transcendental philosophy will illuminate the constitution of the life-world.

INTRODUCING TRANSCENDENTAL PHENOMENOLOGY
IN THE *CRISIS*

The topic of transcendental subjectivity emerges rather hesitantly in the *Crisis* and is merely touched on in passing in the opening sections (C 5; K 3). Initially, Husserl alludes to various enigmas – of subjectivity, of reason and its relation to being – 'the enigma of all enigmas' (C 13; K 12), as well as the need to overcome naïve 'objectivistic

---

[5] Eugen Fink, 'The Phenomenological Philosophy of Edmund Husserl and Contemporary Criticism', in Roy Elveton, ed., *The Phenomenology of Husserl: Selected Critical and Contemporary Readings*, 2nd edn. (Seattle: Noesis Press, 2000), pp. 70–139.

philosophy' (C 59; K 60), the need for a critical self-understanding of the transformation that took place whereby, in modern philosophy (Hume), objectivism transmuted into 'transcendental subjectivism' (C 68; K 69). One has to wait until *Crisis* § 14 for the terms 'phenomenology' and 'transcendentalism' to emerge. It is not until *Crisis* § 18 that the discovery of subjectivity ('the greatest of all enigmas') in Descartes is discussed. Husserl refers several times in passing to the ego and its 'functions' and 'achievements' (*Leistungen*), but the full sense of 'the life of consciousness as the life of accomplishment' is not revealed until *Crisis* § 24, where it is attributed to Hume's ambiguous influence. Indeed, the first mention of the 'transcendental ego' is in *Crisis* § 43 (as uncovered 'in one leap' in the *Cartesian Meditations*, see C 155; K 158), and it is not until *Crisis* § 73 (in Biemel's numbering) that Husserl justifies his use of the term 'transcendental' to describe phenomenology as a genuine science of the entire 'transcendental field' of subjectivity such as earlier German Idealism had sought unsuccessfully to develop. Overall, Husserl's approach is indirect: he prefers the historical mode of exposition of the manner in which subjectivity has been understood by the philosophical tradition.

In *Crisis* § 14, Husserl explains that we have to understand our concept of world (e.g. ordinary world), the meaning that it has for us, its 'sense of being' (*Seinssinn*), as built upon our concept of pregiven, everyday experience. The *scientific* structure of the world is a specific accomplishment, a 'structure on a higher level' (*Gebilde höherer Stufe*) built on the pregiven world.[6] The mistake of traditional objectivism was to assume this pregiven world as primarily existent, whereas what is really primary is the (transcendental) *subjectivity* that accomplishes it (*Crisis* § 14): 'it is not the being of the world [*Sein der Welt*] as unquestioned, taken for granted, which is primary in itself … rather what is primary in itself is subjectivity, understood as that which naïvely pregives the being of the world and then rationalizes or (what is the same thing) objectifies it' (C 69; K 70). This is a crucial passage. It boldly announced the project of studying world-constituting subjectivity (although it does not present this here as 'transcendental subjectivity)'.

---

[6] The German, term '*Gebilde*' carries the connotation of something that has a *Bildung*, an educational formation, suggesting a cultural product rather than a standalone 'structure'.

One has to wait until *Crisis* Part IIIB for Husserl's fuller discussion of transcendental idealism, which centres around his discussion of the 'paradoxes' of subjectivity. Transcendental idealism is presented in response to what he calls 'the paradox of human subjectivity' (*Crisis* § 53). The paradox is easy to express: how is it possible that human beings are both subjects 'for the world' and also objects 'in the world'? Husserl presents this paradox as a serious difficulty and challenge to his investigation of what he calls the 'pure problems of correlation' (C 174; K 178) opened up by the 'phenomenological-transcendental *epochē*' (elsewhere called the 'full transcendental *epochē*', C 263; K 267).

Transcendental phenomenology, as he explains in his 'Author's Preface' to Boyce Gibson's translation of *Ideas* I, is to be an ultimate science that encompasses 'the universal horizon of the problems of philosophy' ('Epilogue', *Ideas* II, p. 408; Hua v 141). It exemplifies the essence of transcendental philosophy as such and, indeed, is the fully justified form of 'first philosophy'. Transcendental phenomenology finally lays hold of a method of incontrovertible, apodictic evidence (K 431) that shakes off the obscurities inherent in post-Kantian transcendental philosophy. Indeed, as Husserl always insists – and here one sees the continuity between the *Cartesian Meditations* and the *Crisis* – it is Descartes as the discoverer of the infinite apodictic evidence to be explored in the transcendental ego who, more than Kant, deserves the title of the founder of transcendental philosophy (K 431). This new transcendental phenomenology offers a *revision* of Kantian philosophy through its grounding and conceptual fixing of transcendental subjectivity in 'living intuition' (K 431).

Husserl is concerned not just to articulate the nature of transcendental subjectivity, but also to explain how it is that it 'objectifies' or 'enworlds' or 'mundanizes' itself as an embodied subject in the real world of time, space and history.[7] In *Crisis* Part III he uses the 'way into transcendental philosophy from psychology' as his methodology for expounding the paradox. At the beginning of *Crisis* § 59, Husserl gives an insight into how he will address the paradox by showing how the focus on psychological subjectivity in modern science and

---

[7] The late Husserl speaks of natural human 'mundane' living. The transcendental ego is said to be 'mundanized' (*mundanisiert*, C 206; K 210, or 'enworlded', *verweltlichen* K209) as a human being in the natural, social world.

philosophy involves an essential misconstrual of transcendental functioning subjectivity:

> In psychology, the natural, naïve attitude has the result that human self-objectifications [*Selbstobjektivationen*] of transcendental intersubjectivity, which belong with essential necessity to the makeup of the constituted world pregiven to me and to us, inevitably have a horizon of transcendentally functioning intentionalities [*Horizont von transzendental fungierenden Intentionalitäten*] which are not accessible to reflection, not even psychological-scientific reflection. (C 208; K 212)

All positive sciences – including psychology – function in the prevailing natural attitude, and it belongs to the very essence of this attitude to obscure entirely the conditions which make such living possible, namely what Husserl here calls the transcendental life of 'functioning intentionality' (*fungierende Intentionalität*). The natural attitude can never uncover the phenomenon of world at all, never mind the intentional accomplishments that make possible the experience of world.

The terms 'functioning intentionality' or 'functioning subjectivity' are of crucial significance (see *Crisis* §§ 13 and 72, and Hua XXIX 169, where it is linked with 'consciousness of the world'). 'Functioning subjectivity' is a rare term in the later Husserl used to refer to the kind of anonymous, background, pre-reflective, passively experiencing subjectivity that is continuously functioning in passivity to produce the unified experience of the world as pregiven in experience. Functioning intentionality was in fact highlighted by Fink and Merleau-Ponty. In his Preface to his *Phenomenology of Perception* (1945), Merleau-Ponty speaks of 'functioning intentionality' (*fungierende Intentionalität*, PP, pp. xviii; xiii, which he translated as 'operative intentionality', see also PP, pp. 418, 478) which he contrasts with active, positing or 'thetic' intentionality that involves the activity of the ego. Merleau-Ponty's source for this distinction is Husserl's *Formal and Transcendental Logic*, where the term 'living ... functioning intentionality' appears (FTL § 94, p. 235; Hua XVII 208).

This functioning subjectivity or, in other words, the transcendental conditions which make life possible (as common life within a shared world), can only be uncovered by a deliberate change of direction or orientation in intention, one that itself belongs to the nature of transcendental life. As Husserl writes in the first draft (Draft A) of his *Encyclopaedia Britannica* article on 'Phenomenology': 'The transcendental reduction opens up, in fact, a completely new kind of experience that can be systematically pursued: transcendental experience. Through the transcendental reduction, *absolute* subjectivity, which functions everywhere in hiddenness [*in Verborgenheit fungierende absolute Subjektivität*], is brought to light along with its whole transcendental life [*mit all ihrem transzendentalen Leben*]' (*Trans. Phen.*, p. 98; Hua IX 250). It is this process of bringing transcendental intentional life from hidden obscurity into clarity that Husserl explores in *Crisis* Part III. Here and elsewhere Husserl will make a distinction between 'psychological', 'natural or mundane' subjectivity and transcendental subjectivity – which is designated as 'absolute'. For Husserl, 'achieving subjectivity', or as Carr translates it 'functioning subjectivity' (*die leistende Subjektivität*, C 67; K 68) – that is, the intentionality that constitutes the sense of the world itself and that will later be distinguished from active intentionality – cannot be adequately understood by the science of psychology.

Husserl claims that transcendental subjectivity (or intersubjectivity), understood as constituting the world, was unknown in previous philosophy. Thus, in a draft paper written in 1935 (Hua XXVII 228–31), he maintains that the ancient world has no knowledge of functioning, constituting subjectivity:

Even the teleological worldview of Aristotle is objectivist. Antiquity did not yet envisage the great problem of subjectivity as functioning, accomplishing subjectivity of consciousness, as world and in-the-world-existing human subjectivity, experiencing, cognizing, acting – and in this subjective achieving, bringing about 'the' world, which is obviously pregiven, bringing it about in streaming, manifold 'presentations' [*Vorstellungen*] as that in which is accomplished the concordant, validating sense 'existing world', etc. (Hua XXVII 228, my translation)

Traditionally, philosophy has as its theme knowledge of the world as a whole, but it neglected (until Descartes introduces radical scepticism about the very existence of the world) how the world appears in consciousness as a common, shared, intersubjective world with horizons of past and future. Husserl's transcendental phenomenology, then, as it appears in the *Crisis*, is a phenomenology of our *intersubjective constitution of the world*. But let us briefly explore the evolution of Husserl's phenomenological idealism.

THE EVOLUTION OF HUSSERL'S TRANSCENDENTAL
IDEALISM (1908–38)

As we have seen, Husserl insists that *his* transcendental idealism is the
most radical form to have emerged in the whole history of modern
philosophy (although he does express some admiration for Berkeley).
Furthermore, he maintains that his approach is absolutely not the
result of a wilful, speculative adoption of a philosophical position
or a theory. Although he characterizes his position as an *idealism*, he
certainly does not mean to put the existence of the world in any form
of doubt or to denigrate its status in any way. On the contrary, the
aim is to uncover why and how the world comes to have such a constant meaning for us. As he puts it in his 'Author's Preface' to Boyce
Gibson: 'Its [phenomenological idealism's] sole task and accomplishment is to clarify the sense of this world, precisely the sense in which
everyone accepts it – and rightly so – as actually existing' ('Epilogue',
Ideas II p. 420; Hua V 152). While 'clarification of sense' had always
been associated with the phenomenological project, this focus on the
world is new.

Husserl's early phenomenology was particularly appreciated for its
direct realism concerning the apprehension of ideal entities.[8] As Edith
Stein later recalled: 'The *Logical Investigations* had caused a sensation
primarily because it appeared to be a radical departure from critical
realism which had a Kantian and a neo-Kantian stamp. It was considered a "new scholasticism" because it turned attention away from
the "subject" and toward "things" themselves.'[9] Husserl's supposed
Neo-Scholasticism consisted of his realist defence of ideal objects as
directly intuited by eidetic and categorial intuition. Husserl himself,
however, classified his defence of the objectivity of categorial unities and universals as 'idealism'. Thus, already in the *Second Logical
Investigation* in the first edition of the *Logical Investigations* (1901), he
states that the defence of the objectivity of ideal objects 'is the point
on which relativistic, empiricist psychologism differs from idealism,
which alone represents the possibility of a self-consistent theory of
knowledge' (Hua XIX/1 112). He then goes on to add, in the second

---

[8] See, for example, Roman Ingarden, *On the Motives Which Led Husserl to Transcendental Idealism*, trans. Arnór Hannibalsson (The Hague: Nijhoff, 1975).

[9] Edith Stein, *Life in a Jewish Family 1891–1916: An Autobiography*, trans. Josephine Koeppel, *Collected Works of Edith Stein* Vol. I (Washington, DC: ICS Publications, 1986), p. 250.

edition of 1913: 'To talk of "idealism" is of course not to talk of a metaphysical doctrine but of a theory of knowledge which recognizes the "ideal" as a condition for the possibility of objective knowledge in general, and does not interpret it away in psychologistic fashion' (LU II, *Intro*. I, 238; Hua XIX/1 112). Husserl's early idealism recognizes ideal entities and the validity of the eidetic intuition that grasps them. Gradually, however, Husserl's phenomenological exploration of subjectivity led to idealism in a stronger sense.

In his private research writings, Husserl had begun to describe his philosophical outlook as 'transcendental' from around 1908, primarily influenced by a reading of Kant.[10] Furthermore, although, strictly speaking, the term 'idealism' does not appear in *Ideas* I (1913),[11] there is no doubt that the readers of that work took it as indicating an idealist direction of interest. Husserl's commitment to idealism after 1913 was well known among his students and followers (especially in Göttingen, where Hedwig Conrad-Martius (1888–1966), Moritz Geiger, Roman Ingarden and Edith Stein commented critically on it). It provoked – in Husserl's own words – a 'scandal' (Hua V 150) among most of his followers.

Husserl himself seems to have adopted the term 'transcendental idealism' (*transzendentaler Idealismus*, see C 100; K 103, and also K 427) for his own position around 1915. It features in his *Fichte Lectures* of 1917–18,[12] for instance, but really comes to the fore in his subsequent publications, e.g. the *Encyclopaedia Britannica* article (1928), *Formal and Transcendental Logic* (1929, especially §§ 94–100), the *Cartesian Meditations* (1931, especially §§ 11, 34, 40 and 41) and, of course, in the 'Author's Preface' to Boyce Gibson's English translation of *Ideas* I (1931). In his 1924 lecture to the Kant Society, entitled 'Kant and the Idea of Transcendental Philosophy', Husserl explains the new approach of *Ideas* I as a discovery of phenomenology as the eidetic science of *pure* consciousness itself:

With the *Ideas* the deepest sense of the Cartesian turn of modern philosophy is, I dare to say, revealed, and the necessity of an absolute self-contained

---

[10] On the evolution of Husserl's transcendental idealism, see Dermot Moran, *Edmund Husserl: Founder of Phenomenology* (Cambridge: Polity Press, 2005), pp. 174–201.

[11] It was, however, included as a term in the index of matters compiled by Husserl's Göttingen student Gerda Walther.

[12] See Edmund Husserl, 'Fichte's Ideal of Humanity [Three Lectures]', trans. James G. Hart, *Husserl Studies* Vol. 12 (1995), pp. 111–33, esp. p. 118; Hua XXVII 276.

eidetic science of pure consciousness in general is cogently demonstrated – this, however, in relation to all correlations [*Korrelationen*] grounded in the essence of consciousness, to its possible really immanent moments and to its noemata and objectivities intentionally-ideally determined therein. (KITP, p. 12; Hua VII 234)

The realm of intentional consciousness is uncovered, but it is now described in the explicitly Kantian sense as 'pure' (*rein*), i.e. containing no empirical content. To reveal consciousness in its purity requires the phenomenological-transcendental reduction, Husserl always insists. This reduction is so radical that the reflecting subject practising the *epoché* must no longer consider himself or herself as a human subject in the real world. All links with mundane human life have to be put in brackets. The effect of the *epoché* is precisely to exclude everything 'human' and thereby all presuppositions concerning psychological subjectivity.

Not only is human nature put to one side under the *epoché*, but the *world* also loses its ontological status as actual (as conferred by the natural attitude) and becomes *world as phenomenon* (*Crisis* § 51). Genuine transcendental philosophy enquires about the *phenomenon* of the world, how a world is presumed in all our experiencing and is indeed latent in our experience. It is because of this focus on world that, for Husserl, the real breakthrough to transcendental philosophy was brought about not by Immanuel Kant (who is always associated with the terminology of 'transcendental' enquiry) but actually by Descartes' radical exclusion of the world, leading to his discovery of the apodictic *cogito ergo sum* and its life of experiences. In the *Crisis*, Husserl situates his own use of the term 'transcendental' in relation to the 'regressive enquiry' inaugurated by Descartes. He writes:

I myself use the word 'transcendental' *in the broadest sense* for the original motif … which through Descartes confers meaning on all modern philosophies … It is the motif of enquiring back [*das Motiv des Rückfragens*] into the ultimate source of all the formations of knowledge, the motif of the knower's reflecting upon himself and his knowing life [*des Sichbesinnens des Erkennenden auf sich selbst und sein erkennendes Leben*] in which all the scientific structures that are valid for him occur purposefully, are stored up as acquisitions. (C 97–8; K 100–1)

Husserl goes on to insist that transcendental philosophy is an 'ultimately grounded universal philosophy' (*letztbegründeten Universalphilosophie*), grounded in my own self.

According to Husserl's 'Cartesian' formulation, transcendental philosophy is a self-reflexive philosophy of subjectivity that begins from the conscious ego reflecting on itself and its experiences (no longer considered as events in the mundane world but as intentional meaning-constitutings on an a priori level). This egological self-reflection is to provide the universal basis of all scientific knowledge. Husserl's formulation in *Crisis* § 26 is consistent with his earlier elaboration of transcendental idealism in the *Cartesian Meditations*. These two texts – so often juxtaposed – in fact represented in Husserl's mind two different expositions of the *same* doctrine of transcendental, phenomenological idealism. Husserl had already firmly articulated this egological 'primal fact' in 1929:

First of all, before everything else conceivable, I am… Whether convenient or inconvenient, and even though (because of no matter what prejudices) it may sound monstrous to me, it is the primal matter-of-fact [*Urtatsache*] to which I must hold fast, which I, as a philosopher, must not disregard for a single instant. For children in philosophy, this may be the dark corner haunted by spectres of solipsism [*die Gespenster des Solipsismus*] and, perhaps, of psychologism, of relativism. The true philosopher, instead of running away, will prefer to fill the dark corner with light. (FTL, § 95, p. 237; Hua XVII 243–4)

For Husserl, one cannot remove the fact that all experience begins from the certainty of the self; transcendental philosophy must both acknowledge and explore the inner meaning of this fact.

Husserl's realist students were particularly troubled by his insistence that the realm of transcendental or pure consciousness was a realm of 'absolute being' (*absolutes Sein*) over and against which everything objective has to be considered merely relative being. Husserl had asserted this very boldly in *Ideas* I, repeated it in the *Cartesian Meditations* and never abandoned it. In *Ideas* I, he speaks of an 'essential detachableness [*prinzipielle Ablösbarkeit*] of the whole natural world from the domains of consciousness' (*Ideas* I § 46, p. 104; Hua III/1 87), which he presents as the fundamental insight implicit in the Cartesian *cogito*. The transcendent world is such that it has meaning only in essential interconnection with consciousness – and not just possible consciousness but *actual* consciousness. Husserl even introduces a notorious thought experiment concerning the annihilation of the world, according to which the world is thought of as losing all sense and coherence. Even in this thought experiment, according to Husserl, constituting consciousness can-not be thought away (*Ideas* I § 49). Many years later, in his 'Author's Preface' to Boyce Gibson, Husserl conceded that this bold, Cartesian-inspired claim in *Ideas* I was 'incomplete' and 'suffered from imper-fections' ('Epilogue', *Ideas* II, p. 417; Hua V 150), because it left out of consideration the nature of *transcendental intersubjectivity*, of subjects operating together in the co-constitution of a harmonious world of possible experience. But he never *renounced* the claim that transcendental consciousness has *absolute being*. Indeed, in the *Crisis*, he continues explicitly to characterize transcendental subjectivity as 'the sphere of absolute being' (*die absolute Seinssphäre*, C 189; K 193) and absolute self-evidence. By 'absolute' evidence Husserl seems to mean an evidence that is self-explanatory – a self-contained form of evidence: 'Having arrived at the ego, one becomes aware of standing within a sphere of self-evidence of such a nature that any attempt to enquire behind it would be absurd' (C 188; K 192). Furthermore, it must be borne in mind that, despite Husserl's emphasis in the *Crisis* on the communal, intersubjective life-world, he never abandons his commitment to the *ontological priority of the transcendental ego* as that which constitutes world and hence has primacy over the world. This ego, however, has to be rethought in terms of its harmonious inter-twinings with other egos in what he calls 'transcendental intersub-jectivity'. It also becomes a serious question how the transcendental ego is to be related to the mundane ego of natural experience.

THE *CRISIS* RECONSTRUCTION OF THE HISTORY OF MODERN PHILOSOPHY

In the *Crisis* – as indeed in the *Cartesian Meditations* (although this usually goes unnoticed, as in the latter work the historical focus is restricted to Descartes alone) – Husserl initially introduces transcen-dental philosophy through a reconstruction of the history of modern philosophy as inaugurated by Descartes. In the *Cartesian Meditations*, Husserl is effectively re-performing Descartes' own meditations leading to the discovery of the *ego cogito*, whereas, in the *Crisis*, he provides a critical history of modern philosophy, reflecting on its 'inner' meaning and teleology. Thus, especially in the *Crisis* Part II (§§ 25–32), he sketches the 'history of transcendental philosophy'

(C 199; K 202), involving a sustained critique of Kant (he had earlier offered a shorter version of this story in *Formal and Transcendental Logic* and indeed in *First Philosophy*, 1923–24).

Husserl introduces transcendental phenomenology in terms of a story about the history of modern philosophy. Although, as we saw above, 'transcendental phenomenology' features in the very title of the *Crisis*, in fact he first introduces the concepts of *idealism* and the *transcendental* in Part II §§ 13 and 14, in terms of two opposed tendencies in modern philosophy, namely *naturalism* and *transcendentalism* (by which he means any philosophy that opposes naïve objectivism and recognizes that all objectivity is an achievement of transcendental subjectivity). Modern philosophy after Descartes consists of a series of 'tensions' (*Spannungen*, C 70; K 71) between transcendentalism and objectivism. In *Crisis* § 14, 'transcendentalism' is presented as protesting against the *psychological idealism* that emerged in the modern philosophical concept of the subject (in, for instance, Berkeley and Locke). Locke's naturalistic psychology simply takes over Descartes' concept of the soul as 'something self-contained and real by itself', i.e. a domain of inner experiences. Locke's attempt to ground the sciences by reducing them to what is experienced in the soul had the effect of stimulating a 'paradoxical idealism' that ended in 'absurdity' (C 86; K 89). By the time of Hume, *objectivism* itself had become transmuted into 'transcendental subjectivism' (C 68; K 69). Thus, transcendental psychology 'uproots' (*entwurzelt*, C 70; K 71) the original naturalistic and sensualist sense of psychology. Modern philosophy collapsed in Hume's 'fictionalism' or philosophy of 'as if', leading to an 'unhealthy academic scepticism' (C 193; K 195).

According to Husserl's reconstruction (his 'critical history of ideas', as he calls it in *First Philosophy,* Hua VII 3), the first revolutionary 'breakthrough' was made by Descartes, whose discovery of the *ego cogito* as transcendental ego was the 'seed' of transcendental philosophy, giving it its 'primal form' (C 199; K 202). As Husserl had already outlined in his *Paris Lectures* (the earlier draft of the *Cartesian Meditations*), the Cartesian discovery of the ego leads to a new concept of foundation: namely transcendental foundation (PL, p. 11; Hua I 11). However, he immediately went on to misinterpret the ego in objectivist terms as a 'substance', leading to the objectivism found both in the rationalist and empiricist traditions, e.g. Hobbes and Locke. However, for Husserl, problems in this objectivist tradition were already identified in a brilliant manner by Berkeley and Hume (*Crisis* § 56).

Descartes' revolutionary breakthrough to subjectivity lost its original impetus, however, by interpreting the transcendental ego as a thinking thing, *res cogitans*, or thinking substance, *substantia cogitans* (CM § 10, p. 24; Hua I 63). Descartes had correctly identified the ego as 'the greatest of all enigmas' (C 80; K 82) but unfortunately went on to misconstrue it in naturalistic fashion as an objective substance in the world. Descartes, as Husserl puts it in his *Cartesian Meditations*, treated this ego as a 'little tag-end of the world' (*ein kleines Endchen der Welt*, as he says in CM § 10, p. 24; Hua I 63) – as a real entity rather than as the condition for the possibility of unified experience and as a domain of meaning-constitution. Or, as Husserl puts it in the *Crisis*, Descartes treated the pure subject or ego as a 'residuum' (*Residuum*, C 79; K 81) left in the objective world.

In the *Crisis*, Husserl emphasizes Descartes' 'double-sidedness', i.e. the ambiguities inherent in his foundational moves. Descartes is responsible for the 'primal foundation' (*Urstiftung*) of transcendental philosophy (the discovery of the absolute evidence of the *ego cogito*), but he also inaugurates its naturalistic and objectivist misinterpretation. Descartes' breakthrough to transcendental subjectivity led to him uncovering 'functioning subjectivity', thereby giving philosophy a new *telos* (C 81; K 83): 'Thus in truth, there begins with Descartes a completely new manner of philosophizing which seeks its ultimate foundations in the subjective.'

In his *Crisis* reprise of the account of Descartes found in the *Cartesian Meditations* (and indeed earlier in *First Philosophy* (1923–24) and the *London Lectures* 1922),[13] Husserl also credits Descartes with uncovering the *infinity* of the ego (K 426), a discovery that Emmanuel Levinas will also underscore in his *Totality and Infinity*, which discusses the discovery of the idea of infinity within the ego in the Third Meditation.[14] But this infinity of transcendental subjectivity

---

[13] See Husserl's London lectures in *Einleitung in die Philosophie: Vorlesungen 1922/23*, ed. Berndt Goossens, Hua xxxv (Dordrecht: Kluwer, 2002).

[14] See E. Levinas, *Totality and Infinity*, trans. Alfonso Lingis (Pittsburgh: Duquesne University Press, 1969), pp. 49–50 and 92–3. The knowledge of the *ego cogito* leads to a recognition of an infinity which is not immanent in it or an object of its intention.

is lost in naturalistic psychology, which treats humans as animals in the real world (see Hua xxix 203ff.).

According to Husserl's interpretation, Descartes remained captivated by mathematical physics as a science and always had as his guiding ideal the Galilean-inspired concept of nature as the mathematical domain of pure bodies distinct from their sensible qualities (C 79; K 81). Descartes, furthermore, failed to think through the true meanings of *immanence* and *transcendence* (a familiar theme from Husserl's *Idea of Phenomenology* lectures of 1907). He did not ask how it was possible to think of God, the world of bodies and other people as somehow 'outside' this ego. The very notions of inside and outside, immanent and transcendent were not properly interrogated by him (*Crisis* § 19). Descartes ought to have understood that to carry out the *epoché* one must do more than slice away the body and material entities: one must let go of the whole natural, human dimension of worldly life. The ego with its flowing life of experiences (*cogitationes*) should never have been construed as a 'subject matter *in* the world' (C 82; K 84). Hence, Descartes never set himself the task of examining this ego for whom the sense of world is gained through its own 'functions' (C 82; K 84) and furthermore never asked how it is possible that this ego can co-exist with 'fellow egos' (*Mit-Iche*, K 84). Instead, Descartes misunderstood his newly discovered transcendental 'egology' (*Egologie*) as a positive science – psychology, thereby opening up the possibility of the problematic and theoretically insecure science of psychology in the modern sense (as we saw in Chapter 4).

The philosophical tradition *after* Descartes – both rationalism and empiricism – took on an *objectivist* shape that coincided with the methodological objectivism of the physical sciences. Husserl regards this objectivism as one of the greatest tragedies to befall philosophy (see his Prague Treatise, Hua xvii 209). It rigidified all thinking about subjectivity. Yet this objectivist rationalism (as it developed in Spinoza, for instance) could not remain stable, precisely because of its suppression of the entire subjective domain. Inevitably, a transcendental impetus had to burst through. A particular transformation took place, according to Husserl, when 'transcendental objectivism' was turned into 'transcendental subjectivism' (C 68; K 69), which occurred with Berkeley, Hume and Kant.

Husserl is the first to admit that there is a natural tendency towards objectivism in all knowledge. Objectivism is, as it were, the first reflex of the natural attitude, because it presumes and builds on the existence and reality of the world. It is possible only on the basis of the 'ground of the world', on the 'experience of the taken for granted pregiven world' (C 68; K 70). In contrast to this naïve objectivism, transcendentalism maintains that 'the ontic meaning [*der Seinssinn*] of the pregiven life-world is a subjective structure [*subjektives Gebilde*], it is the achievement [*Leistung*] of experiencing, prescientific life' (C 69; K 70). Modern philosophy, moreover, had construed subjectivity solely in a psychological manner, and psychology, for Husserl, can only treat subjectivity in terms of the psychological states of actual worldly beings, organisms in the world. A 'change of attitude' was needed to motivate philosophy to move in a transcendental direction and to awaken a completely different understanding of subjectivity. In this regard, Husserl has to confront the legacy of Kant. It is primarily Kant who is Husserl's focus; he touches on Hegel and 'the great systems of German Idealism' only in a most sketchy and unsatisfactory manner (see C 99; K 102 and C 198; K 201), e.g. when he speaks of the 'collapse of the Hegelian philosophy' (C 198; K 201). Husserl is insistent, furthermore, that *his* transcendental philosophy should not be seen as a continuation, amelioration or advancement of Kant's idealist philosophy (K 431). Nevertheless, it must involve a *revaluation* of Kant's achievement.

HUSSERL'S CRITIQUE OF KANT'S 'TRANSCENDENTAL SUBJECTIVISM'

Husserl's career-long relationship with Kant is extremely complex and difficult to summarize in a few paragraphs. Under the influence of Brentano (who was virulently anti-Kantian), he had initially been somewhat antagonistic towards Kant (as he later admitted in a letter to Ernst Cassirer), but his main target for many years was the Neo-Kantians, whom he accused of psychologism and anthropologism. Under the influence of his close friend, the Marburg Neo-Kantian and classicist Paul Natorp, however, he gradually began to reinterpret himself in relation to Kant's critique of pure reason. Natorp had favourably reviewed *Prolegomena to Pure Logic*, the first volume of the

Logical Investigations, in *Kant-Studien* in 1901, portraying Husserl as broadening the essentially Kantian enquiry into the necessary conditions of the possibility of experience.[15] Natorp predicted that Husserl would move further in the direction of Kant as he overcame what he considered Husserl's naïve opposition between the empirical psychological realm and the realm of abstract idealities.[16] Of course, Husserl himself regarded his separation of the psychological from the ideal as one of the particular strengths of the *Logical Investigations* and the first step towards establishing a properly grounded epistemology. But, by 1905, Husserl's discovery of the *epochē* and reduction led him to conceive of the subjective realm in a new manner. By 1907, in his *Idea of Phenomenology* lectures, Husserl deliberately presents his own approach in terms of revisiting the Kantian problem of how subjectivity can transcend itself in order to arrive at objectivity, by introducing a new conception of transcendence: *immanent transcendence* or transcendence in immanence (see IP, p. 35; Hua II 46).

Especially in his Freiburg years (1916–38), as is evident from the letters exchanged between the two, Husserl moved closer to the Neo-Kantian Heinrich Rickert, his predecessor in the Chair at Freiburg. Husserl is concerned to demystify Kantian transcendental philosophy, which he regarded as a speculative edifice not constrained by the intuitive givenness. Husserl also saw his own position as quite distinct from and more radical than Neo-Kantianism (of either the Marburg or Freiburg schools). Husserl had been criticized by the Kantians for his supposedly naïve, unclarified assumption about the status of intuition and his lack of an appreciation of the role of conceptuality in all knowledge, including perceptual knowledge. Husserl, however, rarely responded to his Neo-Kantian critics, and he left it to his assistants (Stein and Fink) to defend his phenomenology from the Neo-Kantian critique (see Hua XXV 226–48), as we shall discuss in Chapter 8.

Husserl criticizes many aspects of Kant, including an ungrounded 'mythic' approach to the categories and for maintaining a too stark

[15] Paul Natorp, 'On the Question of Logical Method in Relation to Edmund Husserl's Prolegomena to Pure Logic', in J. N. Mohanty, ed., *Readings on Edmund Husserl's Logical Investigations* (The Hague: Nijhoff, 1977), pp. 55–66.

[16] See Iso Kern, *Husserl und Kant: Eine Untersuchung über Husserls Verhältnis zu Kant und zum Neukantianismus*, Phaenomenologica 16 (The Hague: Nijhoff, 1964), p. 31.

contrast between sensibility and understanding. Thus, in his 1924 address to the Kant Society, Husserl says:

Naturally, we must from the outset go beyond all of the, in the worst sense of the word, 'metaphysical' stock elements of the critique of reason (like the doctrine of the thing-in-itself, the doctrine of *intellectus archetypus*, the mythology of the transcendental apperception or of the 'consciousness in general,' etc.), that oppose the phenomenological transcendentalism and with it the deepest sense and legitimacy of the Kantian position; and for his still half-mythical concept of the *a priori* we must substitute the phenomenologically clarified concept of the general essence and law of essence. (KITP, p. 13; Hua VII 235)

Generally speaking, Husserl considers Kant to be much less radical than Descartes. Descartes' stance of 'radical self-responsibility' is further-reaching than Kant's efforts to find the conditions of possibility of the accepted scientific knowledge. Furthermore, Kant somewhat naïvely accepted that the natural sciences gave the undisputed account of the nature of reality, whereas Descartes put the sciences under suspension (K 424). In *Crisis* Part II § 27, Husserl makes the point that Kant had already recognized the subjective grounding of the sciences without thereby making the discoveries and successes of the natural sciences into illusions:

As was already the case with Kant, the opinion is not that the self-evidence of the positive-scientific method is an illusion and its accomplishment [*Leistung*] is an illusory accomplishment [*Scheinleistung*] but rather that this self-evidence [*Evidenz*] is itself a problem; that the objective-scientific method rests upon a never-questioned, deeply concealed subjective ground [*tief verborgenen subjektiven Grunde*] whose philosophical elucidation will for the first time reveal the true meaning of the accomplishments of the positive sciences and correlatively, the true ontic meaning [*Seinssinn*] of the objective world – precisely as a transcendental-subjective meaning (C 99–100; K 103)

Husserl also sees Kant's attempt to secure 'a priori synthetic judgements' as a similar attempt to Descartes' efforts to secure the rationality beyond the subject.

On Husserl's account, David Hume had made Kant supremely sensitive to the problem of how an a priori normative reason could comprehend what was given in irrational sensible experience. Kant has a too narrow conception of what is given in sensuous experience, an outlook he inherited from the empiricists. Kant followed the empiricists in thinking that what was received were simply sense data from the outside: 'As for sensibility … it had generally been assumed that it gives rise to the merely sensible data, precisely as a result of affection from the outside. And yet one acted as if the experiential world of prescientific man – the world not yet logicized by mathematics – was the world pregiven by mere sensibility' (C 93: K 96). Husserl is critical of Kant's solution, which involved bifurcating reason: with a normative reason operating autonomously, and a second, hidden reason, 'constantly functioning in concealment' (C 94; K 97), which reached into the sensible world to order it. The entire world of things becomes a construction of subjectivity, with only the sense-data coming in from outside (*Crisis* § 25). Kant correctly identifies transcendental 'knowing subjectivity', but, because of his rationalism, he ends up in 'transcendental subjectivism' and did not deliver an account of *subjectivity* based on intuitive evidence. A new conception of transcendental subjectivity is called for.

Furthermore, along with transcendental subjectivity, phenomenology must give a transcendental account of the obvious self-evidence of the world that is taken for granted in all sciences and, indeed, in Kantian philosophy. Husserl believes that recognizing the world as an accomplishment of subjectivity, of the 'life of achievement' (*Leistungsleben*), is a hugely transformative insight. Naturalism, positivism and objectivism, are, properly understood all forms of loss or distortion of subjectivity.

THE PARADOXES OF TRANSCENDENTAL SUBJECTIVITY

In his mature writings, e.g. the *Encyclopaedia Britannica* article and *Cartesian Meditations*, Husserl frequently reiterates that everything in the world gets its 'being and sense' (*Sein und Sinn*) or 'ontic sense' (*Seinssinn*) from transcendental subjectivity. The claim that there is an a priori correlation between objectivity and constituting subjectivity is the core of Husserl's mature transcendental idealism. But the emphasis changes from stressing the transcendental ego as the source of all being and meaning to stressing the role of *transcendental intersubjectivity*, i.e. subjects cooperating together, integrating past achievements and projecting forwards to produce what he sometimes calls 'all-subjectivity' (*Allsubjektivität*, K 468; see also K 506, K 530) in the production of the world. Thus, in *Crisis* Supplement XX (relating to *Crisis* § 39, not translated by Carr), he says that 'thingly' being, that is, the sense of a common world, can only be understood as being in relation to the correlation with 'all-subjectivity'. Husserl writes, 'the ontological form of the world is that of world for all' (*Die ontologische Weltform ist die der Welt für alle*, K 469).

The subject–object correlation is omnipresent, for Husserl; being has no sense unless it is being for consciousness. But consciousness only exists as first-person consciousness which necessarily constitutes and *validates* this correlated objectivity (K 469). To appreciate this, one must withdraw from one's active participation in the world (which Husserl calls 'living-in', *Hinein-leben*, K 470) and uncover the hidden 'intentional life' of subjectivity with all its 'alterations of appearance, synthetic forms of unity, modes of validity, and possibilities' (see K 530, my translation). Husserl, furthermore, never tires of insisting on the act of 'validation' (*Geltung*) which I as egoic subject give to the world and its objects. I am affirming their legitimacy all the time in a continuous, streaming, intentional life of the ego.

We now have to face an important and puzzling feature of Husserl's transcendental idealism, namely his account of the nature and status of the transcendental ego and its relation to other subjects – the problem of transcendental intersubjectivity. Husserl's conception of the transcendental ego deeply alienated many of his closest followers, including Ingarden, Heidegger, Schutz, Merleau-Ponty and others. Yet, in all his later writings, Husserl insisted that the transcendental ego was at the very heart of his phenomenological investigations. In 1927 he could write: 'The clarification of the idea of my pure ego and my pure life – of my psyche in its pure specific essentiality and individual uniqueness – is the basis [*das Fundament*] for the clarification of all psychological and phenomenological ideas' (Hua XIV 438, my translation). In the *Cartesian Meditations*, the 'self-explication' (*Selbstauslegung*, Hua XXXIV 228) of the transcendental ego is presented as a set of 'great tasks' (CM § 29) of transcendental philosophy. Similarly, in the *Crisis*, Husserl proposes a 'critical reinterpretation and correction of the Cartesian concept of the ego' (C 184; K 188), continuing on from the *Cartesian Meditations*.

In *Crisis* Part IIIA, especially §§ 52–5, Husserl articulates the transcendental phenomenological approach in terms of certain 'unexpected and at first insoluble' paradoxes that centre around the mysteries of the correlation between objectivity and subjectivity. Husserl distinguishes between two aspects of subjectivity – it is 'subject-being for the world' (*Subjektsein für die Welt*, C 178; K 182) and also 'object-being in the world' (*Objektsein in der Welt*, C 178; K 182). In outlining these contrasting senses of being, Husserl quite deliberately uses the term 'object' (*Objekt*) rather than *Gegenstand* (which normally means for him an object in the epistemological sense). He had already introduced this contrast in *Crisis* § 28:

In this world we are objects among objects [*Objekte unter Objekten*] in the sense of the life-world … On the other hand, we are subjects for this world [*Subjekte für diese Welt*], namely, as the ego-subjects experiencing it, contemplating it, valuing it, related to it purposefully; for us this surrounding world has only the ontic meaning [*Seinssinn*] given to it by our experiencings, our thoughts, our valuations, etc. (C 104–5; K 107)

Husserl acknowledges that there is a certain qualified truth in naturalism – human beings are physical, corporeal objects in a physical, corporeal world. Through their bodies, humans interact causally with the world and are subject to the same forces (e.g. gravity) as other physical objects. Human beings also have minds or psyches which are also – through embodiment – real parts of the world. But the world has 'being and sense' not because of this physicality, but precisely because of the achievements of the transcendental ego and indeed the open-ended plurality of transcendental egos acting in consort.

In his later writings, especially in the *Cartesian Meditations*, Husserl struggles to articulate a clear account of the transcendental ego in its relation to the empirical, natural or 'mundane' ego as well as in its relation to other transcendental egos. He had been aware of the problematic and indeed had pointed out the circular manner of the approach at least since *Ideas* I (1913). Thus, for instance, in *Ideas* II § 53 Husserl writes that we appear to be in a 'vicious circle'. If we think of nature as natural scientists do, then humans are parts of nature (*Naturobjekte*). If, on the other hand, we understand humans as persons, then nature is approached as 'something constituted in an intersubjective association of persons' (*Ideas* II § 53, p. 220; Hua IV 210). The solution is to distinguish between the naturalistic and the personalistic attitudes, as discussed in Chapter 6. How the world appears is determined by the particular attitude adopted. The naturalistic attitude, which displays humans as objects in nature as described by the natural sciences, does not have an exclusive claim on comprehensive truth.

In the last section of the *Crisis* Part IIIB, Husserl tries to articulate the concepts of this transcendental correlation and transcendental life as an interconnecting network of subjectivities: 'But the transcendental correlation [*die transzendentale Korrelation*] between the world in the transcendental life of constituting subjectivity and the world itself, as it constantly outlines and confirms itself in the life community [*Lebensgemeinschaft*] of transcendental intersubjectivity as a pole-idea [*Polidee*], is not the puzzling correlation which occurs in the world itself' (C 262; K 266). Rather, the transcendental cooperation between subjects which is the basis of the experience of the world has to be understood not as something itself worldly but as something that precedes the world, and the world has to be understood as an intentional object constituted like any other intentional object.

In the *Cartesian Meditations* § 35, Husserl talks of the 'concrete transcendental ego' and its counterpart, the 'human ego', and at CM § 36, he talks of the 'de facto transcendental ego'. This leads to serious questions. Is there a different transcendental ego for every human empirical ego in the world? Or is there one collective transcendental ego governing all human egos? How can the ego which constitutes the world also be that which is concretized, mundanized and corporealized in the world? Husserl's account in the *Crisis* is far from clear and demands closer scrutiny.

Let us step back from the problem to examine how the transcendental ego emerges in the phenomenological reduction. Husserl constantly emphasizes the difficulty of the 'transposition' (*Umstellung*, C 148; K 151 (Carr translates it as 'transformation')), 'transformation' (*Umwandlung*, C 154; K 157), 'reversal' or 'inversion' (*Umkehrung*, C 200; K 204), that is required to turn our perspective around from the natural attitude of blind acceptance. As Husserl writes (confirming the interpretation that Fink would offer in 1933): 'The transcendental problem arises from a general turning around of the natural focus of consciousness' (*Amsterdam Lectures* § 11, *Trans. Phen.*, p. 238; Hua IX 331). To systematically reflect on the nature of the natural attitude itself requires a kind of 'bracketing' (the 'universal' *epochē* or 'transcendental reduction') of all our commitments to the factual domain, including all 'belief in the world'.

Under this most radical *epochē*, all epistemic commitments are suspended 'in one blow' (C 150; K 153; see also C 76; K 78), changing the 'index' under which they operate. This serves to 'interrupt' (*unterbrechen*, C 151; K 154) the natural attitude: 'all natural interests are put out of play' (C 152; K 155), but my stream of consciousness remains, and the correlated world remains *my* world. The manner in which the phenomenologizing self is able to reflect on the living self in natural life involves what Husserl elsewhere calls – although he does not elaborate on it in detail – the 'splitting of the ego' (*Ichspaltung*, CM § 15, p. 35; Hua I 73). This crucial concept is not explicitly found in the *Crisis*. According to this splitting, the meditating self leads a double life. On the one hand, the ego continues to live naturally, absorbed in the temporal course of everyday life with its ontological commitments and positings, and yet, at the same time, the ego becomes aware of itself as the functioning of world-constituting subjectivity within that natural life and adopts the position of a disinterested onlooker of its own life with inevitable change in the manner in which it lives its temporality. As Husserl puts it elsewhere: 'First the transcendental *epochē* and reduction release transcendental subjectivity from its self-concealment [*Selbstverborgenheit*] and raise it up to a new position, that of transcendental self-consciousness' (Hua XXXIV 399, my translation). The inevitable result is that natural worldly life is lived in a new register, aware of the transcendental operations that make it possible. The natural ego is, as it were, enlightened by the transcendental onlooker.

The phenomenological aim is to uproot from ourselves and from our 'prejudices', which now means from all that is distinctively *human* in our way of being plugged into the world. As Husserl writes in a dense passage in *Crisis* § 40:

An attitude is arrived at which is *above* the pregivenness of the validity of the world [*über der Geltungsvorgegebenheit der Welt*], *above* the infinite complex [*Ineinander*] whereby, in concealment, the world's validities are always founded on other validities, above the whole manifold but synthetically unified flow in which the world has and forever attains anew its content of meaning and its validity of being [*Sinngehalt und Seinsgeltung*]. In other words, we have an attitude *above* the universal conscious life (both individual subjective and intersubjective) through which the world is 'there' for those naïvely absorbed [*für die naiv Dahinlebenden*] in ongoing life, as unquestionably present, as the universe of what is there [*als Universum der Vorhandenheiten*] (C 150; K 153)

According to Husserl, taking up this transcendental stance is by no means a temporary action but requires a 'habitual attitude' (*eine habituelle Einstellung*, C 150; K 153) that we resolve to adopt once and for all. This, of course, is what Husserl describes as the 'attitude of the disinterested or non-participating spectator' (see Chapter 6 above). Husserl, however, sees this disinterested theoretical stance as a first-person attitude that has arrived at final 'clarity' about its own nature. Furthermore, for Husserl, the initiation of the reduction from within the natural attitude is a matter of complete freedom of the will (akin to his understanding of the initiation of Cartesian doubt). Transcendental reduction requires an 'act of will' (*Trans. Phen.*, p. 247; Hua IX 341). This leads to the ego being understood in a completely new sense.

The meditating philosopher performing the universal *epoché* is now situated '*above* [*über*] his or her natural being and *above* [*über*] the natural world' (C 152; K 155). As Husserl puts it over and over, the world and the self within that world have become *phenomena*, which means they present themselves as meaning-clusters to be understood but whose initial ontological configurations have been suspended or disengaged. Moreover, the outlook of the transcendental spectator or onlooker is not a mere 'grasp' or 'apprehension' (*Auffassung*) or 'interpretation' (*Interpretation*, C 152; K 155) since all interpretations and apprehensions are based on the world; it is, for Husserl, a *wholly new attitude* that is not partial but absolute and completely grounded. This attitude of the disinterested spectator is an extraordinary discovery and indeed is a relatively recent acquisition of human culture. Although it had its 'primal founding' (*Urstiftung*) in history with Descartes, it now becomes a permanent acquisition of humankind as the transcendental attitude. The new philosophical attitude reveals the 'universal, absolutely self-enclosed and absolutely self-sufficient [*eigenständig*] correlation between the world itself and world-consciousness' (C 151; K 154).

It is important to note in the radical and universal *epochē* as here defined by Husserl that not only is the *world* preserved as phenomenon but also the ego or 'I' is preserved, although it too can no longer be approached simply as the *human* ego as found in the personal world. After the application of the reduction, all experience is still *my* experience, even though I am supposed to have left behind everything *human*. This is Husserl's deep Cartesian conviction – the ego is what remains stable and connects the natural to the transcendental standpoint. It is this continued presence of the 'I' across the natural and the transcendental domains that allows for the continuity of our experience. The ego is now understood as 'subject *for* this world', as Husserl puts it also in his Preface to Boyce Gibson (Hua V 146).

HUSSERL'S PATH TO THE TRANSCENDENTAL EGO

Originally, in the first edition of the *Logical Investigations* (LU v II, § 8, p. 92; Hua XIX/1 374), Husserl had claimed not to be able to find this 'pure' ego. His focus was on the structure of individual, lived experiences and not on the ego or *sum* (LU v § 6). He avoided *metaphysical* claims about the mental or the physical. As he says, in ordinary speech the 'I' is understood as an individual, empirical object, a thing, like a tree (LU v § 4). The self is an 'animate I-body' (*Ich-Leib*, LU v § 4) in the world, and hence already an object, but phenomenology treats it as an interconnected unity or 'complex of experiences' (*Erlebniskomplexion*, LU v II, § 4, p. 86; Hua XIX/1 363). The ego is, at best, a constant pole running through my experiences, a 'unity of change' (*Einheit der Veränderung*, LU v II, § 6, p. 88; Hua XIX/1 369). In *Logical Investigations*, for instance, Husserl had an almost Humean 'bundle' account of the self.[17] In the revised version of the *Logical Investigations* (1913), influenced by his reading of Natorp, Husserl states that 'the empirical ego is as much a case of

---

[17] Both Jean-Paul Sartre and Aron Gurwitsch similarly elaborated a non-egological account of consciousness in Husserl on the basis that the ego is not experienced in our flowing psychic stream and that it becomes the objects of judgements or assumptions.

transcendence as the physical thing' (LU v II, § 6, 352n.6; Hua xix/i 368). The ego has its own kind of transcendence.

In *Ideas* II, where the same account is given as in the revised LU, the ego is said to be a kind of 'transcendence' or 'transcendency' of a very peculiar kind: 'a transcendency within immanency' (*eine Transzendenz in der Immanenz*), one which in a certain sense is not constituted (*Ideas* II § 57, p. 133; Hua iii/i 110). However, under the *epochē* and reduction, I can exclude this 'human being' (Hua iii/i 160) along with the world, and I am still left with the irreducible 'pure I' which, Husserl says, has no 'explicatable content': it is 'pure ego and nothing more' (ibid.), although he promises to investigate it further in *Ideas* II. In the latter work, the ego emerges in the personalistic attitude as an evolving self with a history, with habits, characteristics that attach to it and form its character. The ego is now a living self, what he soon will call a 'monad'.

In his 'Author's Preface' to the Boyce Gibson translation of *Ideas* I, Husserl says that his 'questioning back' leads to 'transcendental subjectivity', which he says is 'an old term given a new sense' ('Epilogue', *Ideas* II p. 406; Hua v 139). He also acknowledges that 'what specifically characterized the ego' had not yet been broached in *Ideas* I (*Ideas* II p. 426; Hua v 159). Critics of phenomenology, moreover, do not understand the 'ascent' from mundane subjectivity to 'transcendental subjectivity' (*Ideas* II p. 407; Hua v 140). According to the 'Author's Preface', the domain of the transcendental ego is, for Husserl, 'an absolutely autonomous domain of direct experience' (*Ideas* II p. 408; Hua v 141). The transcendental ego, furthermore, is characterized as 'absolute' with 'being absolutely in itself' (*Ideas* II, p. 413; Hua v 146), in contrast to the relative being of the mundane ego. Husserl claims that the same content can be viewed in the mundane sense as psychological and in the transcendental sense as transcendental phenomenological. There is a 'remarkable thoroughgoing parallelism' here (*Ideas* II p. 413; Hua v 146).

This doctrine of the *parallelism* between the mundane and the transcendental ego has particularly troubled critics.[18] Husserl always speaks of the transcendental attitude as 'primary' and 'absolute', as

---

[18] See John J. Drummond, 'The Transcendental and the Psychological', *Husserl Studies* Vol. 24 No. 3 (2008), 193–204.

opposed to the 'relative' nature of the natural attitude. Rather than seeing human consciousness as rooted in the world, we must now see the world itself as 'rooted' in transcendental subjectivity: 'Natural being is a realm whose "being-validity" is secondary; it continually presupposes the realm of transcendental being' (CM § 8, p. 21; Hua I 61). Husserl even speaks in his *Cartesian Meditations* of 'the essential rootedness [*Verwurzelung*] of any objective world in transcendental subjectivity' (CM § 59, p. 137; Hua I 164). Transcendental philosophy brings to awareness that 'conscious life is through and through an intentionally accomplishing life [*intentional leistendes Leben*]' (C 204; K 208). As Husserl makes clear in the *Cartesian Meditations*: 'Every sort of existent [*Art Seiendes*] itself, real or ideal, becomes understandable as a "product" [*Gebilde*] of transcendental subjectivity, a product constituted in just that performance [*Leistung*]' (CM § 41, p. 85; Hua I 118). I have quoted these passages to show the continuity – often disputed – between the *Cartesian Meditations* and the *Crisis* in terms of Husserl's overall account of transcendental subjectivity. Husserl's *Crisis* offers a different emphasis (on transcendental intersubjectivity), but the overall doctrine is unaltered.

THE MEANING OF THE 'PRIMAL EGO' OF *CRISIS* § 54(B)

There has been a great deal of dispute over the nature and status of the transcendental ego in Husserl's *Crisis* and related texts, especially in regard to his invocation of what he calls 'the primal ego' (*das Ur-Ich*).[19] David Carr is emphatic that there is no question but that Husserl conceives of the transcendental ego as an individual ego and speaks in the plural about transcendental egos.[20] For Dorion Cairns (1901–73), also, there is a transcendental ego as a counterpart of each individual mundane ego. Eugen Fink, on the other hand, points to that particular section in the *Crisis* where Husserl speaks of a primal ego and suggests that there is a kind of anonymous impersonal primal ego which underlies individual egos as their ground (see C 184; K 187).

---

[19] See especially Dan Zahavi, *Husserl and Transcendental Intersubjectivity*, trans. Elizabeth A. Behnke (Athens, OH: Ohio University Press, 2001), pp. 65–84.

[20] See David Carr, *Interpreting Husserl: Critical and Comparative Studies* (Dordrecht: Kluwer, 1987), p. 143.

This should be understood as a kind of primal undifferentiated life, prior to the opposition between ego and its other or *alter ego*.[21] Fink's interpretation is perhaps overly influenced by a kind of metaphysical Neoplatonism that treats the *Ur-Ich* as the unnameable One, the indeclinable source of all further oppositions. On this interpretation, the primal I would actually be a non-individual, impersonal 'ego' which would hardly deserve the name of 'ego' at all.

In fact, Husserl's explicit references to the primal ego or *Ur-Ich* are extremely rare. The term appears only twice in the *Crisis* text itself (actually only in the table of contents and in the title to *Crisis* § 54(b), although it is found in associated texts).[22] Husserl speaks of an *Ur-Ich* and of its 'personal indeclinability', indicating that there is a certain absoluteness to the primal ego which does not admit of a 'you', a 'we' and so on. It is worth quoting at some length the key passage in *Crisis* § 54(b):

The 'I' that I attain in the *epoché*, which would be the same as the 'ego' within a critical reinterpretation and correction of the Cartesian conception, is actually called 'I' only by equivocation – although it is an essential equivocation since, when I name it in reflection, I can say nothing other than: it is I who practice the *epoché*, I who interrogate, as phenomenon, the world which is now valid for me according to its being and being-such, with all its human beings, of whom I am so fully conscious; it is I who stand above all natural existence that has meaning for me, who am the ego-pole of this transcendental life, in which, at first, the world has meaning for me purely as world; it is I who, taken in full concreteness, encompass all that. (C 184; K 188)

Husserl here – as elsewhere – is laying stress on the inner *unity* of and continuity between the transcendental ego and natural ego. It is the *same* 'I' who inhabits both stances; there is a continuity and identity between the natural I and the reflective I. At issue is the kind of temporal life possessed by the transcendental ego.

Husserl does speak of the primal ego several times in his Bernau manuscripts on time. The term *Ur-Ich* is to be found in his mature works; it appears already in a text from 1918, where he writes: 'Each empirical ego begins as a primal-ego, thus each wholly identical

---

[21] Eugen Fink, *Nähe und Distanz* (Munich: Karl Alber, 1976), p. 223.
[22] See Shigeru Taguchi, *Das Problem des 'Ur-Ich' bei Edmund Husserl: Die Frage nach der selbstverständlichen 'Nähe' des Selbst* (Dordrecht: Springer, 2006).

according to the matter pregiven to it and the manner of its sharing in immanent time. Accordingly, each primal ego develops differently from every other one' (Hua XIII 407, my translation).[23] As we shall see below, each ego has its own immanent unity in time and its own form of temporalization. There are different temporal 'streams' which ultimately produce different personal lives. Husserl is here suggesting that each ego has its own fundamental self-identity, its *Ur-Ich* structure (see Hua XIII 408). The *Ur-Ich*, then, is the basic underlying *form* of the ego; it should not be interpreted as a separate ego as such but as highlighting its mode of temporal dwelling. The *Ur-Ich* also appears in the Bernau manuscripts (see Hua XXXIII 284) where Husserl is talking about the ego of hyletic (i.e. sensory) experiences and especially of the temporal flow itself:

If we go back to the original constituting stream of life, then it has its own essential structure, which takes place fittingly in an incessant primal origination of sensual primary impressions, with contingent content (limited only by formal laws). In unity with and correlative with it, a singular primal I belongs to the flow, not contingently as an objective datum, but essentially accordingly as a numerical singular subject-pole of I-affections and I-ways of comporting, which on its side again underlie its temporal objective constitution. (Hua XXXIII 286, my translation)

The concept of the *Ur-Ich* also appears in the late C-Manuscripts on time.[24] In every form of reflection, there is the ego that is reflected on and the reflecting ego which at that moment resides in anonymity (see Materialen VIII 2). The ego in its most original mode is not in time at all – this is the 'primal ego' (*Ur-Ich*, Materialen VIII 197). He identifies this *Ur-Ich* with the 'functioning ego' (see Materialen VIII 198). However, he also distinguishes the '*Ur-Ich*' from the originary 'not-I'. But then he goes on, confusingly, to say that both are one:

Thus: Constitution of beings of different levels, of worlds, of times, has two primordial presuppositions, two originary sources, which spoken temporally (in each of these temporalities) henceforth as 'ground-laying' (1) my originary ego as functioning, as the primal ego in its affections and actions with all essential-forming modes belonging therein (2) my original

---

[23] Text Number 15, from Bernau, 1918, entitled 'On the Doctrine of Empathy'.
[24] See Edmund Husserl, *Späte Texte über Zeitkonstitution (1929–1934): Die C-Manuskripte*, ed. Dieter Lohmar, Husserl Materialen Vol. VIII (Dordrecht: Springer, 2006), hereafter 'Materialen VIII'.

not-I as the original form of temporalizing, and itself as the original form
of temporalizing, constituting a temporal field, that of originary-factuality.
But both primal grounds are one, inseparable and thus considered abstractly
for themselves. (Materialen VIII 199, my translation)

According to this obscure text, the *Ur-Ich* is the original source of all
acting and affection, but it is also a kind of non-ego as the original
source of temporalizing. On this reading, beneath the ego that acts as
unifying centre or 'pole' of experiences there lies a 'primal ego' which
is more properly a non-ego, but which is responsible for structuring
the ego's temporality and therefore its constitution. Husserl's account
of the relations between not-I, primal-I and transcendental-I is simply not clear, but he does overall maintain that the ego is involved in
its own *self-constitution*.

In an effort to sort out the confusion, Eugen Fink and Aron
Gurwitsch identify three distinct egos in the late Husserl. In his 1933
article in *Kant-Studien*, Fink distinguishes between the mundane ego,
the transcendental ego and a third ego which is the ego of the meditating phenomenologist. Aron Gurwitsch appears to endorse this
position when he speaks of the problem of the interrelation of the three
egos: 'the empirical and worldly ego, the transcendental ego within the
conscious life of which the whole world, the former ego included, is
constituted, the ego-spectator which operates the phenomenological
reduction and contemplates the constitution'.[25] Gurwitsch, however,
also endorses the Sartrean view that normal 'positional' consciousness
has no ego. The ego is an object created by reflection and is transcendent to the experiencing. Gurwitsch writes:

In fact the ego is connected not only with the act experienced and grasped
at the time being, but also with other acts, even with an infinite number of
them, and it is this way that the ego appears. It offers itself as a permanent
entity, as continuing existing, beyond the grasped act which, like all mental
states, is substantially perishing. The ego thus appears through rather than
in the grasped act. All this is in conformity with the ego's being a transcendent existent.

On Gurwitsch's account, the mundane self is constituted by
the transcendental self, but there is a third self – the meditating,

[25] See Aron Gurwitsch, 'A Non-Egological Conception of Consciousness', *Philosophy and
Phenomenological Research* Vol. 1 No. 3 (March 1941), 325–38, esp. 331 n.11.

phenomenological self – which apprehends the first two but which is also somehow identical with them. Gurwitsch believes that Husserl never solves this problem. Fink insists that the phenomenologizing ego is to be even more radically distinguished from the transcendental ego than from the empirical ego. Thus, in his Sixth Cartesian Meditation he writes: 'with the performance of the phenomenological reduction a *radical split* takes place within transcendental being. The phenomenologizing I of reflection stands in stronger contrast to the transcendental life it thematizes … than an I of reflection ever does to the egoic life that is reflectively grasped.'[26]

This sharp distinction between the transcendental ego and the meditating ego of the phenomenologist clearly goes beyond what Husserl actually claims in the *Crisis* and elsewhere. Husserl is primarily intent on distinguishing the naturally lived, so-called 'mundane' self (which has its own psychological reflection) and the transcendental self with its transcendental reflection; he does not go further and identify a split (*Spaltung*) within the transcendental ego itself. Or rather, Husserl will insist that the split within the transcendental ego is precisely the split between natural and transcendental life. In other words, he turns naturalism on its head. The natural ego and its natural life are actually expressions and products of the transcendental ego.

Husserl does want to distinguish between different layers or levels in the transcendental ego while at the same time also insisting on the unity whereby all these egos deserve still to be called 'I'. His real interest is in the manner in which the ego both constitutes itself in time and can also explicate itself infinitely, generating or uncovering a realm of infinite self-experience (something he believes Descartes completely missed). Furthermore, it is difficult to support any interpretation that divides the ego up in the face of the many instances where Husserl emphasizes that the *same* ego is shared both by the mundane and the transcendental ego. The ego that is doing phenomenology in the transcendental perspective is the very same ego that is living a mundane life.

[26] See Eugen Fink, *VI. Cartesianische Meditation. Teil 1: Die Idee einer transzendentalen Methodlehre*, ed. Hans Ebeling, Jann Holl and Guy Van Kerckhoven, Husserl Dokumente Vol. 11 (Dordrecht: Kluwer, 1988), pp. 11–12; trans. With an Introduction by Ronald Bruzina as *Sixth Cartesian Meditation: The Idea of a Transcendental Theory of Method*. With Textual Notations by Edmund Husserl (Bloomington: Indiana University Press, 1995), p. 12.

The primal ego is not something *beyond* or *behind* my own ego; it is a basic layer of the one ego. It is best to understand the *Ur-Ich* as the absolute 'I'. In this sense, to say 'I' in a genuine way is to admit of no plural: the 'I' is absolutely singular and unique. To be an 'I' in itself always and already means to be singular. In *Crisis* § 55, Husserl proposes to resolve the enigmas of subjectivity by insisting on the 'absolute ego as the ultimately unique centre of function in all constitution' (C 186; K 190). The ego is always one but, on the other hand, it is immensely complex in 'the system of its constitutive levels and its incredibly intricate [patterns of] validity-founding' (C 187; K 191). In the *Crisis*, then, Husserl continues to affirm the absolute priority of transcendental ego or transcendental subjectivity, even though it always exists in consort with others. There is, from another point of view, however, the 'I' that stands in contrast to a 'you'. This personal 'I' can only be understood relatively: it is always co-constituted by its relations with others. As person, I am a father, brother, spouse, son and so on, all indicating a relation to another. Egos are in part defined by their being different from one another, and in their recognition of other egos as literally 'alter' egos.

In contrast to the interpretations of Husserl that give emphasis to the primal ego, Merleau-Ponty, among others, claimed that the late Husserl conceived of transcendental subjectivity primarily as an *intersubjectivity* (see PP, p. xiii; vii), and some have interpreted this to mean that Husserl dispenses with the ego as *solus ipse* in favour of some kind of communally shared experience of selfhood. There are undoubtedly important passages where Husserl speaks of cooperating intersubjectivity as that which is responsible for the sense of objectivity as well as for the constitution of the natural, historical and cultural worlds.

Elsewhere, Husserl borrows from Leibniz's monadology in his attempt to articulate the manner in which each ego mirrors and is mirrored in other egos, although he insists he is not trying to revive speculative metaphysics (CM § 49). From around 1908, Husserl employs the term 'monad' (see also Hua IV 108; XIV 42), borrowed from Leibniz (1646–1716), to refer to the person or concrete ego.[27]

---

[27] See Hua XIII 5–8. The term 'monad' appears already in 1910–11 (see BPP p. 79; Hua XIII 183 and PRS p. 269; Hua XXV 30).

A monad is Husserl's term for an individual human being as a living, dynamic, unified whole (CM § 56, p. 128; Hua I 157; *eine lebendige Einheit*, Hua XIV 34), established over time (CM § 33), with its own temporal field (*Zeitfeld*, Hua XIV 43) and capacity for self development (Hua XXV 322). It is a 'unity of becoming' (*Werdenseinheit*, Hua XIV 34), a *life*. The monad is a self that includes his or her history. Monads also seem to contain within themselves the possibilities of what they may become. Although monads are unique and 'absolutely separate' individuals (CM § 56, pp. 128–9; Hua I 157), nevertheless they are 'communalized' in a community or 'harmony of monads' (CM § 49, p. 108; Hua I 138). Unlike Leibniz's monads, Husserl's monads have windows and communicate with one another. There is a transcendental 'universe of monads' (*Allheit der Monaden*, *Monadenall*, Hua XV 609).

The term 'monad', however, is extremely rare in the *Crisis* (in contrast to the *Cartesian Meditations*), and indeed there is only one paragraph in the whole of Hua VI that discusses monads. This is *Crisis* Supplement VIII, a very late text – probably written in May 1937, and unfortunately not translated in Carr (K 417). According to this text, each ego constitutes itself as an ego that has, opposing it, other egos, each of which is an 'in and for itself' functioning subjectivity. He further distinguishes between this transcendental, intermonadic community and the community of embodied human beings in the world. Husserl writes obscurely:

I, the ego, thus have a world through an accomplishment [*Leistung*], in which, on the one hand, I constitute myself and my horizon of others, and the homogeneous we-community [*Wir-Gemeinschaft*] in unity with it, and this constitution is *not world-constitution*, but the accomplishment which can be described as the monadization [*Monadisierung*] of the ego – as the accomplishment of personal monadization, of monadic pluralization. In the ego, in its accomplishment, is constituted an ego that has other egos, each one being one and being in and for itself an absolute functioning subject, which is unique for all constitutive accomplishments, each monadizing itself and constituting its monadic 'we-all', and each one constituting the other as implicating an other, and his *we* as a *we*, and in his *we* all *we* are implicated and homogenized, and so on. (K 417, my translation)

On this obscure account, monadization is somehow brought about by the transcendental ego, which at the same time also constitutes other egos as themselves constituting subjects and joins them together as a transcendental plural community which itself is responsible for the constitution of the world. Of course, this invocation of an intermonadic community is at best an analogy and does not solve Husserl's problem as to how communication and communalization are possible. In the end, Husserl's intention appears to be that the monadic transcendental ego constitutes other monads which constitute it in turn. Even the strongest emphasis on the uniqueness of the transcendental ego cannot ignore its mutual implication with others.

INTERSUBJECTIVITY AND THE 'OBJECTION' OF SOLIPSISM

As Husserl acknowledges in his Author's Preface to Boyce Gibson's translation of *Ideas* I, he was conscious that the initial presentation found in *Ideas* I could be construed as solipsistic ('Epilogue', *Ideas* II p. 418; Hua V 151), whereas his own view was merely that his presentation there was 'incomplete' and 'one-sided'. He constantly acknowledged the danger that phenomenology might be construed solipsistically – what he routinely refers to as the 'objection of solipsism' (see the *Cartesian Meditations*, especially §§ 13 and 42). Phenomenology inevitably appears as an 'egology', and so the existence and nature of other egos seem hard to establish. Hence, it appears as a 'transcendental solipsism' (CM § 13). But Husserl insists this is just a 'subordinate stage philosophically' and ultimately the problem of transcendental intersubjectivity must be tackled. In fact, in opposition to this supposed 'solipsism', Husserl is always insistent that his position is that transcendental subjectivity is at the same time a *transcendental intersubjectivity*. As he writes in the *Crisis*: 'But in *living with one another* [*Miteinanderleben*] each can take part in the life of others. Thus in general the world exists not only for isolated humans but for the human community; and this is due to the communalization [*Vergemeinschaftung*] of even what is straightforwardly perceived' (C163; K 166, translation. modified). The phenomenon of *communalization* is that through which distinct egos come together to cooperate in the constitution of a single world – just as, in cultural terms, they constitute cultural products such as the one shared language.

Husserl's transcendental idealism claims that the objectivity of the transcendent real world outside of us is an achievement of 'transcendental intersubjectivity'. This is already articulated in his 1910–11 lectures, *The Basic Problems of Phenomenology* (e.g. Hua XIII 184), but it is constantly reiterated in later works, e.g. the 1928 *Amsterdam Lectures*:

Transcendental intersubjectivity is the absolute and only self-sufficient foundation [*Seinsboden*]. Out of it are created the meaning and validity of everything objective, the totality of objectively real existent entities, but also every ideal world as well. An objectively existent thing is from first to last an existent thing only in a peculiar, relative and incomplete sense. It is an existent thing, so to speak, only on the basis of a cover-up of its transcendental constitution that goes unnoticed in the natural attitude. (*Trans. Phen.*, p. 249; Hua IX 344)

Everything we experience as transcendent has the 'value' written on it 'valid for all' (*für jedermann*).

Dan Zahavi (b. 1967), has pointed out that intersubjectivity cannot be thought about objectively as if it were some objective set of relations out there in the world. This would be to objectify and reify what is essentially subjective and intentionally constituted:

For Husserl, intersubjectivity is not some relation, within the world, that is to be observed from the outside; it is not something transcendent to consciousness, or some sort of system or structure in which consciousness would be found … The very opposite is the case: intersubjectivity is a relation between me and the other or others, and correspondingly, its treatment and analysis must necessarily take the I's relation to others as its point of departure.[28]

We cannot take a third-person view on intersubjectivity; we are always already caught up in the intersubjective domain, just as we are in language and culture. Rather, intersubjectivity has to be understood transcendentally in terms of the ego having its other, its 'you', its 'we'. There can be no 'you' or 'we' except from the standpoint of an ego, and this gives the ego a certain primacy. But, as Husserl constantly points out, this is also true for other egos, which have

---

[28] Zahavi, *Husserl and Transcendental Intersubjectivity*, p. 79.

their own 'you's' and 'we's' as well. Nevertheless, the exercise of the transcendental reduction is supposed to lead beyond this intersubjectively communicating self to uncover the transcendental ego as an absolute singularity:

> In this solitude I am not a single individual who has somehow wilfully cut himself off from the society of mankind … or who is cut off by accident, as in a shipwreck, but who nevertheless knows that he still belongs to that society. I am not *an ego* which has always still his *you*, his *we*, his universal community of co-subjects in natural validity. (C 184; K 188)

This paragraph shows that the reduction to ownness, which Husserl explicitly attempts in the *Cartesian Meditations*, is also endorsed in the *Crisis*. There is an egoic core to the self which is essential to it at a level prior to intersubjective engagement.

In Husserl's late musings on the transcendental ego and on transcendental life, he raises the question of the transcendental meaning of 'natural' phenomena such as birth and death (discussed briefly in *Crisis* § 55 and also in supplementary texts, e.g. 'The Anthropological World', especially Hua XXIX 327–38). Husserl does not accept Heidegger's reading of death as signalling an end that marks human existence as essentially finite and essentially always unfinished, ending without closure and fulfilment. Husserl in fact thinks that birth and death have one sense as phenomena associated with worldly human existence; but they have another, transcendental sense. In this transcendental sense, death is, rather, the 'separation of the transcendental ego from its self-objectification as human being' (Hua XXIX 332, my translation). Husserl goes further and accepts that the natural human being lives and dies, but he asks whether being an entity in this spatio-temporal world is the only sense that being has. Can there be another sense, according to which I am co-constituted by others, just as I constitute my own childhood again from memory (Hua XXIX 333)? In this sense, for Husserl, world constituting life as such cannot begin or end. It is immortal (Hua XXIX 338; see also APS 467; Hua XI 378). It makes no sense to think of it living or perishing: 'We would have the absurdity that the absolutely existing ego, in the duration of its being, would encounter itself as not being' (*Ideas* II § 23, p. 110; Hua IV 103). The transcendental ego is that which makes givenness and worldhood possible. Without the ego there is no phenomenality, no givenness and hence no world.

THE 'SELF-TEMPORALIZATION' OF THE
TRANSCENDENTAL EGO

In the *Crisis*, Husserl makes compressed and obscure remarks not just about the primal ego, but also about the 'self-temporalization' (*Selbstzeitigung*) of the 'immediate' (*aktuelle*) ego. In a famously obscure passage in *Crisis* § 54(b) – commented on, for instance, by Merleau-Ponty, as well as by Fink – Husserl speaks about the temporalization of the ego:

Self-temporalization through depresentation [*Ent-Gegenwärtigung*], so to speak (through recollection), has its analogue in my self-alienation [*Ent-Fremdung*] (empathy as a depresentation of a higher level – depresentation of my primal presence [*Urpräsenz*] into a merely presentified [*vergegenwärtigte*] primal presence). Thus, in me, 'another I' achieves ontic validity as co-present [*kompräsent*] with his own ways of being self-evidently verified, which are obviously quite different from those of a 'sense'-perception. (C 185; K 189)[29]

The idea is that the self in recollection has to unify itself with the earlier recollected self. Both present self and past self have to be unified into a single flow of time, a single 'history'. This self-temporalization allows the ego to spread itself into past experiences and thus overcomes the problem of being a series of unconnected I-poles locked inside each fleeting experience. Husserl describes this as finding another 'I' within myself.

Husserl's brief invocation of 'self-temporalization' of the ego in the *Crisis* (the topic is not discussed in the *Cartesian Meditations*) has two main implications. On the one hand, it is, for Husserl, the primal ego which in its self-temporalizing constitutes the full, transcendental ego. Secondly, this self-temporalization of the ego allows the ego to posit variations of itself, and this plays a role in the constitution of other egos. Husserl never manages to sort out these transcendental relations between ego, temporality and the constitution of the other, but his efforts include some of the deepest analyses of his philosophical oeuvre as a whole.

CONCLUSION

Especially in his later writings, Husserl often talks of the *self-objectification* of the transcendental ego as a mundane worldly ego.

---

[29] The term 'depresentation' (*Ent-Gegenwärtigung*) only appears in this passage in the *Crisis*.

He also speaks of the *concretization* of the transcendental ego and of its *self-temporalization*. It is hard not to think of this process as akin to the Christian theological account of the infinite, divine being outside time incarnating itself in the finite corporeal and temporal world. Certainly, there are many passages in the late Husserl that speak in these terms, and there is no doubt that Fink's Hegelian interests tended to push Husserl in this direction also. There is a second – one can call it a Leibnizian – tendency in Husserl which wants to treat of the transcendental egos as together forming a 'community of monads' which constitutes the entire world, the 'world-all' or the 'world for all'. As Fink puts it: 'Transcendental egology becomes transcendental "monadology".'[30] As we saw, this tendency is invoked but not explored in depth in the *Crisis*. There is a third way of reading Husserl's paradoxical formulation of the relation between the ego as subject for the world and as object in the world, and that is to treat the natural and the transcendental as *two points of view* – two 'attitudes' (*Einstellungen*) which one can take to the same human life. Unfortunately, a definitive interpretation is not possible, given the fragmentary nature of Husserl's late texts on these topics.

There is no doubt but that Husserl is deadly serious in his claim that phenomenology must be understood both as transcendental philosophy and as transcendental idealism (in his admittedly new sense). The central claim is that there is simply no way of thinking of 'being in itself' that is not the product of constituting subjectivity. Likewise, there is no way of thinking of transcendental subjectivity without acknowledging that it is involved in relations of mutual recognition with other subjects and that the truly concrete transcendental subjectivity is an open-ended plurality of transcendental subjects operating together in a harmonious way to constitute the experience of the *world* as such.

---

[30] Fink, 'The Phenomenological Philosophy of Edmund Husserl and Contemporary Criticism', p. 121.

CHAPTER 8

The ongoing influence of Husserl's Crisis

THE INTERNAL AND EXTERNAL INFLUENCE OF THE *CRISIS*

In this chapter I shall summarize the range and nature of the influence of Husserl's *Crisis* on twentieth-century philosophy and, at the end of the chapter, suggest briefly the ongoing relevance of the *Crisis* for the twenty-first century.

The *Crisis* was generally welcomed as representing a considerable advance over Husserl's previous publications in terms of the depth, range and clarity of the analysis. The publication of Biemel's expanded *Crisis* text in 1954 (following the publication of *Ideas* II in 1952) offered a new vision of Husserl as the phenomenologist of the experience of otherness or 'alterity', intersubjectivity, personhood, social experience and the kind of 'worldly' or 'mundane' living in the life-world. This assessment of the 'new' Husserl is ongoing and continues to be augmented and revised in the light of the publication of his research manuscripts.[1]

In particular, the *Crisis* was decisive in permanently changing the pervasive interpretations of Husserl's phenomenology (promulgated, as we have seen, even by Martin Heidegger) as a narrow, more or less solipsistic and definitely outmoded Cartesian philosophy of consciousness. Ludwig Landgrebe, Husserl's assistant in the 1920s, writing in 1961, presents the late Husserl as departing from Cartesianism.[2]

---

[1] See, for instance, the essays in Donn Welton, ed., *The New Husserl: A Critical Reader* (Bloomington: Indiana University Press, 2003), and see also his *The Other Husserl* (Bloomington: Indiana University Press, 2001).
[2] See Ludwig Landgrebe, 'Husserl's Departure from Cartesianism', in Landgrebe, *The Phenomenology of Edmund Husserl: Six Essays*, ed. D. Welton (Ithaca: Cornell University Press, 1981), pp. 66–121; reprinted in D. Moran and L. Embree, eds., *Phenomenology: Critical Concepts in Philosophy* (New York, London: Routledge, 2004), Col. v, pp. 59–101.

Husserl himself, however, never saw his Cartesian way as replaced by the later turn to the life-world. Rather, in the *Crisis*, he continues to advocate his 'new Cartesianism', which, however, has to be open to the extraordinary phenomenon of the intersubjective constitution of the world.

The *Crisis* simply explores a different route to reduced transcendental consciousness, namely through what he calls an 'historical-teleological' analysis. The methodology of the *Crisis*, with its self-declared historical teleological reflections, broadened the perceived subject matter and method of phenomenological reflection. Phenomenology is now presented not so much as the effort of the isolated thinker but as a sustained cultural *reflection* (Husserl's *Besinnung*) on the nature of the 'meaning achievement' of both the natural and social sciences, including the meaning of history. As we saw in Chapter 7, the meaning of Husserl's transcendental phenomenology, including his complex relation to Kant, is a theme that receives substantial treatment in the *Crisis*.

In addition to offering a deep meditation on the nature of 'reflection' (*Besinnung*), the *Crisis* introduced or made popular many new concepts, specifically, the life-world, discussed in Chapter 6, but also more controversial concepts such as the notion of the 'primal I' (*Ur-Ich*) – a term that does not appear at all in the *Cartesian Meditations*, for instance. In addition, as James Dodd has pointed out, several important and interconnected themes are introduced in the *Crisis* (even if only incidentally treated), namely: 'flowing in' (*Einströmen*, see *Crisis* §§ 59–60, further discussed in Hua XXIX 77–83) and 'inwardness' or 'interiority' (*Innerlichkeit*, see C 73; K 74).[3] We shall return to these concepts later in this chapter.

The *Crisis* can be seen as having an impact both 'internal' (relating to the understanding of Husserl's own evolution and the work of his immediate students) and 'external' (relating to other philosophers' engagement with Husserl's work). Husserl's students, such as Fink, Landgrebe, Ingarden and Gurwitsch, were all deeply influenced by the *Crisis*, as was Heidegger. Through Koyré, the historian of science Thomas S. Kuhn (1922–96) was also indirectly influenced

---

[3] See James Dodd, *Crisis and Reflection: An Essay on Edmund Husserl's Crisis of the European Sciences*, Phaenomenologica 174 (Dordrecht: Kluwer, 2004), p. 215.

by Husserl's conception of modern scientific revolution.[4] Another historian of science, Jacob Klein (1899–1978), discussed Husserl's account of the origin of mathematics and gave it a constructive critique.[5] More recently Hilary Putnam has acknowledged the importance of Husserl's analysis of the transformation effected by modern science (by Galileo and Robert Boyle 1627–91) in distinguishing between primary and secondary qualities and thereby transforming the modern conception of the world. Putnam acknowledges Husserl's conception of the life-world as important for articulating his own attempt to overcome the false dichotomy Putnam has diagnosed in contemporary philosophy between the 'furniture of the universe', on the one hand, and our projections, on the other.[6]

Social and political philosophers, such as Alfred Schutz,[7] Hannah Arendt,[8] Thomas Luckmann (b. 1927) and Peter Berger (1929),[9] developed their views on the nature and structure of the life-world and the relationship between theory and praxis from their close engagement with the themes of the *Crisis*.[10] German thinkers such as Theodor Adorno,[11] Hans-Georg Gadamer, Helmuth Plessner, Jürgen

---

[4] Thomas S. Kuhn, *The Structure of Scientific Revolutions* (University of Chicago Press, 1962). For Husserl's influence on Kuhn, see Brendan Larvor, 'Why Did Kuhn's Structure of Scientific Revolutions Cause a Fuss?' *Studies in History and Philosophy of Science Part A* Vol. 34 No. 2 (June 2003), 369–90.

[5] See Jacob Klein, *Greek Mathematical Thought and the Origin of Algebra*, trans. Eva Brann (Cambridge, MA: MIT, 1969; reprinted New York: Dover, 1992) and his earlier article 'Phenomenology and the History of Science', in Marvin Farber, ed., *Philosophical Essays in Memory of Edmund Husserl* (Cambridge, MA: Harvard University Press, 1940), pp. 143–63.

[6] Hilary Putnam, 'After Empiricism', *Realism with a Human Face* (Cambridge, MA: Harvard University Press, 1990), p. 50.

[7] See especially Alfred Schutz's early *Der sinnhafte Aufbau der sozialen Welt* (Vienna: Julius Spronger, 1932; reprinted Frankfurt: Suhrkamp Taschenbuch, 1974), trans. George Walsh and Frederick Lehnert as *The Phenomenology of the Social World* (Evanston, IL: Northwestern University Press, 1967; London, Heinemann, 1972) and also Alfred Schutz and Thomas Luckmann, *The Structures of the Life-World*, Vol. 1, trans. Richard M. Zaner and H. Tristram Engelhardt, Jr. (Evanston, IL: Northwestern University Press, 1973). Schutz gives the most detailed account of the structures of the life-world in the natural attitude.

[8] See Hannah Arendt, *The Human Condition* (University of Chicago Press, 1958) for the discussion of Galilean science (although Husserl is not explicitly cited).

[9] See Peter L. Berger and Thomas Luckmann, *The Social Construction of Reality: A Treatise in the Sociology of Knowledge* (New York: Anchor Books, 1967).

[10] See Martin Endress, George Psathas and Hisashi Nasu, eds., *Explorations of the Life-World: Continuing Dialogues with Alfred Schutz* (Dordrecht: Springer, 2005).

[11] See, for instance, Theodore Adorno, 'Husserl and the Problem of Idealism', *Journal of Philosophy* Vol. 37 No. 1 (1940), 5–18. In this text, Adorno makes reference to Husserl's *Philosophia* articles as situating psychologism in the whole history of modern philosophy from Descartes.

Habermas,[12] Herbert Marcuse,[13] Hans Blumenberg,[14] Klaus Held,[15] Bernhard Waldenfels,[16] Ernst Wolfgang Orth (b. 1936), Dieter Lohmar[17] and Elmar Holenstein[18] have all been directly influenced by Husserl's late reflections in the *Crisis* on philosophy, science, instrumental reason, the life-world, familiarity and otherness.

From the initial moment of its appearance in *Philosophia* in 1936, and especially with Walter Biemel's expanded Husserliana edition of 1954, Husserl's *Crisis* has had a powerful, persistent and radicalizing influence on some of the greatest of twentieth-century European philosophers. Strictly speaking, this influence begins, even before the *Crisis* publication, with Husserl's lectures in Vienna and Prague in 1935. In particular, Husserl's own students, including Alfred Schutz, Aron Gurwitsch, Eugen Fink, Jan Patočka and Ludwig Landgrebe, were deeply influenced by Husserl's late vision of phenomenology. The *Crisis* was next influential in France, on Maurice Merleau-Ponty, Paul Ricoeur and Jacques Derrida. Ricoeur translated Husserl's

---

[12] See Jürgen Habermas, *The Philosophical Discourse of Modernity*, trans. Frederick Lawrence (Oxford: Polity Press, 1987), pp. 314–326 where Habermas discusses the conception of the life-world as an unquestioned background of common understanding and suggests that it needs to be expanded by recognizing its *normative* function on social relations. See also Kevin Paul Gaiman, 'Habermas' Early Lifeworld Appropriation: A Critical Assessment', *Man and World* Vol. 23 No. 1 (January 1990), 63–83. Habermas was influenced by Alfred Schutz and Helmut Plessner in reconceiving the Husserlian life-world. See Kenneth Baynes, 'Crisis and Life-World in Husserl and Habermas', in Arleen B. Dallery, Charles E. Scott and P. Holley Roberts, eds., *Crises in Continental Philosophy* (Albany, NY: SUNY Press, 1990), pp. 57–68.

[13] See Herbert Marcuse, *One-Dimensional Man: Studies in the Ideology of Advanced Industrial Society* (Boston: Beacon Press, 1964), pp. 162–6, where he discusses Husserl's analysis of Galileo and the way in which a 'cloak of ideas' (*Ideenkleid*) has been cast over the natural world by the mathematical sciences. Marcuse takes Husserl's point further in emphasizing that the sciences have always linked the projects of the domination of nature and the domination of humankind (see p. 166).

[14] See Hans Blumenberg, *The Genesis of the Copernican World*, trans. Robert M. Wallace (Cambridge, MA: MIT, 1987). Blumenberg was deeply influenced by Husserl and wrote his Habilitation thesis on Husserl in 1950.

[15] See Klaus Held, 'Husserl's Phenomenology of the Life-World', trans. Lanei Rodemeyer, in Welton, ed., *The New Husserl*, pp. 32–63.

[16] See, for instance, Bernhard Waldenfels, 'Experience of the Alien in Husserl's Phenomenology', *Research in Phenomenology* Vol. 20 No. 1 (1990), 19–33 and Waldenfels, 'The Other and the Foreign', *Philosophy and Social Criticism* Vol. 21 nos. 5/6 (1995), 111–24.

[17] See the essays in R. A. Mall and D. Lohmar, eds., *Philosophische Grundlagen der Interkulturalität* (Amsterdam: Rodopi, 1993).

[18] Elmar Holenstein, *Kulturphilosophische Perspektiven: Schulbeispiel Schweiz; europäische Identität auf dem Prüfstand; globale Verständigungsmöglichkeiten* (Frankfurt: Suhrkamp, 1998).

'Vienna Lecture' into French and Jacques Derrida in 1962 translated and commented extensively on Husserl's 'The Origin of Geometry',[19] which had first appeared in print in the commemorative issue of a French journal *Revue Internationale de Philosophie* in 1939.

One had to wait until the Second World War ended to see Husserl regain some influence in Germany. The post-war German reaction to Husserl's *Crisis* (aside from its impact on the *Crisis* editor, Walter Biemel) can be found primarily in the work of Hans-Georg Gadamer, Hans Blumenberg and Jürgen Habermas. Gadamer discusses the *Crisis* (1954) in his *Truth and Method* (1960).[20] Jürgen Habermas acknowledges the vitality of Husserl's conception of the life-world and of 'pre-reflective life' practices and world experience in the context of the critique of reason. He notes Husserl's recognition of the 'we' nature of the communal life-world and also applauds Husserl's recognition of the historical development of the concept of reason itself, but criticizes Husserl for not sufficiently recognizing the role of normativity and the communicative dimension of rationality.

In the United States, former students of Husserl, whether émigrés such as Aron Gurwitsch, Alfred Schutz, Felix Kaufmann and Herbert Spiegelberg (1904–90) or Americans such as Marvin Farber and Dorion Cairns, promoted Husserl's mature phenomenology. Since 1970 David Carr's English translation has played a vital role in disseminating the influence of Husserl's *Crisis*. In North America, Husserl's *Crisis* has influenced such thinkers as the social phenomenologist Maurice Natanson (1924–96), Charles Taylor (b. 1931) and Hilary Putnam, among many others, in more recent times.[21]

Especially in the United States, Husserl's Eurocentrism and ethnocentrism (even alleged latent racism) have been criticized by many

---

[19] Jacques Derrida, *Edmund Husserl's Origin of Geometry: An Introduction*, trans. J.P. Leavey Jr., ed. D. B. Allison (Sussex, NY: Harvester Press/Nicolas Hays, 1978).

[20] See Hans-George Gadamer, *Truth and Method*, 2nd rev. edn, trans. Joel Weinsheimer and Donald G. Marshall (London: Sheed and Ward, 1989), especially pp. 243–54, where he discusses Husserl's later conception of life in relation to Dilthey, Count Yorck and Heidegger. According to Gadamer, Husserl shares with Dilthey a distrust of the Neo-Kantian conception of the lifeless cognitive subject. Both wanted to infuse the transcendental subject with life. Husserl, however, in his later work, realized the importance of the phenomenon of world which is constituted by a 'fundamentally *anonymous* intentionality' (p. 246).

[21] See, for instance, the recent collection of essays edited by David Hyder and Hans-Jörg Rheinberger, eds., *Science and the Life-World: Essays on Husserl's 'Crisis of European Sciences'* (Stanford University Press, 2010).

commentators, including Robert Bernasconi, whereas aspects of his universalism have been defended by Seyla Benhabib,[22] for instance. On the other hand, precisely because of its conception of Europe and the bearing of its discussions of universality and supranationality on the problematics of globalization and interculturality, Husserl's *Crisis* is now widely read outside Europe, for example in Asia, especially due to the pioneering work of Bernhard Waldenfels, Elmar Holenstein (b. 1937) and others, on the phenomenology of intercultural understanding.[23]

THE IMMEDIATE IMPACT OF THE *CRISIS*

Husserl's *Crisis*-project occupied him more or less exclusively from 1934 until his death in 1938. As only a small portion of the *Crisis* text appeared in *Philosophia* in 1936 (this was, in fact, the only version that appeared in his life-time), the initial diffusion of the text was somewhat haphazard, due to the National Socialist prohibition on publishing works by Jewish authors. As a result of Husserl's exclusion from academic life in Nazi Germany after 1935, the *Crisis* first had an impact not in Germany itself but in Czechoslovakia, through Husserl's former student Ludwig Landgrebe, who held a professorship in Prague, as well as through the brilliant young student Jan Patočka, among others. Patočka heard Husserl's Prague lectures in 1935 and was the first to review the *Crisis Philosophia* articles in a Czech journal in 1937.[24] He was also the first to discuss seriously and critically Husserl's concept of the 'life-world' (which he renders as the 'natural world') in his Habilitation thesis, *The Natural World as a Philosophical Problem* (1936), written in Czech.[25] Patočka summarizes

[22] See Seyla Benhabib, 'Another Universalism: On the Unity and Diversity of Human Rights', Presidential Address to the Eastern Division of the APA, *Proceedings and Addresses of the American Philosophical Association* Vol. 81 No. 2 (November 2007), 7–32.

[23] See Bernhard Waldenfels, *The Question of the Other*, The Tang Chung-I Lecture for 2004 (Hong Kong: The China University Press, 2007). See also the essays by Tze-Wan Kwan, Chan-Fair Cheung and Kwok-Ying Lau in David Carr and Chan-Fai Cheung, eds., *Space, Time and Culture*, Contributions to Phenomenology 51 (Dordrecht: Kluwer, 2004).

[24] Jan Patočka's review was published in *Česká Mysl* Vol. 33 Nos. 1–2 (1937), 98–107. An English translation is in preparation for *The New Yearbook of Phenomenology and Phenomenological Philosophy*.

[25] An English translation of Jan Patočka's dissertation is currently in preparation. See also Jan Patočka's 1967 essay, 'The "Natural" World and Phenomenology', trans. Erazim Kohák, in

Husserl's central discovery thus: 'It is subjectivity in its relationship with the universe: the world as a function of subjectivity, and subjectivity as the wellspring of the world.'[26]

After Husserl's death, his loyal students Ludwig Landgrebe and Eugen Fink continued to promote Husserl's phenomenology, especially in the newly founded Husserl Archives in Leuven, Belgium, in 1939 (opened in October 1938), with the assistance of the young Belgian Franciscan priest Herman Leo Van Breda (1911–74).[27] It was in the Husserl Archives that the young French phenomenologist Maurice Merleau-Ponty first read the typescript made by Fink of the then unpublished Part III of the *Crisis*.[28] Merleau-Ponty took the late Husserl to be modifying his earlier claims about the all-embracing character of the transcendental reduction and that he had come to recognize, with the notion of the irreducible life-world, the impossibility of carrying the reduction through to the end. One always runs up against the life-world. In his *Phenomenology of Perception* (1945), Merleau-Ponty proclaims that 'to see the world and grasp it as paradoxical, we must break with our familiar acceptance of it', but he concludes that 'from this break we can learn nothing but the unmotivated upsurge of the world [*le jaillissement immotivé du monde*]. The most important lesson which the reduction teaches us is the impossibility of a complete reduction' (PP xiv; viii). Merleau-Ponty never loses his respect for Husserl's transcendental effort to understand the natural attitude. As he writes in a later essay, 'The Metaphysical in Man', the aim of his philosophy is 'to rediscover, along with structure and the understanding of structure, a dimension of being and a type of knowledge which man forgets in his natural attitude'.[29] In other words, the turn to the transcendental reveals nothing more than

Erazim Kohák, ed., *Jan Patočka: Philosophy and Selected Writings* (University of Chicago Press, 1989), pp. 239–73.

[26] I want to thank Lubica Učnik for providing me with a draft translation of Patočka's review of Husserl's *Crisis*.

[27] See, for instance, Ludwig Landgrebe, 'The World as a Phenomenological Problem', *Philosophy and Phenomenological Research* Vol. 1 No. 1 (September, 1940), 38–58, which refers to Husserl's 1936 *Crisis* articles and discusses his conception of the 'life-world'.

[28] See Herman Leo Van Breda, 'Merleau-Ponty and the Husserl Archives at Louvain', in Maurice Merleau-Ponty, *Texts and Dialogues*, ed. Hugh J. Silverman and James Barry, Jr. (Atlantic Highlands, NJ: Humanities Press, 1991), pp. 150–62.

[29] Maurice Merleau-Ponty, 'The Metaphysical in Man', trans. Hubert Dreyfus and Patricia Allen Dreyfus, *Sense and Nonsense* (Evanston, IL: Northwestern University Press, 1964), p. 92.

the inescapable pull of the world on consciousness and its constant irruption into consciousness. Furthermore, Merleau-Ponty correctly emphasized that the late Husserl was reinterpreting transcendental subjectivity as an intersubjectivity. In *Crisis* § 50, Husserl says that 'subjectivity is what it is – an ego functioning constitutively – only within intersubjectivity' (C 172; K 175). In his Preface, moreover, Merleau-Ponty directly refers to the then unpublished *Crisis* as teaching that transcendental subjectivity is only possible as an intersubjectivity (PP, p. xiii; vii). In his 1945 work, Merleau-Ponty acknowledges Husserl's efforts to root all reflection in the 'world of living experience (*Lebenswelt*)' (PP, pp. 365n; 419n). But he also criticizes Husserl for not seeing the positive contribution of Gestalt psychology (see PP, pp. 50–1n. 1; 62–3n).

Little by little, fragments of Husserl's last works trickled out in various publications through the 1940s. In 1939 Eugen Fink published a tract associated with the *Crisis* entitled 'The Question of the Origin of Geometry as an Intentional-Historical Problem' in an issue of the *Revue Internationale de Philosophie* that marked Husserl's death. In 1940 Marvin Farber published two short tracts (manuscripts D17 and D18), one, now familiarly known as 'The Earth Does Not Move', in his *Philosophical Essays in Memory of Edmund Husserl*,[30] and the other, 'Notes on the Constitution of Space', in a new journal *Philosophy and Phenomenological Research*,[31] which had been explicitly set up as the successor to Husserl's original *Yearbook for Philosophy and Phenomenological Research*.

It was not until after the Second World War that Husserl studies took root again in Germany, through the efforts of Eugen Fink, Landgrebe and others, especially in the work of the newly founded Husserl Archives in Freiburg and Cologne. Through Van Breda's efforts, in particular, during the Second World War, French philosophers such as Jean Cavaillès (1903–44), Maurice Merleau-Ponty and Paul Ricoeur came to know of many of Husserl's late unpublished works. Ricoeur visited the Husserl Archives in Leuven in 1947

---

[30] Edmund Husserl, 'Grundlegende Untersuchungen zur phänomenologischen Ursprung der Raumzeitlichkeit der Natur' [Groundlaying Investigations on the Phenomenological Origin of the Spatiality of Nature], in Farber, ed., *Philosophical Essays in Memory of Edmund Husserl*, pp. 307–25.

[31] Edmund Husserl, 'Notizen zur Raumkonstitution' [Notes on the Constitution of Space], *Philosophy and Phenomenological Research* Vol. 1 No. 1 (September, 1940), 21–37.

and translated one of the drafts of the 'Vienna Lecture' into French; this was published in 1950 before Biemel's German edition, which appeared in 1954. While lecturing at the University of Strasburg Ricoeur set up a Husserl Archive there. The contents were eventually transferred to Paris, where Merleau-Ponty and others established the Husserl Archives in 1957.[32]

THE INFLUENCE OF THE *CRISIS* IN GERMANY

Martin Heidegger – the life-world and science as technicity

In Germany, Husserl's standing as a phenomenologist was gradually being eclipsed by the rise of Martin Heidegger, who gave phenomenology a new impetus by combining it with hermeneutics (a methodology more normally associated with the theology of Schleiermacher (1768–1834) but which Dilthey had adapted for the human sciences). Heidegger's *Being and Time* (along with his radical reading of Kant in his 1929 *Kant and the Problem of Metaphysics*) excited a new generation of students, including not only Hannah Arendt and Hans-Georg Gadamer, but also Husserl's own assistant, Eugen Fink.[33]

The first readers of the *Crisis*, familiar with the solipsistic self-examination promulgated by the *Cartesian Meditations*, primarily interpreted Husserl's text as a reaction to the discussions of temporality, historicity and finitude elaborated in Heidegger's *Being and Time* (1927). Much to the frustration of Husserl, the *Crisis* was read alongside *Being and Time* as a parallel reflection on natural living in the world (being-in-the-world), historicity and temporality. The posthumous publication of the Husserliana volumes, especially those on empathy and intersubjectivity (Hua XIII, XIV and XV), in fact shows that Husserl had been working on intersubjective

---

[32] The Husserl Archives (Centre d'Archives Husserl) in Paris was founded by Paul Ricoeur, Gaston Berger, Jean Wahl, Jean Hyppolite and Merleau-Ponty in May 1957. Merleau-Ponty was its first director; the current director is Jocelyn Benoist. See T. Vongehr, 'A Short History of the Husserl Archives', in Vongehr and Herman Leo Van Breda, *Geschichte des Husserl-Archivs/History of the Husserl Archives* (Dordrecht: Springer, 2007), pp. 105–6.

[33] See Martin Heidegger, *Kant and the Problem of Metaphysics*, trans. J. S. Churchill (Bloomington: Indiana University Press, 1962). For Husserl's response to Heidegger's Kant book, see Richard Palmer, 'Husserl's Debate with Heidegger in the Margin of *Kant and the Problem of Metaphysics*', *Man and World* 30 (1997), 5–33.

and cultural phenomenology for many years before *Being and Time* appeared. Husserl was, in many ways, Heidegger's interlocutor while *Being and Time* was in gestation. The *Crisis* should be seen, then, as an evolution within Husserl's thought, rather than a response to external challenges (although these undoubtedly played some role in the manner in which Husserl articulated his views in his late years).

The intellectual interconnection between Husserl and Heidegger in the 1930s is still a matter of considerable scholarly debate. Personally, they had become estranged after 1929, and Husserl was disgusted by Heidegger's embrace of National Socialism and his taking-up of the rectorship in Freiburg in 1933. Given this estrangement, did the late Husserl exert any influence on Heidegger in the 1930s, especially on the latter's meditations on technology? The precise influence (if any) of the *Crisis* on Heidegger is a problematic issue and very difficult to determine. It is not clear that Heidegger ever read the published text of the *Crisis* in *Philosophia*, and – to my knowledge – the later Heidegger does not advert to the Husserliana edition of the *Crisis* edited by Walter Biemel, which is curious, since Biemel had studied under Heidegger in Freiburg and had written his doctoral thesis on Heidegger's conception of 'world', and Heidegger had himself made use of the concept of the life-world.[34] It is, of course, well known that Heidegger had access to Husserl's draft *Ideas* II text, but it is unlikely that Heidegger paid much attention to Husserl after the success of *Being and Time* (1927). In that work, Heidegger deliberately eschewed the Husserlian themes of intentionality and the phenomenological reduction, and he rejected Husserl's so-called 'Cartesianism'.

Husserl's later discussions of the life-world and our absorbed 'living-in' (*Hineinleben*) the world are often thought to be his response to Heidegger's conception of 'being-in-the-world' as it emerged in *Being and Time* (1927). In fact, both Husserl and Heidegger had employed the concept of the *Lebenswelt* in their lectures in the decade prior to the appearance of *Being and Time*. For instance, Heidegger frequently uses the term 'life-world' (*Lebenswelt*) in his 1921–2 lectures (GA 61, p. 94) only a few years after Husserl, who had begun to

---

[34] See Walter Biemel, *Le Concept de monde chez Heidegger* (Leuven: Nauwelaerts, 1950; 2nd edn, Paris: Vrin, 1981).

use the term around 1917. It is more likely that Heidegger drew his influence here from Dilthey, Simmel and the life philosophers rather than from Husserl. Husserl and Heidegger do seem close in their analysis of technology.

Both Husserl in the *Crisis* and Heidegger in several influential essays written during the 1930s reflected on the meaning of 'technicity'. Both held that the evolution of Galilean science had led to scientific enquiry becoming a form of pure technique, a 'technology' or 'technicity' (German *Technik*). In this regard, it is worth comparing Husserl's reflections in the *Crisis* with Heidegger's almost contemporaneous essay 'The Age of the World Picture' (1938),[35] which enquires about the essence of modern science. In this essay, Heidegger denies (in a manner that anticipates Thomas Kuhn's notion of incommensurability) that it is possible to simply compare Aristotle's and Galileo's accounts of falling bodies. One should not be considered 'true' and the other 'false'; rather, different conceptions of space and being are in play. According to Heidegger, ancient Greek science had no need for exact precision and did not set it as a goal. The essence of ancient Greek science lay in a different direction, and it is misunderstood if it is treated as merely a more primitive version of modern physics.[36] Heidegger maintains that modern science is essentially what he calls 'research' (*Forschung*), that is, the project of finding out what it has already predefined in a restrictive manner in advance. Scientific research measures only what has already been constituted as exact. Elsewhere Heidegger speaks of the self-establishing essence of technology which is focused on 'mastery' (*Herrschaft*) and which is responsible for the modern division of the world into subject and object.[37] Heidegger's views here are remarkably close to those of Husserl. Both Husserl and Heidegger cite Descartes' claim that

---

[35] See Martin Heidegger, 'Die Zeit des Weltbildes', *Holzwege*, GA 5, pp. 75–113; trans. by the editors as 'The Age of the World Picture', in Heidegger, *Off the Beaten Track*, Julian Young and Kenneth Haynes, eds. (New York: Cambridge University Press, 2002), pp. 57–85.

[36] See Heidegger, 'The Age of the World Picture', p. 58, where Heidegger maintains that no one would say that Shakespeare's poetry is more advanced than Aeschylus' and that similarly one cannot simply compare Galileo with Aristotle.

[37] See, for instance, Heidegger's remarks on technology in his 1946 essay 'Wozu Dichter?', *Holzwege*, esp. p. 290; trans. by Kenneth Haynes as 'Why Poets?' in Heidegger *Off the Beaten Track*, esp. p. 217.

modern science enables humans to become 'masters and possessors' of nature.

How did science end up as a kind of applied technique? After all, doesn't Husserl say elsewhere in the *Crisis* (in the 'Vienna Lecture', for instance) that Greek science was born out of a purely theoretical insight and broke with the traditional practices which were linked to the life-world and enmeshed in myth and tradition? Greek science broke with the engaged practical attitude of earlier times and proceeded to think about nature in a new way, interested in a purely theoretical account of it. How then did this very theoretical science, with its correlate of nature understood as a kind of idealized mathematical construct, become a form of applied technology? Husserl's – and Heidegger's – view is that there is a complete difference in kind between ancient pragmatic approaches to scientific problems and modern scientific-technological ones.

Heidegger in particular contrasts the modern scientific approach with medieval technology. Medieval craftsmen, architects and engineers were able to construct Gothic cathedrals, with their columns, arches and load-bearing flying buttresses that have stood for nearly one thousand years. In order to do that, their engineers had to be able to capture the forces of nature, handle the weight of the walls and roof, develop buttresses to distribute the load and so on. This construction was based on a kind of craft or technical 'know-how'; the medievals did not have physics manuals to guide them. The relevant theoretical framework was not yet available (the law of universal gravitation, for instance, whereby every mass in the universe attracts every other mass, had not yet been identified by Isaac Newton). The medieval artisans (incorporated in masonic guilds and passing on secrets to their apprentices) were – if one applies Husserl's guiding ideas – following more practical intuitions which themselves were deeply imbued with older scientific views concerning motion, force and so on. Yet this practical technique could be refined sufficiently to meet practical demand – for instance, that buildings stay standing for an immemorial time. These practical interests can lead to great technical sophistication, e.g. the Incas could construct buildings that were earthquake-proof.

Modern mathematical science, on the other hand, approaches matters entirely in the reverse order. It begins from the theoretical laws of physics and applies them to a predefined domain. Thus, for example, scientific idealization assumes there is something that is truly 'H_2O', although, of course, we know this is an idealization since, at best, our ordinary water contains trace elements and bacteria, is hard or soft, and so on; in fact, even distilled water is ionized and does not contain just pure H_2O molecules. Science deals with the *ideal*. When Galileo performed his experiment dropping balls of different materials from the Leaning Tower of Pisa, in fact they fell at different rates. He had to discount all the *real features* of the situation (e.g. wind, resistance due to surface texture) and focus on the *ideal* in order to formulate his universal law (in the manner today in which physics students can in diagrams replace the physical object on an inclined plan with vectors indicating direction of gravitational pull from what is considered the centre of the object). It is this discounting of the actual in favour of the ideal that marks out modern science.

Husserl believes modern science is a form of *technique* because it now takes for granted the mathematical construction of nature as if it were self-evidently the real world of nature. Nature is now called to account according to a presupposed conception; a grid is applied to it. Every point in space is essentially the same as every other. Similarly, in 'The Age of the World Picture', Heidegger says science involves 'projection' (*Entwurf*) of a 'ground-plan' (*Grundriss*) onto a sphere of predefined objects. In this essay, Heidegger too – again very close to Husserl – calls mathematical physics 'the earliest of modern sciences which is, at the same time, normative for the rest'.[38] Mathematical physics is applied to nature which is already determined in advance as 'the closed system of spatio-temporally related units of mass'.[39] Mathematical physics is bound to a set of objects that have the character of exactness, and hence they can be described with exact precision and calculation. Moreover, the manner in which these objects are approached is in terms of a method based on lawfulness and regularity: 'Only from the perspective of rule and law do facts become clear as what they are,' Heidegger writes.[40] Similarly, for Husserl Galilean science interprets the whole world as given in 'prediction' (*Voraussicht*, C 51; K 51). Galilean science is 'nothing but prediction extended to infinity' (C 51; K 51).

---

[38] Heidegger, 'The Age of the World Picture', p. 59.   [39] Ibid., p. 60.   [40] Ibid., p. 61.

All life rests on 'prediction' or 'induction'. Thus, even perception involves a moment of inductively working out what the unseen aspects will look like. All seeing involves a certain *Vormeinen*, or 'intending in advance' (C 51; K 51).

Both Husserl and Heidegger deny that the modern mathematical sciences achieved their essential character through empirical investigation and experiment (and in this sense, for Heidegger, the medieval philosopher-scientist Roger Bacon (1214–94) cannot be considered a forerunner of modern experimental science). Rather, this form of enquiry was determined in advance by the character of mathematical physics as applying law to what is considered to be changeable in an exact manner. Heidegger writes: 'It is only because contemporary physics is a physics that is essentially mathematical that it is capable of being experimental.'[41] This precisely reverses the traditional story of gradual development through increasing precision and experimental scruple. Husserl and Heidegger believe in Kuhnian-style revolutions of mindset: 'change of attitude' (*Einstellungsänderung*).

Eugen Fink's critique of the late Husserl

As we have seen, Eugen Fink played an important intermediary role as Husserl's student, assistant, editor and interlocutor for Husserl's last decade, from 1928 to 1938.[42] He assisted Van Breda in the rescue of Husserl's *Nachlass* and moved to Leuven to begin the work of transcription and publication, but he was deported by the Germans. After the war, he continued to promote Husserl's philosophy as director of the Husserl Archives in Freiburg until 1971. Indeed, in this respect, he has been described as 'the custodian of phenomenology in Germany'.[43]

Fink was never an uncritical reader of Husserl; indeed, he was a creative co-worker with original ideas, and many of his formulations

[41] Ibid.
[42] See Ron Bruzina, *Edmund Husserl and Eugen Fink: Beginnings and Ends in Phenomenology 1928–1938* (New Haven: Yale University Press, 2004).
[43] See Gabriella Baptist, 'German Phenomenology from Landgrebe to Waldenfels', in Anna-Teresa Tymieniecka, ed., *Phenomenology Worldwide: Foundations, Expanding Dynamics, Life-Engagements* (Dordrecht: Kluwer, 2002), p. 256; and Herman Leo Van Breda, 'Laudatio für Ludwig Landgrebe and Eugen Fink', in Walter Biemel, ed., *Phänomenologie Heute* (The Hague: Nijhoff, 1972), pp. 1–13.

pushed Husserl further in a speculative direction than perhaps he
would consciously have wished to go.[44] Fink believed that phenomenology, in order to be fully grounded, had to undergo a radical
self-criticism. Its central concepts had to be put under interrogation,
'thematized' rather than merely employed 'operatively'. For Fink, the
transcendental-phenomenological reduction is absolutely central. It
puts the being of the world in question, and the world itself is shown
to be a product of constitution, 'end-constitution' (*Endkonstitution*).
He characterizes his own aim as producing a 'cosmogony' – how the
world is constituted.[45] Furthermore, Fink raises the issue of the *being*
of the transcendental ego, and he is especially critical of the manner in which Husserl seeks to solve the paradox of the relationship
between transcendental and mundane subjectivity. For Fink, Husserl
fails to offer a reason why infinite transcendental subjectivity would
make itself finite and embodied in the natural, corporeal world. In
other words, Husserl gives no grounds for the self-constitution of
human finitude.[46] Fink is, of course, raising a Hegelian theological
problem in the Husserlian context: why does the infinite become
finite? Hegel's answer, part of his speculative metaphysics, is that the
infinite needs the finite for its completion. Such a speculative metaphysical answer is not available within Husserl's phenomenological
philosophy. Fink's answer is to absorb Husserlian phenomenology
within the mantle of a speculative metaphysics.

During the early 1930s, prior to Husserl's commencing work
on the *Crisis*, Fink defended him in an influential 1933 essay that
appeared in *Kant-Studien*, just before the National Socialists made
it impossible to write positively about Jewish thinkers.[47] Fink's published essay includes a Preface by Husserl endorsing it: 'it contains no
sentence which I could not completely accept as my own or openly

---

[44] For a detailed critical analysis of their working relationship, see Bruzina, *Edmund Husserl and Eugen Fink.*
[45] Eugen Fink, *Sixth Cartesian Meditation: The Idea of Transcendental Theory of Method. With Textual Notations by Edmund Husserl*, trans. with an Introduction by Ronald Brazina (Bloomington: Indiana University Press, 1995), p. 142.
[46] See Eugen Fink, 'Welt und Geschichte', in Herman Leo Van Breda, ed., *Husserl et la pensée moderne. Husserl und das Denken der Neuzeit* (The Hague: Nijhoff, 1959), p. 153.
[47] See Eugen Fink, 'The Phenomenological Philosophy of Edmund Husserl and Contemporary Criticism', in Roy Elveton, eds. *The Phenomenology of Husserl: Selected Critical and Contemporary Readings*, 2nd edn (Seattle: Noesis Press, 2000), pp. 70–139.

acknowledge as my own conviction'. It is a matter of considerable controversy, however, whether Fink's views really coincide with Husserl's.[48] Fink's essay is important because it anticipates many of the themes Husserl was to articulate in the *Crisis* three years later and because it offers an interpretation of Husserl's transcendental idealism that contrasts it to Kant's.

Fink defends Husserl against Neo-Kantian criticism in relation to two main charges – summarized under the labels 'intuitionism' and 'ontologism'. With regard to the accusation of 'intuitionism', the Neo-Kantians maintained that phenomenology's reliance on what is given in intuition is naïve because of the assumption that intuitions are given directly and immediately, whereas Kant maintained that intuitions are always mediated by concepts. Husserl, on this assessment, simply does not recognize the ineliminable role of conceptuality in the constitution of experience and therefore falls back into pre-critical dogmatism. The very notions of 'essential insight' and 'categorical intuition' show this naïve prioritizing of the intuitive given. Fink writes, summarizing the Neo-Kantian accusation: 'In this way Criticism lets it be known that the characterization of the phenomenological method as a form of intuitionism carries with it the reproach of dogmatism.'[49]

The Neo-Kantians (especially Rickert) regarded phenomenology as pre-critical because it failed to problematize the basic notion of a *self-giving intuition* and played down the essential role of discursivity (i.e. reasoning) and the contribution of the conceptual in the formation of knowledge. Furthermore, the Neo-Kantians (e.g. Natorp) insisted that description is always a retrospective *reconstruction* of experiences, not an immediate intuitive grasp of the given.

The second charge of 'ontologism' refers to Husserlian phenomenology's supposedly naïve – and Platonic – ontological treatment of *essences*, which it treats as extant ideal entities (although not sensuously intuitable) as opposed to Kantian 'validities' (*Geltungen*) which have the status of norms or laws regulating conduct rather than being reified as 'things', albeit of an ideal, timeless kind. Fink summarizes this Neo-Kantian criticism: 'Phenomenology's blindness with respect to values, its ontologizing of validity in general, excludes

---

[48] Ibid., p. 71.   [49] Ibid., p. 74.

it from passing beyond the "affairs" to the sphere of the theoretically valid, a sphere which for Criticism can be exposed through construction and which serves to establish the actuality of all affairs.'[50] In short, Husserlian phenomenology does not understand the meaning of normativity.

Fink's defence of Husserl emphasizes the continuities between Kant and Husserl. Both seek to overcome naïve dogmatism in regard to knowledge of the world, whether in everyday practices or in science.[51] Fink also sees an identity between Kant's transcendental apperception and Husserl's transcendental ego.[52] Fink, however, understands Husserl's transcendental philosophy as an attempt to transcend (through the *epochē*) the world as given in the natural attitude. Neo-Kantianism only wants to explain the conditions that make possible the world as revealed in the natural attitude, whereas Husserlian phenomenology precisely wants to transcend this world but in order to understand and reveal the manner in which the pregiven world is constituted. Fink writes:[53]

By contrast [with Neo-Kantianism], phenomenology's basic problem involves a transcendence with a completely different orientation. It is a transcendence beyond the *world* [*über die Welt hinaus*] and not only beyond inner-worldly beings; nevertheless it is not, as with dogmatic-speculative metaphysics, a transcendence to some other-worldly 'absolute.' Phenomenology … wins back the world from within the depths of the absolute in which – *before* the phenomenological reduction – the world itself lies concealed.[54]

On Fink's account, Husserl's great discovery is the phenomenon of *world* and its transcendental constitution. Fink lays great stress on phenomenology's efforts to break free from 'imprisonment' in the natural attitude through which we are engrossed in the world. The aim of phenomenology is to break through to the nature of 'absolute life', which is 'the ultimate intentionally constituting life'.[55]

Fink is correct in the emphasis he places on breaking with the natural attitude as the distinctive characteristic of Husserl's mature transcendental philosophy in opposition to Kant. As we have seen, already in 'Philosophy as Rigorous Science' (1910–11), and especially in *Ideas* I § 27, Husserl introduces the natural attitude as the commonsense

[50] Ibid., p. 76.   [51] Ibid., p. 85.   [52] Ibid., p. 86.   [53] Ibid., p. 95.   [54] Ibid.
[55] Ibid., p. 106.

outlook of naïve realism with which humans of all cultures and in all periods of history normally engage with the world. People live in a distinctly personal and interpersonal social and communal world, surrounded by other human beings and within social, historical and cultural groupings. Although this is obvious to the ordinary person in the street, this 'obviousness' has in the past not been interrogated by science or by philosophy. Moreover, there are remarkable features to this supposed 'obviousness' or 'taken-for-grantedness' of our social communal world. First of all, there is the sense of the *unity* of world, its 'tendency to concordance' (*Einstimmigkeit*), that is, to unfold in consistent, harmonious ways. There is also the sense of *horizon*, the manner in which all experience (and Husserl always takes perceptual experience as his starting-point) is against a backdrop of co-intended meanings. There is the sense of a visual and spatial world beyond what is immediately seen, the sense of the stability of objects despite the passing of time, the sense of the continuity of experience and personal identity across time, and so on. The contemporary positive sciences assume (with the Kantians) that the real world is the world of physical forces, spatio-temporal objects and so on. But living humans experience a somewhat different and, for them, no less real world which has within it such entities as persons, animals, tools, works of art, money and so on. Husserl recognizes that all of these 'senses' or meanings are not just encountered 'ready-made' in the world, but are always experienced as already unified. They are literally 'achievements' (*Leistungen* – the word can also be translated as 'productions', or 'accomplishments', see C4; K 2, C 5; K 3 and C 29; K 26, etc.) in a very particular sense. Husserl calls them 'achievements of subjectivity'. The essence of phenomenology, then, is the radicalization of the Kantian 'critical' insight that there is no objectivity without subjectivity, and a freeing of phenomenology of naïve assumptions about the givenness of the world in natural experience. Fink's 1993 defence of Husserl was widely read and significantly influenced subsequent Husserl scholarship.

GADAMER AND HABERMAS: THE COLONIZATION OF THE LIFE-WORLD

In his *Truth and Method* (1960) Hans-Georg Gadamer acknowledges the importance of Husserl's relation to hermeneutics and pays particular attention to Husserl's concepts of horizon, world and life-world.[56] Gadamer notes that, already by 1918 (in a letter to Natorp), Husserl had sought to overcome the static approaches of his earlier phenomenology and to bring the issue of transcendental genesis to the very core of his phenomenology. Gadamer is primarily influenced by Husserl's conception of 'horizon', which he himself adopts. For Gadamer, mutual understanding takes place through a certain 'overlapping' of horizons. In *Truth and Method*, he explains a horizon as 'not a rigid boundary, but something that moves with one and invites one to advance further'.[57] Everything belongs to a world; the life-world, for Gadamer, is 'the whole in which we live as historical creatures'[58] and is what is pregiven in all our experience, but it never becomes an object for us in the natural attitude. For Gadamer, this concept of the life-world is the exact opposite of objectivism and is, as we saw in Chapter 6, an 'essentially historical concept'.[59] It has to be contrasted with the infinite idea of a true world which is at the core of the scientific conception of the world. Gadamer commends Husserl for recognizing the unity of the flow of life as prior to the discrete, lived experiences (that had been his focus in *Logical Investigations*). Gadamer, however, criticizes Husserl for importing the speculative concept of life from German Idealism and attempting to fit it into an essentially epistemological framework. Furthermore, according to Gadamer, Husserl pursued his investigations without any knowledge of the prior philosophical tradition (including Simmel and others) that had previously made life into a theme.

The German critical theorist Jürgen Habermas' relation to Husserl is more problematic, but it also centres around his conception of the life-world, especially as mediated by sociological treatment of this concept in Alfred Schutz. Habermas, like Husserl, feels the need to respond to the crisis of modernity, but he also draws on Marxist analyses of the structure of late capitalist societies to show the manner in which the desire for liberation has been thwarted.[60] Like Husserl, Habermas is aiming for a society of rational, free human agents

---

[56] Hans-Georg Gadamer, *Wahrheit und Methode: Grundzüge einer philosophischen Hermeneutik*, 2nd edn (Tübingen: Lohr, 1965), trans. Joel Weinsheimer and D. G. Marshall, *Truths and Method*, 2nd rev. edn (London: Sheed & Ward, 1989).

[57] Gadamer, *Truth and Method*, p. 245.   [58] Ibid., p. 247.   [59] Ibid.

[60] See Jürgen Habermas, *Legitimation Crisis*, trans. Thomas McCarthy (London: Heinemann, 1976), pp. 1–7.

acting cooperatively. Influenced by Durkheim and others, Habermas sees a movement in worldviews towards a demand that norms be legitimized discursively.

In general, Habermas moves away from Husserl's emphasis on 'the philosophy of consciousness' to emphasize the importance of the life-world as the background for mutual understanding, for action and for the development of communicative rationality.[61] In his *Theory of Communicative Action*,[62] Habermas acknowledges that he borrowed his concept of the life-world from Husserl and Schutz,[63] and adopts its 'always already there' character of immediate certainty.[64] According to Habermas, Husserl's life-world 'forms a counter-concept to those idealizations that first constitute the object domain of the natural sciences'.[65] However, he goes on to criticize Husserl for not also recognizing (due to his blindness to 'linguistic intersubjectivity') that the life-world itself demands certain idealizations, namely the validity claims that transcend local circumstances and are carried by the linguistic practices of the community. The life-world is made possible only through intersubjective communicative action. This critique needs to be addressed, especially since Husserl brings the theme of intersubjectivity to the fore in the *Crisis* more than in any other of his published writings.[66] Moreover, in the *Crisis*, Husserl expressly links the experiential communal life-world to what is linguistically expressible: 'for the life-world – the "world for us all" – is identical with the world that can be commonly talked about' (C 209; K 213).

---

[61] Jürgen Habermas, *The Theory of Communicative Action*, trans. Thomas McCarthy, 2 vols. (Cambridge: Polity Press, 1984–7), especially Vol. II, which is subtitled in English *Lifeworld and System: A Critique of Functionalist Reason.*

[62] Habermas, *The Theory of Communicative Action* Vol. II.

[63] See David M. Rasmussen, '*Lebenswelt*: Reflections on Schutz and Habermas', *Human Studies* Vol. 7 No. 2, Schutz Special Issue (1984), 127–32.

[64] See Jürgen Habermas, *On the Pragmatics of Communication*, trans. and ed. Maeve Cooke (Cambridge, MA: MIT, 1998), p. 243.

[65] See Jürgen Habermas, 'Actions, Speech Acts, Linguistically Meditated Interactions, and the Lifeworld (1988)', in Habermas, *On the Pragmatics of Communication*, p. 239.

[66] Furthermore, Husserl does recognize the centrality of language in the formation of intersubjective community, and indeed, in 'The Origin of Geometry', the importance of writing for the making permanent of the idealizations of science and culture, but it is certainly true that he does not explicitly discuss the role of language in a more thematic way. That the life-world has an inherent normativity is discussed by Husserl under the notions of 'abnormality' and 'normality' as structural features of our experience of the familiar and the strange.

In other words, for Husserl, the human community is a 'language community' (*Sprachgemeinschaft*, C 209; K 213).

Habermas understands the life-world primarily as the culturally transmitted and linguistically structured horizon within which human beings *act*. Society can be conceived in terms of the activities of agents or simply as a self-regulating system. The systematic approach tends to neglect the roles of the individual agents. For Habermas, the social world is mediated, materially reproduced and symbolically structured. It can also be 'colonized' by different processes (including the economic), which he labels 'system' (drawing on systems theory), leading to a distortion of communication, reification and alienation. Habermas focuses on the manner in which the life-world has to reproduce itself through socialization, communication, integration, stabilization and so on. The life-world underpins communicative action, whereas preoccupation with systems tends to distort the life-world.

The German historian of ideas Hans Blumenberg, was also influenced by Husserl's conception of the life-world and his account of modernity. In his *Lifetime and Worldtime*, he writes: 'The world won an infinite breadth as soon as the actual life-world, the world in the "how" of its lived-givenness, was considered.'[67] The life-world as that which cannot be surpassed by science is a theme in the German sociologist Niklas Luhmann (1927–98), who was interested specifically in the kind of collective agency that belongs to social systems as complex, self-referential communicating systems.[68] Karl-Otto Apel acknowledges the 'quasi-transcendental status' of the pregiven life-world in Husserl but sides with Heidegger in believing this world to be historically conditioned, public and linguistically mediated, conceptions he believes erroneously (as we have shown in Chapter 6) to be missing from Husserl's 'evidence-theoretic' conception.[69]

---

[67] Hans Blumenberg, *Lebenszeit und Weltzeit* (Frankfurt: Suhrkamp, 1986), p. 10.
[68] See Niklas Luhmann, *Social Systems* (Stanford University Press, 1995), pp. 69ff., where he explicitly invokes Husserl's notion of the world as the horizon of all meaning and the life-world' as the 'unproblematic background of assumption' (p. 70).
[69] See Karl-Otto Apel, *From a Transcendental-Semiotic Point of View*, trans. Marianna Papastephanou (Manchester University Press, 1998), pp. 106–7.

The Crisis *in the work of Maurice Merleau-Ponty*

In terms of the external influence of Husserl's *Crisis*, the French philosopher Maurice Merleau-Ponty offers perhaps the most philo- sophically significant and provocative reading of Husserl. Merleau- Ponty's initial exposure to phenomenology came through reading Aron Gurwitsch's dissertation, which offered a phenomenological critique of the constancy hypothesis of the Gestaltists.[70] But he was deeply influenced by the *Crisis*, which he read in typescript (Sections 28 to 72, along with the typescript for *Ideas* II and *Experience and Judgement*) at the newly founded Husserl Archives in Leuven in April 1939, where he spent a week reading texts and in discussion with Herman Leo Van Breda.[71] The *Crisis* had a profound influence on Merleau-Ponty's interpretation of Husserl's phenomenology[72] as is evident from his Preface to his *Phenomenology of Perception* (which appeared in 1945, almost a decade before Biemel's 1954 Husserliana edition of the *Crisis*), where he insists that Husserl's reduction was by its very nature impossible to carry out in full, since it always brings us back to the life-world from which we cannot extricate our- selves on account of our status as embodied beings in the world.[73] Merleau-Ponty tended to portray the *Crisis* as if it were – in David Carr's words – a deathbed conversion away from 'intellectualism' (as Merleau-Ponty called it) towards existentialism. Merleau-Ponty portrays the late Husserl as having practised the reduction to the point where he has uncovered the irreducible 'pregiven' life-world as the backdrop to all intention. This life-world can never be bracketed completely, and hence Husserl had to abandon his totalistic claim to

---

[70] See Ted Toadvine, 'Phenomenological Method in Merleau-Ponty's Critique of Gurwitsch', *Husserl Studies* Vol. 17 (2001), 195–205, esp. 196.

[71] See Vongehr, 'A Short History of the Husserl Archives', p. 105.

[72] Theodore Geraets claims that Merleau-Ponty's exposure to Husserl's later thought first came through the 1939 special issue of the *Revue Internationale de Philosophie*, which contained 'The Origin of Geometry'; see T. Geraets, *Vers une nouvelle philosophie transcendentale* (The Hague: Nijhoff, 1971).

[73] See, for instance, Maurice Merleau-Ponty, 'The Philosopher and Sociology', in Merleau- Ponty, *Signs*, trans. Richard McCleary (Evanston, IL: Northwestern University Press, 1964), pp. 106–7. (The original French version, *Signes*, was published in 1960 (Paris: Gallimard).) Hereafter '*Signs*', followed by the page number of the English translation.

be able to reduce everything to the achievements of transcendental subjectivity. As he puts it in his late essay 'The Philosopher and His Shadow' (1959): 'We constitute constituting consciousness by dint of rare and difficult efforts. … Originally a project to gain intellectual possession of the world, constitution becomes increasingly, as Husserl's thought matures, the means of unveiling a back side of things that we have not constituted' (*Signs*, pp. 159–81, and see especially p. 180).

Merleau-Ponty is here emphasizing – following Fink – that the late Husserl is primarily concerned with the experience of the world and the manner in which it is always present in our experience. Similarly, as we have seen, Merleau-Ponty places considerable emphasis, as we discovered in Chapter 6, on Husserl's account of anonymous 'functioning intentionality' (*fungierende Intentionalität*) as 'that which produces the natural and antepredicative unity of the world and of our life' (PP, xviii; xiii) and on his notions of embodiment and intersubjectivity, which he sees as running counter to the Cartesian tendency in Husserl's thought. Our bodily intentions already lead us into a world constituted for us before we conceptually encounter it in cognition.

Merleau-Ponty is also largely responsible for reinterpreting certain statements of Husserl in the *Crisis* to claim that transcendental subjectivity is always also an intersubjectivity. Merleau-Ponty claims that 'the *Cogito* must reveal me in a situation, and it is on this condition alone that transcendental subjectivity can, as Husserl puts it, *be* an intersubjectivity' (PP, xiii; vii). Merleau-Ponty frequently invokes this claim, citing the then unpublished *Crisis*. However, no exact statement of this form can be found in the *Crisis*; the nearest remark is the statement that subjectivity is what it is, namely an ego functioning constitutively only within intersubjectivity (C 172; K 175).[74]

Merleau-Ponty had a gift for picking out the great originality of Husserl's contribution. Frequently he identifies elements in Husserl that have otherwise passed unnoticed, e.g. Husserl's one-off use of the term 'depresentation' (*Entgegenwärtigung*) in his discussion of 'self-temporalization' (in C 185; K 189), as well as his use of

---

[74] See Herbert Spiegelberg, *The Phenomenological Movement: A Historical Introduction*, 3rd edn, with the collaboration of Karl Schumann (Dordrecht: Kluwer, 1982), pp. 580–1 n.2.

the concept of 'sympathetic understanding' (*Nachverstehen*) in 'The Origin of Geometry' (C 360; K 371). Merleau-Ponty contrasts our sense of 'original self-presence' (*Urpräsenz*) with our sense of the absence (*Entgegenwärtigung*) of self from self and of the other from oneself. He writes:

The problem of the existential modality of the social is here at one with all problems of transcendence. Whether we are concerned with my body, the natural world, the past, birth or death, the question is always how I can be open to phenomena which transcend me, and which nevertheless exist only to the extent that I take them up and live them; how the presence to myself [*Urpräsenz*] which establishes my own limits and conditions every alien presence is at the same time depresentation [*Entgegenwärtigung*] and throws me outside myself. (PP, pp. 363; 417)

Merleau-Ponty continued to engage with Husserl to the end of his life. This is evident in 'The Philosopher and His Shadow', written to commemorate the centenary of Husserl's birth, published in *Signs*, (see p. 125), as well as in his lectures on 'Husserl at the Limits of Phenomenology'[75] given at the Collège de France in 1959 and published in 1960, shortly before his own death in May 1961. In particular, Merleau-Ponty's late conception of 'intertwining' or 'chiasm' is deeply influenced by Husserl's concepts of 'interweaving' (*Verflechtung*) and 'in-one-another' (*Ineinander*), especially as encountered in the *Crisis* texts. Merleau-Ponty himself explicitly credits Husserl with what he calls his 'prophetic' discovery of the concept of *Verflechtung*. In 'The Philosopher and His Shadow' he writes:

No doubt this is why Husserl does not seem to be too astonished at the circularities he is led to in the course of his analysis ... There is another circularity between Nature and persons ... No doubt this is also why Husserl, in a prophetic text in 1912, did not hesitate to speak of a reciprocal relation between Nature, body and soul; and as it has been well put, of their 'simultaneity'. (*Signs*, pp. 176–7; 222–3)

In a footnote, Merleau-Ponty references Marly Biemel's editor's introduction to *Ideas* II (Hua IV xvii),[76] which cites a passage from (the

---

[75] Maurice Merleau-Ponty, 'Husserl aux limites de la phénoménologie', *Annuaire du Collège de France* (Paris: Imprimerie Nationale, 1960), pp. 169–73, trans. John O'Neill, as 'Husserl at the Limits of Phenomenology', in Merleau-Ponty, *Themes from the Lectures at the Collège de France 1952–1960* (Evanston, IL: Northwestern University Press, 1970), pp. 113–23.

[76] In her editor's introduction to *Ideas* II, Marly Biemel goes on to talk about the 'simultaneity' (*Gleichzeitlichkeit*) in the constitution of thing, lived body and soul (Hua IV xvii), which she

then unpublished) *Ideas* III (Hua V 124).[77] Biemel quotes a text that reads 'an important result of our treatment is that "nature" and lived body, in their intertwining [*Verflechtung*] with each other and also with the soul, are constituted altogether in a reciprocal relationship with one another' (Hua V 124). The full passage in *Ideas* III reads:

> But if we limit ourselves to the mere data of theoretical experience, if we exclude all values and all practical objectivities, then it is an important result of our consideration that '*nature*' and *animate organism* [*Leib*] and, in its interconnection [*Verflechtung*] with the latter, the *psyche are constituted in mutual relationship to one another*, at one with another. (*Ideas* III, p. 112; Hua V 124)

In this context, Merleau-Ponty speaks of Husserl's 'adventures of constitutive analysis – these encroachments, reboundings and circularities' (*Signs*, pp. 177; 223). Merleau-Ponty's interpretation of Husserl was greatly influenced by his discussions with his friend Eugen Fink.

Jacques Derrida on Husserl's 'The Origin of Geometry'

The French philosopher and deconstructionist Jacques Derrida was also deeply inspired by the *Crisis*, although he did not publish his first response to it until 1962.[78] In that year, he translated Husserl's short text, 'The Origin of Geometry', which had originally been published in France in the 1939 special issue of *Revue Internationale de Philosophie*, and later included in the *Crisis* 1954 Husserliana edition (C 353–78; K 365–78).[79] When Derrida was preparing this text for publication, Merleau-Ponty, then general editor of the project to translate Husserl's works into French, wrote to him asking whether he would

---

puts in quotation marks but without giving a specific reference to Husserl's text (the term does not appear in Hua V).

[77] *Ideas* III contains further references to *Verflechtung*; see also Hua V 2; V 117.

[78] See Edmund Husserl, *L'Origine de la géometrie, traduction et introduction par Jacques Derrida* (Paris: Presses Universitaires de France, 1962), trans. with a Preface by J. P. Leavey as Derrida, *Edmund Husserl's Origin of Geometry*.

[79] This essay first appeared in print in 1939 as 'Die Frage nach dem Ursprung der Geometrie als intentional-historisches Problem', *Revue Internationale de Philosophie* Vol. 1 No. 2 (1939), 203–35, in a special commemorative volume marking Husserl's death. The title appears to have been given by Fink. This supplement remains untitled in Biemel's edition. The first two paragraphs in Biemel are omitted by Fink in his edition, and there are some other differences between the editions.

be interested in translating the entire *Crisis*. This led to an exchange of letters between Derrida and Merleau-Ponty, but the project never came to fruition, because Merleau-Ponty died soon afterwards.[80]

Already in 1953–54, Derrida had written a thesis, *The Problem of Genesis in Husserl's Philosophy*, under the direction of Jean Hyppolite and Maurice de Gandillac. While researching this work, Derrida had consulted the Husserl Archives in Leuven. Although Hyppolite urged the young Derrida to publish it, the thesis did not appear in print until 1990.[81] In this early work, Derrida shows himself to be well grounded in Husserl's texts and also to have been strongly influenced by the French philosopher and resistance martyr Jean Cavaillès and by the Vietnamese phenomenologist and Marxist, Tran Duc Thao.[82] In his Preface, Derrida examines Husserl's oppositions (e.g., eidetic/empirical; transcendental/worldly; original/derived; pure/impure; genetic/constitutive), arguing that Husserl ignored the manner in which these oppositions in fact enter in some kind of 'dialectic', and, as Derrida says, 'contaminate' each another.[83] For Derrida, Husserl's late texts make clear that the problem of 'genesis' and 'origin' is always at the heart of Husserl's work.

Derrida's commentary on 'The Origin of Geometry' takes the form of an immanent critique of Husserl, concentrating on an account of signs and writing, and on his assumptions concerning the nature of historicity. He recognizes the 'programmatic and exemplary' import-ance of 'The Origin of Geometry' for bringing together in one place

---

[80] I owe these details to a personal communication with the late Jacques Derrida, during his visit to University College Dublin in February 1997.

[81] Jacques Derrida, *Le Problème de la genèse dans la philosophie de Husserl* (Paris: PUF, 1990) trans. Marian Hobson as *The Problem of Genesis in Husserl's Philosophy* (University of Chicago Press, 2003).

[82] Tran Duc Thao was born in Hanoi and studied at the École Normale Supérieure in Paris in the 1930s, where he met Merleau-Ponty and became interested in phenomenology. He wrote his doctoral thesis on Husserl. His major work is *Phénoménologie et matérialisme dialectique* (Paris: Minh Tan, 1951); trans. Daniel J. Herman and Donald V. Morano as *Phenomenology and Dialectical Materialism* (Boston: D. Reidel, 1985). In the Preface to that work he claims that reading Husserl's *Crisis* led him to abandon phenomenology; see Tran Duc Thao, Preface to *Phénoménologie et matérialisme dialectique*, p. 5. See also Tim Herrick, 'A Book Which Is No Longer Discussed Today: Tran Duc Thao, Jacques Derrida, and Maurice Merleau-Ponty', *Journal of the History of Ideas* Vol. 66 No. 1 (January 2005), 113–31.

[83] Derrida, *Le Problème de la genèse dans la philosophie de Husserl*, p. vii; *The Problem of Genesis*, p. xv.

Husserl's central concerns with ideality and the self-identity of the ideal object, and also his concerns with historicity and genesis. In 'The Origin of Geometry', Husserl poses a specific problem: 'Our problem now concerns precisely the ideal objects which are thematic in geometry: how does geometrical ideality (just like that of all sciences) proceed from its primary intrapersonal origin, where it is a structure within the conscious space of the first inventor's soul, to its ideal objectivity?' (C 357–8; K 369). Derrida highlights the tension in Husserl between the a priori essentialist (eidetic) approach of phenomenology, which attempts to give an essential characterization of the nature of the objects of experience, and his concerns with historical genesis and contingency that work to prevent the possibility of such essential description. Derrida recognizes that the ideal status of mathematical objects had been a preoccupation of Husserl's since *Philosophy of Arithmetic* (1891). He notes that Kant too attempted to remove geometry from all factual situations regarding its relation to the world. History, for Kant, is merely the external circumstance which made visible the a priori content of the concept. Kant lacks the notion of a material a priori. In *Ideas* I, Husserl had presented geometry as a pure science from which all positing of existence had been excluded. In the *Logical Investigations*, eidetic entities had to have historicity as one of their eidetic components. But Husserl already recognizes eidetic singularities; not just universals are ideal. Derrida recognizes the particular complexity of Husserl's notion of the peculiar 'timelessness' (*Zeitlosigkeit*) of ideal objects – their holding true at all times, their 'omnitemporality'. In fact, this characteristic of omnitemporality is achieved through the medium of written signs or language. This recognition of language and of the cultural milieu is a new insight in Husserl, according to Derrida. Derrida, drawing from the *Crisis* itself, focuses on the manner in which written language is the medium which allows scientific insights to be inscribed such that they could be reiterated and cast as 'the same', e.g. the same 'Pythagorean theorem' whenever it appeared in scientific discourse in whatever actual language. Derrida raises the problem of language that Husserl only partly addresses. Husserl never seems to raise the question of the origin of language as a whole.

In 'The Origin of Geometry', as we saw in Chapter 3, Husserl proposes a regressive-historical method that involves a thoughtful reconstruction of the human practices and mental acts that gave birth to geometry. It originally emerged from the practice of land-surveying and, through a set of idealizations and transformations, solidified into a pure eidetic science. Removed from the founding intuitions of the original geometers, geometrical discoveries become objectified in written forms. In writing down symbols, the addressee is removed, and what is written down becomes a 'sedimentation' which can be reactivated by new acts of understanding (OG, p. 164). Husserl, who was always preoccupied with the question of how symbolic thought functions in the absence of the entities symbol-ized, here proposes that written language functions to underpin the ideality of meaning. The objectivity of geometry is made possible through what Husserl calls the 'body of language' (*Sprachleib*, C 358; K 369). As Derrida puts it elsewhere, Husserl is the first philosopher to recognize that writing is 'the condition of the possibility of ideal objects and therefore of objectivity'[84] and in *Writing and Difference* he remarks: 'Meaning must await being said or written in order to inhabit itself, and in order to become, by differing from itself, what it is: meaning. This is what Husserl teaches us to think in *The Origin of Geometry*.'[85]

In his long and subtle analysis, Derrida highlights ambiguities and difficulties latent in Husserl's notions of transcendental phenomen-ology, his notions of ideal history and ideal origins, his concept of an 'historical a priori' and so on. While Husserl had believed the very essence of the historical could be understood through imaginative variation and essential insight, Derrida argues that phenomenological imagination is never rich enough to reconstruct the intellectual lives of people of radically different cultures. Husserl is forced to admit 'an irreducible, enriching, and always renascent equivocity into pure historicity' (OG, p. 103). Derrida also criticizes Husserl's view of an absolute emerging in and through history, claiming instead that 'the absolute is present only in being *différant*' (OG, p. 153), here utilizing the conception of *différance* that he had introduced in 1959 to capture the idea of something that is at once both different and not present

---

[84] See Jacques Derrida, *De la grammatologie* (Paris: Éditions de Minuit, 1967), pp. 42–3; trans. G. Spivak as *Of Grammatology* (Baltimore: Johns Hopkins, 1976), p. 27.

[85] Jacques Derrida, *L'Écriture et la différence* (Paris: Éditions du Seuil, 1967), trans. Alan Bass as *Writing and Difference* (London: RKP, 1978), p. 11.

because deferred. In his *Introduction* to 'The Origin of Geometry', furthermore, Derrida refers to Kurt Gödel's notion of 'undecidable propositions' (OG, p. 53), which he later (e.g. in his *Dissemination*) adapted for his own purposes, applying it to other fields as well, giving rise to talk of a general 'logic of undecidability'.[86] The *Crisis*, then, was seminal in the formation of Derrida's own thought.

The influence of Husserl's 1935 letter to Lévy-Bruhl

An interesting feature of Derrida's Introduction is his discussion of Husserl's 1935 letter to the French anthropologist Lucien Lévy-Bruhl.[87] Derrida criticizes Merleau-Ponty's reading of that letter – one of the few places in Derrida's work where he confronts Merleau-Ponty's philosophy. In 1942 Herman Van Breda met Merleau-Ponty in Paris and gave him a copy of his own doctoral dissertation (defended in 1941) which included a long appendix of ninety pages of Husserl's own texts, including the German text of the letter to Lévy-Bruhl. Merleau-Ponty subsequently discussed Husserl's letter in his essay on 'Phenomenology and the Sciences of Man'.[88] There he writes:

It is important to note the extraordinary interest aroused in Husserl by his reading of Lévy-Bruhl's *Primitive Mythology* (*La Mythologie primitive*) which seems rather remote from his ordinary concerns. What interested him here was the contact with an alien culture, or the impulse given by this contact to what we may call his philosophical imagination. Before this, Husserl had maintained that a mere imaginative variation of the facts would enable us to conceive of every possible experience we might have. In a letter to Lévy-Bruhl which has been preserved, he seems to admit that the facts go beyond what we imagine and that this point bears a real significance. It is

---

[86] Jacques Derrida, 'Hospitality, Justice and Responsibility', in R. Kearney and M. Dooley, eds., *Questioning Ethics: Contemporary Debates in Philosophy* (London: Routledge, 1998), p. 81.

[87] Husserl's letter to Lucien Lévy-Bruhl was originally included in Van Breda's thesis and was later reprinted in *Briefwechsel*. VII, *Wissenschaftlerkorrespondenz* (Correspondence with Scientists), ed. Karl Schuman and Elisabeth Schuhmann, Husserliana, *Dokumente*, Vol. III (Dordrecht, Boston, London: Kluwer, 1994), pp. 161–4. An English translation by Dermot Moran and Lukas Steinacher can be found as 'Edmund Husserl's Letter to Lucien Lévy-Bruhl, 11 March 1935', *New Yearbook for Phenomenology and Phenomenological Philosophy* Vol. 8 (2008), 349–54.

[88] See Maurice Merleau-Ponty, 'Phenomenology and the Sciences of Man', reprinted in *The Primacy of Perception*, trans. James M. Edie (Evanston, IL: Northwestern University Press, 1964), esp. pp. 90–2.

as if the imagination, left to itself, is unable to represent the possibilities of existence which are realised in different cultures.[89]

On Merleau-Ponty's reading, the letter shows that the late Husserl had come to realize that imaginative variation performed in a purely theoretical manner was not sufficient to gain access to the various types of humanity, and that Lévy-Bruhl had shown that empirical explorations in the life-world of others were necessary also. Lévy-Bruhl's work forces Husserl to recognize real possibilities for human existence not reachable by imaginative variation. Merleau-Ponty reads the letter as disclosing Husserl's overall recognition of the impossibility of the complete reduction. Merleau-Ponty concentrates on the manner in which people belonging to historical societies (whether they feel themselves in continuity with the past or not) are capable of envisaging 'stagnant', self-enclosed societies that are history-less. For Merleau-Ponty, this requires 'a joining of effort between anthropology as a mere inventory of actual facts and phenomenology as a mere thinking through of possible societies'.[90] He continues: 'the eidetic of history cannot dispense with factual investigation'.[91] Understanding must begin by living through the concrete experience of others' lived environments, and Merleau-Ponty concludes: 'at this point phenomenology, in Husserl's sense, rejoins phenomenology in the Hegelian sense, which consists in following man through his experiences without substituting oneself for him but rather in working through them in such a way as to reveal their sense'.[92]

Jacques Derrida challenges Merleau-Ponty's reading of the letter to Lévy-Bruhl as an admission of the failure of phenomenology as a purely a priori eidetic science. According to Merleau-Ponty's interpretation, Derrida writes, 'we might think … that Husserl renounced the historical a priori discovered by imaginary variation and recognized that the pure phenomenology of history had to pay attention to the content of the empirical sciences, ethnology in particular'.[93] But Derrida denies that Husserl ever moved in this supposed empirical direction and offers a different reading of the letter. According to Derrida, Husserl is actually seeking to move in the reverse direction,

---

[89] Ibid., p. 90.   [90] Ibid., p. 91.   [91] Ibid., p. 92.   [92] Ibid.

[93] Derrida, *Edmund Husserl's Origin of Geometry*, p. 111. Note that the English translation here conveys precisely the opposite sense of that intended by Derrida.

from the empirical to the a priori. He wants to 'wrest from historical relativism' the 'a priori of historical science itself'.[94] The supposed facts that support a kind of ethnological relativism of different cultures are in fact determined as historical facts only by a presupposed conception of historical truth in general. In other words, Derrida argues, in order to understand something as 'history', one must already understand what history is and under what conditions it is possible. Similarly, ethnological groupings can only appear within the horizon of universal humanity. In fact, Derrida's reading is more accurate than Merleau-Ponty's in divining Husserl's intention. Husserl never abandons the search for the absolute a priori foundations of all aspects of life, including historical life.

HUSSERL IN AMERICA: ALFRED SCHUTZ AND ARON GURWITSCH

Due to the forced emigration from Germany of Husserl's Jewish students in the late 1930s, phenomenology developed in a new way in the United States. In particular the sociologist Alfred Schutz (originally 'Schütz') was deeply influenced by the *Crisis* and drew on it for his discussions of intersubjectivity, sociality and the life-world.[95] Schutz was a very perceptive and critical reader of Husserl. In his first book, in 1932, translated as *The Phenomenology of the Social World*,[96] he had attempted an early characterization of the life-world. This book is particularly noteworthy because it appeared several years before the publication of Parts I and II of the *Crisis* in *Philosophia* in 1936. Schutz is acting as a harbinger of Husserl's views, about which he is clearly well informed and which he articulates with greater clarity and more precision than Husserl.

Schutz interprets the life-world primarily as the social world with its presupposed context of shared meanings that lay the basis for social

---

[94] Ibid., p. 109.
[95] See Schutz and Luckmann, *The Structures of the Lifeworld*, Vol. I, trans. Richard M. Zaner and Tristram Engelhardt Jr. (Evanston, IL: Northwestern University Press, 1973); Vol. II, trans. Richard M. Zaner and David J. Parent (Evanston, IL: Northwestern University Press, 1989).
[96] Alfred Schutz, *Der sinnhafte Aufbau der sozialen Welt* (The Meaningful Construction of the Social World) (Vienna: Julius Springer, 1932; reprinted Frankfurt: Suhrkamp Taschenbuch, 1974), trans. George Walsh and Frederick Lehnert as *The Phenomenology of the Social World* (Evanston, IL: Northwestern University Press, 1967; London: Heinemann, 1972)

action and interaction, what Husserl and Schutz call the 'we-world' (*Wir-Welt*) or 'with-world' (*Mitwelt*). Schutz correctly saw Husserl's intentional description of social acts as having enormous importance for the social sciences.[97] For Schutz, Husserl has clearly articulated that the focus of the social sciences is on the *everyday* social world. In this regard, Schutz opposed the attempt by philosophers of science such as Ernst Nagel and Carl Hempel, who wanted to model the methodology of the social sciences on the natural sciences. Schutz writes:

> It seems to me that Edmund Husserl and the phenomenological school have demonstrated more clearly than any other philosophy of which I know that even our logic is rooted in this world of everyday life, which he calls the *Lebenswelt*, and that 'nature' in the sense of the natural sciences is nothing else but a layer of this common life-world of all of us, a product of a systematic process of abstraction, generalization, and idealization in which man with his subjectivity is not included.[98]

In this early work, Schutz situates Husserl's discussions in the context of the German sociological discussion, specifically Max Weber and others. Weber was responsible for the development of a scientific descriptive sociology that refrained from value judgements. Weber began from the recognition of social action and from the identification of different ways of grouping or associating in society.

In an important subsequent article, 'The Problem of Transcendental Intersubjectivity in Husserl' (originally delivered at the Husserl Colloquium in Royaumont in 1957),[99] Schutz sketches the emergence of intersubjectivity as a theme in Husserl's writing from *Ideas* I to the *Cartesian Meditations*. He enumerates deep theoretical problems in Husserl's account of the recognition of the other subject precisely as *another subject* rather than as a modification of myself. Specifically, Schutz asks how Husserl is able to exclude all reference to others in performing what Husserl calls the 'second' *epochē* to reduce all experience to the sphere of ownness and then go on to discuss social

[97] See Alfred Schutz, 'Husserl's Importance for the Social Sciences', in H. L. Van Breda and J. Taminiaux, eds., *Edmund Husserl 1859–1959* (The Hague: Nijhoff, 1959), pp. 86–98.

[98] Alfred Schutz, 'Positivistic Philosophy and the Actual Approach of Interpretative Social Science: An Ineditum of Alfred Schutz from Spring 1953', *Husserl Studies* 14 (1997), 123–49, esp. 133.

[99] Alfred Schutz, 'The Problem of Transcendental Intersubjectivity in Husserl', in Schutz, *Collected Papers III: Studies in Phenomenological Philosophy*, ed. I. Schutz (The Hague: Nijhoff, 1966), pp. 51–91.

predicates. Is there not an experience of the 'we' already constituted within the self?[100] Furthermore, Schutz believes Husserl's apperception of the other's body as analogue of my own is faulty, as we do not at all perceive or experience the other's body in the inner manner in which I experience my own (as Schutz says, Scheler, Sartre (1905–80) and Merleau-Ponty had also pointed this out).[101]

But, interestingly, Schutz also goes on to discuss the *Crisis*, especially Section 54, where Husserl attempts to describe the constitution of the other person and also the group of persons from the viewpoint of the individual ego. Schutz's problem is how Husserl ever arrives at the 'transcendental we', which for him is the 'primal ground of all communities'. Schutz is particularly critical of Husserl's proposed solution to the problem of the constitution of intersubjectivity and is also deeply unhappy with Husserl's invocation of the 'primal ego' in *Crisis* § 54. Schutz sees Husserl as believing that every personal ego's experience of itself also includes an experience of itself as a member of a community, as part of a 'we' and as also recognizing another as a 'thou'. Yet at the same time Husserl insists that the *epochē* creates a unique kind of philosophical solitude where I cannot co-validate the presence or experiences of others. The problem Schutz identifies in Husserl is that there is no guarantee that the community that I constitute from within myself coincides with the community that the other constitutes for herself or himself. This is an important criticism, to which, I believe, Husserl has no response. In general, in Husserl's intersubjective monadology, as we saw in Chapter 7, it is not clear how these transcendental subjects communicate. Schutz refers to *Crisis* § 71, where Husserl suggests an answer to this problem. Husserl writes:

But this means at the same time that within the vitally flowing intentionality in which the life of an ego-subject consists, every other ego is already intentionally implied in advance by way of empathy and the empathy-horizon. Within the universal *epochē* which actually understands itself, it becomes evident that there is no separation of mutual externality [*Aussereinander*] at all for souls in their own essential nature. What is a mutual externality for the natural-mundane attitude of world-life prior to the *epochē*, because of

---

[100] Schutz, 'The Problem of Transcendental Intersubjectivity in Husserl', p. 59.
[101] Ibid., p. 63.

the localization of souls in living bodies, is transformed in the *epochē* into a pure, intentional, mutual internality [*Ineinander*]. (C 255; K 259)

Husserl speaks of the manner in which ego 'implicates' other egos – but what is the meaning of this intentional 'implication'? Husserl's claim is that transcendental egos overcome the mutual externality (*Aussereinandersein*) produced by being localized in physical bodies and gain a new kind of intersubjective community where all belong as internal members in 'internality' (*Ineinandersein*). But what evidence does Husserl offer for this transformation of mutually exclusive externality into shared internality? Schutz comments: 'It is completely unclear how an intentional in-one-another could account for the reciprocal implication of streams of life belonging to single subjects, and even to all psyches.'[102] In this important paper, Schutz also draws attention to Fink's remark in his 1933 paper on Husserl in *Kant-Studien* that one cannot simply transfer the relation between individual and plural humans to the transcendental sphere and that Husserl's use of the term 'monad' is simply an index of a larger problematic and not a solution to the problem of transcendental intersubjectivity.

In the United States, Schutz was responsible for the Husserlian phenomenological approach to social life joining the mainstream of American sociology. In particular, Schutz had a powerful influence on the German-Slovenian sociologist Thomas Luckmann, with whom he collaborated on a book, *Structures of the Life-World*.[103] Luckmann himself went on to co-write *The Social Construction of Reality* (1966) with the Austrian sociologist Peter Berger (b. 1929), which had an enormous influence on American sociology.[104] Berger and Luckmann argue that traditional sociology has a too restrictive conception of what theoretical knowledge about society is, and they want to widen it out to everything that is communicated in society. Theoretical knowledge is only a small part of 'the sum total of "what everybody knows" about a social world', which is 'an assemblage of maxims, morals, proverbial nuggets of wisdom, values and beliefs, myths, and so forth'.[105] On their own, ideas are not as important

---

[102] Ibid., p. 78.
[103] See Schutz and Luckmann, *The Structures of the Life-World*, Vol. I.
[104] Berger and Luckmann, *The Social Construction of Reality*.   [105] Ibid., p. 65.

in society as everyday communications and conversations. Berger and Luckmann, inspired by George Herbert Mead, assign a larger role than Husserl did to language and signs as important for separating out different dimensions of meaning (semantic fields) and communicating different roles. Humans are socialized through their involvement in this intersubjective process. Socialization is a collective achievement of intersubjective constitution: 'the social order is a human product. Or, more precisely, an ongoing human production.'[106] Berger and Luckmann, following Husserl, place a great deal of emphasis on the importance of habitualization, a concept that Husserl developed in his later work.[107] Husserl's late work, then, continued to have a subterranean influence through the writings of Berger and Luckmann in particular.

Another of Husserl's students, Aron Gurwitsch, who had also emigrated to New York to the New School for Social Research and was a close friend of Alfred Schutz, wrote a number of intelligent and thoughtful assessments of Husserl's later work, especially the *Crisis*,[108] in *Philosophy and Phenomenological Research* in 1956 and 1957. Interestingly, he portrays the *Crisis* as a continuation of Husserl's earlier concerns and not a radical volte-face, as Merleau-Ponty had presented it. He later wrote studies on Schutz's and Husserl's conceptions of the life-world,[109] and also on the nature of Galilean science.[110] Gurwitsch writes very perceptively of the manner in which Husserl's phenomenology of the life-world rehabilitates the world of belief (*doxa*) usually contrasted with scientific knowledge (*epistēmē*):

Under the heading of the *Lebenswelt*, the world of common experience is rehabilitated by phenomenology as *the reality* from which all conceptions and constructions of other domains of existence start and to which these

---

[106] Ibid., p. 52.

[107] See Dermot Moran, 'Edmund Husserl's Phenomenology of Habituality and Habitus', *Journal of the British Society for Phenomenology* Vol. 42 No. 1 (January 2011), 53–77.

[108] See Aron Gurwitsch, 'The Last Work of Edmund Husserl', *Philosophy and Phenomenological Research* Vol. 16, No. 3 (March 1956), pp. 380–99; and 'The Last Work of Edmund Husserl: II–IV.', *Philosophy and Phenomenological Research* Vol. 17 No. 3 (March 1957), 370–98.

[109] Aron Gurwitsch, 'Problems of the Life-World', in Maurice Natanson, ed., *Phenomenology and Social Reality: Essays in Memory of Alfred Schutz* (The Hague: Nijhoff, 1970), pp. 35–61.

[110] Aron Gurwitsch, 'Galilean Physics in the Light of Husserl's Phenomenology', in Ernan McMullin, ed., *Galileo, Man of Science* (New York: Basic Books: 1967), pp. 388–401.

domains essentially refer. Accordingly, the *doxa* is reinstated in its rightful place. Moreover, defined in a broad and all-inclusive sense, the *Lebenswelt* comprises the products and accomplishments of all cultural activities, hence also the sciences, their results and theories. This means that *epistēmē* in the traditional sense, e.g., specific scientific *epistēmē*, also falls under the concept of *doxa*, differences of level and scope notwithstanding. Yet phenomenology does not relinquish the search for *epistēmē*. However, *epistēmē*, in the specific phenomenological sense is not *epistēmē*, as opposed to *doxa*. Rather it is the *epistēmē*, of the very *doxa*, of all possible *doxa*. It is *epistēmē*, concerning the mind and its life in which originate the *Lebenswelt* as well as whatever other domains of being and existence there are, along with their specific objectivities and validities.[111]

Phenomenology develops a new interest in life in the natural attitude.

RECENT DISCUSSIONS OF THE *CRISIS*: NEW THEMES AND INFLUENCES

Although it is not widely recognized, Husserl's discussion of the natural attitude, the life-world and the transformation of Galileo influenced the American philosopher Wilfrid Sellars (1912–89), who contrasts the 'manifest image' and the 'scientific image' as two idealized conceptual frameworks of the world.[112] Sellars himself sometimes characterizes the 'manifest image' as the world understood by *common sense*.[113] The manifest image (and 'image' is clearly a metaphor for an overall world-conception) is, for Sellars, the conceptual framework of human beings in pre-scientific life before the revolution of the ancient Greeks (such as Democritus) transformed our way of thinking about the world.[114] In his original paper, 'Philosophy and the Scientific Image of Man', and in his Notre Dame lectures, Sellars

---

[111] Gurwitsch, 'The Last Work of Edmund Husserl: II. The *Lebenswelt*', 370–98, esp. 397–8.

[112] See Michael Hampe, 'Science, Philosophy and the History of Knowledge: Husserl's Conception of a Life-World and Sellars' Manifest and Scientific Images', in Hyder and Rheinberger, eds., *Science and the Life-World*, pp. 150–63. I do not believe Hampe is correct in portraying Husserl as attempting to unify the natural and the scientific outlooks.

[113] But see James O'Shea, *Wilfrid Sellars: Naturalism with a Normative Turn* (Cambridge: Polity Press, 2007), p. 13.

[114] See Wilfrid Sellars, 'Philosophy and the Scientific Image of Man', in Robert Colodny, ed., *Frontiers of Science and Philosophy* (University of Pittsburgh Press, 1962), reprinted in Sellars, *Science, Perception and Reality* (London: Routledge & Kegan Paul, 1963).

introduces the manifest image with reference to Husserl's procedure of bracketing:

Thus, for methodological reasons I shall, to borrow Husserl's useful term, *bracket* the theoretical picture of the world and concern myself with explicating what I have called elsewhere the manifest image roughly that common sense conception of the world where the phrase 'common sense' indicates a framework of categories, a way of conceiving man and the world rather than a collection of uneducated beliefs.[115]

Sellars explains bracketing as applied to these images as 'transforming them from ways of experiencing the world into objects of philosophical reflection and evaluation'. The 'manifest image' operates under what Husserl would have called the personalistic attitude; it is oriented to persons, values, practices, meanings. The manifest image has a certain historical primacy. The scientific image or 'theoretical image',[116] by contrast, presents a rival way of understanding the world and ourselves. The challenge of philosophy, for Sellars, is to integrate the two images into a single stereoscopic vision of the world. Husserl, however, would disagree with Sellars' naturalism and his claim that modern science is to be accepted as the ultimate measure of all things. For Husserl, it is important to delimit the scope of science's claims and methodological idealizations against the backdrop of the life-world as the constant ground of validity for *all* claims. The two must remain in tension, but the life-world, for Husserl, has more than epistemic and historical priority: it is that which makes human, meaningful endeavour possible.

In his 2004 study on the *Crisis*,[117] James Dodd has pointed to certain new themes which he believes have not been sufficiently noticed by critics, specifically 'flowing in' and 'inwardness'. Dodd identifies 'flowing in' or 'influx' (*Einströmen*) as a central but neglected transcendental concept in Husserl. He explains:

The mechanism whereby transcendental philosophy enriches the sense unities of natural life is designated in Husserl's later writings by the term '*Einströmen*,' which describes the manner in which the transcendental dimension, or the consciousness of the subjectivity of meaning on a

---

[115] Wilfrid Sellars, *Wilfrid Sellars' Notre Dame Lectures: 1969–1986*, ed. with an Introduction by Pedro Amaral (2009), p. 174.
[116] See O'Shea, *Wilfrid Sellars*, p. 13.   [117] Dodd, *Crisis and Reflection*.

transcendental register, 'flows into' natural life, enriching its content, above all the content of the sense of 'subjectivity' itself.[118]

On this account, transcendental philosophy and the transcendental standpoint, although in one sense detached and adopting a bystander approach, is, in another sense, engaged, active and participating in natural life. Husserl characterizes the manner in which transcendental life mingles with natural life as a kind of flowing of the transcendental into the mundane. This kind of intervention of the transcendental is supposed to bring mundane subjectivity to a new level of self-awareness, to incorporate it into transcendental life. As Dodd puts it: '*Einströmen* is supposed to result in the rejuvenation of psychology as a science of the subject',[119] but it is also supposed to modify the sense-content of the surrounding world itself.

In fact the term *Einströmen* is quite rare in Husserl's *Crisis*, although there are a number of supplementary texts in Hua xxix which point to its growing importance for the late Husserl.[120] The 'problem of "flowing in"' features in the very title of *Crisis* § 59, and, in Section 60, he speaks of the manner in which the transcendental 'flows in[to]' psychic being and life, overcoming naïveté.[121] The concept of 'flowing in' is intimately related to temporal flowing. The problem is a version of the problem of the relation between natural and transcendental reflection. Natural reflection has a certain inbuilt naïve assumption not only about the reality of its objects, but also about the kind of temporal reality of its own acts of reflecting. They are real events in the natural world. Transcendental reflection changes the stance towards this naïve concept of temporal flowing. Unfortunately, Husserl lacks a detailed account of how the transcendental life, once discovered, can flow back into and transform mundane life.

The second notion highlighted by Dodd is 'inwardness' (*Innerlichkeit*), a term that appears about half a dozen times in the *Crisis*.[122] Husserl uses the term in several different senses. Perhaps the

---

[118]   Ibid., p. 219.   [119]   Ibid.
[120]   See, for instance, Text No. 7, '*Einströmen* (Sommer 1935)', Hua xxix 77–83.
[121]   The term appears just once in the 'Vienna Lecture' in quite a different and non-technical context, where he speaks of the 'influx' of mythical elements into thinking in the religious-mythical attitude (C 284; K 330).
[122]   See C 247; K 250, C 255; K 258 and K 266, K 348, K 413 and K 515.

most important sense is found in his first use of the term, when he speaks of the 'hidden unity of intentional inwardness which alone constitutes the unity of history' (C 73; K 74), which can only be understood once the 'final establishment' (*Endstiftung*) has taken place. This is a very Hegelian notion – the idea that history has a hidden inner unity which is not shown in the self-interpretations of the agents acting in history. Similarly, at the end of the 'Vienna Lecture' Husserl invokes the idea of 'a new life-inwardness' (*Lebensinnerlichkeit*) that must arise phoenix-like from the ashes of the collapsed rationality of European culture (C 299; K 348). But Husserl also – and more frequently (see Hua xxxix 272ff. or xxvii 142, 175, for instance) – uses the term 'inwardness' to speak of the inner lives of individual subjects or 'souls' (see C 247; K 250 and also C 255; K 258 – where Carr translates it as 'interiority'). Here inwardness simply refers to the fact that embodied subjects (human and animal) have inner conscious lives that are lived through by them in a first-person way. Indeed, it has always been the task of psychology to try to chart this inner life of embodied, conscious animals.

At *Crisis* § 72 (C 263; K 266), and more in keeping with the meaning Dodd finds most interesting, Husserl distinguishes transcendental from mundane innerness. The psychologist is interested in mundane subjectivity and interiority as that taking place in real human beings in the context of their social and communal existence. It is much more difficult to determine what constitutes 'transcendental interiority', as David Carr has pointed out in his review of Dodd's book:[123]

Dodd finds it very difficult to express what this inwardness really amounts to for Husserl, apart from 'a heightened sensitivity to the historical rootedness of concepts and a newfound sense of subjectivity.' In the end he is disappointed: the concept of transcendental inwardness 'is really only a gesture … not enough to fulfill the promise of demonstrating how it is that pure reason, to use Kant's formulation of the problem, can be "practical."' Inwardness, he concludes, is no more than a 'latent potential of Husserlian thought,' something we have to work out for ourselves 'in a very different time and in a very different philosophical climate than was the case when Husserl was working on the *Crisis*.'

[123] See David Carr, '*Crisis and Reflection: An Essay on Husserl's Crisis of the European Sciences* by James Dodd', *Graduate Faculty Philosophy Journal* Vol. 27 No. 1 (2006), 195–205.

Dodd acknowledges that Husserl offers very little elaboration on the meaning of 'inwardness' or 'innerness'. Indeed, Husserl refers to it in relation to the Kantian and Fichtean philosophies in his *Fichte Lectures* (Hua xxvii 279). Husserl's concept of a transcendental innerness must mean something like a life lived in full self-awareness, fixed on the goals of rationality, clarity and groundedness. But it is not clear how this is possible. Dodd suggests that inwardness refers not to the life of the transcendental subject itself but rather to the manner in which it inserts itself into the historical and mundane subject: 'That is, it seems to be not so much the inwardness of a reflecting subject as it is the resulting inwardness that takes hold in a concrete subjective existence in the wake of reflection.'[124] This is an intriguing notion, but I do not find precise evidence in Husserl's own text for this interpretation. Dodd is correct to see this inwardness as itself the product of the history of philosophical reflection which has made such inwardness possible. It is, furthermore, a kind of inwardness that belongs only to the life of rationality. Dodd reads inwardness as signifying the opposite of the Kantian call to be a moral subject independent of nature. Rather, for Dodd, Husserl's inwardness signifies an 'awareness of a selfhood that is never absolutely, completely absorbed by its commitments, its valuations, its understanding, even the consciousness to which it belongs'.[125] It is a rational responsibility attuned to living temporally and historically as an embodied, finite person. For Dodd, to be a finite being who grasps the fact of infinity leads to the kind of transcendental inwardness that enriches the sense of life. But does Husserl offer us enough content concerning this transcendental life of inwardness? And does it not overemphasize the purely rational dimension of human life? Heidegger, by contrast, always opposes moments of such authenticity to the more usual sense of inauthenticity and self-alienation that pervades humanity in its '*das Man*' character. It is hard not to read Husserl as holding a certain naïveté about the possibilities of a fulfilled transcendental life.

CONCLUSION: THE FUTURE OF THE *CRISIS*

The *Crisis* texts we have discussed in the course of this study were composed by the ageing but still mentally vigorous Husserl in his last

---

[124] Dodd, *Crisis and Reflection*, p. 220.   [125] Ibid., p. 223.

years, primarily from 1934 to 1937. They represent his final efforts to explain and justify his transcendental phenomenology and to argue for its relevance in addressing the serious crises facing the sciences and culture in the West. As I hope we have demonstrated, even in its incomplete and programmatic form, the *Crisis* is a remarkable and visionary work – a work that analyses the past history of philosophy only in order to understand its future mission.

Perhaps the most immediately obvious and easily documented effect of the *Crisis* is that it introduced the term 'life-world' into the human sciences, where it has now become a standard, if not well-defined, term. In fact, in Husserl's account the term is really the 'title of a problem' (*Problemtitel*) rather than simply naming the experienced social surrounding environment,[126] and those interested in clarifying the sense of the life-world would be well advised to study Husserl's formulations very closely. As we have shown, the concept of the life-world is deeply problematic, but in a productive way – it stimulates new thinking about the manner in which human beings live in a pregiven world.

Secondly, the *Crisis* articulated in some detail a new way of conducting phenomenological 'backward reflection' (*Rückbesinnung*) that forced Husserl's own students and followers radically to rethink his earlier work. Earlier statements of the phenomenological method, e.g. as found in *Ideas* I or the *Cartesian Meditations*, now had to be understood as merely provisional and one-sided. In the *Crisis*, Husserl offers his new historical approach to phenomenology as indeed primary and encompassing the other earlier approaches. Furthermore, this 'historical' approach is not to be construed as a factual history (of the emergence of modern science or the evolution of modern philosophy), but rather as an intellectual thought-reconstruction of the key foundational moments (*Urstiftungen*) in the formation of Western rationality and scientific knowledge. According to this historical account, phenomenology is the most mature and self-reflexive form of transcendental philosophy as inaugurated by Descartes and

---

[126] As Ernst Wolfgang Orth comments in his book, *Edmund Husserls Krisis der europäischen Wissenschaften und die transzendentale Phänomenologie* (Darmstadt: Wissenschaftliche Buchgesellschaft, 1999), p. 165. In the *Crisis*, Husserl says that every form of evidence is actually 'the title of a problem' (*Problemtitel*, C 189; K 192); cf. also C 83; K 85, where he says that intentionality is the title of a problem.

misconstrued by Kant. Phenomenology must now be understood not merely as a 'static' descriptive science aiming to identify the a priori necessary conditions that structure all human experience and knowing, but must be understood as a 'genetic' science, aiming to uncover the manner in which meanings originate (in a 'primal foundation', *Urstiftung*), become habitualized and ultimately settle down, becoming sedimented into the background assumptions and horizons that then shape new insights and discoveries. In other words, phenomenology has to come to terms with the dynamics of socialization and historicity.

Another major impact of the *Crisis*, which continues to have powerful after-effects, is its challenge to all forms of objectivism and naturalism. For Husserl, transcendental philosophy highlights the inescapably subjective dimension to all human knowledge and exposes naturalism and objectivism as essentially self-contradictory. Husserl's *Crisis*, as we have seen, also mounts a serious challenge to all forms of scientific psychology in terms of its claim to scientific status and its claim to be the genuine science of subjectivity. The *Crisis* offers a deeper and more reflective account of subjectivity and intersubjectivity that continues to be drawn on by philosophers of the social sciences.

One of the most inspiring features of the *Crisis* is Husserl's dogged insistence that philosophy has to begin from the *first-person perspective* and is a kind of self-meditation where the thinker's own being, values and epistemic commitments have to be put in question. Philosophy is radical self-questioning, and the philosopher is the 'self-thinker' (*Selbstdenker*). In this regard, Husserl has an extremely high regard for Descartes' turn to subjectivity, as well as for his radical *epoché*, which stands for Husserl as the model for all philosophical enquiry. Only the carrying-through of the 'full transcendental *epoché*' (C 263; K 267) will lead to a genuine liberation from prejudices and set philosophy on the road to science. Husserl is insistent that the *epoché* itself is not a return to natural subjectivity (as Locke and Hume thought), but rather uncovers a new domain whose existence has never before been noticed. As Husserl says at the end of Part III of the *Crisis*:

But great difficulties had to be overcome in order not only to begin the method of *epoché* and reduction but also to bring it to full understanding of itself and thus for the first time to discover the absolutely functioning subjectivity, not as human subjectivity, but as the subjectivity that objectifies itself … [at least] at first, in human subjectivity. (C 262; K 265)

Husserl's real target is to understand transcendental subjectivity and its 'self-objectification' as natural human life. With this emphasis, Husserl has resolutely joined his phenomenology to the tradition of German Idealism. In the *Crisis*, Husserl is a committed transcendental philosopher, and his defence of the transcendental approach remains provocative and indeed has inspired new approaches to the understanding of what Husserl deliberately calls 'transcendental life'.

Perhaps above all else, Husserl offers in the *Crisis* a new way of thinking about reason and rationality. Human beings – and philosophers especially who are tasked by Husserl to be custodians of culture or 'functionaries of humankind' – have the duty to promote and protect reason and to oppose all forms of irrationalism. Philosophy since the Greek breakthrough has committed human culture to strive endlessly towards rational ends and to create what Husserl optimistically calls a 'new humanity' that transcends all local allegiances to cultural particularism and embraces an open-ended universality. A number of scholars have criticized as naïve Husserl's approach to reason and his underlying assumption that philosophy is the driving force towards the rationalization of society. In this regard, Philip Buckley has criticized Husserl's approach to reason in the *Crisis* as too voluntaristic: to be rational is to *will* to be rational.[127] It is as if the decision to be rational, to set one's goal as rationality, is sufficient to embark on the rational course of history. This decision was, of course, supposedly made already in Greek philosophy. David Carr, among others, has pointed out that Husserl was simply wrong to think that phenomenology, even in its most transcendental form, could save humanity. Husserl's defence of the saving power of philosophy is in contrast to the late Heidegger, who abandons hope that philosophy can save Western culture (recall his famous claim 'only a god can save us now', *nur noch ein Gott kann uns retten*).[128]

---

[127] See Philip R. Buckley, *Husserl, Heidegger, and the Crisis of Philosophical Responsibility*, Phaenomenologica 125 (Dordrecht: Kluwer, 1992), pp. 136–47.

[128] '"Nur noch ein Gott kann uns retten", Spiegel-Gespräch mit Martin Heidegger am 23 September 1966', *Der Spiegel* (31 May 1976), 193–219, trans. Maria Alter and J. Caputo as 'Only a God Can Save Us: *Der Spiegel*'s Interview with Martin Heidegger (1966)', in

Philosophers interested in issues of cultural pluralism and multi-culturalism have also taken issue with Husserl's explicit Eurocentrism in the *Crisis*, with his view that Western science is essentially 'European' and even 'Greek' in origin. In particular, they have expressed concern that Husserl explicitly excludes nomadic Gypsies from the concept of 'Europe' as the centre of scientific rationality.[129] Others have raised questions about Husserl's espousal of human universalism and his apparent devaluation of non-European cultures and societies in this regard. Husserl believes there is an essential teleology to Western cultural development; it is committed to the universalization of reason (and, furthermore, other cultures will embrace Europeanization, and never vice-versa: the European will, for instance, never feel an urge to 'Indianize' (C 275; K 320)). Husserl always stresses this universality and breakthrough to infinity brought about by the Greek philosophical 'theoretical attitude', which he regards as opening up a path of universality and infinity that is now available to all cultures that engage in self-criticism. Husserl, moreover, is a critic of narrow versions of rationalism that have been pursued since the Enlightenment. The main problem facing the 'renewal' (*Erneuerung*) of reason is that in the modern period reason has become construed in a one-sided manner, due to the success of the mathematical sciences. In other words, Husserl – like Heidegger, who made similar criticisms in his essays of the 1930s,[130] and later Herbert Marcuse[131] – is criticizing the *one-dimensionality* of the framework of technologically organized, calculative reasoning. Today's rationalism is in the grip of *objectivism* and *naturalism*, and it is transcendental phenomenological reflection (*Besinnung*), especially on the genesis of these meaning-formations, that will lead our concept of reason to a new form of 'groundedness of existence' (*Bodenständigkeit des Daseins*, Hua XXVII 238). Husserl's critique of

R. Wolin, ed., *The Heidegger Controversy: A Critical Reader* (Cambridge, MA: MIT, 1993), pp. 91–116.

[129] See, for instance, William Casement, 'Husserl and the Philosophy of History', *History and Theory*, Vol. 27 No. 3 (October, 1988), 229–40. See also Benhabib, 'Another Universalism: On the Unity and Diversity of Human Rights'.

[130] See, for instance, Heidegger's 1938 essay 'The Age of the World Picture', in Heidegger, *Off the Beaten Track*, ed. and trans. Julian Young and Kenneth Haynes (Cambridge University Press, 2002), pp. 57–85.

[131] See Marcuse, *One-Dimensional Man*.

one-dimensional, technized reason needs to be understood alongside the better-known positions of Heidegger, Marcuse (1898–1979) and the Frankfurt School.

Husserl never considers philosophy to be a fixed body of knowledge. Philosophy is first and foremost radical, open-ended, questioning. Perhaps we can do no better than to end with Husserl's own words in the *Crisis* regarding his hopes for his own transcendental phenomenology:

Questions never before asked will arise; fields of endeavour never before entered, correlations never before grasped or radically understood, will show themselves. In the end they will require that the total sense of philosophy, accepted as 'obvious' throughout all its historical forms, be basically and essentially transformed. Together with the new task and its universal apodictic ground, the *practical* possibility of a new philosophy will prove itself: through its execution. (C 18; K 16–17)

Bibliography

EDMUND HUSSERL COMPLETE WORKS

The complete critical edition of Husserl's works is: Husserl, Edmund. *Gesammelte Werke*. Husserliana. Dordrecht: Kluwer (now Springer), 1956 –. Forty-three volumes have been published to date.

RELEVANT INDIVIDUAL HUSSERLIANA VOLUMES

Husserl, Edmund. *Aufsätze und Vorträge 1911–1921*. Hrsg. Hans-Rainer Sepp und Thomas Nenon. Hua xxv. Dordrecht: Kluwer, 1986.

Aufsätze und Vorträge 1922–1937. Hrsg. Thomas Nenon und Hans-Rainer Sepp. Hua xxvii. Dordrecht: Kluwer, 1989.

Cartesianische Meditationen und Pariser Vorträge. Hrsg. Stephan Strasser. Hua i. The Hague: Nijhoff, 1950.

Die Krisis der europäischen Wissenschaften und die transzendentale Phänomenologie: Eine Einleitung in die phänomenologische Philosophie. Hrsg. W. Biemel. Hua vi. The Hague: Nijhoff, 1954. Reprinted 1976.

Die Krisis der europäischen Wissenschaften und die transzendentale Phänomenologie. Ergänzungsband. Texte aus dem Nachlaß 1934–1937. Hrsg. Reinhold N. Smid. Hua xxix. Dordrecht: Kluwer, 1992.

Die Lebenswelt: Auslegungen der vorgegebenen Welt und ihrer Konstitution. Texte aus dem Nachlass (1916–1937). Hrsg. Rochus Sowa Hua xxxix. Dordrecht: Springer, 2008.

Die Idee der Phänomenologie: Fünf Vorlesungen. Nachdruck der 2. erg. Auflage. Hrsg. W. Biemel. Hua ii. The Hague: Nijhoff, 1973.

Erste Philosophie (1923/24). Erster Teil: Kritische Ideengeschichte. Hrsg. R. Boehm. Hua vii. The Hague: Nijhoff, 1965.

Ideen zu einer reinen Phänomenologie und phänomenologischen Philosophie. Erstes Buch: Allgemeine Einführung in die reine Phänomenologie i. Halbband: Text der 1–3. Auflage. Hrsg. K. Schuhmann. Hua iii/i. The Hague: Nijhoff, 1977.

Ideen zu einer reinen Phänomenologie und phänomenologischen Philosophie. Zweites Buch: *Phänomenologische Untersuchungen zur Konstitution.* Hrsg. Marly Biemel. Hua IV. The Hague: Nijhoff, 1952.

Ideen zu einer reinen Phänomenologie und phänomenologischen Philosophie. Drittes Buch: *Die Phänomenologie und die Fundamente der Wissenschaften.* Hrsg. Marly Biemel. Hua V. The Hague: Nijhoff, 1952.

Natur und Geist: Vorlesungen Sommersemester 1927. Hrsg. Michael Weiler. Hua XXXII. Dordrecht: Springer, 2001.

Natur und Geist: Vorlesungen Sommersemester 1919. Husserl Materialen Band IV. Hrsg Michael Weiler. Dordrecht: Springer, 2002.

Transzendentaler Idealismus: Texte aus dem Nachlass (1908–1921). Ed. Robin Rollinger and Rochus Sowa. Hua XXXVI. Dordrecht: Kluwer, 2003.

OTHER WORKS BY HUSSERL

Husserl, Edmund. *Briefwechsel.* Ed. Karl Schuhmann in collaboration with Elizabeth Schuhmann. *Husserliana Dokumente*, Vol. III, 10 vol. Dordrecht: Kluwer, 1994.

'Die Frage nach dem Ursprung der Geometrie als intentional-historisches Problem', *Revue Internationale de Philosophie* Vol. 1 No. 2 (1939), 203–35.

Erfahrung und Urteil: Untersuchungen zur Genealogie der Logik. Redigiert und hrsg. Ludwig Landgrebe. Prague: Academia-Verlag, 1938. 7th edn. Hamburg: Felix Meiner, 1999.

La Crise de l'humanité européenne et la philosophie. Traduit par Paul Ricoeur. Édition bilingue avec une préface de S. Strasser. Paris: Aubier, 1977.

La Crise des sciences européennes et de la phénoménologie transcendentale. Traduit de l'allemand et préfacé par Gérard Granel. Paris: Gallimard, 1976.

Méditations cartésiennes: introduction à la phénoménologie. Trans. G. Peiffer and E. Levinas. Paris: Almand Colin, 1931.

Natur und Geist: Vorlesungen Sommersemester 1919. Hrsg. Michael Weiler. Husserl Materialen Vol. IV. Dordrecht: Springer, 2002.

'Notizen zur Raumkonstitution'. *Philosophy and Phenomenological Research* Vol. 1 No. 1 (September 1940), 21–37.

Späte Texte über Zeitkonstitution (1929–1934). Die C-Manuskripte. Ed. Dieter Lohmar. Husserl Materialen Vol. VIII. Dordrecht: Springer, 2006.

'*Umsturz der kopernikanischen Lehre* in der gewöhnlichen weltanschaulichen Interpretation. Die Ur-Arche Erde bewegt sich nicht. Grundlegende Untersuchungen zum phänomenologischen *Ursprung der Körperlichkeit der Räumlichkeit der Natur* im ersten naturwissen-schaftlichen Sinne. Alles notwendige Anfangsuntersuchungen', in Marvin Farber, ed., *Philosophical Essays in Memory of Edmund Husserl.* Cambridge, MA: Harvard University Press, 1940, pp. 307–25.

WORKS BY HUSSERL IN ENGLISH TRANSLATION

Husserl, Edmund. *Analyses Concerning Passive and Active Synthesis: Lectures on Transcendental Logic.* Trans. Anthony J. Steinbock. Husserl Collected Works Vol. ix. Dordrecht: Kluwer, 2001.

The Basic Problems of Phenomenology. From the Lectures, Winter Semester 1910–1911. Trans. Ingo Farin and James G. Hart. Husserl Collected Works Vol. xii. Dordrecht: Springer, 2006.

Cartesian Meditations. Trans. D. Cairns. The Hague: Nijhoff, 1967.

The Crisis of European Sciences and Transcendental Phenomenology: An Introduction to Phenomenological Philosophy. Trans. David Carr. Evanston: Northwestern University Press, 1970.

Early Writings in the Philosophy of Logic and Mathematics. Trans. Dallas Willard. Husserl Collected Works Vol. v. Dordrecht: Kluwer, 1994.

Experience and Judgment: Investigations in a Genealogy of Logic. Revised and edited by L. Landgrebe. Trans. J.S. Churchill and K. Ameriks. London: Routledge and Kegan Paul, 1973.

'Fichte's Ideal of Humanity [Three Lectures]', trans. James G. Hart *Husserl Studies* Vol. 12 (1995), 111–33.

Formal and Transcendental Logic. Trans. D. Cairns. The Hague: Nijhoff, 1969.

'Foundational Investigations of the Phenomenological Origin of the Spatiality of Nature. The Originary Ark. The Earth Does Not Move', trans. Fred Kersten, rev. Len Lawlor, in M. Merleau-Ponty, *Husserl at the Limits of Phenomenology.* Ed. L. Lawlor and B. Bergo. Evanston: Northwestern University Press, 2002, pp. 117–31.

Husserl. Shorter Works. Trans. and ed. Frederick Elliston and Peter McCormick. University of Notre Dame Press, 1981.

The Idea of Phenomenology. Trans. Lee Hardy. Husserl Collected Works Vol. viii. Dordrecht: Kluwer, 1999.

Ideas Pertaining to a Pure Phenomenology and to a Phenomenological Philosophy, First Book. Trans. F. Kersten. Husserl Collected Works Vol. ii. Dordrecht: Kluwer, 1983.

Ideas Pertaining to a Pure Phenomenology and to a Phenomenological Philosophy, Second Book. Trans. R. Rojcewicz and A. Schuwer. Husserl Collected Works Vol. iii. Dordrecht: Kluwer, 1989.

Ideas Pertaining to a Pure Phenomenology and to a Phenomenological Philosophy, Third Book. Trans. Ted E. Klein and W.E. Pohl. Husserl Collected Works Vol. i. The Hague: Nijhoff, 1980.

Introduction to Logic and Theory of Knowledge: Lectures 1906/07. Trans. Claire Ortiz Hill. Husserl Collected Works Vol. XIII. Dordrecht: Springer, 2008.

Introduction to the Logical Investigations: Draft of a Preface to the Logical Investigations. Ed. E. Fink. Trans. P.J. Bossert and C.H. Peters. The Hague: Nijhoff, 1975.

'Kant and the Idea of Transcendental Philosophy', trans. Ted E. Klein and William E. Pohl, *Southwestern Journal of Philosophy* Vol. 5 (Fall 1974), 9–56.

Logical Investigations 2 vols. Trans. J.N. Findlay. Edited with a new introduction by Dermot Moran and new preface by Michael Dummett. London, New York: Routledge, 2001.

On the Phenomenology of the Consciousness of Internal Time. Trans. J.B. Brough. Collected Works Vol IV. Dordrecht: Kluwer, 1990.

The Paris Lectures. Trans. Peter Koestenbaum. The Hague: Nijhoff, 1970.

Phenomenological Psychology: Lectures, Summer Semester 1925. Trans. J. Scanlon. The Hague: Nijhoff, 1977.

The Philosophy of Arithmetic. Psychological and Logical Investigations with Supplementary Texts from 1887–1901. Trans. Dallas Willard, Husserl Collected Works X. Dordrecht: Kluwer, 2003.

'Philosophy as Rigorous Science', trans. Marcus Brainard, *The New Yearbook for Phenomenology and Phenomenological Philosophy* Vol. 2 (2002), 249–95.

Psychological and Transcendental Phenomenology and the Confrontation with Heidegger (1927–31). The Encyclopaedia Britannica Article, The Amsterdam Lectures 'Phenomenology and Anthropology' and Husserl's Marginal Note in Being and Time, and Kant on the Problem of Metaphysics. Trans. T. Sheehan and R.E. Palmer. Husserl Collected Works Vol. VI. Dordrecht: Kluwer, 1997.

'Static and Genetic Phenomenological Method', trans. Anthony J. Steinbock, *Continental Philosophy Review* Vol. 31 (1998), 135–42.

Thing and Space: Lectures of 1907. Trans. R. Rojcewicz. Husserl Collected Works Vol. VII. Dordrecht: Kluwer, 1997.

Welton, Donn. Ed. *The Essential Husserl*. Bloomington: Indiana University Press, 1999.

SELECTED FURTHER READING

Arendt, Hannah. *The Human Condition*. University of Chicago Press, 1958.

Avenarius, Richard. *Der menschliche Weltbegriff*. Leipzig: O. R. Reisland, 1891. Reprinted Elibron Classics, 2005.

Banfi, Antonio. 'Husserl et la crise de la pensée européenne', in *Husserl: Cahiers de Royaumont III* (Paris: Éditions de Minuit, 1959), pp. 411–27.

Baynes, Kenneth. 'Crisis and Life-World in Husserl and Habermas', in Arleen B. Dallery, Charles E. Scott and P. Holley Roberts, eds., *Crises in Continental Philosophy* (Albany, NY: SUNY Press, 1990), pp. 57–68.

Belousek, Darrin W. 'Husserl on Scientific Method and Conceptual Change: A Realist Appraisal', *Synthese* Vol. 115 (1998), 71–98.

Benhabib, Seyla. 'Another Universalism: On the Unity and Diversity of Human Rights', Presidential Address to the Eastern Division of the APA, *Proceedings and Addresses of the American Philosophical Association* Vol. 81 No. 2 (November 2007), 7–32.

Berger, Peter L. and Thomas Luckmann. *The Social Construction of Reality: A Treatise in the Sociology of Knowledge*. New York: Anchor Books, 1967.

Bernasconi, Robert and Sybol Cook. Eds. *Race and Racism in Continental Philosophy*. Bloomington: Indiana University Press, 2003.

Blumenberg, Hans. *The Genesis of the Copernican World*. Trans. Robert M. Wallace. Cambridge, MA: MIT, 1987.

Bossert, Philip J. 'A Common Misunderstanding Concerning Husserl's *Crisis* Text', *Philosophy and Phenomenological Research* Vol. 35 No. 1 (1974), 20–33.

Bruzina, Ronald. *Edmund Husserl and Eugen Fink: Beginnings and Ends in Phenomenology 1928–1938*. New Haven: Yale University Press, 2004.

Buckley, R. Philip. *Husserl, Heidegger, and the Crisis of Philosophical Responsibility*. Phaenomenologica 125. Dordrecht: Kluwer, 1992.

Cairns, Dorion. *Guide for Translating Husserl*. The Hague: Nijhoff, 1973.

Carr, David. '*Crisis and Reflection: An Essay on Husserl's Crisis of the European Sciences* by James Dodd', *Gradnate Philosophy Journal* Vol. 27 No. 1 (2006), 195–205.

Phenomenology and the Problem of History: A Study of Husserl's Transcendental Philosophy. Evanston, IL: Northwestern University Press, 1974.

Carr, David and Chan-Fai Cheung. Eds. *Space, Time and Culture*. Contributions to Phenomenology 51. Dordrecht: Kluwer, 2004.

Casement, William. 'Husserl and the Philosophy of History', *History and Theory* Vol. 27 No. 3 (October 1988), 229–40.

Crowell, Steven Galt. *Husserl, Heidegger and the Space of Meaning: Paths toward Transcendental Phenomenology*. Evanston, IL: Northwestern University Press, 2001.

Dallery, Arleen B., Charles E. Scott and P. Holley Roberts. Eds. *Crises in Continental Philosophy*. Albany, NY: SUNY Press, 1990.

De Gandt, François. *Husserl et Galilée: sur la crise des sciences européennes*. Paris: Vrin, 2004.

De Gandt, François and Claudio Majiolino. Eds. *Lectures de la Krisis de Husserl.* Études et Commentaires séries. Paris: Vrin, 2007.

Derrida, Jacques. *Edmund Husserl's Origin of Geometry: An Introduction.* Trans. J.P. Leavey Jr. Ed. D. B. Allison. Sussex, NY: Harvester Press/ Nicolas Hays, 1978.

Of Grammatology. Trans. G. Spivak. Baltimore, MD: Johns Hopkins, 1976.

The Problem of Genesis in Husserl's Philosophy. Trans. Marian Hobson. University of Chicago Press, 2003.

Speech and Phenomena and Other Essays on Husserl's Theory of Signs. Ed. and trans. David Allison. Evanston, IL: Northwestern University Press, 1973.

Writing and Difference. Trans. Alan Bass. London: RKP, 1978.

Dilthey, Wilhelm. *The Formation of the Historical World in the Human Sciences.* Trans. Rudolf Maakreel and John Scanlon. Dilthey Selected Works Vol.III. Princeton U. P., 2002.

'Ideas Concerning a Descriptive and Analytical Psychology', in *Dilthey's Descriptive Psychology and Historical Understanding.* Trans. Richard Zaner and K. L. Heiges. The Hague: Nijhoff, 1977, pp. 23–120.

Dodd, James. *Crisis and Reflection: An Essay on Edmund Husserl's Crisis of the European Sciences.* Phaenomenologica 174. Dordrecht: Kluwer, 2004.

Drake, Stillman. *Galileo at Work.* University of Chicago Press, 1978.

Drake, Stillman. Trans and ed. *Discoveries and Opinions of Galileo.* Garden City, NY: Doubleday, 1957.

Drake, Stillman, Noel M. Swerdlow and Trevor Harvey Levere. *Essays on Galileo and the History and Philosophy of Science.* 3 vols. University of Toronto Press, 1999.

Drummond, John J. *Historical Dictionary of Husserl's Philosophy.* Lanham, MD: Scarecrow Press, 2008.

Edie, James, Francis Parker and Calvin Schrag. Eds. *Patterns of the Life-World.* Evanston, IL: Northwestern University Press, 1970.

Embree, Lester. Ed. *Schutzian Social Science.* Dordrecht: Kluwer, 1999.

Endress, Martin, George Psathas and Hisashi Nasu. Eds. *Explorations of the Life-World: Continuing Dialogues with Alfred Schutz.* Dordrecht: Springer, 2005.

Farber, Marvin. Ed. *Philosophical Essays in Memory of Edmund Husserl.* Cambridge, MA: Harvard University Press, 1940.

Fink, Eugen. 'The Phenomenological Philosophy of Edmund Husserl and Contemporary Criticism', in Roy Elveton, ed., *The Phenomenology of Husserl: Selected Critical and Contemporary Readings*, 2nd edn. Seattle: Noesis Press, 2000, pp. 70–139.

Sixth Cartesian Meditation: The Idea of a Transcendental Theory of Method. With Textual Notations by Edmund Husserl. Trans. with an Introduction by Ronald Bruzina. Bloomington: Indiana University Press, 1995.

'What Does the Phenomenology of Edmund Husserl Want to Accomplish? (The Phenomenological Idea of Laying-a-Ground)', trans. Arthur Grugan, *Research in Phenomenology* Vol. 2 (1972), 5–27.

Finocchiaro, Maurice A. Ed. *The Galileo Affair: A Documentary History.* Berkeley: University of California Press, 1989.

Flynn, Bernard Charles. 'Michel Foucault and the Husserlian Problematic of a Transcendental Philosophy of History', *Philosophy Today* Vol. 22 (Fall 1978), 224–38.

Friedman, Michael. 'Descartes and Galileo: Copernicanism and the Metaphysical Foundations of Physics', in Janet Broughton and John Carriero, eds., *A Companion to Descartes*, Oxford: Blackwell, 2008, pp. 69–83.

Gadamer, Hans-Georg. 'The Science of the Life-World', in Anna-Teresa Tymieniecka, ed., *Analecta Husserliana* Vol. 11 *The Later Husserl and the Idea of Phenomenology: Idealism-Realism, Historicity and Nature*, Dordrecht: D. Reidel, 1972, pp. 173–85.

Truth and Method. Trans. Joel Weinsheimer and Donald G. Marshall. 2nd rev. edn. London: Sheed and Ward, 1989.

Gaiman, Kevin Paul. 'Habermas' Early Lifeworld Appropriation: A Critical Assessment', *Man and World* Vol. 23 No. 1 (January 1990), 63–83.

Galileo Galilei, 'The Assayer', trans. Stillman Drake, in Drake, ed., *Discoveries and Opinions of Galileo* (New York: Anchor Books, 1957), pp. 237–8.

Sidereus Nuncius or the Sidereal Messenger. Trans. Albert Van Helden. University of Chicago Press, 1989.

Garrison, James W. 'Husserl, Galileo, and the Processes of Idealization', *Synthese* Vol. 66 No. 2 (February 1986), 329–38.

Gens, Jean-Claude. Ed. *La Krisis de Husserl: approches contemporaines.* Le Cercle Hérmeneutique No. 10. Paris: Vrin, 2008.

Grunsky, Hans Alfred. *Der Einbruch des Judentums in die Philosophie.* Schriften der Deutschen Hochschule für Politik. 1. Idee und Gestalt des Nationalsozialismus, Heft 14. Berlin: Junker und Dünnhaupt, 1937.

Gurwitsch, Aron. 'Galilean Physics in the Light of Husserl's Phenomenology', in Ernan McMullin, ed., *Galileo, Man of Science*, New York: Basic Books, 1967, pp. 388–401.

'Husserlian Perspectives on Galilean Physics', in Lester Embree, ed., *Phenomenology and the Theory of Science*, Evanston, IL: Northwestern University Press, 1974, pp. 33–59.

'The Last Work of Edmund Husserl', *Philosophy and Phenomenological Research* Vol. 16 No. 3 (March 1956), 380–99.

'The Last Work of Edmund Husserl: II. The *Lebenswelt*', *Philosophy and Phenomenological Research* Vol. 17 No. 3 (March 1957), 370–98.

Hart, James G. *The Person and the Common Life: Studies in a Husserlian Social Ethics*. Phaenomenologica 126. Dordrecht: Kluwer, 1992.

Heidegger, Martin. *Being and Time*. Trans. John Macquarrie and E. Robinson. New York: Harper and Row, 1962.

Off the Beaten Track. Ed. Julian Young and Kenneth Haynes. New York: Cambridge University Press, 2002.

Pathmarks. Ed. William McNeill. New York: Cambridge University Press, 1998.

The Essence of Reasons. Trans. Terrence Malick. Evanston, IL: Northwestern University Press, 1969.

Hopkins, Burt C. 'Crisis, History and Husserl's Phenomenological Project of De-sedimenting the Formalization of Meaning: Jacob Klein's Contribution', in *Graduate Faculty Philosophy Journal* Vol. 24 No. 1 (2003), 75–102.

'Derrida's Reading of Husserl in *Speech and Phenomena*: Ontologism and the Metaphysics of Presence', *Husserl Studies* Vol. 2 (1985), 193–214.

The Philosophy of Husserl. Durham: Acumen, 2011.

Hyder, David. 'Foucault, Cavaillès, and Husserl on the Historical Epistemology of the Sciences', *Perspectives on Science* Vol. 11 No. 1 (2003), 107–29.

Hyder, David and Hans-Jörg Rheinberger. Eds. *Science and the Life-World: Essays on Husserl's 'Crisis of European Sciences'*. Stanford University Press, 2010.

Ingarden, Roman. *On the Motives which led Husserl to Transcendental Idealism*. Trans. Arnór Hannibalsson. The Hague: Nijhoff, 1975.

'What is New in Husserl's "*Crisis*"', in Anna Teresa Tymieniecka, ed., *Analecta Husserliana*, Vol. 11. Dordrecht: Kluwer, 1972.

Johnson, Galen A. 'Husserl and History', *Journal of the British Society for Phenomenology* Vol. 11 No. 1 (January 1980), 77–91.

Kant, Immanuel, *Critique of Pure Reason*. Trans. Norman Kemp Smith with a new preface by Howard Caygill. 2nd edn. Basingstoke: Palgrave Macmillan, 2007.

Katz, David. *The World of Color*. Trans. R. B. McLeod and C. W. Fox. London: Kegan, Paul, Trench, Trubner and Co., 1935. Reprinted London: Routledge, 1999.

Kaufmann, Fritz. 'The Phenomenological Approach to History', *Philosophy and Phenomenological Research* Vol. 2 No. 2 (December 1941), 159–72.

Klein, Jacob. *Greek Mathematical Thought and the Origin of Algebra*. Trans. Eva Brann. Cambridge, MA: MIT, 1969. Reprinted New York: Dover, 1992.

Kockelmans, Joseph J. *Edmund Husserl's Phenomenological Psychology*. Pittsburgh, PA: Duquesne University Press, 1967.

Kohák, Erazim. Ed. *Jan Patočka: Philosophy and Selected Writings*. Chicago, London: University of Chicago Press, 1989.

Koyré, Alexander, *Études galiléennes*. Paris: Hermann, 1939. Trans. John Mepham, *Galileo Studies*, Atlantic Highlands, NJ: Humanities Press, 1978.

From the Closed World to the Infinite Universe. Baltimore, MD: Johns Hopkins, 1957.

'Galileo and Plato', *Journal of the History of Ideas* Vol. 4 No. 4 (October 1943), 400–28.

'Galileo and the Scientific Revolution of the Seventeenth Century', *The Philosophical Review* Vol. 52 No. 4 (July 1943), 333–48.

Kwan, Tze-Wan. 'Husserl's Concept of Horizon: An Attempt at Reappraisal', in Dermot Moran and Lester Embree, eds., *Phenomenology: Critical Concepts in Philosophy*, London, New York: Routledge, 2004, pp. 304–38.

Landgrebe, Ludwig. *The Phenomenology of Edmund Husserl: Six Essays*. Ed. D. Welton. Ithaca, NY: Cornell University Press, 1981.

'The World as a Phenomenological Problem', *Philosophy and Phenomenological Research* Vol. 1 No. 1 (September 1940), 38–58.

Lofts, G. S. 'Husserl, Heidegger, Cassirer: Trois philosophes de crise', *Revue philosophique de Louvain* Vol. 90 (1992), 570–84.

Machamer, Peter K. Ed. 1998. *The Cambridge Companion to Galileo*. Cambridge University Press, 1998.

McMullin, Ernan. Ed. *The Church and Galileo*. University of Notre Dame Press, 2005.

Galileo Man of Science. New York: Basic Books, 1964.

Mann, Doug. 'Does Husserl Have a Philosophy of History in *The Crisis of European Sciences?*' *Journal of the British Society for Phenomenology* Vol. 23 No. 2 (May 1992), 156–66.

Marcuse, Herbert. *One-Dimensional Man*. Boston: Beacon Press, 1964.

Merleau-Ponty, Maurice. *Husserl at the Limits of Phenomenology*. Ed. Leonard Lawlor and Bettina Bergo. Evanston, IL: Northwestern University Press, 2002.

Phénoménologie de la perception. Paris: Gallimard, 1945.

Signs. Trans. Richard McCleary. Evanston, IL: Northwestern University Press, 1964.

The Phenomenology of Perception. Trans. Colin Smith. London, New York: Routledge and Kegan Paul, 1962.

Mishara, Aaron. 'Husserl and Freud: Time, Memory and the Unconscious', *Husserl Studies* Vol. 7 (1990), 29–58.

Moran, Dermot. *Edmund Husserl: Founder of Phenomenology*. Cambridge: Polity Press, 2005.

Moran, Dermot 'Edmund Husserl's Phenomenology of Habituality and Habitus', *Journal of the British Society for Phenomenology*, Vol. 42 No. 1 (January 2011), 53–77.

'"Even the Papuan is a Man and not a Beast": Husserl on Universalism and the Relativity of Cultures', *Journal of the History of Philosophy* Vol. 49 No. 4 (October 2011), 463–94.

'Fink's Speculative Phenomenology: Between Constitution and Transcendence', *Research in Phenomenology* Vol. 37 No. 1 (2007), 3–31.

'Husserl and the Crisis of the European Sciences', in M. W. F. Stone and Jonathan Wolff, eds., *The Proper Ambition of Science*. London, New York: Routledge, 2000, pp. 122–50.

Introduction to Phenomenology. London, New York: Routledge, 2000.

Ed. *The Routledge Companion to Twentieth-Century Philosophy*. London, New York: Routledge, 2008.

Moran, Dermot and Joseph Cohen. *The Husserl Dictionary*. London, New York: Continuum, 2012.

Moran Dermot and Lester Embree. Eds. *Phenomenology: Critical Concepts in Philosophy*. 5 vols. London, New York: Routledge, 2004.

Morrison, James C. 'Husserl's "Crisis": Reflections on the Relationship of Philosophy and History', *Philosophy and Phenomenological Research* Vol. 37 No. 3 (March 1977), 312–30.

Nenon, Tom. 'Some Differences between Kant's and Husserl's Conceptions of Transcendental Philosophy', *Continental Philosophy Review* Vol. 41 No. 4 (2008), 427–39.

Nenon, Tom and Philip Blosser. Eds. *Advancing Phenomenology: Essays in Honor of Lester Embree*. Dordrecht: Springer, 2010.

Orth, Ernst Wolfgang. *Edmund Husserls 'Krisis der europäischen Wissenschaften und die transzendentale Phänomenologie': Vernunft und Kultur*. Darmstadt: Wissenschaftliche Buchgesellschaft, 1999.

Owensby, Jacob. 'Dilthey and Husserl on the Role of the Subject in History', *Philosophy Today* Vol. 32 (Fall, 1988), 221–31.

Rasmussen, David M. '*Lebenswelt*: Reflections on Schutz and Habermas', *Human Studies* Vol. 7 No. 2, Schutz Special Issue (1984), 127–32.

Richir, Marc. *La Crise du sens et la phénoménologie. Autour de la Krisis de Husserl suivi de Commentaire de L'origine de la géométrie*. Grenoble: Jérôme Millon, 1990.

Ricoeur, Paul. 'Husserl and the Sense of History', in Ricoeur, *Husserl: An Analysis of his Phenomenology*. Trans. Edward G. Ballard and L. Embree. Evanston, IL: Northwestern University Press, 1967, 143–74.

Schuhmann, Karl. Ed. *Husserl-Chronik: Denk- und Lebensweg Edmund Husserls*. The Hague: Nijhoff, 1977.

Schutz, Alfred. *Collected Papers. I. The Problem of Social Reality.* Ed. Maurice Natanson. The Hague: Nijhoff, 1967.

The Phenomenology of the Social World. Trans. George Walsh and Fredrick Lehnert. Evanston, IL: Northwestern University Press, 1967.

Sepp, Hans Reiner. Ed. *Edmund Husserl und die phänomenologische Bewegung: Zeugnisse in Text und Bild.* Freiburg, Munich: Karl Alber Verlag, 1988.

Soffer, Gail. 'Philosophy and the Disdain for History: Reflections on Husserl's *Ergänzungsband* to the *Crisis*', *Journal of the History of Philosophy* Vol. 34 No. 1 (January 1996), 95–116.

Spiegelberg, Herbert. *The Phenomenological Movement: A Historical Introduction.* 3rd edn with the collaboration of Karl Schuhmann. Dordrecht: Kluwer, 1982.

Steinbock, Anthony J. *Home and Beyond: Generative Phenomenology after Husserl.* Evanston: Northwestern University Press, 1995.

'The New "Crisis" Contribution: A Supplementary Edition of Edmund Husserl's *Crisis* Texts', *Review of Metaphysics* Vol. 47 No. 3 (March 1994), 557–84.

Toadvine, Ted. 'Phenomenological Method in Merleau-Ponty's Critique of Gurwitsch', *Husserl Studies* Vol. 17 (2001), 195–205.

Trotignon, Pierre. *Le Coeur de la raison: Husserl et la crise du monde moderne.* Paris: Fayard, 1986.

Vetter, Helmuth. Ed. *Krise der Wissenschaften – Wissenschaft der Krise? Wiener Tagungen zur Phänomenologie im Gedenken an Husserls 'Krisis'-Abhandlung (1935/36–1996).* Frankfurt: Peter Lang Verlag, 1998.

Wagner, Helmut. 'Husserl and Historicism', *Social Research* Vol. 39 No. 4 (1972), 696–719.

Waldenfels, Bernhard. 'Experience of the Alien in Husserl's Phenomenology', *Research in Phenomenology* Vol. 20 No. 1 (1990), 19–33.

'Homeworld and Alienworld', in Ernst Wolfgang Orth and Chan-Fai Cheung, eds., *Phenomenology of Interculturality and Life-World, Phänomenologische Forshungen Sonderband* (Freiburg, Munich: Karl Alber, 1998), pp. 72–87, esp. p. 72, reprinted in Dermot Moran and Lester Embree, eds., *Phenomenology: Critical Concepts in Philosophy,* Vol. IV. London, New York: Routledge, 2004, pp. 280–91.

The Question of the Other. The Tang Chung-I Lecture for 2004. Hong Kong: China University Press, 2007.

Welton, Donn. Ed. *The New Husserl: A Critical Reader.* Bloomington: Indiana University Press, 2003.

Zahavi, Dan. *Husserl and Transcendental Intersubjectivity.* Trans. Elizabeth A. Behnke. Athens, OH: Ohio University Press, 2001.

Zahavi, Dan. *Husserl's Phenomenology.* Stanford University Press, 2003.

Index

For EU product safety concerns, contact us at Calle de José Abascal, 56–1°,
28003 Madrid, Spain or eugpsr@cambridge.org.

www.ingramcontent.com/pod-product-compliance
Ingram Content Group UK Ltd.
Pitfield, Milton Keynes, MK11 3LW, UK
UKHW020322140625
459647UK00018B/1975